PUT
Another Pin
IN THE MAP

The Interesting Places I've Seen and the Food I've Eaten

GEORGE S. FLEETWOOD

authorHOUSE°

AuthorHouse™
1663 Liberty Drive
Bloomington, IN 47403
www.authorhouse.com
Phone: 1 (800) 839-8640

Published by AuthorHouse 09/01/2016

ISBN: 978-1-5246-2283-1 (sc)
ISBN: 978-1-5246-2282-4 (e)

Print information available on the last page.

INTRODUCTION

I AM A TRAVELER. IN fact, I consider myself a world traveler. I have lost count of the number of countries I have visited, but it is well over a hundred and I continue to add to my list. I think that I came by it naturally as my mother, maternal grandmother, and her parents were all travelers. Some of my earliest memories were of my mother telling me stories about her travels as a youth.

She described in vivid detail to my brothers and me several trips she took. My favorite was a train trip she took with her mother and sister through western Canada and the United States. We hung on her every word as she described the journey in a glass domed-roofed observation car through the craggy, snow-peaked Rocky Mountains. She told us of glistening azure lakes which reflected the mountains that surrounded them.

They stayed in large, rough timbered hotels along the railroad route and in national parks. They ventured out to explore the surrounding wilds in these parks seeing large grazing animals like bison, elk and moose. They even spotted a huge black bear and big horned rams. The spouting geysers and bubbling mudpots of Yellowstone were almost too much for me to fathom.

Their journey took them further west to the great, young cities of the Pacific coast. Their first stop was Seattle which she described as a rough and tumble place in the 1930s, filled with mariners who were preparing to set sail for the Orient. Next it was down the coast to San Francisco home to the newly opened, Golden Gate Bridge. She loved the rolling nature and natural beauty of this her favorite city. The final leg of the journey would take them to Los Angeles, where they visited the lots of several movie studios watching production of early talking movies. This was all too exciting for this young boy and I tried to convince her to recount this journey so often that I knew all the stories as well as her.

My mom was a home economics teacher, as they called it back in her day. She had a passion for food, as did my father who owned several restaurants while I was growing up. She was an excellent cook, more of in the Betty Crocker mode, than Julia Child. My father also knew his way around a kitchen. Meals were special occasions in our house filled with good food, freshly baked treats, and lively conversation. Because of this, I think my two brothers and I all became fond of good food at a very early age.

One of the parts of her journey she would love to describe in detail to us was the food she ate on these trips. She ate what we thought were terribly exotic items from far-off lands in her travels. Heck, for a kid growing up in small-town Indiana, Italian food was exotic. But things like Peking duck and buffalo steak were difficult to comprehend. All I know is as I grew older I became a more adventurous eater and wanted to see what other cultures had to offer from a culinary prospective.

Although as a child and through early adulthood, I was not in a position to travel much because of financial and time considerations, I hoped one day I could. Thanks to achieving some professional success I was able to accumulate the necessary capital to afford to travel. Although I have seen a great deal of the United States, my interests quickly became international in nature and I must confess to having a strong desire to "see the world."

I began traveling internationally with a buddy of mine, Bill Schreiber. We first took a trip to Cancun, Mexico, to see how we meshed as travel partners. We had a great time for five days and decided it was time to give a trip to Europe a try.

The next year, after we had saved the necessary funds, we booked a trip to Europe for 15 days. We decided to wait for the airline fares to drop for the winter season to book our trip. One morning in late August of that year, Bill called me as he was reading the morning paper. There was a big advertisement in the Indianapolis Star, our hometown paper, announcing a winter fare sale on TWA.

Before the day was over we had made reservations for Europe, traveling into, and returning from Amsterdam. We chose this location to embark on the trip, not only because it was at the top of both of our lists, but also it was the cheapest place we could get on the European continent. We would also discover that the Netherlands is a very easy place for Americans to travel because virtually everyone speaks English, and they are not put off by speaking our language.

We would leave on November 1 and return on November 15, 1989. We now had the starting and ending points of our journey firmed up, now all we had to do was decide on an itinerary. We determined that we should pack as much into the trip as possible, so we went for an aggressive agenda. We both bought Eurail passes, which you must do before leaving the United States. This would enable us to travel anywhere we wanted in Western Europe for the entire time we were gone.

You have to remember this was a time before the internet had developed, so we spent a lot of time in the library examining rail schedules and travel guides. We relied heavily on the Thomas Cook European Timetable, a compendium of passenger rail schedules in Europe. This very helpful and voluminous document also provided us with maps of rail lines allowing us to figure out how major cities were connected and the easiest routes to travel.

We finally arrived at a proposed itinerary. We would visit Amsterdam, then Paris, on to Munich, Florence, Rome, back through Berne and Basil in Switzerland and one final night in Amsterdam.

We made hotel reservations at a small hotel in Amsterdam, the Museumzicht, for our first two nights, and the last one. We left the other days free intentionally, thinking we might want to change our agenda along the way.

We adopted a rule on the journey which I still adhere to when I travel. We called it the "Beech Grove Rule." You see, Beech Grove is a suburb of Indianapolis and the rule goes like this: "if you can do it in Beech Grove, you can't do it on vacation." In practical terms it means that if Beech Grove has a McDonald's, no McDonald's on the trip, a Holiday Inn in Beech Grove, can't stay in one in Europe, a miniature golf course in Beech Grove, no playing miniature golf on vacation.

Hopefully, you can follow this to its logical conclusion. What this rule means to us is, that we could stay home if we wanted to do these things.

A vacation was for exploring new things and visiting different sights. And explore we did.

We packed every day of those two weeks, covering as much territory as possible. To assist in our efforts to see as much as practical we even rented couchettes on trains, sleeping overnight five of the nights as we were traveling to new destinations. This does allow you to see more sights by traveling overnight while you sleep, but I would not recommend that many nights in two weeks. I do not find it very restful.

The upshot of this trip was I had a blast and was now addicted to travel. Bill and I traveled several more times together until his untimely passing from cancer. I picked up several other vacation pals along the way and have enjoyed the company of these folks. However, it was not until I met, started dating, and married my wife, Jenny, that I found a permanent and most enjoyable travel companion. Heck, we even got married barefoot on the beach in Belize.

In 2005, an event changed our lives for the better, as our son was born. George Henry Fleetwood, II, who goes by "Hank," has made us a family of three. I was 51 years old when Hank was born, a time when most men my age are welcoming grandchildren. I felt quite blessed to be a father, an experience I almost missed in life and one I surely would not have had without the love and persistence of Jenny. Hank began traveling at three months when we took him to Ireland and Northern Ireland. Now at the age of eleven he has visited over 100 countries and revels in the experience. We also believe it is contributing greatly to his education and understanding of the world, its diversity, and cultures.

I give Hank a lot of the credit for pushing me into writing this book. I had told him that I had the idea of writing a book on my travels, and would like to include a story about my favorite meal in each country I had visited. Well, with the time constraints created by being a business executive and having a young family, I made little, to no, progress on the project.

On Hank's last day of school his kindergarten year I came home and found my way to my easy chair in the den. The little man came up to me and stood right next to my chair nearly face-to-face with me. He proclaimed, "Daddy, I can read now, when are you going to write that book."

Well, I began to feel the pressure as he would periodically ask me about my progress. I would unfortunately have to respond that I had done nothing. I finally decided I had enough of corporate life and it was time to write the book. Not only was I going to write the book, but I was going to write it to Hank. I wanted him to better understand a large part of my life and passion: travel. I hope he is able to enjoy what I have written and will benefit from the advice I have put forth.

I appreciate all the encouragement I received from Hank and Jenny. In fact, this document might not have been possible without the assistance of my beautiful wife. She is a bit of a pack rat and has saved all manner of things from our trips. This includes the guidebooks my assistant, Elyse Rumely, would so meticulously assemble for us, and notes Jenny had taken, business cards she gathered from hotels, restaurants, and shops, even credit card receipts for our purchases. This made the recounting of our journeys a more practical matter.

I need to level set a couple of things to assist you with a better understanding of this book. First, I not only consider myself an international traveler, but a value-conscious one. By that I mean I am somewhat frugal and I look for a good deal in all things. We do not need to stay in five stars hotels, and rarely do. We prefer smaller, locally-operated establishments that are not overrun by American tourists. We want to mingle with the people of the countries we are visiting, or other foreigners, not other Americans. If we wanted to hang out with people from our country we would stay in the United States.

Second, I do not consider that for something to be good, it has to be expensive. A prime example of this is dining. I have had folks that worked for me who were of the belief that the only good meal was an expensive one. The higher the cost of the items on the menu directly correlated to the quality of the food and enjoyment of the meal. I firmly disagree with this proposition. Many of the meals I describe in this book were not necessarily costly, but I would submit to you that the quality of the ingredients and preparation of the food was indeed top-notch.

Third, I believe that by doing a little homework before I travel I can greatly enhance the experience. In this internet age there is a ton of information that is available to assist you in finding the right accommodation for your needs, the proper time to visit the sights, and even that perfect "little" restaurant. Some of the guidebooks and internet sites that I have found valuable are Frommer's, Lonely Planet, Rick Steve's and more recently, Trip Advisor. A cautionary note about the latter is they cannot filter their content, so sometimes their reviews are written by people who really have no business traveling. So, I just find it helpful to throw out the extremes when reading their reviews.

Fourth, be sure you check out what items are locally produced before you travel to an area. You may find that this will set you up for some outstanding deals on items that are very affordable at your destination, but are quite expensive here. An example of this is my wife has acquired a lot of jewelry containing precious and semi-precious stones that are indigenous to areas we have visited, that she probably would not have otherwise. Every time she wears these pieces she is also reminded of the circumstances and places where they were acquired, a very special, positive thought.

Finally, we try not to overlook the cultural experiences when we travel. These opportunities can take various shapes and sizes, from simply sitting at an outdoor café sipping a coffee and watching the pedestrians go by with the locals, to attending music and sporting events. We have been to see musical performances from Amsterdam to Vienna, and basketball and baseball games, and soccer and hockey matches all over the world. These can be very rewarding experiences. We also do what we can to engage the locals in conversations to learn from them more about how they live.

In fact, I believe that one of the greatest examples of local culture can be found in their food and beverage. I enjoy trying new things and this certainly extends to indigenous cuisine and drink. I have attempted to chronicle my favorite meal in each country I visited. Additionally, I have reached out to the restaurants in an effort to provide the recipe for these dishes. I hope that you are able to enjoy them also.

In the pages that follow I will attempt to share with you some travel tips that I have learned along the way. Hopefully, these will one day come in handy for you. I hope you are able to value the experience of travel as highly as I do. Enjoy the ride.

I feel compelled to add one final thought about the title of this writing. Put Another Pin in the Map was the idea for the title of this work by my wife, Jenny. It refers to a long-held practice in our household. Several years ago, Jenny bought me a large world map. She had it framed and mounted. It now resides on a wall in our home. When we return from a new destination we stick a color-coded pin in the map for each country we have visited. We utilize three different colors of pins. Blue for places I have visited, red for locales Jenny and I went, and green for the three of us. As you can imagine, the map is dotted with pins and filled with memories.

I would like to dedicate this book to my lovely wife, Jenny, and my son, Hank, without whom I don't think it would have been possible.

TABLE OF CONTENTS

CHAPTER 1

BENELUX COUNTRIES

HANK, MY SON, I WISH you would have known my great friend, Bill Schreiber. He was quite the character, almost larger than life to me. He was a man of great intellect, a wonderful sense of humor, and was extremely resourceful. I am confident you two would have enjoyed each others perspective on life and would have been good friends also. I want to tell you a little about him that will give you more insight into his capabilities.

Bill grew up in Indianapolis and was fiercely proud of our hometown. He earned an undergraduate and master's degree from Indiana University in political science. As he was matriculating through school the Viet Nam War was beginning to escalate. Unlike previous foreign encounters in our history, this war was extremely divisive of the American public. American youth became very disenchanted with the skirmish and the resentment grew while our efforts heightened. As the war wore on open demonstrations against the hostilities became commonplace.

In order to muster the forces necessary to fight the war, the federal government was forced to reinstate the process of conscription into the armed services. The prospect of being drafted into the service was a daunting notion to the majority of our young adults. To them, this was a one way ticket to Asia to fight in a war they did not believe in. Although he was hardly a leader in the movement against the war, it is safe to say Bill was not a supporter of the encounter.

In fact, he began to do everything in his power to avoid being drawn into the encounter. After completing his undergraduate work he taught high school for a year, insuring his exempt status from the draft. While teaching, Bill met a woman, fell in love, and married which gave him another avenue for avoiding being called into the service.

The marriage deferment allowed him to quit teaching and pursue a career in politics, his true passion. He went to work for a local congressman. While in this position, over coffee at the federal building, he sought out and befriended an employee of the local draft board. Eventually, his new friend kept him abreast of future changes that were to occur in the Selective Service process.

He was informed that he would soon need to have a child to maintain his exemption from the draft. So, he and Patty started their family. Not long after they had their first son, his friend told him he may need to have a second offspring to further avoid induction. So, Bill and his wife tried for several months to conceive, to no avail. They then decided to adopt an infant girl which enabled Bill to continue his deferred status. Oddly enough, soon after they brought their new daughter home, they became pregnant with their second son. But, all his maneuvering enabled Bill to successfully avoid military service in this tumultuous era.

A few years later and not even thirty years old, he was elected Marion County Democratic Chairman. In 1975 while serving as chairman, Bill decided to run for mayor of Indianapolis. He ran a spirited campaign, but was defeated by a much better funded local businessman in the primary. (I supported his opponent, a mistake he would never let me live down.)

Later that year Bill traveled to Iowa to campaign for Senator Birch Bayh of Indiana who was making a foray into the Democratic Presidential sweepstakes. Bill returned from Iowa very impressed with the organization that little-known governor, Jimmy Carter of Georgia had built. After Senator Bayh dropped out of the race early in 1976, Bill announced his support for Carter. This early endorsement of Carter by Bill would accrue to his benefit.

Bill spent the remainder of the election campaigning for Carter for President. In fact, while campaigning in Indiana, Carter stayed at the Schreiber home as their guest. When Carter was successful, Bill immediately set his sights on an appointment. He zeroed in on the position of the International Boundary Commissioner. This rather obscure role had been established by treaty between the United States and Canada decades before, to ensure a clearing along the joint borders of the two countries. It was a very low profile position, but paid well, and Bill thought it was a perfect fit for a political professional.

Soon after President Carter's Inauguration, Bill began angling for the position. Nothing occurred for several months. In the early spring, Bill attended a swearing in ceremony in the Rose Garden at the White House for a fellow Hoosier being appointed U.S. District Attorney. While there Bill ran into a friend from the Carter campaign who was now a high ranking official in the White House. His friend asked him about how his appointment was coming. Bill responded that it had become bogged down in the bureaucracy at the State Department.

His friend immediately ushered him into the White House to pay a visit on Hamilton Jordan, President Carter's Chief of Staff. When they arrived at Jordan's office they were immediately waved in. After a warm greeting and catch-up conversation, Jordan asked Bill about the status of his job application. Bill informed Jordan that it had apparently become stymied at the State Department because he was not fluent in French. At this Jordan erupted. He told Bill's high ranking friend to call the State Department and tell them, "Ham says f**ky vous!" Bill said that at that moment he knew he had the job. This was another example of Bill's ingenuity working to his benefit.

When the Carter Administration began to falter, Bill moved his family home to Indianapolis and began searching for other employment after his term ended. Eventually, he and I would come to work together in the Indiana General Assembly and we started a consulting business together. We traveled together often on business and soon would become international traveling companions.

In the late winter of 1992 I began to see television ads that were proclaiming an amazing deal on trips to Europe. The deal seemed too good to be true, $449 for roundtrip airfare and five night's accommodation including breakfast daily and all taxes. I realize this has been over two decades ago, but even then this was a terrific deal. After seeing the commercial a couple of times I decided to share this information with my buddy and traveling companion, Bill. At this time Bill and I worked closely together and were former business partners.

I dropped by Bill's office first thing the next morning to try to encourage him to consider another trip to Europe. I walked in the door and before I could tell him what I had discovered he told me about having seen the ad the night before, and could hardly believe what he had seen and heard. We immediately pulled out our calendars to see if there was a feasible opening in our mutual schedules prior to the March 15 deadline. Sure enough, there were two different weeks we could make a trip work.

We decided that the first step was to attempt to ascertain the legitimacy of the offer. So, we called the number provided on the ad to see what the catch was. As it turned out, there was no catch. Apparently, the fact was TWA had excess capacity on its transatlantic routes and was looking to fill its planes. Consequently, they had teamed with a travel company, who had paired up some of their inventory with a number of small hotels that dot Europe with the same capacity issues as TWA and, presto, the mother of all travel sales was born. The travel agency was running the ads, filling the orders, and we were in business for the best deal I have had, before or since, on travel.

Bill and I realized that a deal this good would not last long and we needed to make some decisions quickly. First, we needed to choose from the various destinations that TWA served in Europe, because that was where the special was offered. And, secondly, we need to arrive on the dates of travel.

After surveying the potential destinations, we decided to return to Amsterdam, the city where we had started and ended my initial European visit a couple of years before. However, we decided to see if it was possible to extend our time abroad from five to eight nights and see not only Amsterdam, but include more of the Netherlands and the other two Low Countries. We also decided to push as close to the deal deadline as possible and travel the second week in March in hopes of having a little better weather.

These decisions made, we called the travel agent to make our arrangements. Sure enough, there was still space available to Amsterdam on our preferred dates. We were also able to extend the trip by three nights without penalty, nor having to purchase rooms for those days. We found out that our hotel in Amsterdam would be the Slotania in the western suburb of Slotermeerlaan, a hotel and area neither one of us had heard of. Hank, you may not believe this, but these were the days before the internet existed and finding much out about either the hotel or the area was difficult. Yes, Hank, there was actually a time not too long ago that the internet did not exist. After searching all the related travel guides available at the Indianapolis Public Library we finally found a small reference to the hotel and its remote area. We also were able to get directions to the hotel from the travel agency.

As an aside, I learned from this experience that some of the best deals in travel are packages that pair, at least, airfare and accommodations together. By doing so, you are able to often times realize significant savings. These types of deals are available around the globe by travel agents that specialize in travel in a particular region. These agencies become well acquainted with hoteliers in their area of specialty and will help them with a consistent clientele by allowing the agency to sell limited inventory at a reduced rate. At the same time these agencies make similar arrangements with airlines that fly to these destinations and they will pair air, hotel and sometimes ground transportation, into unbeatable deals.

These types of arrangements can often be made directly through airlines. Airlines will typically co-brand with a travel agency that puts together exclusive packages using the airline. We are loyal Delta customers and have realized great savings through Delta Vacations packages on numerous occasions. These deals are readily available and should be strongly considered in making travel decisions.

I find that planning for a trip overseas is nearly as much fun as the trip itself. Bill and I both set about scouring travel books to determine which areas of Belgium, the Netherlands, and Luxembourg were not to be missed. We also researched the best way to get around these countries and quickly determined that rail travel made the most sense to us.

Our research also indicated that the most cost effective method was to buy a Benelux rail pass that was good for a specified number of days travel during a prescribed period of time. In our case, we chose a pass good for travel throughout the three countries for five days in a month. These types of passes are available through vendors of Eurail passes and must be purchased in the United States before you go to Europe. There are various types of theses passes which are country specific, or a grouping of countries, that can fit your travel needs. These passes can be great deals and are excellent ways to see European countries.

NETHERLANDS

Our prep work done, our day of departure finally arrived and we boarded our plane from Indianapolis to New York JFK Airport. After an uneventful trip to New York we found our way to the TWA International Terminal and boarded our flight for Amsterdam. In those days TWA (prior to their merger with American Airlines) flew wide-body Lockheed-made L-1011 aircrafts to Europe. My level of sophistication in travel was not what it is today, but I thought these big planes were comfortable. However, their configuration of two seats, an aisle, five seats across the middle and another aisle and two more seats made it nearly imperative that you get a window or aisle seat. Otherwise, you were squeezed between two other passengers and had a difficult time getting comfortable on the long flight.

I remember that the plane was far less than full that night and thinking it is a good thing that they ran the package deal special or no one would be on this flight. The fact that the plane had a number of vacant seats was a good thing for us because we were able to move around and get more comfortable. In fact, I discovered that the seats were designed to be folded over. So, with no one in the seat in front of me I was able to flatten the seat back and stretch out literally. After dinner, I kicked the seat in front of me back down and was able to get a few hours' sleep which is a real bonus in coach when traveling abroad.

We arrived in Amsterdam as the sun was just breaking over the horizon. It was a clear, cool morning and after passing through Customs and Immigration we made the short trek to the Schiphol Airport train station. My buddy, Bill, had put together directions to our hotel which called for us to hop on the train heading toward the Centraal Station, but get off a stop or two before at Sloterdijk. At the base of the train station we were able to connect to an Amsterdam city tram which took us directly to our hotel, the Slotania.

Our short tram ride wound us through a pleasant-looking neighborhood filled with multi-story buildings with commercial activity on the first floors. We hopped off the tram within a few feet of the front door of the hotel. It was now about nine o'clock. Not knowing what to expect of the Slotania, the outward appearance looked good to us. We ducked inside to be greeted by a friendly, English-speaking man who was in charge of the front desk operation. To no great surprise given the early hour, he informed us that our room would not be ready for a couple of hours, but invited us in to store our luggage and have a cup of coffee.

We graciously accepted his offer and placed our bags in a closet near the front desk and grabbed a cup of coffee. We then approached him about the last bit of uncertainty that remained in our travel planning. We were to stay at the Slotania for five nights, but we wanted to divide those nights into three nights at the beginning of our trip and two at the end. This would leave us with three nights in the middle of our trip so we could relocate further south in the Benelux countries to provide us with a better base to explore the southern regions of the area. We had been unable to arrange this through the agency we had purchased our package from; we were only able to arrange for a return flight three days later.

We explained our predicament to this pleasant gentleman running the hotel and he quickly understood what we were trying to accomplish. He reviewed the reservation book and confirmed that our plan was possible and made the appropriate changes to accomplish our needs. Whew! This was a great relief to us and made for an even more pleasant start to our trip.

His offer of coffee, followed with our conversation about our nights of stay, lead to an invitation to breakfast. We again accepted his kindness and moved to the second floor dining room and satisfied our appetites. We then set out to explore the neighborhood around the hotel for a couple of hours until our room was ready to occupy. The majority of our time was spent at an open-air, Saturday market across the street from the hotel that was selling everything from hardware to fresh flowers.

We returned to the room after sating ourselves on sausages at the market across the street and discovered our room was now ready. We quickly moved into the room which was light and airy. After we had both cleaned up from our journey, removing the airplane film from our bodies, we set out to explore Amsterdam.

We had visited Holland a couple of years before and had absolutely fallen in love with Amsterdam. The city had been saved from the ravages of the two world wars and the dominate architecture hails from the 17th Century. These multi-story, brick houses which line this canaled city are beautiful and the water that is everywhere provides an oxygenation, a literal freshness in the air.

In addition to the natural beauty of the city and the crispness of the air, it is the attitude of the Dutch people that I find so endearing. I know that we Americans are fiercely proud of the freedoms we possess and when I return from many of my travels I reflect on how wonderful a country in which we live. However, I have never felt as profoundly free as I do when I am in the Netherlands. The openness of the society, accepting of such practices as prostitution and soft drug use, bespeaks a broader tolerance of views and lifestyles that is not found most anywhere in the world. It is inspiring to me.

One of the beauties of the Slotania is its proximity to public transportation. The ever efficient Amsterdam trams and buses stop right in front of the hotel. We were able to buy a stripenkaart, or multi-ride pass, from the tobacco shop down the block and jump on the tram for a twenty minute ride into the city. Being somewhat familiar with the city from our previous visit we spent the first day roaming around the neighborhood near the Leidseplein, one of the many squares that serve as focal points for the city.

Our real effort was to stay awake until dinnertime, eat, and then go to bed. I am a firm believer that this is the best method in which to acclimate to your new time zone. The last thing you want to do upon arrival in Europe is go to your room and fall into bed for several hours. This can screw up your internal clock for days. We accomplished this by doing a lot of walking and stopping into a couple of bars for a beer.

As night began to fall we returned to Slotermeerlaan and found a nice little restaurant and had a wonderful dinner. I still remember eating the largest and tastiest chicken breast I had ever consumed, before or since. We then returned to the room and quickly fell asleep at the ripe hour of 9 p.m. I recall being awakened around midnight by the sounds of a Las Vegas style show emanating from directly below our room. It turns out that at that time the Slotania was a popular spot for English weekend merrymakers to Amsterdam whose package included this floor show. As best we could tell these folks came to Holland, enjoyed the coffee houses and were treated to the Saturday night show which posed quite a ruckus. But, being as tired as I was, after a few minutes I fell back to sleep and enjoyed a good night's rest.

We awoke refreshed the next morning and, after polishing off a good breakfast, we set out to see the sights of Amsterdam. We decided to explore the oldest neighborhood in Amsterdam, the Jordaan, as our first order of business. We had run out of time on our previous visit and had not been able to nose around this highly recommended area. Little did I know that this would become my favorite area in the city?

The Jordaan is just southwest of the Centraal Station and stretches on southward to the Anne Frank House and the Westerkerk. The former working-class neighborhood was built largely in the 17th Century and maintains a wonderful charm. Although not a major shopping or entertainment center, the area houses many quaint boutiques, restaurants, bars and is home to some of the best "brown cafes" in the city. "Brown cafes" are uniquely Amsterdam eating and drinking establishments that have been in service for hundreds of years. Their name is derived from the brown, or tan, coloring of the walls from years of nicotine build up from the heavy smoking that has gone on inside. Although it is now illegal to smoke indoors in Amsterdam, it was not at this time and it seemed that in the early '90s everyone did.

It was on this day that I stepped foot in what has become my favorite brown and also one of my favorite places to eat in Amsterdam, De Prins. Bill had spied the recommendation for De Prins in Frommer's Travel Guide (our most trusted trip advisor) and as we were getting hungry we decided to seek it out. When we arrived on this cool Sunday it seemed that every hip and attractive person in the Jordaan had the same idea.

We squeezed into the last two seats available and set about trying to figure out what to order. I began to look around at the beautiful young women sitting near us and check out what they were eating. Something quickly caught my eye, a gorgeous, tall blond eating an open-faced sandwich. When the waitress came around I ordered a beer and the sandwich like the blond was eating. It turns out they are called a uitsmijter, which consists of two eggs sunny-side up, thinly sliced ham, and melted gouda cheese served on brown bread. You talk about a slice of heaven, this is it!

We spent the rest of that day visiting some of the major attractions in the city including the Rijksmuseum, a wonderful palace of an art museum. It is the home of my favorite piece of art, *the Nightwatch*. Probably the most famous painting by the Dutch Renaissance artist, Rembrandt, viewing *the Nightwatch* is worth the trip to Amsterdam in and of itself. There are numerous other works by Rembrandt and other famous artists, Dutch and otherwise, and the experience at the museum is a very pleasant one indeed.

Nearby the Rijksmuseum are two other art museums well worth a visit, the van Gogh and the Stedelijk. The van Gogh contains over 200 paintings plus etchings and drawings by Vincent van Gogh. Clearly the most comprehensive collection by the artist, the works were a gift to the Dutch government from family members under the proviso that they would not be taken out of the country. Around the corner is Amsterdam's modern-art museum, the Stedelijk, which is impressive in its own right.

After roaming around the area near the Leidseplein, we settled into a Middle Eastern restaurant for a giant plate of shawarma and French fries. The lamb/beef concoction is very filling and can be well spiced. We polished off our plates along with a couple of beers and headed back to the Slotania and called it a night.

We awoke the next morning after another good night's sleep and we were clearly now acclimated to European time. After breakfast we decided it was time to break out our Benelux rail passes and go exploring other parts of the Netherlands. Exiting the hotel we caught the first passing bus heading toward the Centraal Station. Upon our arrival at the train station we confirmed our earlier research via the train board and got our passes validated for travel by the rail authorities, a must prior to traveling with these type of passes. We then hopped on a train headed west to the city of Haarlem to begin our whirlwind tour.

We would soon discover that the Netherlands is filled with charming cities and towns outside of Amsterdam. Our first stop, Haarlem, is a great little city close enough to Amsterdam that many tourists use it as a base to explore the city and the surrounding countryside. It is a very walkable city and is home to several canals, a trademark of many Dutch communities.

Haarlem is home to a couple of noteworthy sights, the Frans Hals Museum being the foremost of them. The museum is filled with works of Hals and other artists who were of the Haarlem school and is a definite highlight. Additionally, the St. Bravo's Church, or Grote Kerk, is an excellent example of Gothic architecture. Construction was begun in the mid-15th Century and completed early in the next. Probably the most notable feature of the church is a magnificent Christian Muller organ that was built in 1738. Several renowned musicians have ventured to Haarlem to play the instrument including Mozart, Handel, Liszt, and Schubert, to name a few. The instrument is frequently played in recitals that are open to the public free of charge.

After breezing through these sights we returned to the railway station and caught a train for The Hague. The Hague is the seat of government for the Netherlands and is a city filled with impressive palaces and government structures. Realizing that our time in the city was limited and with our interest in government, Bill and I decided to visit the Peace Palace. The imposing structure is the home of the International Court of Justice. This body, which is the judicial arm of the United Nations, is composed of fifteen judges that endeavor to resolve international disputes. The structure and the process are fascinating and worth the visit.

After our brief visit to The Hague, we hopped back on a train for a short, six mile ride to Delft. Delft is a beautiful city with a preserved medieval core, filled with canals and wonderful architecture and is probably best known for the blue and white earthenware that has been made here for centuries. Before setting off to find the Royal Delft factory we had a small matter to resolve, quenching our appetites. By now it was well after noon and it was a very sunny spring day. We headed to the town square, the Markt, found a suitable café and plopped down at a table in the sun to enjoy a nice lunch.

Sufficiently regenerated by a bowl of pasta and a couple of beers, we set out to find the Royal Delft factory for a tour. Here you are able to view the potters at work, finely crafting their wares as they have been for nearly five hundred years. Their artisanry is impressive and examples of their work through the years are on display. Additionally, they have an outlet store onsite and slightly nicked items can be purchased at a very reasonable price. In fact, a tiny tear bottle from this store adorns my dresser, as it has all the years since that visit.

We made our way back to the train station and decided it was time to head back to Amsterdam, as it was moving toward darkness. We boarded a train that took us through Rotterdam and then turned back east toward our destination. As we moved through the countryside the train made a stop in Gouda, famous for their cheese. On a whim we jumped off the train, found the times for future Amsterdam trains and headed out to locate a tavern for a beer and some cheese. We accomplished this in short order and caught the next passing train to Amsterdam in about an hour, but with a beer in our stomach and cheese in our pockets.

Returning to the Centraal Station, we were tired, hungry and ready to find our way back to our hotel. However, Bill had read in a guide book about a good, reasonably priced restaurant at the station and we decided to give it a try. The Grand Café is near platform 2 and has a diverse menu and a very comfortable atmosphere. That evening I dined on beef stroganoff which was delicious and affordable. The meal was a fine ending to a packed, but interesting, day. So, if you find yourself with a layover in Centraal Station and are hungry, know that a very viable alternative is just upstairs. I am quite confident you will be satisfied.

BELGIUM

Bill and I discovered that Holland has a lot more to offer than just Amsterdam, but it is time to move on southward to Belgium. After finishing a breakfast of ham, cheese and hard boiled eggs, we packed up, checked to make sure everything was in order for our return on Friday, and headed to the Centraal Station to catch a train to Antwerp. Bill had done the yeoman's share of the research for this trip and had determined that Antwerp was the most suitable location to serve as a three day home base for our exploration of Belgium and Luxembourg.

After a smooth couple of hours on the train we arrived at Antwerp's Centraal Station. A large and impressive structure, the Centraal Station is near the center of the city and is a great location to begin exploring this interesting locale. It is for this reason, and the fact that we intended to be utilizing train travel to discover other parts of Belgium and Luxembourg, that we decided to find a hotel in the vicinity of the Station.

Bill had found in a guidebook a reference to the Hotel Antwerp Billiard Palace which is located on the same square as the Station. The hotel contained a pool and billiard hall that had apparently hosted the world billiard championships on a few occasions. Bill found this aspect of the hotel particularly appealing because we could play a game of snooker on the same table as the world's greatest players had. So, upon our arrival we walked directly to the Billiard Palace and rented a room.

Hank, if you find yourself in Antwerp without me, do not stay at this hotel. You will not like it!

It turns out that the central location and billiard hall were about all this hotel had going for it at the time. It has been my experience that often times that areas around the main train stations can be a little seedy. This was certainly no exception. I am confident that if your desire was to find some companionship or a controlled substance; it could be done within a few feet of the front door.

As with many budget European hotels at that time, the bathrooms were shared and had seen their better days. Our room was decent sized, but the wallpaper was peeling off. The preponderance of their clientele appeared to be African exchange students who seemed to be enamored with the local brew which led to a good deal of late night noise. All-in-all we could have done a better job of selecting an accommodation. I am sure that our choice of hotel helped to color my impression of the city.

Antwerp is an interesting community and one that is very pedestrian friendly. So after a brief period of settling in, we ventured out on foot to see what the city has to offer. You don't have to wander too far from the Centraal Station before it becomes apparent that you are in one of the diamond centers of the world. The industry is huge here and one aspect of it that I found particularly interesting, as a Midwestern protestant, is that the industry is dominated by the city's Orthodox Jewish community. Thus, you can not only get a glimpse of a new industry, but some insight into a different, and interesting, culture.

Given that both Bill and I were single at the time with no immediate intentions of changing that status; neither of us was in the market to make any serious diamond purchases, but we were intrigued by the industry. We spent the next couple of hours visiting the Diamond Museum and, probably more interestingly, one of the myriad diamond workshops. Here we were able to observe craftsmen cutting and polishing the diamonds into their state of brilliance. To me, this was well worth the visit.

In addition to the diamond activity, Antwerp was home to the famous artist, Peter Paul Rubens. Rubens mansion is now a museum that is quite interesting to visit. The home itself provides you with an idea of the grand style in which the artist lived, but there are several of his and other contemporaries' works adorning the walls. Additionally, Antwerp has a well preserved medieval core that is filled with shops and sidewalk cafes and is a very pleasant area for a stroll.

After our sightseeing was finished we stopped at a restaurant near our hotel that specialized in Middle Eastern fare. I once again opted for a shawarma dinner and a few beers. We then went back to the hotel for that game of snooker that had taken us to the god forsaken place to begin with. This was my first encounter with the game and I found it to be considerably more difficult than its American cousin, pool.

Snooker is a very similar game to pool, but is played on a larger table with more balls. Bill, who had played the game before and held himself out to be knowledgeable of the rules, showed me how to play. Since the table is larger, and the pockets appear smaller, and it is more difficult to sink your ball. Although I would rate the experience an interesting one, it was certainly not grand enough to recommend an overnight stay in the hotel, let alone the three nights we had signed on for.

The next morning we awoke, quickly cleaned up, and ate what they offered for breakfast. We then set out to get our money's worth from our rail passes traversing the Belgian countryside. Specifically, we had decided to make a quick trip to Brussels, Bruges, and Ghent.

Our first stop on this tour was Brussels, the capitol of Belgium and home to much of the European Union government. The Brussels central rail station, Gare Centrale, was our point of arrival and is very well situated for covering the highlights of the city. Brussels is a very walkable town and our first stop was their famous city square, the Grand Place. The Grand Place is one of the largest and most beautiful central squares in all of Europe. The buildings have a medieval feel and include the remarkable Town Hall, the Brussels Museum and several Guild Halls. The sides of the square are lined with outdoor cafes, and given that the March sun was shining we decided to sit down at one, enjoy a cup of strong coffee and get our bearings.

The cobblestone square was teeming with locals and tourists alike, talking, taking pictures and enjoying the beautiful day. Many of the stunning buildings that surround the old marketplace are guild halls representing the various historic craftsmen of the area. It seems as though every other shop sells delicious Belgium chocolate or their signature waffles. Wanting not to offend anyone, we decided to sample the chocolates and they did not fail to live up to their reputations.

Sufficiently buzzed from the coffee and sugar, we decided it was time to venture out a little further and see what else the city had to offer. Our next stop was a very short stroll away, their very famous and much beloved Manneken Pis, a statue of a little boy peeing. In my book this is clearly one of the most overrated and absurd landmarks I have witnessed in my travels. It is so preposterous that it cries out to be viewed to see how different cultures embrace the unusual.

Oddly enough, Bill was so turned off by the Manneken Pis that he believed that it was time to move on from Brussels. I didn't feel like I could make a strong argument against the move particularly since I knew we had another shot at the city the next day if we so desired. So, we returned to the Gare Centrale and hopped on the next train for Bruges.

Bill and I first found out about the wonders of Bruges from two young Canadian women we had breakfast with in our hotel in Paris a few years before. These two fellow travelers joined us at our table one morning and we began to swap tales of our trips. They had just arrived the night before from Bruges and spent nearly the entire meal filling us with stories about their time there and encouraging us to go. I learned two things from those young ladies, first, that there is a lot to be gleaned from conversations with others you meet in your journeys and, they were correct about in their high praise of Bruges.

About an hour away from Brussels by train, Bruges is nearly a place out of a fairytale. Bruges was a major commercial and trading center for northern Europe in the 13th and 14th centuries. Although it was some thirty miles inland it was the largest port city in that part of the world and was a hub for the textile industry. However, in the 15th century the Zwin River, Bruges' access point to the North Sea silted in and eliminated the city's access to the sea. Thus, Bruges fell into suspended animation for centuries until it was rediscovered by travelers in the early twentieth century.

This stroke of misfortune for the city of Bruges at the time has led to its resurgence. Bruges has become a very popular tourist attraction relying on its medieval core, so well preserved, as its primary attraction. The city has a calmness to go along with its picturesque beauty that makes it a natural draw for travelers.

We arrived at the train station, about a ten minute walk from the center of the old city. As we strolled toward the center we noticed the peaceful canals that flow through the city and decided that a canal tour might be in order. We soon arrived at a square where there was a trailer serving Belgian waffles among other drinks and snacks. Since we had passed in Brussels, we decided that we needed to sample one of these delicacies we had heard about. Unlike what we are used to at American waffle establishments, we were handed our treat in wax paper and it was not covered in maple syrup. Rather, the sweetness was included in the waffle mix. Eating it much like you would a cookie in the wax paper; the waffle was a deliciously sweet snack.

Polishing off our tidbits, we noticed a canal boat was preparing to take a load of tourists on a trip around the city. We hurried over to join the tour thinking that, in addition to being an enjoyable experience, this would be a great way to get oriented to the city. We were correct on both counts.

The canal cruise lasted about an hour and took you by many of the most notable sights in Bruges. The ride was serene, interrupted only by the English speaking narration of the guide. One of the most memorable parts on the tour was seeing the number of swans gliding about in the canals. Our guide offered that in 1488, Maximilian of Austria was imprisoned in Bruges during a revolt. His chief advisor was beheaded and when Maximilian was freed he ordered Bruges to keep swans in its canals as a punishment for his imprisonment. I have since been confused whether Maximilian was actually angry with the citizens of Bruges, or whether his fine to the city was to further beautify a place he secretly enjoyed. Regardless, by introducing these magnificent waterfowl to its canals it has enhanced the appearance in my opinion.

Having finished our relaxing water tour of the city and our snack of the waffle had long been digested; we decided it was time to take our midday meal. We ventured into the Markt, or Central Square, and quickly settled on a place to eat. Seated at a table inside the restaurant with a view of the activity on the square, I quickly decided on an order of steak frites. This turned out to be a wonderful decision and we thoroughly enjoyed our lunch and watching the activities on the square.

We felt as though we had gotten a pretty decent overview of this charming city on the canal tour, but there was one major attraction we wanted to see before we ventured on to our next stop. We decided that we needed to see the treasures in the Church of Our Lady next. We walked across the cobbled-stoned square to the church and entered in search of one particular item; Michelangelo's marble sculpture of the Madonna and Child. This magnificent work of art depicts Jesus standing beside Mary appearing to almost step away from his mother. This was the only piece by Michelangelo to leave Italy during his lifetime having been purchased by a Bruges merchant.

After viewing the Madonna and Child and other pieces in the church, we decided it was time to begin our retreat from Bruges. As we wound our way through the narrow, cobblestone streets back to the train station, Bill and I discussed that finding these types of cities teeming with history and ambiance are the best reason we know to travel.

We soon arrived at the train station and, after checking the schedule, we boarded a train for the short, half hour ride to Ghent. Upon our arrival, we learned that the best method to get to the center to see the sights was to take the tram. We hopped on the first tram and about ten minutes later we were standing in the medieval core of this vibrant city of about a quarter of a million. It was now a cool, blustery day and rain was starting to spit and we decided to duck into a nearby pub to gain our bearings.

We entered the establishment and encountered a bartender that was friendly, full of advice and spoke excellent English, three qualities that were perfect for the occasion. We ordered glasses of some fine Belgian ale and began to plan our visit. But first, we engaged our server in a protracted conversation about the wonders of Belgian brews, some of the finest in the world. Clearly, our barkeep was knowledgeable and enthralled with the subject. He gave us a lengthy history of the brewing tradition in his country, from its early beginnings in the Catholic Church, to its continued nurturing by the Trappist's monks, to today's vibrant industry that produces hundreds of hoppy beverages in Belgium. The range of brews is broad, from pilsners to strong ales, to reds, browns and flavored Trappist concoctions.

Two other points were driven home that day. First, the Belgians are very serious about their glassware for their beers and ales with most all having their own specific glasses that they deem appropriate for their beverage. They can be very fancy by our standards and swilling from the bottle would be viewed as something very uncouth. Second, beware! The fermented beverages of this country can be far stronger that our 3.5 to 5 percent alcohol content beers. With nearly twice the punch as what Americans are used to, be cautious about your intake.

We spent about an hour learning about the industry and sampling a couple of different varieties in lovely glassware, and decided it was time to set forth and see some of the sights of the attractive city. Our advisor, nee bartender, suggested that given our limited timeframe, we should explore two landmarks: the Belfry and Cloth Hall and St. Bavo's Cathedral. We bid our friend adieu and set out to accomplish those tasks.

One of the most striking features of Ghent is that three large cathedrals stand nearly in a row in the center of the old town. The most impressive of these St. Bavo's, was our first destination. St. Bavo's was constructed in the 13th and 14th centuries and is really an architectural mishmash but is an impressive, massive structure. The classic art contained inside was the draw for us. The signature piece is a 24 panel work by Jan Van Eyck, The Adoration of the Mystic Lamb. This splendid work was commissioned for the cathedral by a wealthy alderman in 1420. Originally Van Eyck's brother, Hubert, was engaged to create the work, but was finished by Jan in 1432 six years after his death. In addition to this work, there are a number of notable pieces of art including Ruben's, The Conversion of St. Bavo, in a circular chapel bearing the artist's name.

Our next stop was across the street at the Belfry and Cloth Hall. The Cloth Hall was the denizen of the local textile merchants since the 15th century. The grand, ornate structure is certainly worth a perusal, but the attached Belfry is the star of the show. The structure rises nearly 300 feet high and is topped with a gilded copper dragon. The tower houses the bells that have rung out for centuries proclaiming the great moments in Ghent history. An elevator will take you about two-thirds the way up where you can see the bells and enjoy a spectacular view of the city. If you are fortunate, and we were not, you can attend regularly scheduled concerts of the Belfry's bells.

After our visits to these two sights and our education on the Belgian beer industry, we decided it was time to head back to Antwerp as night was beginning to fall. We hopped back on the trusty tram and retraced our steps to the train station. A few minutes later we caught our train for the half hour ride through the verdant Belgian countryside to Antwerp.

Upon our return we scouted out a nearby Italian restaurant which would serve as the location for that evening's dinner. After enjoying a heaping plate of pasta that we washed down with some more fine Belgian beer we returned to the Billiard Parlor Hotel. We determined that this would be a perfect time for a final game of snooker. We went back to the snooker hall on the second floor of the hotel. Snooker is clearly more difficult than a game of standard eight ball or rotation on a pool table. After a couple of lengthy games, largely because of our lack of skill, we were persuaded that we would not be returning to participate in the next world championship to be hosted at the hotel. It was time to turn in as we were off to Luxembourg on an early train the next morning. Our only hope was that we would not be carried away by bedbugs as we slept in the shabby hotel.

LUXEMBOURG

We awoke early, somewhat refreshed and happy that no great trauma had befallen us overnight at the Billiard Parlor Hotel. We took a quick breakfast and walked across the street to the Centraal Station. We caught the first train for Brussels and changed there to complete the four plus hour journey to Luxembourg City. We arrived in late morning having gotten the early start, the day was bright and sunny, a perfect late winter day.

The first impression one has when exiting Gare Centrale in Luxembourg City is that it sits in a picturesque gorge formed by the two rivers that join in the city. The center of the city lies atop a hill above the train station. We decided to hike up the hill and explore the center of the city by foot. After about a twenty minute climb we reached the top of the hill and were greeted by a lovely town plaza and terrific views down on the gorge below.

Luxembourg City is truly a physically beautiful locale created by the ravine which cuts through the city.

We quickly found the tourist information office and armed ourselves with maps and a guidebook. It was such a pleasant day we decided to sit at an outdoor café on the main town square, enjoy a cup of coffee, take in the sights and develop a plan of attack for our few hours in this welcoming city. As we watched the foot traffic and observed the buildings surrounding the square we firmly believed that the standard of living in this community was very high. Even though we were at the end of winter, everything was extremely clean, well-kept and manicured.

We decided to spend the rest of the day on a walking tour of the city. The tourist office had supplied us with all we needed to amble about the old town. We wound our way past such sights as the Notre Dame Cathedral, past several monuments (presumably to war victories), the neoclassical City Hall, the outstanding Grand Ducal Palace (the official residence of the Grand Duke), and, most impressively, the stunning views from the old fortress walls down into the gorge. Did I mention they have a very pretty gorge?

Having ambled through the cobblestone streets for nearly two hours we decided it was time to break for lunch. We had noticed a particularly inviting little bistro down near the train station that we decided to try for lunch. We entered to find an array of neatly arranged dark wood booths and a warm greeting from the staff. We were ushered to a table and presented with menus that were in German and French. Since neither of us spoke either language we did our best to determine something that could quell our appetites.

Our very pleasant server soon arrived and, unfortunately, informed us that she did not speak any English and would be of little help in interpreting the menu. I had by then looked around the room to see what the other patrons were eating and had spied a very well-dressed elderly gentleman eating what appeared to be a steak and fries. I motioned to the waitress that I would have what he was eating and immediately she reacted strangely. She promptly left and quickly returned with a colleague who spoke a little English. This new woman informed me that the gentleman's dish was horse meat and she did not know if Americans eat horse. I promptly thanked her for the warning and told her that did not sound appetizing to me. She suggested that I try the special of the day, beef stroganoff, and I rapidly agreed.

As it turned out the dish was delicious. I had eaten beef stroganoff several times before and since and I believe that to this day this is the best version of that recipe I have ever eaten. It probably tasted all that much better because this kind soul had spared me from eating horse steak, and although I consider myself to be a pretty adventurous eater, the notion of horse is still a foreign thought to me. This event was clearly my most vivid memory of my first day spent in Luxembourg.

However, my favorite meal would come years later when I had the opportunity to return to the Grand Duchy. Hank, as you will recall, we had the pleasure of visiting Luxembourg City in the late fall of 2014. We were ending a trip to visit Christmas markets in which we visited Switzerland, Liechtenstein, and France. We spent our last night of that trip in this lovely city before flying out for home the next day.

We took a room at the Hotel Francais situated on the main city square, the Place d'Armes. After arriving at the early afternoon, we boarded a bus outside the train station which delivered us to a stop a couple of blocks from the hotel. We rolled our bags the short walk through the pedestrian-only area toward the hotel. As we neared our destination we could see a large crowd gathered in the open area in front of our lodging. As it turned out the entire square was filled with temporary chalets comprising a vibrant Christmas market.

We made our way into the hotel, past the teeming crowd and down a small hall adjacent to the thriving restaurant associated with the accomodations. With the help of a waiter from the restaurant we were ushered to a second floor lobby area and checked into our room. Our cozy room was located a floor above the lobby. Although it was rather small, it was well-appointed, had a very nice bathroom and three beds that suited our needs.

After a brief time to freshen up from our couple hour train ride from Strausbourg, we hit the streets to see the sights with the time remaining that afternoon and evening. Our first mission was to explore the Christmas market right out our front door. It was quite nice with local vendors selling native handicrafts and food and drinks. Although we had eaten lunch on the train, feasting on sandwichs and beverages we had purchased in the

Metz train station as we changed trains enroute, Hank you were hungry. We bought you a large sausage sandwich which you promptly devoured while your mom and I sampled some of the delicious hot mulled, red wine.

As we walked around the market Hank spotted a nutcracker which he added to his growing collection of this small wooden figures. As he and I were deciding on which one to buy, Jenny slipped into a tourist information center just across the street to see what was going on around the city. She returned with a map which was marked up, pointing out where another Christmas market was located a couple of blocks away.

We finished our foray through the Place d'Armes market and headed down the street to locate the other market. Really all we had to do was follow the crowd down the street which was devoid of vehicular traffic. We soon arrived at another large, crowded market which occupied a square on the precipice above the ravine. We circulated through the market, stopping to buy a lovely, handblown starshaped ornament with a snowman painted on it.

It was now well past dark, so we decided to head back to the hotel for a short rest before we went out to dinner. We stopped at a nice, little souvenir shop on our way back and purchased some small flags, one of Luxembourg and also the European Union flag. By now, Hank, you had quite a collection of flags of countries you have visited and these seemed to round out that trip.

We began to scout out a restaurant for dinner as we made our way back to the hotel. There was nearly every ethnic variety represented in the center of Luxembourg and several looked inviting. When we arrived back at our hotel we couldn't help but notice that the first floor restaurant, Café Francais, was still packed. Given the crowd as a recommendation, we decided to peruse the menu and see if anything looked agreeable to us. Hank, you immediately spotted a fettucini Bolognese which sounded good to you. Jenny and I both thought there was something we would like so we made a reservation for an hour later.

We went upstairs to our room and spent the time until dinner packing for our departure the next morning. At the proscribed time we hopped the elevator to the ground level and we greeted by the hostess as we came off. She remembered us from making our reservation and ushered us to the best table in the house by the front window overlooking the Christmas market. The dining room was very nicely appointed with tables covered in starched linen and nice art covering the white walls. The place was crowded, but the acoustics were such that it was conducive to conversation, as we like it.

A friendly waiter arrived in due course and presented us with menus. As we looked at the wine card he disappeared and returned with still water and a basket of warm bread. We ordered a bottle of an inexpensive Bordeaux he recommended, which turned out to be quite nice. We then turned our attention to ordering dinner. Hank, you stuck with your earlier decision while your mom and I decided to try the mussels in white wine sauce with French fries.

The meal turned out to be fabulous. The mussels were quite tender and flavorful. As we started to eat them our waiter appeared and gave us proper instruction on how to pry the meat from the shell. He suggested that we take an empty mussel shell and use it to scoop the meat from others. He persuaded us that using a fork was a waste of time.

We complied and worked our way through the huge bowls of mussels that had been placed in front of us. The fries that accompanied the dish came in another gigantic bowl and were perfect, golden on the outside with a slight crunch with a soft interior. Hank's fetticini was prepared perfectly and was heaped with a tangy, thick Bolognese sauce with a side of freshly grated Parmesan cheese that would have pleased even an Italian's palate.

Clearly, this was my favorite meal in Luxembourg. Before I left the restaurant I told the waiter that I would like to include the recipe for the mussels in a book I was writing. Before I knew it the general manager of the establishment came by the table with handwritten notes on the preparation from the chef. After we paid our bill, the chef came out of the kitchen and we were able to compliment him on the outstanding meal. **(See Appendix 1 for the recipe)**

We returned to our room and prepared for our final night's sleep on the trip. Hank, you may recall you grabbed your mom's tablet device and tuned into the Indianapolis Colts and Washington Redskins game which was taking place at Lucas Oil Stadium. With the Colts holding a comfortable lead at the half, we were able to persuade you to turn it off and get some sleep.

We got a fairly restful night's sleep and awoke, cleaned up, and checked out of the hotel. We walked a couple of blocks to the bus stop and caught a packed bus heading in the direction of the Luxembourg Airport. We were barely able to squeeze onto the vehicle and the situation only got worse for the next few stops. Finally, as we moved further from the center we began to deposit passengers in front of modern medium-rise office buildings along the route.

By the time we were halfway through our half hour ride we all found seats and were able to enjoy the ride out from the city. We arrived at the spiffy, efficient airport and were quickly checked in. We whisked through the security checkpoint and found our way to an airline lounge which the Skyteam shared with the Luxair, the flagship carrier of the Grand Duchy. After a bit of a hassle we were admitted and enjoyed a tasty breakfast of cold meats, cheeses, boiled eggs, breads and pastries before we departed. We all left with a very positive impression of this tiny European nation, hoping to return one day when we could stay longer.

And now back to my trip with Bill....

BACK TO BELGIUM

After lunch we had an hour or so to kill before the next train for Brussels was to depart. So we strolled the streets and stopped into a pub for a beer. One thing I remember about the bar was that across the street were these big egg shaped bins. We had seen nothing like them before and after we finished our beers we decided to try and figure out what they were. It turns out that they were three recycling containers for glass, plastic and paper. Thus, we encountered an organized recycling effort long before we were to see similar ones back in the states. What a great idea!

We returned to the Gare Centrale in time to catch our train to Belgium. We settled into a couple of comfortable seats and headed out toward Brussels. Soon the train came to its first stop, only a couple of minutes after departing the station. Uniformed officers came through the cabin inspecting our passports and tickets. This, in all likelihood, would not happen today because of the unifications activities in Europe. In those days, nearly all European countries sent their own customs officials to inspect international trains that passed through their territory. In recent years since the strengthening of the European Union, this is no longer a practice and actually helps to reduce the time of travel.

After the train started to roll again through the Belgian countryside, we both fell asleep for a while. When we awoke we were only a few minutes from Brussels where we needed to change trains to get to Antwerp. We decided that hunger had again overtaken us and we would jump off and find an eatery in Brussels before headed back to the Billiard Palace for the night. We also wanted to see the Grand Place at night.

We were not disappointed with our decision. We took the short walk from Gare Centrale to the Grand Place and found the square to be even more impressive when it is illuminated at night. We drank in the moment, resisted any temptation to take the five minute walk to see the Mannequin Pis again, and set out to find a dinner location.

Bill was carrying several pages from the guidebook he had cobbled together from various sources. He found in his notes a suggestion for a seafood restaurant a couple of blocks from the Grand Place, not far away from the Gare Centrale, that looked interesting. Soon we were standing in front of Chez Leon which specialized in a Belgian tradition, mussels and frites. We quickly glanced in the window and saw there was space available and decide to go for it.

Once inside we discovered a very warm and inviting décor, simple but appealing. We were soon escorted to a checkered table clothed booth and presented with a menu we could read. We both decided to go with the house specialty, mussels and frites. This turned out to be an excellent choice and we washed it down with some more delicious Belgian beer. I have had the good fortune to return to Belgium again a couple of times and this remains my favorite meal I have had in the country. In fact, several years later while traveling through Europe with my pal, Mike Price, we returned to Chez Leon for another sampling of their specialty. It was equally as good the second time it tried it. **(See Appendix 2 for the recipe)**

Fully sated, we returned to the Gare Centrale and caught the next train to Antwerp. We soon arrived back at the Billiard Palace Hotel for our final night in this god forsaken place. We decided to pack up that night so we could make a hasty retreat the next morning and leave this hotel behind for good.

BACK TO THE NETHERLANDS

We awoke the next morning and I walked down the hall for a quick shower before breakfast. When I returned to the room I let Bill know that there was a free shower in the bathroom so we could keep moving. Bill, who had been an apologist for the hotel, let me know that he would shower when we got back to Amsterdam because the place gave him the creeps. I know how hard it was to make this admission to me, but I could not have agreed more and only wish I had possessed the idea of waiting myself.

We quickly polished off the breakfast offering and checked out. We caught the first train to Amsterdam Centraal Station and were really looking forward to our return to the city. Upon arrival we purchased a new strippenkaart at the public transportation office directly across from the train station. Unfortunately these multi-ride tickets are no longer available having been replaced by passes that contain a magnetic strip. These are available in varying lengths depending on your needs and length of your stay. These new multi-day passes are convenient, but I miss the old strippenkaart.

We boarded our bus for the return to the Slotania for our final two nights of our trip. We were once again greeted by the friendly gentleman who had met us when we first arrived. He welcomed us warmly and gave us a key to a nice, clean room with its own bathroom. I don't want to sound too redundant, and the Slotania is far from a five star hotel, but, man, was it nice to be back to a hotel that was clean and safe.

Bill decided it was time for him to take a shower and I decided that I would take a walk through the neighborhood. It was another beautiful, late winter day in Amsterdam. The sun shone brightly and the midday temperatures were probably approaching 50 degrees. I strolled by the strip of shops that lined the main street heading south from the Slotania and came upon a small park. Much to my surprise, the entire lawn that covered the park was awash in crocus. These small, multicolored flowers formed a veritable blanket on the ground.

I later learned from viewing this in other parks over the next two days, that this is a common practice in Holland. In talking to some locals this is a done by simply strewing the crocus bulbs over an area and planting them where they fall. Then, in the spring they are one of the first flowers to bloom making a lovely patchwork of colors in the open space. By the time the lawn needs to be mowed the crocus blooms have run their course for the year and you can mow the lawn without fear of disturbing the handsomeness of the plot. I keep threatening to do this in an area of my lawn, but alas, it sounds like more work that I want to do.

This practice of planting these crocus in a random pattern speaks volume about the Dutch love affair with flowers. It seems as though there is a flower shop, kiosk or peddler on every street corner in Dutch cities and towns. A number of the big tourist attractions in the country revolve around flowers and the flower industry.

In Amsterdam there is a floating flower market, Bloomenmarkt, on the Singel Canal near the Muntplein that is a top spot for visitors. Here you can see numerous shops built on barges on the canal selling assorted flowers and bulbs, as well as, other kitschy tourist keepsakes. One thing to note is that they will ship bulbs anywhere in the world. If it is the wrong season for planting your selection, they will gladly ship them to your desired address at the appropriate time for planting. I know this because we had tulips sent to our home in this manner and they still brighten our property each year.

Flowers are in fact big business in the Netherlands. If you are fortunate enough to visit the country in the spring (and I have been) you should take a train ride through the countryside to visit one of the many quaint towns in Holland. Along the way you are sure to pass fields upon fields of tulips in bloom. It is a veritable checkerboard of colors, reds, whites, yellows and so forth interspersed with green fields which either have not bloomed yet, or have already been harvested. It is quite a sight.

Many tour groups are escorted to Keukenhof Gardens, the world's largest flower garden where over 7 million bulbs are planted each year. Open only from mid-March until mid-May this is a sight to behold. It is easily accessible from Amsterdam by tour, bus, or train. And if this is not enough, you can visit the Aalsmeer Flower Auction which is the world's largest flower market. The market is housed in the largest building in the world by square footage. Over 20 million flowers from around the world are sold at auction every working day at Aalsmeer. Only ten miles from Amsterdam, the market is open to interested visitors.

If you are curious, or flowers don't wind you watch, the Dutch have a corresponding love affair with cheese. In my opinion, a quick trip to Gouda will set you right on some delicious cheese. If you have a greater interest in the business that surround this dairy product, you can visit the one of several cheese markets in addition to Gouda. Alkmaar is probably the most famous, but another worth note is in Edam and, yes, they feature Edam cheese here.

These are two additional, terrific reasons to love the Netherlands and the Dutch people.

Bill and I spent our last two days ambling around Amsterdam ducking into brown cafes and coffee shops. We decided on the afternoon of our return from Antwerp to take a canal boat ride. Again, this was a bright, sunny day and we entered the glass enclosed boat from it mooring across from the Centraal Station. As we cruised the canals receiving an oratory on the history of various sights in Amsterdam, I was interrupted by a loud ruckus coming from my left. I quickly wheeled around to see that my pal, Bill, had fallen asleep and was soundly snoring as one with sleep Apnea would do. I jolted him awake and the disturbance ended, but not before all the other passengers got a good laugh.

Our last day we decided to return to the De Prins thinking it was time for another uitsmijter which we had enjoyed so much on the first part of our journey. By the time we got to the brown café, I was beginning to rethink my order because it was a rainy, blustery day and something hot sounded good. When we arrived I saw that they had pea soup that day and the guy sitting at the next table was consuming a bowl. This, indeed, looked like the ticket for this nasty day.

Our server took our orders, Bill had mushroom soup and I had pea with the obligatory large beer. The server returned in a few minutes with our beers and piping hot bowls of soup. Mine was served with a thick slice of dense, brown bread covered with smoked bacon. The soup was a mélange of peas, carrots, potatoes and ham so thick you could probably stand a spoon up in it. The soup and the open-faced sandwich were delicious and just the recipe for a cold day in Amsterdam. I have come to discover from numerous return visits to the city that pea soup is somewhat of a specialty in Holland. I have tried it in countless places on these visits, but for my money De Prins has the best pea soup in the world. This was my favorite meal in Holland and will be the next time I return to this country. **(See Appendix 3 for the recipe)**

Later that afternoon Bill and I were sitting in a bar on the Leidseplein which had a scrolling, electronic message board, an innovation for the time. As we were sipping our drinks, we noticed that Lyle Lovett, an American singer/songwriter was performing at the Paradiso that evening. Bill had become a big fan of Lovett because of a cover of a Grateful Dead tune, <u>Devil is a Friend of Mine.</u> The song appears on an album that is a one hundred percent cover of various Dead songs by an eclectic group of artists. I had to be convinced because of my limited exposure I believed that Lovett was a country only singer, not a genre I have a great deal of interest in.

Well, Bill was persuasive and the next thing I knew we were striding across the Leiseplein seeking out the Paradiso box office. It turns out the venue was only a couple of minutes away and tickets were available. First, you had to join the Paradiso club, about five bucks as I recall, and then you could buy a ticket, which I think was only twenty guilders, or ten dollars. A good deal in my book. The show was to start at eight o'clock and it was festival seating.

With a few hours to kill, we ventured out to have dinner. In a small restaurant on a canal near the red-light district, we had a fine dinner of Indonesian rijsttafel, or rice table. Rijsttafel is a multicourse meal consisting of small portions of fifteen, or so, entrees served with rice. Some of the dishes are meat based, others vegetable, and one a hard boiled egg, but most all are spicy hot. Indonesia was once a Dutch colony and their cuisine can be readily found in Holland. It can be quite tasty. After dinner, we found our way back to the Paradiso.

The Paradiso is an old church that was converted into a concert (think rock n' roll) venue in the 60's. Consisting of folding chairs on a wooden floor with a small balcony, we arrived about a half hour early in hopes of finding a decent seat. Much to our surprise we could have literally sat in the front row. Instead, for some unknown reason, we took two seats in the center of row two and waited for the show to begin.

In about a half hour, Lovett appears with guitar in hand and three or four other musicians in tow. He soon treated us to a couple of hours of pure pleasure. We were sitting so close we could have reached out and touched him. His dry wit and the range and clarity of his voice thoroughly entertained the crowd. And, yes, my pal Bill got to hear the <u>Devil is a Friend of Mine</u> making for a nearly perfect evening.

Since this chance encounter I now look at what's playing in most all cities I visit. I have attended concerts, numerous basketball and baseball games, ice hockey and soccer matches and enjoyed the experiences. These opportunities provide you with a little insight into the culture of the country you visit because each appreciates these events in a slightly different way.

Bill and I arrived back at the Slotania late that evening after the concert. Tired and with an early wake-up call because of an early flight back to the states we were ready for bed. Much to our chagrin, a large group of British holidaymakers were again enjoying a Vegas-style floor show on the level below our room. These folks had come to Amsterdam for the weekend on a package deal to party, and party they were that night.

Finally able to fall asleep, we awoke early the next morning and took the tram and train to Schiphol Airport. There we boarded our TWA flight for our return to the U.S. After a change at Kennedy we returned home, tired but enriched by the experience. I took another great trip with Bill in 1994 to Berlin, Prague, Budapest and Vienna. We had a great time traveling and working together.

Unfortunately, Bill Schreiber died of lung cancer in January of 1996 at the ripe age of 52. Remarried and a new father to a son of less than six months of age, his death was a tragedy. He was as good a friend as I ever had. I miss my friend.

*Bill Schreiber displaying his sense of humor during a
visit to Vienna in 1994. R.I.P., my friend.*

Chapter 2

UNITED KINGDOM

In the late summer of 1995, my friend, Bill Schreiber and I decided it was time to travel abroad together again. It had been a nearly a year since our last trip, one to Central Europe. We thought it was high time we visited the countries of England, Scotland, and Wales. Bill got the okay from his relatively new wife to travel and we set about arriving at a time and scheduling the trip.

Shortly after making the decision to take the journey, we found out about a deal through American Airlines Fly Away Vacations on an air and hotel package that was very affordable and attractive to us. For about $650 we would get the "Simply London" tour which would provide us with air from Indianapolis to London Heathrow and three night's accommodations on a departure in early December. We were able to split up these nights lodging taking part on the front end and the remainder on the end of the trip. The hotel was a tourist class one in the Bayswater section of London which met our needs perfectly.

With the initial air and hotel in London in place we decided which other areas of the British Isles we wanted to visit. We determined that we wanted to see Edinburgh in Scotland, Cardiff in Wales and I wanted to visit the city of Fleetwood on the northwest coast of England. I had reason to believe that this town might have been my ancestral home and I want to see if I could find out more by visiting the community. Bill was good with the notion, particularly because he had gone to Hungary a couple of years before to see the village where his family immigrated from, so he understood my interest.

We researched the best way to travel from London to these far-flung points on the island and once again came up with the answer that train travel was best. We determined that a BritRail Pass could be tailored to our needs. We eventually purchased one that gave us eight days' worth of travel in fifteen days which would enable us to cover all the area we had time to do.

With our itinerary set and tickets purchase by early September all that was left was waiting for our a couple of months before our departure. Then something nearly unthinkable happened. Bill had been complaining about pain in his right shoulder for several weeks. It didn't go away. He thought he might have torn his rotator cuff and finally decided to go to the doctor for an examination.

The diagnosis took a while to be determined. Several tests were run by different physicians, but the final assessment was a grave one. He did not have a torn rotator, he had lung cancer that had metastasized to his bones. Worse yet, it was an aggressive form of the small cell variety and the treatment options were rather limited. This was crushing news, not only was Bill as good a friend as I have had in my life, but he was happily remarried a couple of years before and was a new father of a bouncing baby boy.

Obviously, we were not going anywhere together. I contacted American Airlines and explained to them the situation and, although the tickets were nonrefundable, they reimbursed us for all our charges. The folks that sold us the BritRail Passes did the same. I must say that I was very pleasantly surprised by their actions. It is nice to see a business stand up and do the right thing even when they do not have to do so.

I did what I could to be a good friend to Bill in this time of dire need. His response was to convince me that I needed to take the trip and come back and tell him all about it. I assured him that I had no real desire to go, but he persuaded me otherwise. He noted that I already had the time blocked off from work and I needed to use it. Further, he reminded me that I would not go with him to Hungary to see the village of his ancestors, and that I needed to make the pilgrimage to Fleetwood.

I finally relented and made alternative plans. I cashed in frequent flier miles with US Air and reserved a roundtrip flight to London Gatwick. I retailored the schedule to better fit my needs and set about reserving a lodging in London, and elsewhere. The time passed quickly and soon I was off on my first trip abroad flying solo.

ENGLAND

Hank, let me offer you a tip. Before you fly on a free ticket, check the routing. I have discovered that when you cash in frequent flyer miles you often times get a rather unfavorable schedule. On a previous trip to Greece with a friend I had used frequent flier miles. The outbound portion of that trip took us from Indianapolis to Dayton, Dayton to Cleveland, Cleveland to Toronto, Toronto to London Heathrow, from Heathrow we were bussed to London Gatwick and after a several hour delay, we finally flew on to Athens. What an ordeal!

Although not quite as trying, it was somewhat the case on this trip to London. I had to fly to US Air's big hub in Pittsburgh and, instead of catching a flight which was available to London from there, after a sizable layover I flew to Baltimore to depart for London. I don't understand the routing. In those days I could have flown the same carrier directly to Baltimore and onward, with no need to make the intermediate stop. I had a similarly confusing schedule on the return.

I had minor status with US Air at the time and was able to get some decent seats on the bulkhead for my long flight across the Atlantic. We boarded up the Boeing 767 and I found bin space for my only bag and settled in for the flight. I was doubly lucky on that flight because no one occupied the window seat next to me. Consequently, I was able to hog up both seats on my side of the aisle and have some adequate room. After our dinner was served, I actually stretched out and fell asleep for a few hours, a real rarity for me on flights in those days.

I awoke in time for breakfast, and before I knew it we were on the ground. Since I only had carry-on luggage and was sitting near the front of the plane I zipped through customs and immigration. I was able to locate the train station and took the Gatwick Express to Victoria Station. At Victoria I found the Underground and figured out how to get to my stop, Queensway. I had taken a room at a small bed and breakfast, the Hotel St. Charles.

Knowing virtually nothing about London, I decided to stay in the same neighborhood as the hotel contained in the American Airlines package. I guess my logic was that if they put us there it couldn't be too bad. I arrived at the Queensway Station and followed the guidebook directions to the hotel, a short couple of minutes' walk away.

I arrived at the entrance of the converted townhouse a little before nine o'clock, much too early to check-in I thought, but what else was I going to do. It was a cool, late fall day and I wanted to get in out of the cold. I opened the front door of the building and was immediately hit by the smell of frying bacon. It was warm inside, and the scent of breakfast cooking was comforting.

The hotel was run by an aging couple, the Wildriges. Mrs. Wildrige met me in the small room that served as a lobby and took my information. She notified me that my room was not quite ready, but offered me a cup of coffee, and said she would do what she could to hurry things along. I settled into a comfortable, overstuffed chair and drank my coffee and fought the effects of jet lag. I remember struggling hard not to fall asleep right there in the cramped surroundings.

In about a half hour Mrs. Wildrige came and led me to my room. The maid had just finished her cleaning of the room when I arrived. The room consisted of a twin bed, a small dresser with a television on it, a closet and one chair. The bathroom was compact to say the least, but I did have a private one. I unpacked what things I needed, disrobed and proceeded to get rid of the airplane grime.

After I had showered and shaved, I decided to lay down on the bed to see how it felt. Well, it felt too good, and I made the cardinal mistake of falling asleep. I didn't just doze off for a few minutes, I slept for a few hours. I finally was awakened by some noise in the hallway at nearly one in the afternoon. This was a mistake I would regret for the next few days as I had a difficult time adjusting to the new time zone, made worse by this foolhardy maneuver.

I awoke with a growling stomach, ready to eat. I attempted to shake off the ill-effects of my sleep and headed out to find some lunch. I retraced my steps toward the Underground station because when I arrived the street it was located on appeared promising for commercial activity. I turned the corner onto Queensway and was correct in my assessment. It appeared that in a couple of blocks there was almost every kind of ethnic cuisine you could ever want.

I spent more time than I should have trying to decide on a lunch spot, but finally settled on an Indian buffet. The food was good and very reasonably priced. I particularly enjoyed the tandoori chicken, dal (a thick, lentil bean stew) and naan, their flat bread. It was all very flavorful and spicy, which I enjoy.

After I finished lunch and paid my bill, I decided to stroll the streets around my hotel and gain my bearings. I had procured a map of the city from Mr. Wildrige at the St. Charles, but I pretty much disregarded it as I meandered largely without purpose for over an hour. Finally, I came upon Paddington Station, one of the major train stations in the city and a transportation hub I would be using to exit and reenter the city.

I spent a little while there exploring the Paddington Station. Because of my future travel plans I wanted to get the lay of the land. By now, it was getting to be late in the afternoon and I decided it was too late to venture out to any of the major tourist attractions. I came upon the idea of visiting Harrods Department Store. I had read how it was a splendid place to see and I needed an activity to occupy my time until dinner and bed to follow.

Just outside of the Paddington station there is a tube stop. I went underground and purchased a ticket and went the few stops to Knightsbridge where Harrods is located. I departed the subway and discovered that there was an actual entrance into the department store directly from the tube. I rode the escalator into the department store and soon was overwhelmed by the ostentatious nature of the store.

The place is enormous. It has over a million square feet of selling space. If you are interesting in purchasing an item, I think you will find it here. From designer clothing, jewels, furniture, to souvenirs, it is all here. The area of the store I found most interesting was the Food Hall on the Lower Level. The Food Hall contains an international collection of food, wine and spirits from around the world. You could easily do your daily food shopping here, if you could afford it.

After walking around the Food Hall for nearly an hour I decided to buy my dinner and take it back to my room to eat. Because I had to travel

I decided a cold meal would be best for dinner. I selected some salami, cheese, bread and a bottle of wine for my supper and hopped the subway back to the hotel. In less than a half hour I was back in my room at the St. Charles with this feast spread out on my bed enjoying the offerings from the most famous department store in the world.

After I finished my meal I realized I was tired from a long day of travel. Determined to stay up until at least nine o'clock I watched a little television and sipped some wine. At some point I dosed off and awoke to the sounds of the television around three in the morning. As much as I tried I was not able to get back to sleep. That darn nap I had taken when I arrived was now taking its toll on me.

Breakfast didn't start until seven and I did the best I could to while away the hours until I could really start my day. I read my travel guide and planned my day to maximize my time in London. I tossed and turned in bed until nearly six o'clock when I showered and went downstairs in search of a cup of coffee. Mrs. Wildrige was in the kitchen starting breakfast preparations and had pity on me and gave me a cup of hot coffee. She invited me to go downstairs to the breakfast room and I could be her first serving of the day.

I took a small corner table in the breakfast room and drank my coffee. In a few minutes my hostess appeared with a plate of English bacon, an egg over easy, some fried potatoes, and white toast. It looked appetizing to me and proved to be just what I needed. She came back shortly with a refill for my coffee and a glass of orange juice.

After I finished breakfast I killed some time before going out to start my day of sightseeing making certain the attractions were open when I arrived. In about an hour I went to the Queensway Underground and caught the subway for Charing Cross. This stop which opens onto Trafalgar Square is the gateway to the political and governmental establishment for the United Kingdom. Simply walk south along Whitehall and you are into the thick of the political infrastructure.

I headed down the street and my first stop was at the Banqueting House. This former dining hall of kings is all that remains of the once opulent Whitehall Palace. I took a quick tour of the building and was most impressed by the ceiling painting by Peter Paul Rubens. The Flemish master's works depict a fantasy view of the crowning of King James I. The structure is worth a brief stop.

Working my way further down the street I came upon Downing Street the next block on my right. I decided to duck down the street and see the home of the Prime Minister at number 10 Downing. I was able to walk down the street and stand in front of the house. Not nearly as impressive as the American White House to me, it nonetheless is worth walking by the residence. I do think with heightened security, you are not able to get as close today as I was then.

Continuing on down Whitehall you come upon the Houses of Parliament which is topped by the famous clock tower, Big Ben. Although I was unable to tour the building because my visit was ill-timed, I walked around the yard and even checked out the view from the far side which faces the Thames River. I was fortunate to be in the area when it was nearing ten o'clock and I lingered across the street from Big Ben until it tolled, a pretty impressive experience.

From the Parliament I ventured practically across the street to pay a visit to Westminster Abbey, one of the greatest religious structures in the world. Not only is the church noteworthy for its architectural significance, it historic importance is even greater. It has played host to centuries of British Royal events from coronations, to funerals, and weddings including that of Prince William and Kate Middleton.

Additionally, a walk through the impressive Gothic building reveals the burial plots of many famous British citizens. Scattered about the church are the tombs of numerous former monarchs of England like Edward the Confessor, Elizabeth I, Richard III and more than one of the Henrys.

Even more interesting to me are the literary giants honored in the sanctuary. In the area known as Poet's Corner, the remains of Geoffrey Chaucer were buried here in 1400. There are tributes to other greats like William Shakespeare, William Blake, Jane Austen, Dylan Thomas, D.H. Lawrence, and many others in this area. In another section of the church, statesmen like Benjamin Disraeli, and Winston Churchill are honored. Additionally great men of science like Charles Darwin and Isaac Newton are remembered with monuments. The Abbey is truly a moving experience and a visit to London would not be complete without stopping by this historic structure.

After nosing around Westminster for nearly an hour I realized that I needed to begin to make my way to Buckingham Palace, the main home of the Royal Family. At 11:30 most days, the Changing of the Guard ceremony takes place and I should have enough time to make this function. I headed north of the Abbey a couple of blocks to St James Park and followed the street on the south side of the park to the Palace, a less than ten minute walk.

As I was nearing the end of St. James I could see Buckingham a few hundred yards away. A crowd was forming and this told me that my chances of the ceremony taking place were good. I found an excellent vantage point, and stood with the several hundred other patrons awaiting this terribly British tradition.

It was a cold and damp day and I was anxious for the proceeding to start. I was not disappointed when I heard the sounds of the marching band, and the orders being shouted by the lead soldiers. The ceremony is interesting, if long. I watch the procession for about half an hour and, as it was nearing a close, I decided to beat the crowd and head out.

I decided to walk along The Mall and return to Trafalgar Square. Had I known then what I know now, I would have headed back across St. James Park to visit the Churchill War Rooms. In subsequent visits to London, first with my wife, Jenny and a second time with Jenny and our son, Hank, we took the tour of this fine facility. The War Rooms are where Prime Minister Winston Churchill and the British military high command ran their efforts in World War II. It is one of the most interesting museums I have visited anywhere. When we returned from a visit to London in the spring of 2013, a friend asked Hank what was his favorite thing we did on the trip. He did not hesitate in naming the War Rooms Museum. So, I think the appeal of the place is fairly broad and I would highly recommend it to anyone.

As I strolled along The Mall back toward Nelson's Column, I realized that I was hungry. It was now past noon and I had last eaten over five hours ago. I decided it was time to begin to look for a place for lunch. As I approached Trafalgar Square I noticed a street running along the other side that looked promising to find a pub to eat.

Sure enough after walking a couple of blocks, I noticed a little place tucked down an alley. The charming and warm little pub turned out to be the perfect spot for a beer and some food. I sat down on a stool at the bar and was warmly greeted by the bartender. He poured me a pint of Boddingtons Ale and got me a menu.

I sucked on the creamy beverage and decided that I should take this opportunity to have my first plate of London's signature dish, fish and chips. The barkeep kept me entertained with stories and recommendations of what I should do while in town, and shortly a cook appeared with my order. The crispy white fish was lightly breaded, and way too hot to eat. I drank on my beer for a minute while it cooled and finally dove into my food. The fish was very tasty, and not too greasy, and the plump little fries were very much to my liking. I ordered another beer and polished off my lunch. I remember having to visit the restroom before leaving and wondering if I would survive the steep descent into the bowels of the building.

Totally satisfied, I paid the bartender and thanked him for the conversation. I slipped back out into the cold, gray day and made my way the few blocks to the National Gallery which was just on the other side of Trafalgar Square. I spent the remainder of the afternoon exploring the paintings contained in this neoclassical structure. The Gallery had a very impressive collection arranged by chronology, making it easy to access.

Their paintings include works by early masters like Leonardo De Vinci and Michelangelo to the Impressionists. There really is something for everybody here. I find myself drawn to the works of Rembrandt, Van Gogh and Monet, to name a few. After a two or three hours of barely scratching the surface of their offerings, I began to tire and decided it was time to head back to Bayswater for a rest.

I caught the Underground right in front of the museum and headed back to Queensway. I arrived at the hotel as night had set in and decided to rest for a few minutes before venturing out for dinner. I got back to my cozy room and flipped on the television and poured a glass of wine from the bottle I had gotten the night before at Harrods. The next thing I knew it was nearly eight o'clock and I had awakened groggily from my nap.

I was a little hungry and knew if I did not go now, I would not get out at all. I forced myself to pull my pants back on and bundled up for the cold walk back out into the night. I walked back to Queensway with the intention of dining at an Italian place I had seen the day before while looking for a lunch spot.

After about a five minute walk in the cold I arrived at the restaurant. The front windows were sweating from the heat inside meshing with the night's cold air. I entered the crowded dining room and was welcomed by an attractive young hostess. She tucked me away at a table on the back wall and provided me with a menu. My young server came by promptly and I order a glass of Chianti and a plate of penne with a Bolognese sauce.

The young man returned promptly with my wine, a fresh green salad with a vinegar and oil based dressing, and a basket of piping hot, garlic bread. I began to eat and check out the activity on this Sunday night in Bayswater. It appeared to be date night as the place was filled with young couples having a good time. It made me wish I was not traveling alone, because I find meal times to be the most difficult time when I am traveling by myself, either on business or pleasure. I have come to realize that good conversation is a fundamental part of a good meal for me.

I finished my salad and the glass of wine about the same time my waiter returned with my penne and I ordered another glass of red wine. I ate my pasta in peace wishing for some female companionship. I finished my meal and the second glass of wine, and decided it was time to return to my hotel. I paid my tab and headed back out into the cold, dark night. There was a lot of activity on the street as Londoners were out enjoying their last weekend evening.

I slipped back into the St. Charles and headed directly to my room. I was not sleepy in the least because of my unwelcomed nap and I pulled out my travel guide and began to plan my next day trip to Scotland. Eventually, the events of the day caught up with me and I did fall asleep after reading for an hour or so.

As you may have gathered by now, I have had the pleasure of visiting London a couple of times since this initial trip. They have both been long weekends, once with my wife, Jenny, and once since with Jenny and our son, Hank. My favorite meal in England actually occurred on one of these trips. Since I do not intend to write about those trips in this book and one of the objectives of my writing is to share my favorite meal from each country, I will proffer it now.

In late March of 2013 we took Hank to London for a four day weekend, at his request. I had gotten a really good deal from Delta Vacations on an air/hotel package flying into London Heathrow with our accommodations at the Lancaster Gate Hotel Hyde Park. The hotel is located in the Paddington/Bayswater area on London only few blocks from where I stayed on this trip.

Being a frugal guy and since we were traveling light for the short trip, I decided that we should just take the Heathrow Express train from the airport to Paddington Station. From there we could walk the few blocks to the hotel rolling our bags. As it turned out it was a little further than I thought, but my family are troopers and did not complain.

Upon our arrival at the hotel we were informed that our room was not ready and would not be so for over an hour. By now it was around noon and, bereft of any other brilliant ideas, I suggested we leave our bags at the hotel and go out to lunch. We all seemed hungry and it sounded good to Jenny and Hank. We decided that a little Italian eatery we had passed on the way from Paddington Station looked good to us and we would give it a try.

We retraced our steps and found the quaint little spot. Taormina is a welcoming little, family-run trattoria on Cravens Terrace a couple of blocks from the Lancaster Gate Hotel. There were only a couple of other patrons when we arrived and the gentleman serving as host could not have been more welcoming. He showed us to a booth in the front window and provided us with menus. Our pretty young waitress came to take our orders and made some recommendations.

As it turns out they were having a real special on a couple of Italian red wines and Jenny and I decided to drink a bottle of Barolo with our lunch. Our waitress brought us the wine, which we tried, and liked a lot, and we all placed our orders. We had been given assurances that all the pastas were homemade, so we all went that direction. Hank got tagliatelle Bolognese, Jenny spaghetti carbonara, and I, the penne with a seafood marinara.

In a couple of minutes the waitress returned with small Caesar salads and a basket of assorted breads. The salads were delicious and Hank absolutely loved the bread. After we finished off the salads, our pastas arrived and were out of this world. My marinara sauce was chocked full of calamari, shrimp and scallops in a red sauce with a nice tangy spice to it. Hank and Jenny both raved about their orders, enough so that when we left they both suggested we come back.

Stuffed from our ample orders, we passed on the lovely looking deserts that were shown to us. Jenny and I finished off the tasty wine and we asked for the check. When the host brought us the bill we received another very pleasant surprise. He explained to us that given the time of day we had visited, we would receive a 25 per cent discount. What a bonus after such a fine meal with my two favorite people. **(See Appendix 4 for the recipe)**

SCOTLAND

I awoke the next morning to the sounds of the street coming through the sole window in my room. It was about six o'clock on Monday morning and I had gotten a good night's sleep and was finally beginning to acclimate myself to Greenwich Mean Time. It was time for me to move on the Edinburgh. I was to depart from London's Charing Cross railway station at nine o'clock. I showered, finished packing and went down for breakfast. It was a slow morning at the breakfast room and Mrs. Wildrige was there to greet me with a cup of hot coffee and seat me at a larger table that usual. Soon she returned with my breakfast, same as usual. I finished the meal and had enough time for another cup of coffee. Then I returned to my room and gathered up my things and met Mrs. Wildrige to settle my account. I thanked her and reconfirmed my room for my return later in the week.

I walked to the Queensway station and got on the Underground headed for Charing Cross. I arrived at the station, found my track and got on board the train for Scotland. The train was a sleek, new, fast one. I had a comfortable seat and enjoyed the ride through the U.K. countryside. My route took me through the cities of York and New Castle and along the East Coast of Great Britain.

We arrived at Edinburgh's Waverly Station a little after two o'clock that afternoon. The station is in the middle of the city and I exited into a cold, damp afternoon. I walked about ten minutes east along main streets to my hotel. The Terrace Hotel sits in a park-like setting, on a tree-lined cobblestone street.

I arrived at the address and found a lovely, old Georgian home converted into a small, 14-room hotel. I entered into a beautiful foyer and was struck by the large curving staircase that leads up to the bedrooms. As I entered further I could see that atop the stairwell was a magnificent skylight which was formed by leaded and stained glass. The proprietress greeted me and got me registered. I was then shown to my room on the second floor, a large corner one with a king bed, lounging area and a desk and chair. The bathroom was huge and was wood-paneled, cedar I believe.

I must tell you that I was taken aback by how nice the hotel was. I would have to say it was opulent, and at a very reasonable price. I could only think that I wished I had more than two days to stay in such pleasant surroundings and a nice woman to share it with. I unpacked and set about to go for a walk around the city to gain my bearings.

I headed out the door in the direction of the train station trying to make the most of the remainder of the day. The center of Edinburgh is divided into two major parts, Old Town and New Town. The Old Town is the original part of the city emanating from the Edinburgh Castle down the Royal Mile to Holyrood House. The New Town, which dates from the 18th Century, lies north of the Old Town, the two being separated by the Princes Street Gardens.

I was staying on the New Town side, and when I got to Princes Street, the main drag of New Town, I saw a hawker touting for a Hop-On, Hop-Off bus. I realized just then that I received a discount for this service with my BritRail information. Although I generally do not take advantage of these types of services, I decided in this instance with a very limited timeframe I might give it a try.

I approached the man from Hop-On, Hop-Off Edinburgh and agreed to the terms of the service. Within a matter of a couple minutes the bus arrived and I boarded. Although it was a cold day I braved the weather and climbed up to the open, upper-deck of the bus. The ride, if you chose to stay on the entire journey without hopping off, took one hour. A good aspect of the ticket for me was it was valid for a 24-hour period making it worthwhile for me most of the next day.

I decided to just take the sixty minute ride and use it to get my bearings, see the important sights, and plot which ones of these I wanted to return to and see in detail in the next day. The bus passed all the significant tourist attractions including castles, museums, monuments, churches and gardens. The ride was a chilly one, aided by the blankets furnished to customers on the upper level, but it certainly helped me to see the entire downtown and to plot a course of action for the next day.

After we arrived back to my starting point I decided it was late enough, and I should make my way toward dinner. I headed out into the commercial center of New Town looking for something of substance, given that I only had a small sandwich on the train from London for lunch. I wandered onto Rose Street and found a number of inviting, little pubs. As I surveyed the situation, I noticed one place that looked particularly good with a sign proclaiming a steak special.

I walked in to find a classic pub atmosphere and the place was crowded with locals that appeared to just get off work. There were a number of attractive, young women to look at so I decided to stay. I found a stool on a curve of the bar so I could look both directions and ordered a pint of the local ale. The bartender was a young guy who was friendly and he convinced me that the steak, a rib-eye, was delicious. I ordered it promptly and turned my attention to people watching.

In a couple of minutes the bartender brought me a crisp, green salad with a thick, red French dressing. It was quite tasty and I realized that my hunger was at a peak. Shortly, the steak and thick-cut fries arrived. The steak was large, tender and quite juicy. I thoroughly enjoyed the meal and the people watching at the pub. I stuck around for a couple of more beers and then paid the bartender and headed toward my hotel.

When I returned home to Indianapolis I learned that a rumored outbreak of the dreaded "mad cow disease" had started in Scotland. It occurred about the same time I ate this large and tasty steak in Edinburgh. I must confess that I was fearful for a number of weeks that my brain was going to turn to mush for having succumb to my desire for red meat. However, I am pleased to report that it all worked out okay.

It had now begun to snow and I was cold on the walk back to my room. It was still early when I reached the Terrace, so I undressed, got in bed and turned on the television. One of the beauties of traveling in Great Britain is that all the television stations are in a language I can understand. I found an American movie that I had not seen running on one of the

BBC channels. I laid in my bed warming up and watched the movie until I became too drowsy. Finally, I shut off the television and went to sleep for the night.

My hotel room was extremely quiet and I got the best night's sleep I had, thus far on the trip, sleeping for over nine hours. I awoke, cleaned up and went down stairs for breakfast. The owner was working hard, fixing breakfast for a couple at another table. She brought me some coffee and provided me with a menu to choose my breakfast. I remember that the menu options were varied, not just a continental, or Scottish breakfast, but you could even have kippers if you liked.

I selected the full Scottish breakfast which consisted of eggs over easy, bacon, assorted sausages, grilled tomato and mushrooms. This was also served with fresh squeezed orange juice and an assortment of breads and toast. It was one of the best breakfasts I have ever had, even the coffee was truly delicious.

Fortified, it was time to head out for a big day of sightseeing. When I walked out of the hotel I realized for the first time that a fresh layer of snow had fallen overnight. As I trudged through the snow I noticed something you do not see back home; a shop offering kilts for hire. I found this amusing enough to snap a picture of the store and sign. I often wondered if you could rent a kilt and it be acceptable for formal occasions in the United States as well. Possibly only if you pick the proper tartan.

I continued my trek until I reach the spot where the Hop-On, Hop-Off bus boarded passengers. Within a few minutes the big, red double-decker arrived and I caught a ride to near the top of the hill in Old Town where Edinburgh Castle sits. I climbed the rest of the way up the hill from the bus stop to the castle entrance. I stopped and paid the entrance and went inside the walls.

The ancient fortifications finds it roots in the 12th century as the residence for Scottish royalty. For the past few hundred years it has served as a military outpost, protecting the city below. There are many interesting historical displays contained inside the castle, not the least among them are the Scottish Crown Jewels. But, I think the most impressive part of visiting the castle is the view from its vantage point.

You can look over the ramparts and see why Edinburgh is considered one of the most beautiful cities in Britain, if not the world. Often referred to as the Athens of the north because of the placement of prominent hills, you can get a look over nearly the entire city from the castle hill and on out to the North Sea. Additionally, from here you get a real sense of the large amount of green space that exists in this lovely city. I finished my visit and set out to walk the Royal Mile to the other end where it terminates at the Palace of Holyrood House.

I window shopped and stopped at various stores along the Royal Mile. The route down the steep hill is lined with very interesting, old buildings which are now largely filled with retail stores, pubs and restaurants. Along the way the snow was continuing to fall and a brisk wind was blowing. I was cold and decided it was time to break down and purchase a hat to help protect me from this chill. As I walked along I noticed that one of the souvenir shops had a St. Andrews Old Course flat cap in the window. I popped into the store and decided that his blue and green plaid number would do an adequate job of protecting my head, so I bought it. One of the advantages of the hat was it could fold up and fit in my pocket when not in use. I like that hat and still use it today.

I reached Holyrood House which is at the opposite end of the Royal Mile from Edinburgh Castle. I entered the large, stone palace which is the official residence of the Queen when she is in Scotland. I paid the entrance fee and had to wait for a time until a tour formed up. Finally, about twenty of us were shown through the Royal Apartments. The palace was home to many rulers, but is closely associated with Mary Queen of Scots, Queen Victoria and Bonnie Prince Charles.

Our tour guide delighted in showing us the spot where Mary Queen of Scots personal secretary, David Rizzo, was stabbed 58 times and succumbed to his wounds at the hands of associates of her jealous husband. In about a year her husband died mysteriously in a gunpowder explosion.

Not a picture from home, only in Scotland!

We also visited the Throne Room, the Great Gallery, containing more than a hundred portraits of Scottish Kings, and the State Apartments which are still used for entertaining royal guests.

I found the tour to be quite interesting and worthwhile. After it ended I again caught the double-decker bus back to the New Town and began looking around for a spot for lunch. I found myself gravitating back toward Rose Street and the string of pubs and restaurants that line both sides. I finally settled on an interesting looking place that featured a chili mac special on a signboard out front. It seemed so out of place in Scotland that I thought I needed to go in and see what it was like.

I found a seat at the bar in this very old-fashioned looking establishment, ordered a pint and a bowl of the chili mac, which the bartender highly recommended. I chatted with the barkeep and drank my ale until my brimming bowl of chili arrived. Much to my surprise the concoction of hamburger, tomato sauce and macaroni was a very pleasant, spicy entrée. The soup was covered with a layer of cheddar cheese and was so thick the spoon would stand up in the bowl. I devoured it thinking that this is something I might find in the southwestern part of the United States, not Edinburgh.

I finished my lunch and beer and set out to continue my exploration of the city. My next stop was the National Gallery of Scotland located in the heart of the city. My short walk led me to the entrance off Princes Street Gardens. The attractive stone, neo-classical structure houses a very surprisingly good collection of fine art ranging from the Renaissance to the twentieth century.

I spend the bulk of the afternoon wandering the gallery. The place really blew me away. I liked how it is organized, its size that is not overwhelming, and the contents are outstanding. There are samplings of all my favorites from Rembrandt to Van Gogh, and de Vinci to Monet. I roamed the entire museum and even took time to inspect the museum shop, which I found to be a pleasant little store. I discovered a lovely Christmas ornament, a delicate, little azure ball with gold stars which I could not resist. Thankfully, it made it home safely and still graces our tree at the holidays.

After over two hours I decided to head out and begin to work my way back to the Terrace Hotel. Along my way I did a little souvenir shopping for friends and associates, particularly timely with Christmas only a few weeks off. I trudged through the cold, snowy evening ducking in and out of shops along my route, if only to warm up from the chilly, windy weather.

After making a few purchases I arrived back at my hotel where the proprietor met me and offered me a cup of hot tea and some freshly baked cookies. I gladly accepted and took them to my room where I warmed up from the cold. I turned on the television and relaxed before going out to dinner. I decided to consult the guidebook for a restaurant suggestion and determined that I should find something nearby the hotel if possible.

I arrived at what I thought was my best choice given the criteria, the Café Royal Bistro. The bar is located less than a ten minute walk from the Terrace and is just a little north of the train station. On this freezing evening I made the trek in record time in an effort to get in out of the cold. When I arrived I was pleasantly surprised by the almost clubby atmosphere of the place. It has dark, wood-paneled walls and loads of stain and leaded glass windows.

I made my way to a stool on the long deep-toned bar with its brass fixtures. The barkeep poured me a pint of a local ale as I studied the menu. I decided that since I was within a stone's throw of the North Sea I should sample some local seafood. I consulted the bartender and he persuaded me that the haddock and chips was my best bet. Since he had not steered me wrong on the ale, which was creamy smooth, I went with his recommendation.

In a little while the server appeared with my dinner, two large, golden haddock filets, lightly battered and fried to perfection, accompanied by a large portion of thick, hand cut chips and a serving of fresh peas. I ordered another beverage and began my assault on this delectable looking plate of food. It did not disappoint. I devoured every morsel on the plate, save the parsley garnish. My only regret was that I had not discovered this place earlier so I could have had this meal more than once.

I washed the fish and chips down with a third pint and settled my bill with the bartender. I must tell you that it is a tough choice for me on what my favorite meal has been in Scotland, the wonderful breakfast at the Terrace Hotel, the rib-eye steak the previous evening, or this haddock. But, I think that the quality and freshness of the fish, and the warm atmosphere of the Café Royal Bar, makes it a winner by a nose. **(See Appendix 5 for the recipe)**

I quickly made my way back to my room and turned on the television as I began to make preparations for bed. I watched part of yet another American movie as I did what packing I could do that night. Since I had an early start in the morning, I flipped off the television and read a book until I was ready for sleep.

I awoke early the next morning knowing that I needed to catch an early train back to England. I showered, packed my things, and went downstairs for one last fabulous breakfast at the Terrace Hotel. I entered the dining room to the warm greeting of the hard-working proprietress. She sat me at a table next to a young Asian couple and gave me the menu. I again chose the full Scottish breakfast, orange juice and coffee. It had been so enjoyable the previous morning that the other offerings on the tempting menu were not a serious consideration.

I noticed that the owner was taking the order of the couple to my right. The young man was particularly challenged with the English language, and did not fully understand the menu. So, he just decided to order all the options that appeared on the card. The proprietress and the young woman with him were having a difficult time explaining to him that what he was selecting was way too much food. They were finally able to convince him that he should *only* order the Scottish breakfast with a side of pancakes and a plate of kippers.

When his food did arrive in a few minutes, you should have seen his face. The three plates would not all fit on the table and the owner had to wheel in another side table for his food. I don't think the young man understood what he had over ordered, even when he had reduced it from six or seven options to three. I will say he did make a valiant effort to eat it all, finishing most everything on all three plates.

I sat and enjoyed my breakfast and scanned all I could see of the hotel. It truly was a far nicer place than I normally stay while traveling abroad on my own nickel. I hoped that I could find as nice a place to stay the rest of the trip and in all my future journeys.

I finished my breakfast and settled my bill with the owner, thanking her genuinely for the pleasant stay. I grabbed my things and headed out into the morning, a blustery, snowing one. I reached Waverly Station in about ten minutes and quickly located the track and my train. I settled in for a several hour trip which would take me across Scotland and back into England along its west coast.

FLEETWOOD, ENGLAND

The train departed in a timely manner and I quickly purchased another cup of coffee from the vendor working his way through the cars with his snack cart. I drank my beverage and watched the train roll through the countryside. Our first stop was Glasgow, the industrial hub of Scotland. We were then off through lightly populated areas with rolling hills and pleasant looking valleys. I remember we passed through Lockerbie, the sight of a terrible plane crash caused by a terrorist bombing.

As we made our way, I became excited about the prospects of visiting a city in England that shared my same last name. A few years earlier I had been in Ireland at the picturesque Cliffs of Moher and had visited a tourist's center where they assisted Irish descendants with locating their ancestral heritage.

Just for kicks I looked up my mother's maiden name, McKinney, and was provided with little, to no, information. I was taken aback by this, because I was under the impression that this was an Irish surname and they would be able to help me locate what part of Ireland my maternal ancestors were from. I, then, decided on a lark to enter Fleetwood and see what happened. Well, much to my surprise, the computer came back with a response. We were from the area around what is now Fleetwood, England, on the northwest coast of the country.

I had been aware of the existence of the City of Fleetwood in England because of looking at an encyclopedia as a kid, in the days before the internet. There is also a small city of the same name in Pennsylvania. I wanted to see if I could find more out about the area and my family history, so I decided to visit the city.

After making a change of trains in Preston, England, I arrived in the blue-collar resort town of Blackpool on the coast of the Irish Sea. Blackpool is a little north of Liverpool, a much larger city and famous for being the home of the Beatles. From Blackpool I was able to take a local bus north to the heart of Fleetwood, an even smaller neighbor of about thirty thousand people. My first order of business was to go to the Visitor's Information Center to see what they could do to help me.

Upon arrival in what appeared to be the commercial center of town, a kind man at the bus stop directed me to the visitor's center a couple of blocks away toward the sea. I walked in to the shop and was greeted by two women who were working there. I asked first if they were able to help me find a reasonably priced room for the night. They let me know that the options were not as great as in the summer, when all the little resort properties were open, but it should be no problem.

They showed me information about various lodgings they believed were open in December, and I chose the one that best fit my needs. They called the bed-and-breakfast and asked about availability and price. They informed me a nice room was ready at a very reasonable cost, which I accepted. The tourist center woman then asked for my name so the small hotel could hold the room until I arrived in a little while.

I told the woman my name was Fleetwood and she looked at me in disbelief. She asked me a second time and I repeated it for her. She told the person on the other end of the line and promptly hung up. Well, at this point the other worker in the office and a few patrons came to a stop. They all looked at me strangely. It seems they had never met someone with my last name and I was, indeed, a welcomed guest. Hank, you would have enjoyed the attention I received. It was like having a daylong birthday celebration without being your birthday. I thought for a while that the mayor was going to show up shortly and provide me with a key to the city.

The four or five people assembled wanted to know all about me and why I was visiting the city. I explained to them that I was in search of information about my family and had reason to believe that they might have come from the area. I also told them that I wanted to visit the library to see if they had any historical information that might be helpful to me. It was around noon now and they let me know that the library was closed in the afternoon on Wednesday, so I was out of luck on that angle.

They were disappointed to learn that I was only staying the one night and would be unable to consult with the librarian the next day. They then immediately sprang into action and began to provide me with whatever information they had on the community, historical and otherwise. Although the town appeared old to me, it seems the place had been founded in the 1830s as a green-field site by Peter Hesketh-Fleetwood, a member of the British Parliament from nearby Preston.

The Fleetwood family had owned the local manor for over three hundred years and Fleetwood envisioned the community as a beachside resort for the vacationing working class of northern England. He also saw its protected harbor as a possible port onto the Irish Sea. The city did become a thriving seaport, largely relying on fishing. At its peak the local fishing fleet numbered in excess of three hundred boats, but by the time of my visit, changes in the industry had shrunk that number to about thirty vessels.

What I learned from the good people at the tourist office was enough for me to know that in all likelihood my family was not from the city of Fleetwood. I have good reason to believe that my ancestors were in America before the War of Independence took place. This was several decades before the founding of the English city. Clearly, my family could have been from that area, but by all accounts were firmly enounced in the colonies well before the area was platted.

Slightly disappointed with the news, I thanked the nice, helpful people at the visitor's center and took off walking to check into the hotel they had arranged for me. Following their directions, I walked to the street that parallels the sea and turn south for a couple of blocks. I did just that and after a couple of blocks of walking along the Esplanade, I came to my bed and breakfast.

I mounted the steps leading into the lodgings when the front door threw open. The proprietors, a very nice middle-aged couple met me at the door and welcomed me to their establishment. It was like the earlier scene at the tourist office where my last name gave me instant celebrity. The couple checked me in and showed me to a quite nice room at the top of a short staircase beyond the front desk.

They also ran a small restaurant/bar in the front of the building and wanted to know if I would be having dinner at the hotel that evening. They strongly encouraged me to do so, and said that they would be going to the market for fresh fish which they would be serving that night. They guaranteed me the fish would be delicious and the meal would be special. Since I had an early departure in the morning and they were so insistent, I decided to take them up on the offer and said I would eat around seven.

I went to my room and got settled. I tried to decide what I should do next given my whole mission in Fleetwood had been dashed. I realized that I was now very hungry and decided that top of the agenda should be to find something to eat. I went back downstairs and asked the owner for a suggestion for lunch, since he did not open until the evening that time of year.

He recommended a little pub across the street on the Fleetwood pier, a summertime amusement center for holiday makers. I took his advice and made my way to the pub. It was now early afternoon and when I entered the place there were a couple of patrons and one server behind the bar. I went to the bar and ordered a pint of ale and immediately they recognized I was not a local by my accent. When I informed the bartender of my name, and why I had come to their fair city, I was asked to join the man and woman sitting at the only occupied table.

Again, the celebrity treatment began. I was told under no uncertain term was my money good in this establishment, and I was their guest for as long as I wanted to stay. I ended up spending a couple of hours eating a sandwich and drinking beer with all three of the folks. It seems that my appearance in the bar was a convenient excuse for a party, and even the bartender felt compelled to join in. I listened to the oral history of the community, the decline of the fishing industry, and its impact on the city, and the importance of tourism to the local economy.

After three or four pints, I decided I needed to leave, or I never would. By now, my fellow revelers who had a head start on me were pretty much on their way. They appeared genuinely disappointed that I was leaving and wished me well in my travels and in unearthing my family history. I departed into a dark and blustery afternoon. I spent the next hour or so walking around the town checking out the port area, the city's lifeblood, and admiring the trademark lighthouse.

There really was not too much else to see, so I decided to return to the hotel and rest a while before having this much ballyhooed dinner. I arrived back at the hotel and the owner beckoned me to join him at the bar. It seems he wanted me to meet his two customers who were visiting the bar. The gents were both locals and were intrigued to meet someone with the surname the same as the city's moniker. They insisted I join them in a beverage, which I did.

I finally wished the locals well and went upstairs to rest for about an hour before dinner. Fearing I would nod off on my bed, I returned to the restaurant a little early and ordered a beer. I was the only patron in the place. The owner came by my table in the front window and told me that his wife was going to start on my dinner and I should relax and enjoy my drink. Before too long, the owner returned with a crisp dinner salad with a blue cheese dressing.

I ate the delicious salad, and just as I was finishing, my entrée was brought to me. The owners were correct, the food looked terrific. The fish was a halibut that had been lightly dusted in flour and had been sautéed to perfection. It was served with a large baked potato with butter and sour cream on the side. The meal was absolutely heavenly. I was so glad that they had convinced me to stay in that evening. The food was as advertised, extremely tasty, and it was a nasty, raw night outside.

As I was finishing up my meal the owner came to my table carrying a couple of beers. He placed one in front of me and sat down in the chair across from me. He tried to talk me into some dessert claiming that his wife fixed an outstanding custard tart. I thanked him for the offer, but I was full. I still wonder to this day if I made a big mistake not trying this dessert, I bet it was really good.

I drank my beer and asked the owner if I could settle my bill because I had to leave very early in the morning to start my journey to Wales. His first concern was that I was going to miss the fine English breakfast they served in the morning. He insisted on leaving a continental breakfast for me outside my room at five-thirty, as I told him I would be leaving by six in the morning. I reluctantly agreed and he finally allowed me to pay my bill.

The seaside amusement in Fleetwood which has subsequently burned down.

WALES

By now the rigors of the day were upon me and I needed to go to sleep because of my early start. I thanked the owner of this fine, little establishment and slipped off to bed. The next morning I awoke to my five o'clock alarm, showered and prepared to leave. Promptly at five-thirty

I heard someone outside my door. I opened the door to find a tray with a full English breakfast, a bowl of cereal, toast, a small pot of coffee and orange juice. These extremely nice folks had gone way out of their way to please me and I appreciated it.

I, of course, did not want to offend them so I ate everything they served me. I grabbed my bag and headed out for the bus stop about a ten minute walk from my hotel. I got to the stop a few minutes early and waited in the dark and cold for the bus to arrive. Soon it came roaring up and my journey to Cardiff, the Capitol of Wales was underway.

We arrived at the Blackpool train station and shortly I was on my first of three trains that day. From Blackpool we travel to Preston, with a change of trains onward to Crewe for another change, which would take me directly on to Cardiff. I remember that train from Preston was running late which made my change in Crewe very tight. I had to make a mad dash from one track to another and barely made it saving myself over an hour delay.

When I boarded the train in Crewe I was in such a rush, I grabbed the first seat I could find and stowed my bag in overhead storage. The train was pulling out when I turned around to see that the seat I selected was facing a very pretty, young woman. This was clearly a bonus.

I sat down across the table and, after a while, struck up a conversation with the young beauty. It seems that she was from Liverpool and was on her way to Newport, Wales, where she had just graduated from the university, and was on her way to visit friends still there. She had dark brown hair, fair skin and piercing blue eyes. She had the shape a woman should wish to have. Our conversation was very amiable. Although we both spoke English as our language, there were times that I had a difficulty understanding her, and she me.

I must confess a serious weakness for attractive women, and this young lady certainly made the next two plus hours a very enjoyable ride. I learned about her hometown of Liverpool and about the university city of Newport. It was with some sadness that we parted company when we arrived at her station. I wished her well and wondered what might have happened if I had asked her to come with me to Cardiff. One will never know.

We chugged into Cardiff's Central station a little past noon. My first order of business was to find a room for the night. I had decided to search along Cathedral Road for one of several interesting-looking, budget accommodations I had read about in my Frommer's Scotland and Wales guide. As I was walking through the station, I noticed a tourist information office and decided to duck in for a free map of the city.

When I entered the office a pleasant woman offered to assist me. She gave me a nice map of the city and asked me if I needed a place to stay. I told her I was thinking of walking to Cathedral Road and mentioned a couple of places that I was going to check for availability. She said she would call them for me, but she had another suggestion that was a little closer and of comparable quality and cost. I told her to check with the hotel and she was able to book me a room at Austin's Hotel, a small inn less than a ten minute walk from the station. She also offered me a few "must see" ideas for my short stay in Cardiff.

I thanked the woman for all her help and headed out into the gray, blustery day to check into my hotel. The Central Station is truly in the center of town and the walk to the bed and breakfast was not a difficult one. After exiting the station you take a left and look for a bridge over the River Taff. Once across the river you turn right follow the street for several blocks and the guesthouse is on your left, overlooking the river and the large rugby stadium on the other side.

I arrived at Austin's and was warmly welcomed and shown to a twin room because a single was not available. My room was on the front side of the building overlooking the river and stadium beyond. The well-appointed room had two twin beds, a couple of chairs, desk and table, with a television mounted on the wall. It also contained a compact bathroom with a shower.

I dropped my bags and decided to head out for lunch before my day of sightseeing. I consulted my guidebook for a recommendation and decided that the area on the other side of the river near the train station and rugby station had some good prospects. I retraced my steps to the train station and found my way onto St. Mary's Street which is jammed packed with pubs, certainly enough eateries for my stay in Cardiff.

For lunch, I chose the Cardiff Cottage, a traditional, old pub. The narrow building hosts a long bar with a lively atmosphere. I determined by now that the worst part of traveling alone is eating without company. Thus, I had concluded that sitting at a bar for my meals was the superior way to go because there was a better chance of engaging in conversation, at least with the bartender, if not with fellow patrons.

So, I took a seat at the bar and ordered a pint of the local ale, Brains Smooth. The creamy concoction was indeed smooth and tasty. I ordered a ham and cheese sandwich on a dark, dense bread. The sandwich was delivered quickly and was served with chips. The sandwich was quite good, with the ham a very thick cut. I finished my sandwich and ale and decided to begin my short day of sightseeing in Cardiff.

I decided to begin my tour with a visit to the Cardiff Castle which was only a few blocks to the west of the pub. I walked out into heavy wet snowfall that had just begun. I quickly made my way to the castle. I reached the castle just in time to meet up with a tour of the fortress. The original structure on the site was built by the Romans nearly two centuries ago, with Normans and Anglo-Saxon versions to follow.

Not only do the walls of the imposing structure continue to exist, you are afforded an opportunity to stroll through the impressive manor, visiting selected rooms in the apartments, including the huge banquet hall, and former living quarters of the nobility who inhabited the buildings. There is an imposing clock tower and there are tunnels in the castle walls that served as bomb shelters in World War II. I was not prepared to be so impressed with this castle, but I was. It sits directly in the center of the city which is another alluring quality which makes it easily accessible. As our tour came to an end I stopped briefly in the castle museum shop which I found to be of high quality.

Since it was now past three o'clock I was feeling my time in Cardiff slipping away and I decided to try and fit in a few more sights before my time ran out. I walked down to the City Hall and viewed the impressive structure, continued on to the Central Indoor Market to inspect the offerings for sale there and stumbled across an outdoor Christmas Market nearby. Of course, I am a sucker for these festive marketplaces and I spent the remainder of the afternoon noising around its shops. I did find a beautiful, heavy, hand-blown, irregularly-shaped oval bulb which I purchased. The green orb with gold accents is an unusual piece and looks wonderful on our tree each year.

I decided to walk around the large, rugby stadium on my way back to my hotel. The snow was beginning to accumulate and I determined I needed to get off my feet for a while before I ventured out for dinner. My lower back was acting up a bit, a chronic issue since my sophomore year in college, and I thought a rest might do it some good.

I returned to my room and it was downright frigid. I decided it must be going to warm up, or it was a figment of my imagination. But, after about fifteen minutes of watching television, I noticed I could see my breath. I decided that I needed to point this out to the management of the hotel and sought them out. The kind lady running the place came to my room and pointed out to me that the heat was motion activated and since I was in the room it would warm up soon.

I laid on one of the beds in the cold for another half hour and decided that I may as well go out to dinner and warm up. I decided to return to the St. Mary's Street area and find another pub to have my evening meal. I ended up at a tavern just down the street from the Cardiff Cottage where I had lunch. The Borough Arms is a decidedly old, but inviting tavern. I worked my way through a crowd near the front and found a stool at the bar.

I ordered a pint of ale and asked the barkeep what he recommended to eat. He strongly urged me to try the fish and chips, so I did. It was delivered to me about the time I was ready to re-order another beer. It was a large helping with three pieces of white fish and a mound of fries. The batter on the fish was a little thicker than I prefer, but overall the food was tasty.

I was tired and decided to call it a night, so I paid my bill and headed out into the cold evening. I returned to my room to find it was even colder than when I left it. I tried to get the motion detector to work, kicking on the heat, but to no avail. I went to the front of the house and couldn't find anyone working. So, I returned to my room and finally decided to turn on the hair dryer in the bathroom, attempting to knock off a little of the chill.

After the hair dryer had been somewhat successful, I put the hair dryer away and quickly got in bed. I was still cold. I decided to pull the duvet off the other bed and cover myself with both these comforters. I wrapped myself up as tightly as I could and finally fell asleep shivering.

When I awoke the next morning, I swear there was frost on the inside of my bedroom window. I went into the bathroom and turned the shower as hot as it would go in hopes it would help warm the room. I quickly disrobed and jumped in the tub, taking one of the quickest showers in my life. I think I dried off even faster and hurriedly pulled on my clothes.

Immediately, I went to the back of the hotel to the breakfast area and got a hot cup of coffee. The manager that I had dealt with the day before came by my table and asked me how I slept. Wrong question! I told her about the heating situation in my room and how it never improved. I seemed to get little sympathy from her, only that she would look into the issue further before she rented the room again.

The one silver lining that morning was the breakfast. I don't know if the manager took a little pity on me, or what, but she served me an outstanding meal. I had a full Welsh breakfast, rashers, three different sausages, broiled tomato, mushrooms and baked beans, yes, baked beans. This was my first time to experience baked beans for breakfast and I truly enjoyed them. In fact, this became my favorite meal in Wales. **(See Appendix 6 for the recipe)**

I finished my third cup of coffee, returned to my room, grabbed my things and checked out of the hotel. I made my final walk along the river and crossed over to the Central Station. I didn't have much of an expectation for Cardiff, I really wanted to just get a taste of another capital. But, I will tell you that I was leaving the country with a very positive impression. I thought there was a very good vibe about Cardiff, and I hope to return someday.

BACK TO ENGLAND

I caught my train back to London, a trip that takes slightly over two hours. I arrived at Paddington Station a little past eleven that morning and decided just to walk back to the St. Charles Hotel. When I arrived Mrs. Wildrige had my room ready, so, I checked-in and took my bag to my room. I resolved to make a move for it, as I had decided that I would go to Oxford the next day. I only had the rest of the day to cram in what I wanted to see in London.

I wanted to try and accomplish three things that day; see the Tower of London, St. Paul's Cathedral and, most importantly, the British Museum. I went to the Underground and bought a day pass and headed toward the Tower of London. My real objective was not to visit the Tower and all its trappings, but rather to see the Tower Bridge, an icon of the city.

The day was at least partly sunny which made this trip more appealing. I took the tube to Towers Hill and exited the station heading south toward the Thames River. I rounded the corner of a building and beyond the imposing Tower of London, the Tower Bridge came into full view. The massive medieval-looking towers and the blue steel drawbridge are an impressive sight. I set out to walk across the bridge, but got to the first tower and decided I had enough of a view to satisfy my curiosity.

As I peered back in the direction from which I had come, I was afforded a very good look at the Tower of London. I decided to walk around the Tower and inspect it to see if I wanted to visit the fortress. As it turned out, I felt my time was running short, and I really wanted to visit the British Museum, and I knew I didn't have time for both that day. The Tower is also an expensive place to visit, so I would see how my funds were doing when I returned from Oxford the next day. If I had the money, and the time, I might catch it then.

Having exhausted all possibilities in the area I decided to move on. My next stop was to quickly view the St. Paul's Cathedral, the domed structure which has dominated the London skyline for about three hundred years. I caught the Underground for the St. Paul's stop and made my way the next block or so to the entrance.

Here I faced another dilemma in that the church was holding a rare weekday service, I decided to just slip into the back of the cathedral while the service was going on. The worship had already begun when I arrived so I quietly entered the huge naïve and took a seat in the far back corner. Being as unobtrusive as possible I joined in with the parishioners, all the while gawking about at the beautiful structure. One cannot help but be drawn to the imposing domed ceiling which is decorated with mosaic tiles depicting biblical scenes.

After about fifteen minutes I felt too much like an interloper, and decided to depart as gracefully as possible. When the worshipers rose for the next hymn, I slid out of the pew and quietly departed taking great pain to not make any noise. I was successful in making a noiseless exit and now was headed to the tube in the direction of my ultimate objective, the British Museum.

I took the tube a couple of stops to the Holborn station and exited for the several block walk to the museum. It was now in the early afternoon and I decided to try and find a place for a quick lunch along my path to the museum. In a block, or so, of leaving the subway I stumbled upon a little pub which has an open stool at the bar. I entered the establishment and claimed the stool for myself.

The bartender approached and I ordered a pint of ale. He returned with my drink and shared the bill of fare with me. Today's lunch would be simple: a hamburger and fries. After engaging the bartender in conversation for a few minutes he departed only to return with my order. The thick, juicy burger was prepared to my satisfaction, medium, and the fries were home cut with the skin still on. Yummy! I made quick work of my meal, paid and headed to the museum.

The British Museum is so large you hardly know where to begin. I took a look at the floor plan and plotted my strategy. There were a number of things I wanted to see, but two were can't miss items; the Rosetta Stone and the Elgin Marbles. I spent the next few hours plying the halls of the museum marveling at the pieces contained in the collection. I saw my two can't miss items and much, much more.

It seems to me the British Museum is a tribute to the old colonial era when, "the sun did not set on the British Empire." It is amazing how much the British decided to bring back to London to share with their countrymen. As in other national museums of countries that experienced colonial power, it is chocked full of articles that were national treasures in their home countries. Or as my eight-year old son, Hank, put it as we were leaving the museum on a future trip, "Why do they call it the British Museum, when there isn't anything British in it?"

The museum and its holdings are truly outstanding. It is quite possibly the top museum in the world, and depending on your perspective, the number one attraction in all of London. There is way too much to see in one visit and I, too, succumbed to its sheer volume. After about three hours I had enjoyed all I could stand and decided to head back to the hotel.

I took the Underground to Paddington Station. Before heading back to the hotel I resolved to check on the details of a potential trip to Oxford the next day. I was able to locate all the necessary information rather quickly, and decided to just make my way back to the St. Charles on foot from Paddington. Along my route to the hotel I spotted an interesting little pizzeria and stopped in and ordered a small sausage, pepperoni and onion pizza for take away.

I sat and drank a beer while my order was finished. In about fifteen minutes I was headed out of the restaurant with a hot pizza in a box. I stopped at a convenience market and bought a couple of cans of beer to go with the pizza, and returned to my room to eat my dinner. I wanted to catch up on my sleep because I would be leaving in the morning for a day trip to Oxford.

I awoke the next morning, cleaned up, and went downstairs for breakfast. The ever present Mrs. Wildrige was there to greet me and handed me a hot cup of coffee. I sat at a corner table and she soon returned with my full English breakfast. I took my time that morning enjoying the food and coffee. I engaged in a conversation with a couple from Canada seated at the next table about the virtues of Bruges in Belgium.

I had a spare day on my BritRail pass and decided not to waste the opportunity. Thus, I determined for certain on the train ride from Cardiff the day before to go visit Oxford, England. I have friends who attended the university there, and I thought it might make for an interesting day trip out of London. And, it was only a little over an hour from Paddington Station.

I gathered my things after breakfast and headed out on foot for Paddington to catch the train. There are several trains each hour between the two cities, but I wanted to make one around nine o'clock that was a little shorter in duration. I arrived in time to catch my desired train and found a nice, comfortable seat on the modern train. Before I knew it we were clipping through the countryside, often times with the Thames River within our sight.

When we arrived I decided to walk into the center, find the tourist's information center for a map, and any advice they might have for me. I found the office with little difficulty and was given a map. It turns out that Oxford University was not really what I had expected. I thought it would be concentrated in one area like American institutions, but rather it is a number of disparate colleges interspersed throughout the city. The folks at the tourist information center gave me some ideas of a walking tour, sold me a couple of Oxford University t-shirts, and I set out to see the city.

I spent a couple of hours walking the streets of central Oxford simply looking at the historic colleges and structures. I came upon Carfax Tower, all that remains of a medieval church that was on the sight. I decided to climb to the top to get a better view of the city which I believe was a worthwhile venture. From the top of the tower you are afforded a wonderful vantage point to survey the landscape of the historic city.

I finally got hungry and decided to find a welcoming pub for lunch before heading back to London. I started my trek back toward the train station when I ran into a tavern that looked like a good place to stop. The King's Arms sits on a corner near the center of town and boasts a long history, including being the oldest pub in Oxford.

The place was crowded and I luckily found a seat at a railing along one wall. I was pleased that a server took my order for a pint of house ale because I didn't know if finding service in this place would be difficult. When he came back I decided to place a food order while I had him. I went for the fish and chips because I saw a fellow down the way eating it and it looked good. I also didn't want to wait for a menu.

Before too long the server returned with a large plate of food and I reordered a pint. The fish and chips turned out to be quite palatable and the beer delicious. The place was absolutely slammed the entire time I was there. It looked like a mix of students, university types, and a few random tourists like me. I was glad I had found the place because it looked like the genuine article to me, and the food was good.

I finished my lunch and second beer and headed to the train station. I soon arrived back at the station and within a matter of minutes I was boarding a train headed to London. As we pulled out of Oxford, I thought to myself that I was glad I had made this side trip. I had seen one of the greatest university towns in the world and would have a picture of it in my mind for the rest of my life.

We arrived back at Paddington Station in about an hour. It was now moving toward late afternoon and I decided to just take it easy for the rest of the day. I did a little last minute souvenir and Christmas shopping as I made my way back to the hotel. I stopped and bought a couple of beers to drink back in my room as I relaxed before going out to dinner. Back in my room I rested, watched television, and packed for my early departure the next morning.

After I drank my beers I decided to venture out one last time to grab some dinner. I was not feeling too adventurous, so I was determined to just find something in the Bayswater neighborhood. I ended up at the little Italian spot where I had eaten on my second night of the trip. I sat at the same table and had the same server. I even ordered the same meal, penne Bolognese with a glass of Chianti. It turned out to be as good as before, and the right dinner for me on my last night in the city.

I returned to the St. Charles and went to bed. I awoke early the next morning worried I might oversleep and miss my flight. I cleaned up and went to the breakfast room in the basement for my last English breakfast. I lingered for a few minutes talking to the Wildriges and thanking them for all their kindness. I paid them what I owed them and headed out for the airport.

I caught the tube at Queensway for Victoria Station where I changed to the Gatwick Express train for the airport. Once I arrived at the airport I went to the USAir counter to check-in for the flight. I was able to wrangle another good seat, this time in the exit row. I made my way through Customs and was soon on my way back to the United States. The connections were better on the way back, directly to Pittsburgh and home to Indianapolis from there.

Hank, as I flew back, I reflected on the trip. I particularly thought about what it was like to travel alone. Clearly for me, I prefer to have someone to share these moments with. As I mentioned before, eating alone is probably the most difficult thing for me. I wouldn't say I would not do it again, but it is not my preference. Hank, I would have enjoyed it more if you and your mother had been with me.

After I got home I called my friend, Bill, to see when I could get together with him to tell him about my trip. He didn't sound well, but we agreed to meet in a couple of days. I took dinner to his house, and discovered that in the two weeks since I had seen him he had deteriorated dramatically. I told him the story of my trip in great detail, as he requested. As we were departing, he told me that he was entering into a hospice situation. This was the last trip I would tell him about, as he was gone the next month.

CHAPTER 3

THE IBERIAN PENNISULA

HANK, THE YEAR 1996 WAS to be a big year for me which I would not recognize until after it was nearly over. You see that year that there was a big election for governor of our home state of Indiana. The candidates were the early, prohibitive favorite, Mayor Steve Goldsmith of Indianapolis, and Frank O'Bannon of Corydon, the sitting Lieutenant Governor for the past eight years.

All the pundits were calling for Goldsmith, a slick, articulate, well-funded, media savvy, candidate to win the race by a sizeable margin. O'Bannon, by contrast, was a modest, humble public servant and southern Indiana lawyer, who had gone through office, first in the Indiana Senate and then as lieutenant governor, not seeking the limelight. Rather, he simply tried to do what he thought was in the best interest of his fellow Hoosiers. Not noted as a great orator, O'Bannon was viewed as a nice guy, but in this case nice guys surely would finish last.

I had the very good fortune to work for Frank O'Bannon for nearly eight years while he was the Democratic Leader of the Indiana Senate. In 1980 I had just moved back to Indiana from St. Louis after a brief stint in a doctoral graduate program at Washington University. Upon my return I immediately got involved in a statewide campaign which ended unsuccessfully in the May primary.

Looking for work, a friend of mine whom I had met on the campaign trail, Ed Treacy, set me up to meet with Senator O'Bannon and State Representative Mike Phillips, the leader of the Democrats in the Indiana

House. It seems they were hiring someone to run their state legislative campaigns with an eye toward capturing the majority in their chambers. This was a particularly important election for them because of the impending reapportionment which would occur the next year following the decennial census.

As luck would have it, I got the job. Although we were far from successful in gaining the majority in either house, Frank and I had established a rapport which led to him hiring me to work on the staff in the Senate. In less than a year he promoted me to lead his staff in the position of Staff Director. In this role I had the very good fortune to work closely with Frank and to become a close advisor and good friend to him.

I cannot begin to say enough good things about Frank O'Bannon. Hank, I am sorry he passed before you got to know him. He was a true gentleman. He was bright, funny, and a very adept consensus-builder. He was truly the nicest person I have known in my life. He possessed the incredible knack of being able to find something good in every person he met.

I saw numerous times when that ability was severly tested, when I certainly could not find a redeeming quality in a person we were meeting with, but Frank would always do so. I recall one particular occasion when we met with an attorney from Washington, D.C. in Frank's office about a matter. For forty-five minutes we had to endure this man's boarish behavior. When he finally departed I let Frank know on no uncertain terms that I thought the gentleman was rude and obnoxious, and he had been disrespectful to him in his office. When I had finished Frank turned to me and told me that he thought the man had a very nice smile. I couldn't believe this reaction! I was aggravated with Frank, thought he was just too nice, but in hindsight I view it as an unbelievable talent.

Well, as you know by now, good guys sometimes do finish first and that is exactly what happened in 1996 in Indiana. The Hoosier voters eventually saw the two candiates for what they were and Frank ended up winning the race by a comfortable margin. Although I had left my position with Frank eight years earlier for one in the private sector, his victory made me a more marketable commodity. I was so happy for my friend's success that I really had not contemplated the impact it could have on me. I was soon approached by others about opportunities, and although I made no immediate move, it would be a contributing factor in my move to the telecommunications industry the following year. That career change would certainly have a profound affect on my life.

In the summer of that year my friend, Kip Tew, and I began to discuss taking a trip abroad together in November of that year. (Hank, you may remember Kip. You played with his daughter, Riley, when you were very young.) Although we had never traveled together for pleasure, we worked in the same industry, and had traveled at the same time on business. We thought we could get along, have a good time, and were both going to be ready for a break by the time November rolled around. In addition to his regular job as an electric company lobbyist, Kip was serving as the Marion County Democratic Chair at that time. He knew he would be worn out from the exhausting general election that would take place on the Tuesday before our departure. He would be ready for a much needed change of scenery.

We began to contemplate possible destinations and started to search for travel deals. We both had a desire to travel to someplace neither of us had been before, and thought a temperate climate might be enjoyable. We finally decided that we would visit Spain and Portugal. We were able to book an open-jawed ticket into Madrid and back out of Lisbon, thus enabling us to cover more ground and not have to back track. We were able to book these tickets on USAir at a good fare and with a reasonable schedule.

We started to examine the map and determine which localities we wanted to visit. We ultimately decided that the following cities looked most interesting to us: Madrid, Toledo, Granada and Seville in Spain, and, because of limited time, we would confine our foray into Portugal to its capitol of Lisbon. So, we decided to begin to put together an itinerary around these locales.

Once again, I found at this time the most effective and cost efficient way of traveling was by rail.

We were able to buy a combined Spain and Portugal rail pass which gave us a total of five days of travel over a two month period of time. This suited our needs. Additionally, since we were trying to cover a great deal of ground in nine nights in Europe we made reservations for overnight travel a couple of the nights.

In order to accomplish this most effectively and comfortably, we paid a little more for first-class passes. First-class travel enabled us to reserve two-person sleeping compartments for our overnight experiences, rather than being thrown in with four strangers. This truly was not much additional expense for a great deal more comfort, something I would recommend to any fellow traveler.

SPAIN

The day of our departure finally rolled around. We left Indianapolis on the afternoon of Friday, November 8, flying to Philadelphia and onward to Madrid. The flights were uneventful and once again I was able to secure good seats on the bulkhead of the Boeing 767 for the transatlantic flight. After an on-time departure from Philly, we settled in, having a couple of drinks and an uninspiring airline meal of soggy salad and overcooked pasta. I nodded off to sleep watching a movie and awoke a couple of hours later as the sun was just breaking the horizon.

After another less than satisfying meal, an American cheese omelet with a couple of sausage links, we arrived in Madrid in the mid-morning around eight-thirty on that Saturday. The sun was now shining brightly as we alit on Spanish soil. We cruised through the Customs and Immigration process, and entered the arrivals hall in search of public transportation to downtown Madrid. We found the airport bus that took us to near the center of the city, and dropping us off at Plaza Colon.

We had yet to equip ourselves with a fully functional map and were left with rudimentary directions to our hotel from our guidebook. I remember wandering around for much too long a period of time searching in vain for our hotel. The city had yet to awake, so there was virtually no one to ask for directions. It probably was partially a function of lack of sleep, coupled with poor preparation on our part, but we walked aimlessly for what seemed to be a long time.

Finally, we encountered a young man walking towards us and we stopped him to see if he spoke English and could point us in the proper direction. It turned out that this gent was our savior, not only speaking passable English, but he knew our hotel. He gave us directions and we went on our way. As it turns out, we were only a couple blocks from the hotel and were there in a matter of minutes.

The Hostal la Macarena is situated on a little side street, just to the east of the Plaza Mayor. The small hotel which contains 25 rooms is located in a well-kept, centuries old building in a very central part of the city. It is an easy place from which to venture out sightseeing either on foot, or from the nearby subway station. We took the rickety, caged elevator to the second floor check-in area where we were greeted by a pleasant, aging man. He informed us that we were lucky and our room was ready.

We were led down the hall to an airy, clean, twin-bedded room. We settled in, relaxed for a while and then decided to shower up. I went first and was confronted with a handheld shower in the bathtub. Thank goodness I had experience with one of these before and soon had finished a long, hot shower. It became Kip's turn and I tried to show him how to control the handheld device. After he finished his shower he hollered for assistance, it seems he was not too adept at controlling the shower spray and there was over an inch of water on the floor. I am pleased to say he became much better with these gadgets as the trip progressed.

After resting a little while longer, we decided to venture out and find some lunch. We consulted our guidebook and chose a target location nearby our hotel. We crossed the street from our lodging and climbed the stairs to Plaza Mayor. The large open plaza is one of the major squares in the city, and has been for over five hundred years. The large space is surrounded on three sides by a four-story building housing shops, bars and restaurants on the street level and residential space above. Some of the facades are smartly painted making for a very lovely locale.

We crossed the attractive open space on this bright, sunny day heading east a couple of blocks to the Restaurante Rodriguez, a spot highly recommended in our guidebook. Located on a side street we spotted the homey looking restaurant from a couple of blocks away. As we approached the entrance we noticed several people lingering outside on the sidewalk. Undeterred, we forged ahead and entered in search of a table. We could see no tables readily available as we surveyed the dining area.

In a few seconds we were greeted by a hostess wanting to know if we had a reservation. We told her we didn't, and she said it would be a few minutes, asking us to wait outside. When we stepped out, we could hear the audible complaints of those standing on the sidewalk. Neither Kip, nor I, were fluent in Spanish. However, you did not have to be to comprehend that these folks were not happy with us for unknowingly trying to jump the line. We both felt very small for not recognizing our faux pas, and our inability to properly communicate to those assembled that we were sorry for our mistake.

We were so taken aback by our blunder that we really didn't know what to do. We ended up just standing there silently until the young lady came to take us to a vacant table. The restaurant was packed with families out for a Saturday lunch. It was a very comfortable place, in spite of the white lace covering the windows and tables, and the smells filling the room were very pleasant.

The hostess brought us a menu and it was all in Spanish. I had taken three semesters of Spanish in college several years before, but I am hardly a linguist. I believe that Kip had taken German, so the translation duties fell to me. I remember recognizing the Spanish word for chicken, pollo, and told Kip I would be ordering the chicken with rice dish. Kip decide not to order the same dish as I had, so he ordered another pollo preparation.

We sat and drank a beer we had ordered, and shortly our selections were served. Mine turned out to be a lovely chicken breast, grilled in a garlic and sun-dried tomato sauce, served with rice and vegetables. It was a delicious preparation, one that I thoroughly enjoyed. As luck would have it, Kip's was a plate of chicken livers with a little rice. Unfortunately, neither of us like liver, so Kip had a far less than satisfactory meal.

After we finished our lunch, we headed back out into the warm afternoon for a walk and to get our bearings. We ended up strolling around the center of the city for several hours, stopping occasionally at an interesting bar to have a beer, or window shop. I was impressed by the numerous plazas, green space and open areas that Madrid has to offer. It seems to me that for a city its size and age, it has a large amount of open space adding to the livability of the community.

One of the areas we checked out that afternoon was the Mercado de San Miguel. This central market near the Plaza Mayor offers a wonderful selection of meats, fruits and vegetables. Additionally, you can find a nice selection of wines and Sherries. It is all enclosed in a wrought iron and glass building and which I found to be well worth the visit.

Additionally, we visited the Puerta del Sol, a large square a few blocks from our hotel. Puerta del Sol is the Times Square of Madrid, famous for its New Year's celebrations. It is also the geographic center of the city and the point of zero measurement for all of Spain. It was bustling on the fine Saturday afternoon and a great spot for watching beautiful, young Spanish women strut their stuff.

The effects of the long flight and lack of sleep eventually overcame us and we returned to our room to rest a while before venturing back out for dinner. As we laid on our beds and fought off sleep, we watched a little television and I tried to brush up on my Spanish. In particular, I focused on pleasantries like hello, goodbye, thank you, you're welcome and how much does it cost. I think it goes a long way with the locals if you at least attempt a few basic words and phrases. I always endeavor to learn these simple words, or phrases, as a sign of respect for those countries I am visiting.

After a couple of hours we decided to head out for the evening. We had selected another restaurant within a short walk of our hotel, which was not difficult because there were tons of places within a five minute walk. Our guidebook recommended a place in the same block as our choice for lunch, so we decided to give it a try.

Mason Restaurante Pontejos is located near the Puerta del Sol and is far from fancy, but inviting nonetheless. The tiled restaurant has numerous tables covered in blue and white checkered table cloths and we were shown to one in the back of the dining room. Over the bar there were several Spanish hams hanging, seemingly a staple of the local diet, waiting to be consumed.

Our attractive young waitress appeared and we ordered a couple of beers while we read the menu, thank goodness they had an English version for our use. I decided to try the paella and Kip, eyeing the ham hanging above the bar, selected a ham and cheese omelet. Our waitress reappeared with our cold drinks and a basket of tasty bread. In a few minutes our meals were delivered. My paella was great, but unfortunately, Kip's omelet did not meet his tastes. It seems that the Spanish ham is very, very salty and it overpowered the omelet.

I felt very badly for my friend as he picked at his dinner gingerly. He had chocked down a few chicken livers at lunch and now he couldn't stomach the ham in his omelet. I could only hope that there would be meals to his liking in the future. We drank another beer while Kip ate the rest of the bread in the basket. Finished, we settled our bill and decided to take a stroll.

We walked out on the street and joined the legions of Madrilenos in their nightly tradition of taking an evening walk. As we were making our way through a crowded area on the street near the Puerta del Sol, a bit of a commotion started. A middle-aged woman was hollering at a group of young men about something. As it turned out one of these guys had spat on me, landing a large chunk of phlegm on the back of my shirt.

This kind woman had seen what I had not felt and was taking up our cause with these fellows. After shooing these scoundrels off, she turned to me and said that I should check for my wallet because this was a common ploy used by pick-pockets. Thankfully, all my things we intact, but before we knew it several passersby were coming to our aid. People assisted in cleaning the spit from my shirt and others apologized for the behavior of their countryman. It turned out to be quite a nice gesture on the part on these strangers.

As we approached out hotel we noticed a lot of activity on our street and decided to explore further. The area was now coming to life with numerous bars and restaurants wide open for business. The Spanish are notoriously late eaters and they were proving their point as they were coming out in droves as it was now after ten o'clock. We stopped at a little shop selling some locally produced sherry and sampled a glass. It was a superb after dinner drink, dry with just a hint of sweetness, which I thoroughly enjoyed. I decided when we got back to the room that I would return the next day and buy a bottle to take with us on the trip. This proved to be an unwise decision, as when we went back the next night, our final in Madrid, the shop was closed. Another proof point of my mother's theory that if you like it, buy it, don't wait for later, or it might not be there.

Kip and I awoke the next morning refreshed after both of us were able to get a good night's sleep. We cleaned up and went to the hotel's breakfast room to partake in their continental offering. The meal consisted of coffee, juice, bread and jams. It was certainly nothing to write home about, but the price was right, and it was enough to get you started.

We decided to start out our day by visiting the city's largest flea market which takes place on Sundays just down the street from la Macarena. El

Rastro is one of the more amazing outdoor markets I have been to in the world. It winds around numerous streets in a residential neighborhood and spills into a few plazas. It is open on Sundays and you can find most anything you would want here. From books to live birds, antiques to clothing, and art to collectables, you can purchase it here.

We wandered around the market viewing all that was for sale for a couple of hours. Tired, we finally stopped at a bar along the route and order a beer and some tapas. This proved to be a very satisfying stand-up lunch, as we sampled the offerings of a couple of different taverns. Watching the locals interact from this vantage point was quite enjoyable.

After we had our fill, we decided to visit the Palacio Real de Madrid, a nice walk from the flea market. The Royal Palace of Madrid is the home of the Spanish royal family in Madrid, but they choose to live elsewhere. The palace is used for official functions of the state, and is open to the public as a museum. It is surrounded by a series of beautiful gardens which are also open for touring.

We made the several block trek through the city on another bright, sunny day with temperatures now in the high sixties. We arrived at the palace in time for a tour in English that was forming. I must confess that I knew little about the building before we arrived, but I was blown away by it. The baroque structure is one of the largest buildings in Madrid, and the largest royal palace in Europe. Over fifty of the rooms and apartments are available for viewing, and we did just that.

We spent the next couple of hours walking through this massive structure. We visited the Royal Apartments and Reception Room which includes the Throne Room, the Banquet Hall, and the Royal Chapel. Additionally, we viewed priceless art works including paintings, tapestries, and porcelain pieces. After our time in the apartments we moved on to the Royal Armory with its impressive collection of weaponry dating back hundreds of years. We also checked out the Royal Pharmacy with its displays of medicines conceived in years past.

After thoroughly exhausting ourselves and the content of the palace area, we decided to hop the subway across the city to one of the main train stations, Madrid Atocha. We were traveling to the station for two reasons, first, to get our train passes validated before our first trip the next morning and, second, to get our bearings for the trip to Toledo the next day.

The Atocha station is the largest station in Madrid and is the sight of the first train station in the city. The large brick, steel, and glass structure that used to house trains has been converted into a large atrium which contains ticket offices, travel agencies, and restaurants. The actual tracks are now located in adjacent structures, and the station is not only functional, but ascetically appealing.

We quickly got our passes validated and confirmed our first trip of the next day to the historic city of Toledo. By now it was late in the afternoon and we were pretty well spent. We had yet to visit the nearby Prado, Madrid's world class art museum, but we decided to wait until the next day after our return from Toledo, and before our departure to Granada. Instead, we decided to return to our room and rest up for a while before dinner.

We ended up going to dinner almost across the street from our hotel at a place called El Cuchi. A quirky place that advertise that "Hemmingway never ate here," in contrast to several others in the Plaza Mayor area that boast he indeed did. There was also a sign that stated, erroneously I might add, that they did not speak English, but they would not laugh at our Spanish.

The lively joint served mainly Mexican fare, so we ordered a couple of beers and noshed on some chips and spicy salsa as we decide on what to order. I ended up ordering a chicken burrito with rice and beans. We drank our beers and ate chips until our orders arrived. My burrito turned out to be quite tasty, and very large. I could barely eat the whole thing, but did so in a valiant effort.

We drank a couple of beers and flirted with our waitress until we decided it was time to go across the street to bed. We returned to the room and did some packing to lighten our load in the morning. We had to be up fairly early to catch a train to Toledo for the day, return to Madrid, and finally catch an overnight train to Granada the next evening. We knew that we needed another good night sleep, so we turned out the light by ten in an effort to do so.

We awoke the next morning to a cloudy, cooler day. We cleaned up and had another continental breakfast, lingering over a second and third cup of coffee. After breakfast and checking out, we headed for the subway station to go to the Atocha train station. Our train for Toledo departed a little before ten, so we caught the tail end of rush hour on the subway. The train was not overcrowded as we feared and in a matter of minutes we arrived at the station.

We were early in our arrival, so we had plenty of time to find a storage locker to stow our luggage for our day of travel. European train stations and airports typically have storeage space available for just these occasions. However, since terrorist activity has escalated, their usage has become more restricted. We grabbed a cup of coffee and boarded our train for the slow, ninety minute ride to Toledo. The ride was a pretty one through the rolling, green Spanish countryside, and we had an on time arrival into the city.

The train station in Toledo is an old one, but is rather ornate with tile work, and stained and leaded glass windows. Its location is east and a little north of the Old Town of Toledo and as we departed we could see the city on the hill perched above the Tagus River. It looked like a scene from an El Greco painting, the artist who helped make the area famous. The town was above us with dark, brooding clouds beyond, it was quite a sight.

We decided to just walk into town, a move that in hindsight might not have been the wisest given the uphill nature of the climb. As we were walking through a gate into the Old Town the threatening skies opened up and a hard rain began to fall. Fortunately, we were able to duck into a nearby shop and kill some time until the rain lessened.

An offshoot of this stop was that I learned of the gold inlay process that Toledo is known for producing. Toledo jewelers are famous for a process called damascening, which is where a precious metal, like gold, is applied in a decorative pattern over a non-precious metal, like steel or iron. The process had been practiced in Toledo since the Middle Ages and the results are quite beautiful. Before we left the city I was a proud owner of a small globe made from gold using this process.

With my little impromptu shopping spree over, we decided to venture out into the city. As we were leaving the little shop we were overcome by the distinct smell of garlic. Looking to our left we saw a little, Italian eatery open for business with a specials board outside. We checked our watches and stomachs, and decided it was time for lunch.

We entered the small bistro and sat down at one of only about a half dozen tables. A server came rushing out of the kitchen in the back to greet us and provided us with English menus. We placed a drink order and perused the menu. We both decided on one of the luncheon specials, spaghetti with meat balls, how could you go wrong?

Our waiter returned with some freshly baked garlic bread, probably what we smelled to attract us inside, and a small green salad with an oil and vinegar dressing. It was quite fresh and tasty. Our heaping plates of pasta with tomato sauce and two large meatballs followed. The pasta tasted homemade to me, and the meatballs and sauce were spicy and good. We had made an excellent choice by simply following our noses.

Loaded down with carbohydrates, we set out to see this quaint city. The Old Town area is a labyrinth of narrow, winding streets lined by very old buildings and homes. We first encountered the Alcazar, an imposing fortress that dominates the skyline. Unfortunately, our day to visit was a Monday and, as in many cases around the world, it and several other museums in Toledo were closed on that day. We poked around the outside of the centuries old stone structure, seeing what we could from the exterior.

We then wound our way to the Cathedral, a magnificent Gothic structure finding its beginnings over 800 years ago. We took a tour of the church which contains some wonderful works of art by masters, like El Greco and Goya. One of the most impressive features is a wall of white marble and alabaster which contains a sculpture of The Last Supper in alabaster. The cathedral also houses a treasury which contains religious objects reputed to be crafted from gold brought back from the New World by Christopher Columbus.

Our next stop was the Museo de Santa Cruz, an art museum which has been aptly described as the people of Toledo's gift to the world. The museum is housed in a unique, beautiful structure done in plateresque style. The museum contains many works of Toledo's most famous artist, El Greco, and other famous Spanish painters and sculptors. It also hosts an impressive collections of Flemish tapestries.

We continued to wander the cobblestone streets of the town for a several hours, ducking in and out of open shops, and other interesting buildings. We finally decided it was time to head back to Madrid and descended the hill toward the train station. We caught a train back to the Spanish capitol around five which would put us back in the city in about ninety minutes. As we were departing Toledo, we could look back and see the town on the bluff. We both agreed that a trip to Toledo is a must if you are visiting Madrid. It is one of the most memorable places I have visited.

We arrived back at Atocha station around six-thirty. We had originally planned to return from Toledo and visit the nearby Prado Museum, one of the world's finest art museums, but we discovered it was closed that evening. I guess this is a strong reason to return to Madrid one day.

We decided that our best course of action now was to just collect our luggage from the storage lockers and head across town on the subway to the Chamartin Train Station, the other main railway hub in Madrid. We caught the subway directly from Atocha and arrived at Chamartin with nearly two hours until our overnight train departed. We spent some time securing the details of our departure, and then decided it was time to find something to eat before we departed.

The Chamartin train station is not as grand as Atocha. It is a more modern structure, but is quite spacious with all the services one would require. We had several choices for dining, a few besides the usual fast-food suspects, and we finally selected a pizza place. We both ordered individual pizzas, mine was loaded with several toppings, and we sat in sort of a food court area and ate. Hardly fine dining, but it would have to suffice for that evening.

The time to board our train arrived, and we found our car and stowed our luggage in our berth. Our compartment was nice with two somewhat elevated beds, one on each side of the room. Soon our train was chugging out of Chamartin headed south toward Granada. We settled in for the night entertaining each other until we tried to get some sleep. Our berth was hot, so we opened the window to get some cooler, fresh air. Opening the window created a lot of noise, but it was either noise, or heat. Finally, I was able to drop off to sleep for a few hours of fitful rest.

We arrived in Granada before dawn the next morning. Although it was not raining it was a wet, very dark arrival. As was my custom in those days, we did not have a hotel reservation. In order to maintain flexibility, I would reserve rooms for my arrival and departure cities. I would leave the middle of my trips open in case I decided to change plans and possibly stay a longer, or shorter, period of time in an area. After years of not changing my plans and, assuming a position of more responsibility at my company,

I discontinued this practice and began to make all my reservations in advance of my departure.

We had picked out our first option for a hotel, the Macia. We exited the train station and fumbled around trying to figure out how to walk, or find public transportation, to the hotel. Finally, we just gave up and hailed a taxi who took us the several blocks to the hotel. I am glad we did, because understanding the bus system was not simple, and it was a lengthy walk from the station to the hotel.

The Macia sits on a lovely little plaza at the foot of the hill which is home to the Alhambra. Since the primary purpose of our visit to Granada was to spend time at the Alhambra, proximity to this palace was somewhat important. The taxi driver let us off in front of the hotel just as the day's first light was peaking over the horizon.

We sauntered into the hotel across the marble floor to the reception and inquired about a room. The front desk clerk said they had an immediate availability for a twin room on the second floor in the back. The price was good, so we took it. We moved through the modern lobby filled with blond furniture, past the buffet breakfast and entered the elevator. We arrived at our room and entered to find a nice-sized room, newly furnished with two beds and a large bathroom with all the amenities. This place would definitely do.

I stretched out on the bed and got caught up on all the world news on CNN while Kip took his turn in the shower. My time came soon, and I must say it felt good to get rid of the grime that had blown into our compartment the night before with the window open. We had been given a light breakfast on the train, but decided that the buffet downstairs looked so good to us that we would go downstairs and investigate the situation.

We stepped off the elevator and, since there was no one at the restaurant, we went to the front desk and asked if we could have breakfast. The clerk told us to help ourselves, and we did. We found a nice table and proceeded to attack the breakfast buffet. It was a very nice set up featuring cold meats, cheeses, cereals, yogurt, eggs, fresh fruit, juices, assorted breads and a coffee machine capable of making a variety of hot beverages.

We had plenty of time to visit the Alhambra, so we took our time, and ate to our hearts content. We lingered over several cups of coffee which helped us wash down some sweet pastries which we enjoyed at the conclusion of our meal. Sated, we went upstairs and prepared to tackle one of the world's great palaces which was on top of the hill across the street.

As we were departing we asked at the front desk about the best way to get up the hill to the palace. Our new friend at the front desk told us that a public bus existed, but it ran about every thirty minutes and we had just missed it. He thought our best option was to hike it up the hill.

Heeding his advice we headed out the door and started across the Plaza Nueva passing a lovely little fountain directly in front of the hotel. The hike up the hill to the Alhambra was just that. It was steeper and longer than it looked from a distance, and we probably should have waited for the bus. To make matters worse, the threatening skies opened up on us about half the way up the hill. All in all, the walk was less pleasant than we had hoped for on our departure from the hotel.

Finally reaching the top of the hill, we located the ticket office and purchased our ducats. The type of ticket we bought entitled us to a guided tour of several sections of the fortress lasting about three hours.

The Alhambra was originally constructed in the ninth century as a fortress overlooking the Darrow River. Four centuries later the Moorish sultans decided to erect a palace on the site and this truly amazing series of buildings were set in motion. It is difficult to describe the beauty of this UNESCO World Heritage site. Before I launch into a feeble attempt, let me say that I believe the visit to the Alhambra made the entire trip to Spain and Portugal worthwhile, irrespective of any of the other sights we saw, or things we did.

We entered the fortress and headed directly to the first of the three Moorish palaces on the grounds, the Palace of Mexuar. This palace is the most modestly decorated of the palaces and was the functional area of the Alhambra. This palace contains the main chambers where the sultan's ministers met. Also in this palace is the Golden Room where the sultan sat on giant cushions and held meetings with citizens and his ministers.

We then moved to the Palace of Comares, which was the official residence of the sultans. This palace is more ornate than Mexuar and contains the opulent Throne Room. The Hall of Ambassadors is the largest room in the complex and was the reception room with a grand entrance and the throne on the opposite side of the room. The ceiling is a highly-decorated, tiled dome with inlays in the shapes of circles, crowns and stars.

The final Moorish palace we visited was the Palace of the Lions, often considered as the crowning glory of the complex. The centerpiece of this residence is the Court of the Lions and its fabulous fountain. This fountain is made of alabaster and is supported by twelve marble lions which represent the hours of the day and months of the year. Each hour a different lion spouts water from its mouth. Also in the Palace of Lions is the Hall of Two Sisters which is where the favorite member of the harem was housed.

Not only the Moors inhabited the Alhambra, the Holy Roman Emperor Charles V also built a palace on the grounds in early 16th century. Charles did not believe that the Moorish palaces were grand enough, so he commissioned a student of Michelangelo to design and build him a more elaborate residence on the grounds. The classical Renaissance structure which resulted is quite magnificent, if out of place in its setting.

The grounds surrounding the palaces are filled with gardens so beautiful, they also are difficult to describe. We were not able to fully enjoy these gardens because the downpour that greeted us when we arrived at the Alhambra never subsided during our visit. This possibly was a blessing because it kept the throngs away from the palaces which are apparently an everyday occurrence.

Inside the Alhambra

The level of detail in each of the palaces is simply amazing. There are carved wooden ceilings, marble floors and alabaster walls throughout. The inlaid tile work is something to behold. The level of sophistication is a wonder. There is hot and cold running water and bathrooms. There are fountains that flow freely, and this is all in structures that were built by the 14th century. The Moors were finally pushed from the Iberian Peninsula for good in 1492, the same year the Columbus discovered the New World.

As our tour ended, we were wet, tired and hungry. We decided to head back down the hill and see if we could find a quick lunch and take a rest. The rain had begun to slacken as we descended from the Alhambra. I pulled some guidebook pages from my raincoat as we were walking and discovered that an inexpensive restaurant was recommended near our hotel, so we made a bee line for the place.

The Mason Andaluz is a quaint little Spanish restaurant between our hotel and the large cathedral in Granada. We entered the eatery around two and a good crowd still existed. We were seated at a table covered with a red and white table cloth, and ordered a beer. Soon the server brought our beer and a menu which was not in English. Given that our server did not speak English and my Spanish was poor, I looked around to see what the other patrons were having so I could just point. A fellow at the next table was eating what appeared to be a beef stew and this looked good to me on this damp, cool day.

When our server returned I ordered the stew and Kip had the paella. Our orders came out in no time and I had no complaints about the stew which was served with fries, and Kip seemed satisfied with the paella. We drank another beer and finished our lunches. I noticed that we both were beginning to fade, so we paid our bill, and headed back to our room to rest.

In a few minutes we were back at our room and the rigors of overnight train travel had overcome us. Before I knew it we were in our respective beds, and asleep taking a much needed nap. I think we slept for a couple of hours because before I knew it I was awakening and it was five o'clock. We shook off the effects of the sleep and decided to venture out to see more of Granada.

We headed out to see the impressive Cathedral we had seen in the distance while we were going to lunch. But along the way we spotted an Irish pub and decided to stop in for a pint of Guinness. Hannigan and

Sons Irish Pub was alive that evening when we walked in. The dimly lit place with dark wood paneling was set for a party. It seems that Granada is a university town and several of the young co-eds had descended on Hannigan's that evening, and we were in for a night.

Hank, my son, it has been my experience that nearly everywhere you go in the world there is an Irish pub. And, if you are looking for a good time an Irish pub is a place where you can find it. We sidled up to the bar which a very attractive Spanish lass was tending, and ordered a pint. The bartender was outstanding and could pour a good pint. Before I knew it we were engaged in conversation with our server and a number of her friends that were patronizing the bar that evening.

One pint led to another, and so forth. Soon all thoughts of going out sightseeing and having a nice dinner vanished. We ended up spending the entire evening sitting on those bar stools. At some point we ordered big, juicy burgers and fries for dinner. I am sure by then we needed something to soak up the alcohol we were ingesting. After several pints and buying a Hannigan's t-shirt as a souvenir of Granada, we decided to call it a night. The place was still rocking as we said our good-byes.

We stumbled back to the hotel around midnight and fell into bed. I did remember to arrange a wakeup call for next morning, as we were catching a train the next day for Seville. We awoke the next day a little worse for the wear. I will say that a good hot shower and some strong coffee were in order. After another fine breakfast, we packed up our things, checked out of the hotel and caught a cab for the train station.

Our train to Seville was to depart Granada a little before nine o'clock and would arrive in Seville around noon. We found our track and car with little difficulty. We stowed our bags and took our seats for the ride. I immediately went in search of another cup of coffee, as I was still trying to shake off the ill-effects from having falling into bad company the night before.

Successful in my mission, I returned to my seat and watched the lovely Spanish scenery float by as we made our way to Seville. We had an on time arrival and decided to head out on foot toward the Old Town in search of a lodging. It was a sunny, pleasant day probably nearly seventy degrees and the walk felt good, even though it turned out to be longer than we had bargained for.

We finally arrived in the Old Town and quickly located the Hostal Goya, a small hotel smack dab in the middle of the Barrio de Santa Cruz. It was so close to many of the top attractions that even a weak-armed pitcher could throw a ball and hit them. We were in luck as the desk clerk offered us a twin room with full bath at a very reasonable price. He escorted us to the room to check it out before we decided. As we walked down the gleaming white marble hallways past the common areas, I grew quite confident that the room would meet our needs.

Indeed, the room was perfect. It contained two double beds, ample space including a couple of sitting chairs and a large marble bathroom. Given the price, quality, and ideal location, we felt that we had hit a home run. We quickly paid the clerk for the room and moved in for two nights. We decided the first order of business was to find place for lunch because the breakfast we had that morning in Granada was no longer with us.

Stepping back outside into the beautiful sunlit afternoon, there were abundant dining options all around. We strolled down the narrow, cobblestone street toward the Cathedral de Seville and spotted a little pizzeria which we had read about in our guidebook. The Pizzeria de Artesanos is an unpretentious eatery which was serving aromatic pizzas, pastas and sandwiches that day to a young crowd of hungry patrons.

We decided to join the throng, and were lucky enough to find a seat at a table near the front of the dining room. The young, dark, and attractive waitress brought us menus, but I knew from looking around the room what I wanted. It was a pizzeria after all, and they looked and smelled quite good to me. I ordered a ham and onion and Kip selected a pizza also. Still shying away from demon rum, I got a large bottle of cold water to drink.

Before too long our thin-crusted, hot, gooey, cheesy pizzas arrived at our table and we dove in. This was the ideal meal for me in my condition. A little grease from the cheese and ham should go a long way toward healing me of what ailed me. I was right, by the time I had finished off my pie I was feeling much improved and ready to hit the streets in search of all the sights. We paid our bill and vacated our table as quickly as possible because a crowd awaiting a seat was now building outside on the sidewalk.

We slipped past the waiting patrons and headed for our first stop, the imposing Cathedral de Seville. The huge 15th century structure is the third largest church in Europe and the largest Gothic building in the world.

Once inside the cathedral it is even more impressive to me. Works of art abound with beautiful tile works, stained-glass windows, ornate vaulted ceilings and a large frescoed dome. The cathedral is an awesome display of the wealth that existed in Seville at the time of its construction. The church is also the final resting place of Christopher Columbus, whose tomb rests on top of four statues bearing his remains.

As you work your way through the cathedral you exit on the opposite side into a lovely citrus garden. From the garden you can make your way to the Giralda Tower which stands next to the church. The tower is a former minaret of a Muslim mosque which previously stood on the site of the cathedral during Moorish times. It was converted into a bell tower when the church was constructed.

Quite possibly the most recognizable feature of the Seville skyline, you are able to walk to the top of the tower. Kip and I decided to undertake this journey which is accomplished without walking up a single step. Rather, you hike your way up what seems to be a nearly endless winding ramp that takes you to the top. Once reaching the top, you are afforded a commanding view of the metropolitan area of Seville. The scenery is worth the effort, but it requires a certain level of physical conditioning.

After we finished with our tour of the cathedral and tower we decided to go to the Tourist Information Center to pick up some maps and find out about a basketball game. Their office was a short walk from the cathedral, which we made in a matter of a few minutes. The gorgeous young lady working the counter was very helpful. She provided us with maps of the city, gave us some good suggestions for sightseeing, and was able to help us with information about their local professional basketball team.

Our local pro team, the Indiana Pacers, had played a preseason game in Seville earlier in the year which we had seen on television. This probably gave us the idea to pursue the possibility of going to see the team from Seville play while we were in town. We knew that the Spanish league is one of the top professional basketball leagues in Europe, and we thought it might be a great form of entertainment.

It turns out that the top local team, Caja San Fernando, had an international game that evening against a team from Pau, France. Kip and I got all the pertinent details from the kind young lady at the tourist office, along with bus directions to their venue. By now, it was moving on five o'clock and we wanted to get a little rest back at the room prior to leaving for the game.

On our way back to the hotel we stopped by a laundry we had spotted earlier in the day. We wanted to get some clothes washed before we went any further, and this shop looked promising. It turns out that if we would drop them off before ten in the morning, we could pick them up after three that afternoon. This sounded like a very favorable solution to our issue because I was down to one clean change of clothes. We returned to the hotel for a short rest because we had to catch a bus for the game in about an hour.

We rested for a while and decided to leave a little early for the game so we could soak up the atmosphere and catch a dinner of arena food. We walked a couple of blocks through the Barrio de Santa Cruz to the bus stop. Soon a sleek, new bus picked us up, and in about ten minutes it deposited us at the Palacio de Deportes San Pablo, the home of the Seville team.

The exterior of the building was well lit and revealed a modern, large edifice. We located the ticket office without difficulty and purchased a pair of tickets near the end of the court about ten rows up from the floor. We entered the arena and walked out on the floor level to find our seats. The two teams were on the floor warming up as we made our way to our red cushioned chairs.

We sat down for a while and watched the teams go through their drills, and oggled the cheerleaders who were beginning to perform in front of us. After a few minutes we went for a walk to check out the arena, and see what the concession stands had to offer. The arena appeared to be rather new and well-kept. It seated in the neighborhood of ten thousand fans and looked like it would be at least half-full that evening.

We found the concession stand, and settled for the classic beer and tubular snack. We returned to our seats a little before the tip-off. The arena was now well over half-full, and the excitement was building. When the game began the fans were clearly into it and were knowledgeable about the game. The event had much the same trappings as an American basketball game with loud music blaring and dancing girls performing at time outs. The quality of the play was quite high and each team had two, or three, former American college stars on their roster.

The star for Seville was a player from Gary, Indiana, named Tellis Frank. Frank played his college ball at Western Kentucky and went on to play several years in the NBA before taking his game abroad. The local squad ended up winning a very competitive game and the crowd went home happy. Being basketball fans, we were both delighted with how the night turned out, and that a fellow Hoosier led a team thousands of miles from home to victory.

Basketball game in Seville

Kip and I caught the bus back to our neighborhood and decided it was time to check out the town before heading to bed. As luck would have it, we located another Irish pub just down the street from our hotel. Flaherty's Irish Bar is in the shadow of the Cathedral and is another rocking place at night. We entered and ordered a pint of Guinness, which was poured to perfection with a nice creamy head with a shamrock on top. We drank our ale and watched the young crowd mingle, and decided it had been a late night the previous day, a long day today, and it was time to hit the bed.

I was proud of our mature decision. We hoofed it back the couple of blocks and hit the hay. The bed felt particularly good and I remember sleeping like a rock in the very quiet room. We awoke the next morning and it was after eight o'clock. We each took our turns in the bathroom and then grabbed up our dirty clothes and headed for the drop off laundry. We left our clothes and were given full assurance they would be done, and ready for pick-up any time after three that afternoon.

Our room did not include breakfast, so we now went in search of a place for our morning meal. We were both hungry as the hot dog the night before had not proven to last long. As we walked down the street we noticed that Flaherty's had a sign out offering breakfast. We went inside as they had apparently just opened and discovered they had a full breakfast menu.

We both ordered the full Irish breakfast the included eggs, rashers, sausages, baked beans, hash browns, grilled mushrooms, roasted tomato, toast, jam, orange juice and coffee. We sat at a table overlooking the street and thoroughly enjoyed the feast. It was just what we needed to kick start the day. We sat and drank several cups of coffee and watched the street scene play out before our eyes. The whole experience was superb.

After reluctantly determining it was time to move on, we decided to visit the fabulous Moorish palace of Seville, the Alcazar. The Alcazar sits on the opposite side of the Seville Cathedral from our breakfast locale. Literally, all we had to do was walk around the Cathedral and there was the Alcazar. The thirteenth century palace is still used by the Spanish royal family when they visit Seville, and it is the oldest palace in Europe still occupied by royalty.

We entered the palace and were immediately taken by its similarities to the Alhambra in Granada. This seemed very incongruous given this structure was in a very urban area, and the Alhambra sets on a lofty perch in a bucolic setting. We purchased our tickets and joined an English speaking tour of the facility.

As in Granada, the structures contain incredible attention to detail and are filled with expansive rooms for gatherings of officials and large ceremonial functions. The ornate palaces are accompanied by magnificent gardens with large, flowing fountains. This palace and its grounds are a definite can't miss if you are in Seville. In fact, I am not sure which is more impressive, the Alcazar or the much more ballyhooded Alhambra, but both should be on your list.

After spending nearly three hours wandering through the chambers, pavilions, and gardens of the Alcazar, we determined it was time to find some lunch. Given that we were still in the neighborhood where we were staying, it was not difficult finding a place to eat. The only question was on deciding what sounded good at the time.

We ended up in the Cerveceria Giralda which sits on a busy little street right near the Cathedral and the Alcazar. This bar/restaurant is located in a centuries old building that once was an Arab bathhouse. We decided it was time to sample some of the Spanish favorites, tapas, and this place was highly rated for their offering of these small plates.

We took a seat in the bar area with its wonderful arched ceiling supported by columns. We ordered a couple of beers, it seemed almost obligatory given the first name of the establishment was Spanish for beer. Our young waiter brought us a couple of glasses of the cold, frothy beverages and proceeded to give us his thoughts on the day's tapas. We ordered several of the small plates including some calamari, meatloaf, a mushroom dish and a pork with potatoes concoction.

In no time our orders appeared, and we found them quite good and filling. We ordered a couple of more cold beers and enjoyed people watching in the very central location. We sat and discussed our next steps on our last afternoon in Seville, a city we were growing to like very much. Since it was a beautiful, sunny afternoon we decided to take a walk to see a large structure we had seen the previous evening on our way to the ballgame.

After a less than ten minute walk around the Alcazar and through the University of Seville we came to the Plaza de Espana. This urban oasis was the sight of the 1929 Spanish-American Exposition hosted by Seville. This huge main edifice is arranged in a semicircle around a lovely plaza. The accompanying gardens are magnificent.

It is a truly stunning place and was a total surprise to us. We wandered around the buildings and were amazed at the level of detail in the tile work. We checked out the alcoves that contained exquisite tiled maps of each of the regions of Spain. There is a 'river' running through the grounds with small boats available for rental. We spend a couple of hour here just enjoying the nice weather, checking out the wonderful structures, and the locals who were having fun.

The sun was beginning to lower in the autumn sky when we decided to walk back toward our hotel. We remembered to pick up our clean clothes at the laundry on our way back. We returned to our room and repacked our bags with the fresh laundry and rested for a while before heading back out for the evening.

We finally decided to go out for our last night in Seville. Our first stop was a restaurant we had seen earlier in the day which looked interesting and the prices matched our wallets. Pizzeria San Marco was just down around the corner and on the left in half a block. We got there around seven, early by Spanish standards, and had no trouble getting a table.

The restaurant was well-appointed and the menu was far from what you would expect from a pizzeria. Sure, there was pizza on the menu, but pastas, fish and meat dishes dominated the selections. We ordered some red wine and inspected the menu. I ordered a pappardelle with a spicy, tomato seafood sauce. I believe Kip chose the lasagna. All I remember is that my pasta was out of this world, and I think Kip enjoyed his, too.

We finished our plates of pasta and sat back to enjoy our remaining red wine. We watched the crowd of attractive, well-dressed Spaniards just beginning to arrive for their customary late dinners. We sat and discussed our next move and determined that we would just move back down the street to Flaherty's for a pint before turning in for the night. We did just that, had a pint, and went back to the Goya for the night. I was proud of us.

The next morning we awoke, got cleaned up, and went out to find some breakfast. We decided to return to the Cerveceria Giralda because we noticed they opened at nine o'clock for breakfast when we had been there earlier. They had just opened when we arrived, and we ordered our morning coffee. We looked over the menu and both chose omelets, mine ham and cheese and Kip's without the ham. We also each got a glass of fresh squeezed orange juice which was delightful. Our omelets were served with a basket of freshly baked bread with butter and jam. It was another great start to the day.

After we finished our coffee, we decided to go check out one of the local favorites, bullfighting. The Plaza de Toros Real Maestranz is a short walk through an old neighborhood from the Cathedral. As we were walking to the bullring we did some window shopping and stopped into one particularly interesting store. The shop specialized in handmade ceramics painted in colorful patterns.

I decided to buy some particularly fetching candlesticks, and salt and pepper shakers, for my dining room. Since I didn't want to carry the items around I thought I would just stop at the shop on our return to our neighborhood. Kip was also eyeing a couple of items, so we would look forward to our return after our visit to the bullring.

We came upon the Plaza de Toros Real Maestranz shortly after leaving the shop. This bullring is probably the most famous in Spain, and is the oldest in the world with construction starting in 1761. The beautiful Baroque structure is an attractive yellow and white and has seating for 14,000 spectators. Tours are available in English, and Kip and I were able to join one.

The focus of the tour is on the museum associated with the bullring. During the tour you see the chapel were the toreadors pray before the fights, the hospital where they are taken if hurt in the battle, an art collection of paintings and pictures of famous bullfighters, and an array of the colorful costumes worn by various contestants over the years. We were then led out into the bullring to get the same view as a toreador entering the ring. Although I don't think I would enjoy the carnage associated with a bullfight, the visit to the bullring was quite interesting and a real peak into the Spanish culture.

Having finished our tour, we retraced our steps back toward the Barrio de Santa Cruz. We were pleased with our sightseeing mission and were looking forward to making our purchases at the ceramic shop. When we arrived at the shop it was closed. We were shocked that the place had closed, but apparently they observed the old Spanish tradition of closing for siesta, and we missed that iteration. This created a problem because we were leaving that afternoon before the business would reopen. I could kick myself for not buying the item earlier. It was further proof of my mother's axiom, "if you like it, buy it, and don't wait."

We had a little time to kill before we headed to the train station to begin our trek to Lisbon. Since there was no direct rail line along the southern coast of the Iberian Peninsula we were forced to take a train back to Madrid and then change to an overnight train onward to Lisbon. We ambled back toward our hotel to pick up our luggage we had left behind. We ended up stopping along the way for a quick bite of tappas, standing up at some nameless bar next to the Goya.

It turned out our small plates were quite good, especially a tangy pork dish with potatoes. After we finished and grabbed our bags, we headed to the bus stop to catch a ride to the Santa Justa train station. We arrived at the modernized facilities about 45 minutes before our train was to depart. We found our track on the lower level as our train was just pulling in. After a few minutes we were able to board. We were excited for this train ride because it was aboard a high speed, AVE train which traveled at top speeds of nearly 200 miles per hour. I had yet to ride on one of this high speed trains and couldn't wait.

Our rail pass entitled us to first-class ticket, we found our car and took our seats. The super sleek vehicle was more like entering an airplane, than a conventional train. There was a center aisle in the car with two airplane-like seats on each side. We had individual television screens at each seat, and could watch movies on the two and a half hour trip to Madrid's Atocha Station.

I was seated for quite a while without anyone next to me on the window. About five minutes before our departure a beautiful, young Spanish woman entered the car turning nearly all heads. She worked her way down the aisle and claimed the vacant seat next to me. I helped her place her bag in the overhead bin and she sat down. She turned to me and thanked me in Spanish and tried to begin a conversation. I asked her if she spoke English, and unfortunately, she knew fewer words in my language than I did hers.

I was kicking myself where it hurts for not paying more attention in my college Spanish classes. This raven-haired beauty obviously wanted to have a conversation, and I could barely oblige. Kip who was across the aisle from me was trying his best to engage her, but he spoke no Spanish at all. The train roared off and the next thing I knew was this nice person was sharing family photos with me, and trying her best to be understood.

The best Kip and I could ascertain was that she was from a wealthy, landed family from somewhere outside of Seville and she was going to Madrid on business. Frustration with our inability to communicate effectively finally set in, and we all resorted to watching the Steve Martin movie playing on the screens in front of us. A steward came by with drinks and the countryside flew by so quickly it was almost hard to watch. At one point another high speed train passed us headed toward Seville and it nearly scared the dickens out of us. It happened so quickly, rocking the train with such force that it was very alarming.

We arrived at Atocha station a few minutes ahead of schedule. I helped the very pleasant woman with her bag, grabbed mine and said good-bye to her. Kip and I headed out to locate the subway because we needed to transfer to Chamartin station to catch our overnight train to Lisbon. We hopped the subway and arrived at Chamartin with a couple of hours to kill before our train would depart. We found a bar in the station that served sandwiches and killed the time drinking beer and eating hamburgers. There were a couple of young Aussies doing the same thing, and we swapped travel stories and drank beer until our train was posted for boarding.

My favorite meal in Spain would not occur until a later trip to the Iberian Peninsula with my family. Hank, you were on this trip, but were probably too young to remember. So, I am going to take a short break from this trip to discuss a later journey which included my favorite Spanish meal, as well as, in the small country of Andorra. I will rejoin this trip soon.

In May of 2007, we returned to Spain to visit the lovely city of Barcelona. We were on a "pod" type trip which we have come to enjoy. This vacation started with a flight into Geneva, Switzerland, for three nights, an onward flight to Morocco, specifically the exotic city of Marrakech for four nights and we finished our trip with four nights in Barcelona.

We had arrived at this "pod" system of traveling for a few reasons. First, we discovered that we prefer to stay at least three nights in an area because by doing so you can begin to experience what life is like in a locale. Anything less, and we feel you are cheating yourself out of this opportunity. Secondly, after you came along Hank, travel changed for us and we needed to take more time to enjoy an area and not be in a hurry. Finally, with the advent of low-cost airlines in Europe you could cover more ground, in less time, and often cheaper than if you travel by train.

So a driving factor in scheduling these types of trips is who the economy carriers that service an area are, and what destinations do these carriers serve? As an example, on this trip we discovered that Atlas Blue

Airlines, a low-cost airline and a wholly-owned subsidiary of Royal Air Maroc, flew to Geneva and Barcelona from their hub in Marrakech.

With all three cities on our list of places to see, this airline made our trip to all three cities a very reasonable proposition. We simply booked open-jawed flights into Geneva and out of Barcelona on Northwest Airlines and linked the three cities together with tickets on Atlas Blue. It turned out to be a wonderful trip to three very diverse cultures.

We arrived in Barcelona late on a Thursday evening. We hopped a cab from the airport to make it to our accommodation before the front desk closed for the night. We had rented an apartment at the Barcelona Center Plaza, a well-situated lodging just outside the Gothic Quarter in the Eixample neighborhood. You were within easy walking distance of many of the major sites of the city.

After a little difficulty finding the exact address of the Barcelona Center Plaza, our taxi driver dropped us in front of a stone building which had to be pressing the century mark. We pushed open the double wooden doors to find a spacious lobby with an old cage-type elevator which would take up to the second floor where the apartments are located.

We arranged our bags and ourselves on the cramped elevator and were soon at the entrance of the apartments. We entered the small, but comfortable lobby area and were met by a nice young man who had a good command of the English language. Although it was nearly midnight, he took his time explaining everything we needed to know about the apartment and the city of Barcelona.

He took us down to the end of the hall, helping us with our bags. He opened the door to our abode which was rather Spartan, but very clean and functional. We had a nice little bathroom, a kitchenette with everything you needed to prepare meals, a dining area, and a large studio room with a double and a single bed, television and a small balcony. It was certainly not the Ritz, but it suited our needs ideally.

We took no time settling in and were all soon in bed. We awoke the next morning and after showering, we ate breakfast of some items that Jenny had procured the day before in our travels, muffins, breakfast bars and yogurt. After eating, our first order of business was to run to a nearby grocery store to buy some staples.

There was a very convenient and nice grocery store located only about a block from the apartment. The gentleman at the front desk the night before had given us a map of Barcelona and had indicated the location of the grocery for us. We exited the apartment building into a gorgeous spring morning, a bright sunshine and temperatures already in the low 70s. We quickly located the market and stocked up on breakfast items, some snacks and a couple of bottles of local red wine.

We scurried back to the apartment and stored our purchases. It was such a pleasant day we wanted to waste no time getting out into it. We left the building and headed west for the Plaza de Catalunya, arguably the commercial center of Barcelona. Only a couple of blocks away we were soon basking in the sun with hundreds of locals in the square. We stood and snapped photos in all directions before deciding to head down the most famous street in the city, Les Rambles.

This broad avenue features a wide esplanade which is perfect for walking and on a day like this it is the ideal place to be. Judging from the crowd we were not the only ones to agree with this thinking. We started south on Les Rambles and were immediately struck by the number of vendors which line the walkway. The variety of items for sale were impressive from live pets and birds, to flowers and plants.

We continued down the street until we came upon a real find, the large public market. Mercado de la Boqueria sits just off Les Rambles and has been in business for centuries. The large covered market is open on both ends and presents a shed-like appearance. Inside, the place was teeming with business. The vendors were selling everything from fresh fruits to seafood. There were businesses that specialized in spices and delicious chocolates. If you wanted something to eat, you could find it here.

We walked around the market and our senses were nearly overcome by the sights and smells. It didn't take long before we were buying all kinds of foodstuffs to take back to our apartment. We bought fruit, chocolates, nuts, mortadella, salami, and a couple kinds of cheese.

As we were walking toward the back of the market we spotted some open stools at a bar and restaurant. We determined it was time to have lunch. We hopped up on the stools at what I believe was the Central Bar de la Boqueria. This hopping little spot specializes in fresh seafood, and it smelled delicious.

We quickly looked over the English menu and made our decisions. Hank would have sea bass, Jenny went for the tuna, and I decided on the calamari. We ordered some French fries as a side for all, and decided to sample their house red wine. The wine was served almost immediately and it was delicious, a bold red with nice legs.

Our appetizing fish came out soon. We all loved what we had ordered and shared our large plates with each other. This place was a real hit with us, and we arrived at a perfect time. Soon after we grabbed the last three seats, a line formed and there must have been at least a half hour wait when we left.

We gathered up all our bags of food and headed back out on Les Rambles. We walked by all the little shops and cafes until, before we knew it, we were standing near the waterfront looking at the statue of Christopher Columbus. The towering monument to the famous explorer is situated in a circle, right at the water's edge. We ventured on past to check out some yachts which were docked nearby, but decided it was time to start heading back to the apartment.

We retraced our steps back up Les Rambles and noticed that the little man was beginning to nod off in his stroller. It had been a big day of travel the day before, and he had to be tired. As we walked along we couldn't help but notice all the patrons at the sidewalk cafes sipping Sangria.

We decided it looked too good to pass up, and with Hank now asleep we found a table in the sun with a shady spot beside it for the stroller. We ordered a pitcher of the red wine and fruit mixture, and sat in the sun watching the pedestrians pass by for the next hour. Although Sangria is generally a little sweet for my tastes, this blend was particularly pleasant and refreshing on this warm day.

Hank got in a good nap, not really awakening until we returned to our apartment. We got back to the apartment and stowed away the food we had bought to the market, and relaxed for a while watching television. After a couple of hours we decided to have a little party in the room snacking on the delicious meat, cheese and fruit we had purchased.

We decided it was not enough to just snack, it was time to go out to dinner. We consulted our guidebook and picked out a location nearby, just in the old Gothic Quarter. We gathered our things and headed out into a very pleasant evening. After about a five minute walk we arrived at our destination.

Restaurant La Rosca is a well-established, small eatery having been in business for over fifty years. The traditional setting in an old building with a rustic, white dining room was perfect for the occasion. We were greeted by an aging man who spoke no English, but he led us to a table in the front corner of the room.

Although our Spanish is not too good, between Jenny, the kind gentleman and me, we were able to somehow communicate. We ordered a bottle of local red wine, some water and bread for the little man while we tried to figure out the Spanish only menu offerings. The server returned with our drinks and we placed our orders. It turned out to be "pollo," or chicken, for all three of us.

We didn't know exactly what we had ordered, but if it contained chicken we would likely be fine with the dish. Our waiter returned shortly with our wine, the bread and water. We had not hardly had time to sample the wine when he returned with a bowl of soup for all of us. It was a delicious creamy, chicken base with pasta and potatoes. We all liked it, but Hank went crazy for it, eating all he received and part of ours.

The next course arrived as we were finishing our soup. It turned out to be roasted chicken breast in an herb sauce with fresh vegetables and white beans on the side. It was all quite delicious and filling. The excellent red wine helped us enjoy the dish even more. As we were pushing back from the table, very full, a busser cleared our places. He was quickly followed by our waiter who brought us all a dish of dessert. It was a very traditional recipe for crème brulee, called crema catalana. It was delicious, not too sweet and overpowering, it was a nice ending to a wonderful meal.

We returned to the apartment and watched a little television. We quickly realized that the travel from the previous day and our sightseeing had caught up with us. We had a big day planned the next day and needed to get up early in the morning. So we shut everything off and all went to bed in hopes of a good night's sleep.

We awoke the next morning to the buzzing of our alarm at 6:30 a.m. We were up, showering, fixing breakfast, and making other preparations for the day ahead. We had rented a car through Alamo and were going to make a road trip to the final principality on our list, Andorra. We had considered traveling there a couple of years before, but it did not work in with our schedule. This was to be the day.

ANDORRA

We departed our hotel a little after eight and headed up the street to catch the subway. We had a reserved a rental car at Barcelona Sants Railway Station. The easiest way for us to reach the main railroad station in the city was to catch the subway down the street at Plaza de Catalunya.

We made the short walk to the subway on another bright, sunny morning. It looked like a perfect day for a drive. We descended into the bowels of the station, purchased tickets and headed for the Number 3 line. We had Hank in his stroller which we had to lift over the turnstiles because it would not fit between them. I remember it was a heavy lift up with him still strapped inside.

We caught the train and after a half dozen, or so, stops we got off at the Sants stop. We exited the station a couple of blocks from the railway terminal, but were able to find it without any difficulty. When we arrived in the terminal we found the Alamo office tucked away in the back of the building.

The rental car folks had our reservation and everything was in good order. They provided us with a Citroen which was a small three-door, blue car with a manual transmission. We also rented a car seat for Hank, much easier than lugging one all over the world for a few hours of use.

The good folks directed us across the street to a parking garage over a supermarket where our car awaited us. As we started to leave I remembered to ask the agent for a map of Barcelona and Spain. They had little to offer us, and I had a sinking feeling about our chances of getting out of Barcelona without some difficulty. We had a map of the city and some directions I had copied from the internet, but no firm guide. We checked some shops in the train station for a better map situation then we had, but to no avail.

We crossed the street to the parking garage where we picked up our little blue car. After checking out how all the features worked, and going over some directions with Jenny, we headed out. We were following the plan that I had printed out, but before I knew it we had missed a turn. I tried to get back to that point, but to no avail.

I began to rely on my senses as to which direction to turn, but they failed me, and soon we were very lost on a superhighway and were cruising along the Mediterranean Sea. Well, I knew this was the opposite direction we should be going, so we pulled off at the next exit and began to search for help.

What do you do when you are on the road in the United States and are lost? We pulled into the first gas station we could find and asked for help. The only problem with this was no one at the station spoke English. Finally, a truck driver crawled out from under his rig he was working on and came to our aid.

He, along with a young man who spoke a few words of English, figured out where we wanted to go, Andorra. They had no map, but the truck driver took out a piece of paper and a pen and proceeded to hand draw us a map which would lead us out of our predicament. I still have that work of art. He took us through four large intersections and onto a superhighway. He estimated how far we should travel in kilometers until we made a change to another highway and drive through a long tunnel which would put us on the thoroughfare that would take us to the diminutive country.

We thanked him from the bottom of our hearts and hopped back in the car. With Jenny's able assistance we followed the map in exact detail all the while hoping he had not forgotten anything. Within five minutes we were on the superhighway and beginning to feel a lot better. We found the tunnel, exited onto the other freeway, and were soon headed north toward the Pyrenees Mountains. His map had worked and we were on our way. I only wish that I could have repaid him for his kindness, but that was not possible.

The drive to Andorra was a beautiful one. The four lane, limited-access highway was newly paved and smooth. Our journey took us first through rolling green countryside filled with farm fields, and occasional vineyards. The further north we proceeded the more rolling it became until we were clearly in the Pyrenees Mountains.

At some point when we entered the mountains our divided highway gave way to a nice two-lane one which made for slower going. The trip was about 125 miles and it took us about two and a half hours to reach the border. The crossing into Andorra was a breeze with border officials looking at our passports, checking our car briefly, and letting us enter. The return into Spain would be a little more difficult.

Andorra is a micro-state wedged between Spain and France in the Pyrenees Mountains. The politically independent state is officially a co-principality, headed by the President of France and the Bishop of Urgell, which is Catalonia, Spain. The economy of the country thrives largely on tourism. The visitors are attracted to the country for its tax haven status, and winter and summer resorts. The lovely topography makes for great skiing in the winter, and a cool respite from the warm European weather in the summer.

Upon entering the country we immediately drove past shopping centers and retail outlets including very high end merchandise. We passed auto dealers selling Mercedes Benz, Porsches, and Ferraris. There were outlets vending all manner of electronic devices from huge televisions to computers. We also noticed that all the famous fashion houses seemed to be represented with retail establishments.

We had not come to shop, rather we were most interested in driving around, and seeing the country. We pushed past the border town with the heavy retail emphasis, and headed for the capital of Andorra la Villa. We were getting very hungry by now and since we had no real information on dining in Andorra, we keep our eye out for a likely spot.

Within a few minutes we were in the capital cruising the streets in search of something to eat. We spotted a couple of pizza joints and a bar, or two, but nothing that looked too exciting. As we had approached the town we had noticed a small motel-like structure which appeared to have a nice restaurant. We turned our car in that direction to take a closer look.

As we passed by on the road, we noticed tables which were set up under porticos with white linen table cloths flapping in the breeze. I swung the car around at my next opportunity because we knew that this was the place for our lunch. We pulled into the gravel parking lot, and entered the lobby of the motel and restaurant, Borda Can Travi.

We were pleasantly surprised to find a very nicely appointed dining room inside the building, and a pleasant greeter. He asked our preference of seating, and then showed us to one of the tables outside. It was a perfect time for dining alfresco. The temperature was in the low 70s, there was a cloudless blue sky with a gentle breeze, and no insects.

We had no sooner been seated, but a tuxedoed waiter was at our table offering us beverages. Jenny and I were enticed into a bottle of Spanish red he strongly recommended which was priced very reasonably. Hank chose some orange juice, and the waiter disappeared into the building to fetch our drinks.

He returned with the lovely bottle of red wine, a glass of orange juice, and a bread basket. We had been studying the menu in his absence and had arrived at our decisions. They hooked Hank up with some real chicken strips and fries, Jenny decided on the tuna with asparagus, and I went for the white beans and sausage.

We sat and drank in the wonderful views of the Pyrenees countryside, sipping our fabulous wine, and sampling the bread until our lunches arrived. Before we knew it, a dining cart was wheeled up to the table and our lunches were served. We all selected well, if fact, I am not sure one could get a bad meal at this restaurant.

Hank loved his chicken and fries, Jenny enjoyed the tuna, but I hit the grand slam with what I ordered. I really did not know what to expect when I ordered, but this dish was incredible. I now know the origins of the beany-weeny casserole, and what a bastardization of the real thing it is.

The waiter opened the silver serving vessel and scooped the beans and two plump sausages onto my plate. The aroma told me I was about to experience something special. The large, white beans had been cooked in a tomato sauce with onion, garlic and numerous spices. I took my first bite and could not believe the flavors I experienced. It was truly otherworldly.

We all sat and enjoyed our large plates of food. This was a really special meal, one of my all-time favorites. The food was absolutely divine, the service was first rate, the atmosphere was, well what can you say about a perfect day sitting enjoying mountain vistas, and the company was the best of all. This was clearly one meal I will never forget. I would make the drive to Andorra again just to sit and have this meal. It was sublime. (See Appendix 7 for the recipe)

BACK TO SPAIN

When we finished this awesome meal we found it hard to leave. We thought for an instant about taking a room and enjoying dinner and breakfast here. If we had only known about this place, we would have made different arrangements. But, reality kicked in and we hopped back in the car and pointed it south.

We were soon at the Spanish border where the guards inspected our documents and vehicle closely. They looked at us like we were the first people that had ever crossed into Andorra, and not returned in a car brimming with retail bargains. We were finally let go, and we followed the same route back we had taken before. The ride was quite nice, and it seemed in no time we were back in the Barcelona area.

We made all the proper turns this time and were able to return the car to the supermarket garage earlier than expected. We checked out with the Alamo folks, and stopped through the grocery store to look around. We bought a bottle of the red wine we had consumed at the Borda Can Travi and headed for the subway.

Soon we were back in the apartment resting up from our day of travel. Jenny popped the cork on the bottle of red wine we had just bought and we all began relaxing on the beds watching television. When it came time to eat, we decided to stay in the room. We had stocked up so much at the market earlier, we didn't need to leave the room. We enjoyed the meats, cheeses, nuts, fruits and chocolates we had purchased the day before. It really was a very enjoyable evening, and a nice end to a great day.

We slept in a bit the next morning, awakening after eight o'clock. We scurried around fixing breakfast, and cleaning up for the day. We headed out that morning for our last day in Barcelona. It was another sunny, pleasant day and we decided to stay on foot exploring the major sites of the nearby Gothic Quarter. We walked south from our apartment into the old neighborhood and headed for the Barcelona Cathedral.

After about a ten minute walk through the interesting community, we were standing in front of the impressive church. The Gothic structure was built during the 13th to 15th Centuries with the bulk of the work occurring during the 1300s. The exterior features a wide range of gargoyles, including animals, local and mythical.

We arrived between masses, so we were able to tour the large cathedral. The church is dedicated to the Eulalia of Barcelona, the co-patron saint of the city. Lore has it that she was martyred during the Roman occupation of the city. The story goes that she was exposed nude in a public square until a freak spring snow covered her body. Enraged by the occurrence, the Romans then placed her in a barrel with knives stuck through its wooden sides. She was then rolled through the community. The body of Saint Eulalia is entombed in the cathedral.

We toured the church taking in its impressive chapels. Jenny and Hank lit a candle and said their prayers for the souls of departed family and friends. We then decided it was time to move on and ventured further into the area in search of the Picasso museum, which is nearby. It was only a few minutes walking from the cathedral to the museum, the first such structure dedicated to the works of the artist.

The museum is housed in five Gothic palaces which have been joined together. We bought our tickets and began touring the facility which is particularly dedicated to the early life of the artist. The permanent collection contain over 4,000 pieces which have been donated by friends, family and the artist himself. The museum stresses the long-standing relationship Picasso had with the city of Barcelona. It is well worth a visit.

We spent the next couple of hours browsing the fantastic collection of the great artist. We finally realized that Hank was growing tired and hungry, and left in search of a place for lunch. We consulted our guidebook which Jenny was carrying in her day bag, and arrived at a nearby restaurant as our choice.

We walked a few minutes to the bistro Taller de Tapas, a highly recommended eatery, and we thought we should try a tapas meal while in Barcelona. As we were preparing to enter the building a couple of men knocked into us, then hastily moved on. A man who worked at the restaurant had seen the incident and immediately asked us to check to see if our belongings were intact. We quickly examined our pockets, and the bag Jenny was carrying, and nothing was missing.

It seems these two were known pickpockets that work the area. Thank goodness that we always carry our money and credit cards in our front pockets, or zippered cargo ones, thus making it more difficult to have items stolen. This is a good lesson for travelers, always be aware of your surroundings and keep your valuables in a safe place, not in your back pocket.

After we were confident all was well, the kind man who had alerted us, showed us to a table inside. The smells of the food being prepared were enough to tell us that we were in the right place. A waiter came by and dropped off menus, and we ordered a couple glasses of the house red wine and a bottle of water.

We studied the menu and selected a number of small plates including grilled calamari, tuna, spinach, fried potatoes and a cheeseburger for Hank. The lively place was filling up. The décor was attractive with exposed stone and brick walls with polished wooden accents. We sipped our tasty wine, and observed the crowd enjoying their Sunday afternoon.

Our meals arrived and we all enjoyed what we had selected. Jenny and I shared the small plates while Hank went to work on his large sandwich. He, of course, could not help eating some of the calamari which was delicious and one of his favorites. As Hank was finishing his sandwich he noticed someone getting a cup of vanilla ice cream with chocolate sauce. He wanted one so we ordered it, along with a crème brulee for Jenny and me to split. It was an apt ending to a good meal.

We spent the next hour or so wandering the streets of the old neighborhood. We did a little souvenir shopping coming away with some interesting "t" shirts and a few other small things. We noticed that Hank was about to go down on us, and decided it was time to return to the apartment so he could get a little rest.

We had no more than returned to the apartment and Hank was asleep. This gave us an opportunity to start our packing process for the return home the next day. I slipped down to the front desk, paid for our stay, and inquired about a taxi to the airport in the morning. The chap at the desk placed a call for us, and informed us that a taxi would be waiting for us on the street the next morning at 7:15.

I thanked the man and returned to the room to find that the little man had awakened while I had been gone. We all sat around the kitchen table and played a game as we finished the last of the meat and cheese from the market. Jenny and I drank some red wine while Hank had a glass of orange juice.

We finally determined it was time to go out for our last dinner in Barcelona. We had studied the guidebook and come up with what we thought was a good choice for our final night. We pulled on our shoes, grabbed out things and headed out into the pleasant evening air. The walk to the restaurant was quite nice with agreeable weather and good spirits among all of us.

After a little over five minutes we arrived at our choice, Els Quatre Gats, or The Four Cats. The restaurant had been in business for over a hundred years and was reputedly the former hangout of Picasso. In fact, it would seem that anyone of importance in the arts, politics or business from Barcelona in the past century had visited the place.

We entered the small lobby area and were greeted by a man who showed us to a table in the first dining room. The cheerful place had yellow walls, tile flooring and marble topped tables with wooden chairs. Our waiter soon arrived and we quickly selected a bottle of wine from the card. Hank asked for a glass of milk and the waiter disappeared to fill our drink orders.

He returned with our wine and some bread which Hank had requested. We looked over the menu and Jenny and I both selected the lamb shank while Hank went for a piece of fried cod with French fries. As we sat sipping our wine we decided to wander about the dining room a bit taking in the century of memorabilia which covered the walls. There were pictures of patrons, interesting tile works, and other framed objects adorning all the nooks and crannies.

We returned to our table, and soon Jenny noticed a man who had just entered the restaurant standing next to our table. It was Rick Steves, the well-known travel author and PBS television host. I stood and introduced myself to Rick and in turn presented Jenny and Hank to him. He seemed genuinely pleased to meet us, and introduced us to his Spanish friend who was a tour guide of the area.

We stood and talked with Rick and his friend for several minutes while we waited for our dinner to arrive. He assured us that we had selected a nice place for dinner. He also told us that he was in town making another travel show, although he was not filming at the moment. It was a chance encounter, but one I will remember because of his was warm and gracious manner. Now, each time I see him on his program I think of that evening in Barcelona.

The star of the evening arrived just as Rick was moving on. It was the tender, roasted lamb shank, which was absolutely terrific and Hank said the same about his cod. The large portion was accompanied by some roasted potatoes and vegetables. We sat and enjoyed the fine meal and the good Spanish red wine. It was truly a memorable meal, great food, interesting atmosphere, and good company. **(See Appendix 8 for the recipe)**

Knowing that we had to get an early start in the morning we paid the waiter and headed out into the dark night. We were soon back in our little apartment. We did what further packing that could be done that evening and watched a little television before preparing for sleep. We set a couple of travel alarms and switched off the lights.

I awoke to the buzzing of my travel alarm and when I opened my eyes I noticed that Jenny was already in the bathroom getting ready. We all got cleaned up and had a bite of breakfast. A few minutes after seven we headed downstairs to catch our taxi to the airport. As we were exiting the elevator cage the driver was coming in the front door. He helped us with our bags and soon we were off for the airport.

We must have been a little ahead of the rush hour traffic on this Monday morning because we had smooth sailing all the way. Our driver dropped us at the KLM check-in area and we got our seat assignments and were soon winging our way to Amsterdam, then to Memphis and on home. But, not before stopping past Corky's Barbeque in the Memphis airport to sample a little of their outstanding pork. It was a fine trip and I would recommend Barcelona to anyone........

And now back to the original story....

PORTUGAL

Kip and I found our car and climbed into the bunk-bedded berth. We found storage space for our bags and sat down for a while as the train pulled out headed for the capitol of Portugal. After a short while we decide it was time to go to bed and Kip claimed the upper berth, I the lower. This was clearly not the fast train which we were on from Seville, as our journey would take us over nine hours to complete. We had no sooner laid down than the conductor came to our berth to inspect our tickets and passports. Not long after he left, the rocking motion of the train finally put us to sleep.

We awoke the next morning with the sun shining through the window in our compartment. A few minutes later we were visited by the Portuguese customs officials that had boarded the train. They checked our documents and welcomed us to their country. We still had a couple of hours until we were at arrive in Lisbon, so we went in search of the dining car for breakfast. We settled into a small table and ordered up a continental breakfast of coffee, juice and breads with jam. We drank our coffee and enjoyed the views out the window.

We arrived in Lisbon a little after ten o'clock on this sunny, clear Saturday morning. We pulled into the aging Santa Apolonia Train Station, which is near the banks of the Tagus River in the center of the city. It seemed as if the city was slow to awake that day. It was such a pleasant day, probably already in the mid-60s, we decided to head out on foot to find our hotel.

As we made our way we were overcome by the natural beauty of the city. The city is built on seven hills and the broad Tagus flows through its center. A giant suspension bridge, which strongly resembles San Francisco's Golden Gate Bridge, connects Lisbon with Almada on the other side of the river. Despite the resemblance, the bridge was actually built by the same company that built the San Francisco-Oakland Bay Bridge, not the Golden Gate. At any event, maybe it's the water and the bridge, maybe it's the hills, but I was immediately reminded of San Francisco, which is one of my favorite cities in the world.

We walked well over a mile carrying our bags and finally located the Gloria Funicular that would take us to the Barrio Alto, or upper neighborhood, where our hotel is located. The rickety, old train runs up the side of the step hill and has been saving people the difficult climb for well over a hundred years. We hopped aboard the bright yellow and white vehicle and the train slowly, but steadily made its way to the top. When we arrived at the summit there was a lovely little garden with a commanding view over the city below and the hills beyond. We stopped for a while to drink in the wonderful vista.

We continued up the main road from the funicular stop and located, with some difficulty, our accommodation, the Pensao Londres. We had made the reservation in advance and when we entered the hotel, they were expecting us. The small, old hotel had high ceilings and a lot of charm. The aging gentleman at the front directed us to our room up an old elevator a couple of floors. It turned out to be a large space with two double beds, antique furnishings and a functional bathroom. A real bonus was a nice, little balcony with a great view of the city.

We settled in and cleaned up before we set out to see the sights. We were staying in the Barrio Alto, an enclave of narrow, cobblestone streets, lined with fashionable shops, bars and restaurants. We decided to investigate our neighborhood before heading out further into the city. The Barrio Alto has an excellent vibe and we felt we were lucky to be staying in this old, funky neighborhood.

As we strolled the winding, hilly alleys of the area we ran into an interesting little Italian restaurant that we decided would be our choice for lunch. Mama Rosa is the kind of restaurant you might run into almost anywhere in the world; a comfortable trattoria with red checkered tablecloths, fresh pasta, and good pizza.

We were seated at a table near the front door and were able to watch the pedestrian traffic that was passing by. Our dark, attractive waitress brought us each a glass of red wine and a menu we could understand. We both ended up ordering plates of pasta, seemingly a staple of our diet on this trip. Our pasta dishes came out shortly, Kip had a spaghetti with a red sauce and I sampled the lasagna. Both of us agreed that this was a great stop as the food and wine were both tasty, and very affordable.

We finished our lunches and decided to venture on further, and since it was such a nice day we settled on visiting the Castillo de San Jorge which sits atop one of the neighboring, and highest of the seven, hills. The castle dominates the Lisbon skyline and is visible from nearly anywhere in the city. The fortification began under Roman rule, saw further construction by the Visigoths, and the Moors, until they were vanquished in the 12th Century.

We descended from the Barrio Alto and caught a small, historic tram to the Alfama neighborhood which lies at the feet of the castle. From our stop we then climbed up the hill to the fortress on narrow, winding streets past pastel colored houses. Once we were inside the castle we were able to wander about freely, climbing the towers and walking the ramparts. The vantage point from the top of this hill has to enjoy the best views of Lisbon.

From here, you can see why many believe that Lisbon is one of the world's most beautiful cities. As you look out over the red-tiled roofed structures you get a terrific view of the Tagus River and its beautiful suspension bridge. If you look beyond you can even get a glimpse of the Atlantic Ocean in the distance. This was a perfect day for this visit, sunny, and nearly 70 degrees. The locals were out in force appreciating the day and the view. Couples were laying on blankets drinking bottles of local wine and showing their affection for one another.

After we had thoroughly explored the fortress, and sat and taken in the view for quite a while, we decided to make our descent back down the hill. We took our time and explored the Alfama area as we made our retreat. The oldest part of the city appears to be a working-class neighborhood filled with very narrow, winding streets.

The Portuguese affinity for tile work is very obvious as you walk these streets. Not only are there beautiful tile scenes on the sides of buildings and in tiny plazas, there are shops selling these ceramic beauties. Kip and I stopped into a couple of very interesting stores along the way and I purchased a couple of items. One of them is a hand painted metal rooster which serves as a representative of Portugal on our Christmas tree.

As we descended further we came to a church plaza that has one of the most elaborate tile scenes you will see anywhere. The Church of Santa Luzia has some amazing polished tile scenes affixed to its exterior walls. Nearby the small, very old, Catholic parish church, is one of the most scenic overlooks in the city which is also embellished with tile scenery. The Portuguese have a real love affair with tile as an art form, and are experts at is production.

By now the light of day was beginning to fade, and we decided it was time to return to the Pensao Londres for a rest before venturing out for the evening. We caught public transportation to the bottom of the hill, and the funicular back up to the Barrio Alto. We returned to our room and went out on the balcony in time for the sunset. It was a beautiful sight, over a lovely city. We kicked off our shoes and laid down for a while until hunger drove us to find something to eat.

We consulted our guide before leaving our room and discovered a very interesting restaurant nearby our hotel. We exited the hotel into a still nice evening and walked a couple of blocks to our destination. The Cervjaria Trindade is a tavern housed in a remains of a thirteenth century monastery and is owned by the large Portuguese brewer, Sagres.

It seems the place is a cross between a German beer hall and a tile gallery. The walls in the expansive rooms are covered with tile murals with colorful scenes. Before being seated we walked throughout the restaurant and inspected these old works of art. Just a visit to see the tile works would be worthwhile.

The host finally ushered us to a table in a large dining room which was pretty full with a loud crowd. We both order a Sagres brew and began to peruse the menu. Our waiter returned with our cold steins of beer and we placed our orders. We both decided to order a steak since we hadn't had one on the journey. The beer tasted quite good, and we ordered a second one when our dinners arrived.

Our filet mignons were prepared to perfection and were served with golden French fries. I was ready for some red meat, and this steak filled that void for me. The beer was tasting good that evening, and I had a hunch we were going to be in for a long night, for us. We finished our steaks and had another beer as we let the meal digest. Our waiter brought the check and we paid, and set out into the night looking for another place to have a drink.

We walked down a narrow, cobblestone side street not far from the restaurant and happened into a little bar that specialized in tequila. The loud music was blaring from the dark, hole in the wall tavern, but there something that drew us into A Tasca that evening, namely the two women working at the bar. One a petite blond and the other a dark and attractive brunette, beckoned to us as we walked by the door.

Kip stopped and did a double take at the blond, and the next thing I knew we were having a shot of tequila and with a beer chaser. The two very friendly young ladies were bemoaning the fact that business was slow that evening and they were glad we had stopped by. After a short time the small, dimly-lit tavern began to fill up with Saturday night regulars.

We drank and talked to the barkeeps for quite a while until Kip asked if any Irish pubs were in the area. The two young ladies told us about one at the foot of the hill and the next thing I remember was we were out the door, promising to return. The bartenders had pointed us in the direction of the main street in the Barrio Alto and told us to turn right and start walking. Go to where the street flattens out and it would be on our right. If we reached the Tagus River, we had gone too far.

Sure enough, after about a ten minute walk we found O'Gilin's Pub. As we wedged our way into the bar, I felt like I could have been stepping into an establishment in Dublin. The place had the look and feel of many Irish pubs I had visited around the world, including Ireland. The tavern was absolutely slammed, but we finally found a crease at the bar where we could sidle up to and order a pint.

The red-haired Irish lass tending bar poured us a nice glass of stout and we began to check out the clientele. It was clearly a young crowd, probably dominated by international exchange students from universities around the United States and Europe. We struck up a conversation with some of the students who happened to be Irish, but the throng continued to grow. After about a half-hour I felt like the fire marshal should be arriving any minute to clear the house because it was too filled with patrons.

I finally convinced Kip we should walk back up the hill and have a nightcap at A Tasco. There was beginning to be a chill in the night air as we mounted the hill back into the Barrio Alto. Soon we were back at the tequila bar ordering another round, a shot and a beer. We slammed them down and I suggested to Kip that I was nearing the end of my night and needed some sleep. He decided that he would like one more, and I headed back leaving him in the capable hands of the blonde bartender.

I went back, pulled my clothes off and fell into bed. I don't know when, but at some point I heard Kip return, but I rolled over and quickly went back to sleep. The next morning I awoke before Kip, showered and got ready for the day. I stood on the balcony enjoying the fine fall weather as Kip cleaned up for breakfast. We went downstairs for breakfast which proved to be just fine; consisting of cereals, breads, ham, cheeses, juice and coffee. I had an extra cup of coffee that morning because I had stayed up later than normal the night before.

After breakfast we decided that our first stop that day should be a visit to the renowned Museu Calouste Gulbenkian. The weather was so warm that morning that I left the Londres in a short sleeve shirt. We walked to the funicular and rode it down the hill and found the subway station a short distance from the exit point. We went down the stairs and caught the underground a couple of stops to the station nearest the museum. We walked a short way and were soon in front of this modern structure.

Calouste Gulbenkian was an international man of Armenian descent, born in Turkey, but lived in Egypt, France and England. He became very wealthy in the oil business in the first half of the 20th Century. His chief passion was collection of art. Over the years he amassed a priceless collection which was housed in his private museum in a residence in Paris. Gulbendian's desire was to display all his holdings in one place. Because of political wrangling's, which included his participation in the Vichy government in France during World War II, the establishment of the museum became complicated. After his death the directors of his foundation determined that his collection would be housed in Lisbon and the museum was constructed.

This was an incredible stroke of good fortune for the city of Lisbon. The works were housed for a few years in a temporary facility while the museum was built. The beautiful modern structure opened in 1969. The sleek building houses a magnificent collection centering around two primary areas, Oriental and Classical Art, and European Art. A trip through the museum is an easy one to follow because it is laid out in the two areas, and is done chronologically.

A bonus for us was that on Sunday's the museum is free to visit. We spent the next couple of hours wandering through its displays and enjoying all its offerings. The antiquities include magnificent pieces from Egypt, Greco-Roman, and Mesopotamian civilizations. The European collection embraces a lot of my favorites including Rembrandt, Monet, van Dyke and Renoir, to name but a few. Although it is not as imposing a structure or collection, as say, the Louvre or the Hermitage, it is nonetheless an important museum. It is certainly well worth a few hours of your time if you are in Lisbon.

After a couple of hours we decided that we had seen all we wanted and set out to see more of the city. It was such a pretty day that we felt that a stroll back to the center of the city was in order, forgoing public transit. As we were walking we noticed a wonderful green space, Parque Eduardo VII, and decided to walk through it on our return. The park was filled with merrymakers enjoying the beautiful day. We then followed the broad, leafy Avenida Da Liberdade back toward the center.

We were now beginning to get hungry so we pulled out our handy reference and discovered that a highly recommended restaurant was not too far ahead. The Sol Dourado is a seafood restaurant that sits a couple of blocks from where we caught the subway to the museum. We found the place and entered a rustic dining room because all the outside seating was taken.

We were seated alone at a small table and soon our waiter arrived. He took our drink orders and returned in a few minutes with our glasses of cold beer and menus. I asked him for his recommendation and he suggested I try carne de porco a alentejana, a Portuguese specialty. The dish was a pork and clam concoction and sounded odd to me, but the waiter was a convincing chap and you only live once.

In a short while our orders came out, and my hesitation about my selection began to melt away once I saw and, better yet, smelled the dish. The stew-like mixture clearly contained pork, clams, black olives and a lot of garlic among other spices. I took a forkful and told Kip he had made a grave mistake ordering the chicken dish he was eating. The dish was very flavorful with a spicy finish, I wish I had a plate of it now. My meal came with a side of roasted potatoes which was the perfect complement.

Other than the small bite I gave Kip to try the wonderful flavors, I soaked up every morsel. It was one of the tastiest dishes I had eaten. Clearly, this was my favorite meal not only in Portugal, but on the entire trip. We decided to order another beer and enjoy the pleasant setting. After we finished our beers we paid the waiter, and I thanked him profusely for the wonderful entrée suggestion. **(See Appendix 9 for the recipe)**

We were not too far from our hotel, so we just decided to shop our way back to our room. We browsed through several shops making final purchases for family and friends back home. Kip came across an interesting pair of filigree earrings for a friend, which he purchased. I had not encountered filigree, which as it turns out is a popular form of jewelry making in Portugal. The delicate items are formed by fine gold, silver, or copper wires soldered together to make an open patterned piece. They are quite lacy-like and very pretty.

By the time we finished our shopping spree, we decided to return to our hotel and begin the process of packing up for our return journey home the next morning. We took the nearby funicular to the Barrio Alto and stopped for one last, long view over the city from the park at the top. We then walked up the hill to the Londres and took the caged elevator up to our room. Once inside we silently went about the business of packing, both of with mixed emotions, not wanting the trip to end, but eagerly anticipating seeing our friends and family when we got back.

Time passed and we decided to go out for our last meal in Portugal. Staying in the neighborhood was clearly our best option and we perused our travel guide for one last recommendation. We decided on Tasco do Manel, a small eatery down the street that specialized in regional Portuguese dishes, but most importantly it was open on Sunday night when many restaurants seemed to close.

We were successful in locating the little restaurant and were ahead of that evening's crowd so we were seated at a choice table near the front of the small dining room. The room was filled with tables covered in white clothes and slat back wooden chairs. Our waiter brought us menus and asked for a drink order. There were numerous shelves that were stocked with bottles of Portuguese wine, so I asked him for a recommendation for a descent value, full-bodied red.

He returned with a small taste of two different wines from which to choose. They were both quite good, but I made a choice and was very pleased with the selection. We looked over the menu which contained a number of wild game dishes, not to my liking. I also resisted the temptation to order the same dish I had for lunch which I had spied on the menu. Rather, I ordered a pork tenderloin dish and Kip had fish.

The service was good and our dinners came out rather quickly. My pork tenderloin was served with French fries and it was a very tasty dish. I drank another glass of the red wine and watched the bistro fill up with late arriving patrons. We both finished our meals and settled our bill with our waiter.

We decided to go by the A Tasca for a night cap. The same two young women were working and were as friendly as the night before. They insisted we all do a shot of some tequila they pulled off a shelf in the back of the bar. We ordered a couple of local beers, conversed with the bartenders and listened to the good music. The next thing I knew another round was coming at us, shots and all. I didn't want to seem ungrateful for the bartenders' act of kindness, so I drank my share. However, when they tried to do it again, we called it quits and Kip and I headed back to the hotel for a short night of sleep.

We awoke early the next morning and hastily cleaned up. We went downstairs for a quick breakfast and settled our account with the same front desk clerk who had greeted us on our arrival. We grabbed our bags and headed out the door to find a taxi to the airport. Nearly outside the hotel there was a taxi stand and a nice English-speaking driver whisked us to the airport in his new silver, Mercedes Benz. It was a nice, quick ride and we arrived at the Lisbon International Airport is ample time.

The check-in process went smoothly and we breezed through customs. We sat in the airport lounge and waited for a plane to be called. Soon we were boarding the plane and winging our way back to the United States. Our flights home went well and were a fitting ending to a successful trip through the Iberian Peninsula. I thoroughly enjoyed the trip, was blown away by many of the sights, really liked the people we encounter along the way, and thought the local food and beverages were excellent. What else can you ask for in a trip?

CHAPTER 4

RUSSIA

I HAD BEEN READING IN the <u>New York Times</u> Travel Section for years about seemingly fantastic deals on trips to Russia. Certainly in the days before the internet, newspaper advertising was the primary form of finding out about travel deals, with the <u>Times</u> and the <u>Washington Post</u> leading the way from my perspective. The Sunday editions of these papers contained (and still do) myriad ads reflecting very favorable package vacations to destinations around the world. It seems that certain agencies fill niche markets specializing in one locale. I would often go to the library and peruse these papers and dream of taking these discount tours to exotic destinations.

It seems a group of expat Russians living in New York City had started one of these boutique travel agencies, Eastern Consolidated Tours, specializing in tours to Russian and other parts of the former Soviet Union. These trips were advertised for as low as $599 for a week's tour of St. Petersburg and Moscow including airfare from New York, airport transfers, overnight train between the two cities, accommodations, guided tours and some meals. I believe that some form of this organization may be still in business operating similar tours under the name of the Russian National Group.

Hank, I was now dating your mother and suspected that she might be the one for me. However, we determined this was not the time for us to take this type of trip. I had been seeking a friend to take advantage of one of these offers for a few years, and she agreed with me that the time was right. One day I was talking to a young fellow I knew through business, Warren Mathies, and discovered that he was very interested in world travel. He had taken some international trips and was not fearful of tackling more adventurous locales. I mentioned to him that I had seen this trip advertised to Russia and he was extremely interested. We decided to inquire further and see if the trip made sense to us.

I contacted the travel agency in New York and discovered that they preferred to put together small groups for their trips ranging from about five to twenty people. This was ideal for us because the last thing we wanted to do was to be herded about in a large group. We got the details and pricing and decided it all looked favorable to us. We began to negotiate with the travel agents to modify the trip to better suit our needs.

We decided that we would wait for the rates to drop with the beginning of the winter season and would register for a trip that would depart the first week of November 1998. We thought this could potentially give us a small taste of the Russian winter, but certainly not its full force. We found out that the trip would depart from New York's JFK Airport on Finnair through Helsinki and entering Russia through St. Petersburg. We decided to see if we could lay over for three additional days in Helsinki on the way back so we could see the Finnish capitol while we were in the area.

The folks from Eastern Consolidated Tours were able to see to our modifications for a small increase in the tour fee. They accepted our applications for the trip in September, but informed us that they required a minimum number of six travelers for this trip to be confirmed and, at this time we were the only people signed up for that week. After about a month passed they informed us that one other person was interested and they had determined that they could make the trip work with just the three of us. This was terrific news to us, as we would now for all practical purposes be on an individual tour, not attached to a group. Additionally, there would be no increase in the cost of the tour because so few were going.

Sometime in early October we were notified that another person was interested in the same tour and dates as us and they could make the group of four work. Warren and I began to study up on the two cities and their surrounding areas in an effort to maximize our time on our own. Warren picked up a small guide on St. Petersburg that proved invaluable. Given that travel to the Soviet Union, and now Russia, had been limited by both our governments, travel guides on the area were not as plentiful as many other parts of the world. We cobbled some other information together making use of some data that now was coming through via the internet.

Our departure day finally came and we were both very excited. We caught a United plane to Washington, D.C.'s Dulles Airport and connected from there to JFK on another United flight. At the Finnair check-in I was able to sweet talk our way into some bulkhead seats which provide some extra legroom and would make the flight that much more enjoyable. When you are nearly 6'8" tall you will fight for every extra inch of legroom you can get.

HELSINKI, FINLAND

Our flight departed on time and I recall the trip being rather uneventful. I do remember that we had good service and the food was better than normal for an international flight. One thing I do remember distinctly about the flight was an older American, an Iowa farmer, across the aisle was a rather loud talker and he kept saying he could not wait to get to "Hell sinky." Warren and I laughed about this man's pronunciation of the city the entire trip.

We arrived in Helsinki after nearly nine hours and we were both able to get a couple of hours sleep on the plane, a rarity for me at the time. As we broke through the clouds we could see that it was snowing hard as we were landing. Helsinki was getting its first snow storm of the year. We had about a four-hour layover and we had determined that we would take this time to go into the city and get our bearings for our return in about a week. We located storage lockers and stowed our luggage. We had learned that Finnair operated a bus service into the city with a couple of drop off points.

We hopped on the bus and took it to its final stop which was right in the middle of the city. We got out and started to explore the city with our first order of business to locate the hotel we would be staying when we returned, the Hotel Finn. Only a few short blocks walk from our drop off point, we found the building in which the Finn is housed. We entered the building and located the front desk and reconfirmed that they had our reservation for our return. We both grabbed business cards for the hotel and a city map and departed. We spent the next hour walking the streets of Helsinki, slogging through the snow covered walkways.

ST. PETERSBURG AND ENVIRONS

We decided to return to the airport with ample time to ensure we did not miss our departing flight for St. Petersburg. As it turned out, we returned with more than enough time as our flight ended up being delayed for nearly three hours because of the adverse weather conditions. We wasted some time exploring the airport and eating a leisurely lunch. Finally, our flight was called and we boarded the plane. It was a short flight with actual time in the air of only about a half hour. It was pretty bumpy because of the snowstorm, but that didn't prevent them from serving us a drink and a snack, something an American carrier would not even consider.

As we began our approach into St. Petersburg, Warren and I were very excited and filled with anticipation. Neither of us had visited Russia before, our long-time Cold War enemy. The landing was perfect on the snowy runway and we taxied to the aging terminal. Once inside we found a cold, dank atmosphere. We moved slowly through customs and immigration, a very rigid and humorless process. Once we passed through customs we began to search for our tour guide that was to meet us. Sure enough, there she was, an attractive, young Russian woman that spoke excellent English.

More than a little bit relieved to see her, we waited for another member of our party to be located. Very soon we met our travel partner, a recently retired firefighter from Allentown, Pennsylvania, named Frank. Our guide, Katarina, hustled us out the door to an awaiting, large van. We threw our bags in the back and crawled in. The van had ample room for us and was all warmed up for us. Our driver was a very friendly sort, but spoke almost no English.

We were supposed to arrive shortly after noon, but because of the delay it was now after four o'clock. As we made our way to the hotel nightfall was upon us. The snow covered streets of the city were lined with large stone apartment buildings. I recall thinking that these structures, all about five stories high and rather nondescript, were quite substantial. Our excitement built as we neared the hotel and we came closer to the core of the city.

Soon we arrived at our destination, the Hotel Sovietskaya. The Sovietskaya, as its name may imply is a very imposing complex, which was built and operated by the former official travel agency of the Soviet, Intourist. With over a thousand rooms in its two buildings and eighteen stories in the larger one, it was a definite throwback to the Cold War era. Upon arrival our guide led us into the huge lobby area of the main building. I remember it was filled with shady looking characters who looked like they belonged in some cheap spy novel.

Our guide assisted us through the tedious and bureaucratic process of check-in. They insisted on confiscating our passports which was unnerving, but Katarina assured us that they would be returned to us sometime the next day. Finally we were issued room keys and were pointed in the direction of another building across the large parking lot. We all exchanged a few dollars for some rubles in order to have some currency to begin our journey. It was far enough to the other building that Katerina recommended we ride over in the van.

She took us inside the building and gave us a quick tour so we would know our way around. In addition to another much smaller lobby area, there was a large restaurant and a bar on the first floor. Katarina escorted us to the elevator and rode with us up a couple of flights to our floor. As we got off the elevator we were greeted by the floor matrons. These ladies, another nod to a previous era, were in charge of the floors. They checked our keys and led us to our rooms. As we rounded the corner one thing that we noticed was that we could not see the end of the hallway. With Warren as my witness, I swear that the corridor was so long you could not see the end of it. We presumed it had something to do with the lighting at night, but we checked in the morning and still could not see the other end. Thank goodness our room was only about four down on the right, or we might still be waiting for the shuttle to get to our room.

Assured that we had finally arrived, Katarina gave us our instructions for the next morning and departed. We entered our room and quickly discovered that the Soviet theme continued there, too. Certainly not a five-star property, the room met our basic needs. There were two double beds, a desk and chairs, dresser, television and a private bathroom. Exhausted we both feel on our respective beds and rested for a few minutes. Finally, I decided to get rid of the road grudge and take a bath. It took us both a few minutes to figure out how the shower worked, but when it finally got working it felt so good.

I told Warren that we needed to get moving or I would fall asleep, particularly since I was now all warm and clean. We decided to not to venture out into the night, rather we would go downstairs and try the restaurant off the lobby of our hotel. Warren cleaned himself up a bit and we decided it was time to go downstairs.

As we approached the elevator, one of the matrons stopped us. She spoke no English. I had taken two years of Russian in high school, but had not been a star student. But somehow between the three of us, we learned that the matron clearly ran the show. We were to leave our keys with her when we left the floor and recollect them when we returned. Also, she was available to do laundry and ran a small sundry shop out of her office. Basically, if we needed anything, come see her.

We descended to the main floor and entered the large restaurant. It was rather garish with heavy red velvet curtains covering the windows and doors, the woodwork all painted black, with red and black flocked wallpaper and white linen table cloths. Clearly little redecorating had been done since the move to a capitalist society several years before. You could imagine large groups of Eastern bloc tourists being herded in for their meals while touring the mother country.

We were met by a black suited matre'd who showed us to a table in a rather secluded, raised area of the restaurant to the left as you entered. Our waiter soon arrived with a menu which was in Russian. He scrambled around and soon returned with another menu that contained some English and we set about to order. We both decided to order a drink and, when in Russia, why not try the vodka. As you might expect, they carried a large selection of the spirit and we settled on a locally produced one that was of moderate price. Our waiter pointed at the glasses arranged neatly on the table and asked which one we would like to have filled with the vodka. We had noticed that there were four glasses in front of each place setting varying in size from about a jigger to a water glass, but we had no idea that they were there depending on the size of your appetite for vodka. We each chose a small glass and the waiter soon filled it with vodka directly from the freezer.

Next we ordered dinner. I remember that I thought that some sort of beef dish would be the safest bet, along with potatoes. I passed on the salad fearing it might be washed in tap water and might make me sick. I would only eat fully cooked meats and vegetables on this trip. This is a practice I continue to this day when I am in locales that I have concerns about the purity of the water. At that time St. Petersburg was known to have some of the worst drinking water in the world.

The vodka was very pleasant, which we drank while we waited for our meal to arrive. We toasted the fact that we had made it, and were looking forward to seeing the sights in our former enemy's land. Our meals arrived and we quickly realized that this was not going to be a culinary highlight of our travels. My beef, if that is what it was, appeared boiled and was gray, swimming in a greasy gravy and the potatoes were small and boiled. We were both hungry and wolfed it down knowing it was our only option to fill our stomachs. We had ordered a local beer, Baltika Number 9, which tasted good and helped us to wash down this less than satisfying meal.

By now it was about seven o'clock and we decided we needed to kill another hour or two before heading to bed. We paid our bill, which thankfully was very modest, and decided to check out the bar for a drink. We walked next door to the small bar which was staffed by an attractive, English-speaking bartender. We ordered another round of the Baltikas and slumped down at a Formica table which had molded, red plastic chairs surrounding it. We sipped our beers and engaged in conversation with the bartender. We finished our beers and ordered another.

After a drink or two of the second beer, we decided it was time for us to return to the room and call it a night. We rose to leave taking our bottles with us. All at once I realized that I felt a big buzz from the alcohol. I was very surprised by this because a shot of vodka and two beers over a couple of hours generally did not have this effect on me. All I know was that I struggled back to the room and we turned on the television attempting to find a program on we could relate to. I took another swig of beer, went to the bathroom, took off my clothes and laid down.

The next morning I awoke to find three quarters of that bottle of beer sitting on the end table beside me. Warren was rustling by now and I asked him if he had felt an inordinate reaction to a seemingly modest amount of alcohol. He agreed that he had and we looked at the label on the beer and saw it contained seventeen per cent alcohol by volume. No wonder we were wrecked the night before. It seems that the Russian government under Gorbechev had become concerned about the amount of vodka the citizens were drinking and had encouraged the greater production of beer. Well, their appetite for alcohol could not be quenched by the normal four or five per cent beverages we were used to, so they brewed these high alcohol versions. We learned a tough lesson to pay closer attention to alcohol volumes in the future.

We had fallen asleep pretty early and had awakened around six in the morning. Since we were not to be picked up for our day's tour until nine o'clock we decided to take a little walk before we went down to breakfast. We bundled up and headed out into the cold morning. Our hotel sat at the intersection of a couple of main arteries along the Fontanka River. We chose to walk on a concrete sidewalk along the riverside. The river was channelized at this point and concrete-lined with stairways leading down to the water's edge. It looked like it would be a great place to launch a rowboat and take your best girlfriend for a ride on a nice summer's day. This day was anything but that. It was subzero and a fresh layer of snow had fallen overnight.

After walking several blocks we decided we had enough and turned around to head back to the hotel. Morning traffic was stirring and we noticed that unleaded gas had not made it way to Russia yet. As the cars chugged past we were nearly overcome by the fumes from the leaded gasoline. Caught up in conversation about the poor air quality we came upon one of the stairways down to the river. Just then a huge, black German Shepard darted out from the stairway. Barking and straining at the leach of its owner, it scared the crap out of us. Its fangs were showing and saliva was dripping from the corners of his mouth. Thank goodness that it was muzzled or we would have been breakfast for the beast.

The dog's handler mutter something to us as we passed by, but it did not appear to be in a very sympathetic tone. We did not look back the rest of the way to the hotel and we could not get in out of the cold quickly enough. For this and other reasons we ditched the morning walk for the remainder of the trip.

We got back to our room and were still shaken by the encounter with the dog. We quickly showered and dressed for breakfast. We went back down to the restaurant where we had eaten the night before to take our meal. We were seated near the buffet that had been set up for the morning's breakfast. The room was filled with Eastern European travelers. I think Warren and I were the only English speakers in the large room that was nearly filled. We checked out the buffet and discovered it was full of items we do not usually eat for breakfast.

The other patrons were diving headlong into lettuce salads with beets and we were scratching our heads trying to decide what would agree with our palates. Finally I spied a hard-boiled egg, some dark bread and something runny that appeared to be yogurt-like. I grabbed a cup of very strong coffee, a reasonable facsimile of orange juice and returned to my table. I ate the egg with the bread and decided to stick to the bread in the future. The coffee was full of grounds and barely potable. All in all it was another lousy meal. Warren and I had fortunately had the foresight to bring some snacks along and a breakfast bar helped me get through the morning.

As we were finishing our second cup of coffee Katarina appeared. She sidled over to our table to let us know that although she was early, she was ready when we were. We then spied our fellow traveler, Frank, across the room and waved him over to join us. He appeared ready to go and we went back upstairs to grab our coats and cameras to set out for the day.

We returned to the lobby and followed Katarina out to the parking lot where our driver and van sat running, warmed but spewing leaded fumes into the atmosphere. The vehicle was really quite nice and spacious. We headed out down the snow-covered streets for our first destination, a Russian orthodox church. After about a ten-minute drive we arrived at the church which sat back off the street in a park like setting.

We piled out of the van and followed Katarina in the direction of the church. The exterior of the building was very attractive, painted in a bright blue with a stark white trim with gold-like accents. The Cathedral of St. Sampson is one of the oldest churches in St. Petersburg tracing its roots back to 1709. Katarina wanted us to see the structure because it was a fine example of a Russian Orthodox Church. It had been closed for years under the communist regime and used as a vegetable warehouse. It had since been restored and was open for worship.

We entered the building which has several interesting features including an ornate alter that had been discovered during the renovation. It had been meticulously hidden behind marble slabs when the building had ceased to function as a church. The day we visited a funeral service was being held in one part of the building. Unlike our churches there were no pews and worshippers gathered around the alter standing in front of the priest. Incents were prevalently used in the service.

One noteworthy point was the age of those who were in attendance, they were all very old. Katarina informed us that many of the elderly continued to hold their beliefs during the Communist regime, which had taken a dim view of the practice of all organized religions. She said that the return of the church to Russian life was one of the outward signs of change that had occurred since the Soviet regime had fallen.

We departed and spent the next couple hours driving around St. Petersburg visiting other religious, and nonreligious, sights. First, we stopped by the Smolny Cathedral another beautiful structure painted in a robin egg blue and white with gold trimmings. The cathedral is considered to be one of the best pieces of baroque architecture in St. Petersburg. We simply walked around the outside of the structure and took pictures because renovation was underway inside.

After our visit to the Smolny, Katarina decided to take us to a new "supermarket" to show us how the new capitalist state was progressing. As we pulled up to the new grocery store the first thing you noticed was it is the size of a modest neighborhood store in the United States. As we entered the sparkling new digs we were struck with how little was stocked on the shelves. Unlike home, there would only be a few of one item on the racks leaving the appearance of empty shelving.

Katarina pointed out two particular sectors of the store to us; the caviar selection and the space containing vodka. Oddly enough, these two particular areas were well stocked and full of numerous selections. Our fellow traveler from Scranton, Frank, leapt at the chance to buy some good Russian caviar. Katarina helped him with his selection. Not being a fan of roe, Warren and I focused on a vodka and found a particularly agreeing local concoction to our liking. We were confused by the caps that were on some of the vodka bottles. These tops were peel off only, with no real way of recapping the bottle. We asked Katarina about it and she seemed nonplused by our query. We finally determined from her that once you opened a bottle of vodka it was presumed you would finish it, and thus there was no need to recap it. Wow!

Another oddity of the store was the check out process. Instead of proceeding directly to a cashier for check out, you first had to take your goods to a window where someone checked them and presented you with a voucher. You then took the voucher to a cashier whom you paid and they gave you a receipt. You then returned to the first desk, presented the receipt and were finally given the items you had purchased. Clearly, this was confusing to us, but I am guessing this was a remenant of the old communist state which was aimed at providing a job for another person.

After we left the grocery store, we drove to the center of the city and drove around the Church of the Savior of the Spilled Blood. The oft photographed, colorful church sits on the site where Czar Alexander II was assassinated in 1881. The popular czar who had freed the serfs twenty years earlier, was killed by a group of radicals demanding greater reform. The cathedral is an attempt to revive traditional Russian architecture. It has several colorful, beveled domes topped with gold crosses and can be compared to St. Basel's Cathedral in Moscow. It is truly a sight to behold.

After driving around the cathedral our driver located a place to park right off Nevsky Prospect, St. Petersburg's most popular street. Katarina led us to a small restaurant that she likened to the Russian version of fast food. As I recall, the only thing that resembled a western fast food establishment was you ordered and paid at a counter. Katarina helped us through the Russian menu and Warren and I both ordered grilled chicken and French fries. When our order came out the chicken appeared to have been boiled, not grilled. By the time I removed the skin and fat, I was left with about a three ounce piece of unidentified meat. I could hardly eat it, but given how hungry I was I chocked it down. The fries were not bad, however.

After lunch we were driven to a store that featured Russian souvenirs. You could buy Russian nesting dolls, amber, lacquer boxes, scarves, t-shirts and much more. We poked around and found a jewelry case containing some very interesting items. My gaze fell upon a pendant that was a miniature replica of a Faberge egg. Unfortunately, Warren also liked the item and we both perused it thoroughly. After a time Warren decided he had no interest in it and I snapped it up as a Christmas gift for Jenny. I also bought a Stolichnaya Vodka t-shirt for myself, which soon after getting home with it became Jenny's, as it shrunk to a very small size without even entering the dryer.

When we had finished our shopping spree, we loaded back up into the bus and went to see the Peter and Paul Fortress. The citadel contains several tourist attractions including the City Museum, a former political prison, a mint and the famous Peter and Paul Cathedral. The church, erected in 1723, is very recognizable because of its very tall spire which made it the tallest structure in the city until the 20th century. We spent time touring the cathedral which is the final resting place of all the czars and their families from Peter's time until the end of the Romanov dynasty.

By the time we had finished our visit to Peter and Paul's it was getting dark and was time to return to our hotel. As we drove back to our hotel Katarina pointed out several landmarks to us that we could return to on our free time. She also noted that a large number of buildings in St. Petersburg are painted in pastels. She told us that this has been done because the weather in the city is often gloomy and the winter days are so short that this added color helps with the disposition of the locals.

As we arrived back to the Sovietskaya, Katarina informed us that as part of the tour we were entitled to a trip to the ballet that evening, if we desired. None of the three of us had any particular interest in attending the performance, so Katarina offered the driver to us for the evening to take us to a nice restaurant if we had an interest. Warren and I quickly accepted the offer, but Frank declined the opportunity saying he was tired from the day and was still suffering from jet lag. Katarina would make the reservation and the driver would pick us up at the hotel in a couple of hours.

Warren and I returned to our floor and collected our key from the matron. We went into our room and kicked off our shoes and laid down for a short rest. Warren had the ingenious idea of putting our recently purchased bottle of vodka out on the window ledge to chill it down for consumption later. With the temperature below freezing, it would be cold enough for us to have a drink from it before departing for dinner.

We both napped for a short time and before we knew it, it was time to leave for dinner. Katarina had made us a reservation at a very nice place named 1913. The restaurant took its name from one of the most prosperous years in Russian history, and one of the last in the Imperial era. Our driver picked us up promptly at six and drove us to the eatery. He let us know where he would be when we were finished to take us back to the hotel.

We entered the restaurant and were surprised to see it was quite an elegant establishment. We were greeted by a beautiful, coat check woman who insisted that we leave our jackets with her. A well-dressed host showed us to a very nice table on a raised platform toward the back of the restaurant. Our first thoughts were that it was a really good thing that the U.S. dollar compared very favorably to the Russian ruble at the time, or this place might not be affordable for us.

Soon our very attractive, young waitress appeared with menus and talked us into a glass of fine Russian vodka to start our evening. We once again struggled somewhat with the menu, but our server was able to translate for us. We sipped our vodkas and made our dinner choices. Warren selected sturgeon and I ordered the hunter's steak. We snacked on a light appetizer that was brought out to us and finished our drinks. Soon our entrees arrived, and my huge plate of hunter's steak with cooked vegetables and potatoes looked outstanding. Warren's sturgeon, on the other hand, looked problematic.

As I devoured my first truly delightful meal since we had arrived in Russia, Warren struggled with his. Sturgeon is a prehistoric fish that is the source of what is often considered the best caviar in the world, beluga. The fish is not particularly boney, rather is has cartilage. Herein, was the problem for Warren? He wrestled with his fish trying to get to the meat because the cartilage that surrounds its unusual body formation. After a time he simply gave up and watched me enjoy may meal. We laughed for the remainder of the trip about how Warren had missed out on the delicious hunter's steak because he wanted to try something different.

We finished our meals and ordered an after dinner drink. As we enjoyed our beverages and took in the activities in the restaurant we asked our server for the bill. The waitress returned with the check and it was surprisingly inexpensive, again the favorable exchange rate had to have driven the modest amount. We paid our bill, collected our coats and set out to find our driver. Sure enough, he was where we were dropped off with a warm vehicle ready to take us to the hotel. **(See Appendix 10 for the recipe)**

A few minutes later we were back at the hotel. We decided to drop by the bar for one Baltika Number 9 before heading to bed. Our bartender was working so we engaged her in conversation for a while and drank our beers. Shortly, we decided it was time to head upstairs and call it a night. Our first full day in Russia had been eye opening and we were ready for our second.

The next morning we got up, passed on the walk for fear of the dog and the leaded gas, cleaned up, and went downstairs for breakfast. The buffet had changed somewhat for the better. On this day they had some runny scrambled eggs and mini hot dogs as their main attractions. Being hungry, I ate some and wished for some catsup to bring a little taste to the meal. The coffee was still strong and full of grounds, but this didn't stop me from drinking three cups loaded with cream.

As we were finishing up we noticed that Katarina had arrived to take us on our morning tour. We rounded up Frank and headed out for the last of our organized activities in St. Petersburg. Our driver had the van ready and we were on our way to the Winter Palace, home to the Hermitage Museum. The Hermitage is one of the most impressive museums in the world, both for its contents and the structure that house the collections, the Winter Palace.

As we were driving to the Hermitage, Katarina warned us that there could be a disturbance when we arrived. It seems that the remnants of the Communist Party were organizing a rally on the Palace Square adjacent to the museum, protesting various aspects of the current government. The most specific grievance was adjustments in the pensions of former state workers. News accounts quoted organizers predicting crowds in excess of a million people participating. There were also threats of violence.

As we arrived at the Winter Palace we indeed did see a protest underway. However, those engaged numbered in the hundreds, it was very peaceful, and there was no cause for alarm. The almost timid gathering was an assemblage of largely elderly Russian women who were upset about cuts in their pensions by the current government. Their numbers looked pathetically small in the vastness of the Palace Square. Clearly, there was no cause for concern for our safety.

The Winter Palace sits on the banks of the Neva River in the center of St. Petersburg. The original winter residence for the czars was constructed in the early 1700s for Peter the Great and his family. Several of his successors had a hand in reconstructing the palace until Catherine the Great came to the throne in 1762. Although the palace was nearly complete Catherine dismissed the architect, Francesco Rastrelli, but his exterior designs for the structure remain nearly unaltered today. The palace stands 22 meters high and local planning regulations prevent buildings in the center city from rising above its height.

As we approached the building we were struck by its beauty and detail. Its green façade, in keeping with the pastel theme of the city, contains two rows of columns with parapets adorned with statues and vases. The building forms a rectangle with an open courtyard in the center. Access to the courtyard is obtained through three archways leading from the Palace Square. As you enter the building you know that you are in for something special.

Katarina told us as we passed through the main entrance we needed to decide what we wanted to focus on before we set out on our tour. She informed us that the Hermitage collections contained approximately 3 million objects and if we were to spend 45 seconds viewing each one it would take us three years to finish the tour. We quickly perused the plan of the museum trying to decide which direction to turn. Frank offered that he was good with whatever we decided. Warren and I told Katarina that we would like about a three hour tour and she should lead us to what she considered the highlights. We also asked to try and work in the Rembrandts and some French impressionists, if possible.

We set out to explore the museum. I recall that I was simply overwhelmed by the beauty of the structure and the collections. Katarina took us to the most impressive sights, not only the collections, but the most intriguing aspects of the buildings. She led through room after room until it became a blur and we finally cried uncle. Being a huge fan of Rembrandt, I do remember seeing several of his paintings. It seems that for centuries there has been a kinship between the Dutch and Russians and, so, having a good representation of the Dutch Golden Age did not surprise me. Warren was also able to get his fix of French Impressionists, including several Monet's.

Tired from all the walking and awed by the sights, we called it quits after about two and a half hours. We huddled with Katarina for a while at the end of our tour to discuss the next two days. Warren and I had decided we would like to go to see Peter's Summer Palace, Peterhof, and inquired of Katarina what a tour for the two of us would run the next day. She informed us that, all in including a vehicle and driver, it would be two hundred dollars.

Outside the Hermitage Museum

We conferred briefly and decided to pass on the opportunity and just set out on our own. We agreed to meet Katarina the next evening at the Sovietskaya at 8:30 where she would take us to the train station to catch our overnight train to Moscow. She offered to take us back to our hotel along with Frank, but Warren and I declined since we were near the center of the city and were prepared to go exploring. She left us with a phone number in case we needed anything, or changed our minds about the tour to Peterhof, and departed.

Warren and I began a walking tour of the center of St. Petersburg. We headed out to see the statue of Peter the Great riding a horse. The Bronze Horseman is one of the city's most recognizable monuments and stands near the Admiralty and St. Isaac's Cathedral. The statue, which was commissioned by Catherine the Great, shows Peter riding a horse which has reared up on its hind legs. The statue sits on a large piece of granite and is quite impressive for the balance necessary to maintain its upright position on two legs. Legend has it that St. Petersburg will never be taken by a foreign invader as long as the statue stands. Although protected by sandbags and a wooden structure, the statue did not come down during World War II and it survived the 900 day siege of Leningrad, the city's name during the Soviet era.

Since we were in the neighborhood we decided to peek inside the St. Isaac's Cathedral. Built in the early part of the nineteenth century, the cathedral was the main church in the city and the largest in all of Russia. Its style is completely different than the traditional Russian Orthodox, rather the domed structure looks more like St. Peter's in Rome, than St. Basil's in Moscow. At any event, it is an impressive and imposing structure that is a dominant feature of the skyline of St. Petersburg.

By now our stomachs were telling us it was time to head somewhere for lunch. Consulting a map we decided to head toward Nevsky Prospect, the Fifth Avenue of St. Petersburg. As we walked toward the street we noticed that the weather had taken a real turn for the worse. It was spitting snow, the wind was howling, and the temperature had dropped quite noticeably. We decided that we would stop in the first café that we found that looked suitable to us.

After about ten minutes of walking and the bitter cold affecting us, we happen upon an inviting little bistro. We entered and were greeted warmly by a middle-aged woman that was neatly dressed. She showed us to a table in a back corner that looked to be the warmest spot in the room. We quickly decided that a hearty soup would be the order of the day, if available. Our server arrived with Russian only menus and spoke only a little English. We resorted to pointing as we saw other patron's meals.

Warren chose the Russian classic, borsht, a beet-based soup with sour cream. Having experienced this when it was served to my Russian class in high school, and not being a fan of beets, I chose something that looked similar to a beef stew along with a large bottle of still water. Soon our large bowls of soup arrived along with a dense, dark bread. It turns out that I had indeed ordered a variety of beef soup that was quite palatable. Warren said he enjoyed his first experience with borsht, but I noticed that like sturgeon, he did not order it again.

Refueled and warmed up, we finished our lunch and ventured back out into the cold. We decided to head toward the Church of the Savior of the Spilled Blood. We wanted to take a closer look at the impressive structure, as the day before we had only driven past. Also, and more importantly, we noticed that there was an open-air market to the side of the cathedral.

After a several minutes walking, and with the assistance of a good map, we came upon the church. We approached the front doors and for some reason were not able to gain entrance. Apparently the church was not open at that time. Disappointed but undeterred, we decided to move on to the outdoor market that was operating in the shadow of the building. Warren and I made a lap through without making any purchases. We saw several things that interested us and made inquiries about price, but made no offers.

After completing this first lap, we decided to zero in on what we wanted. By now, we were frozen and decided that those goofy-looking, round, rabbit fur hats you see Russian men wearing probably performed a function. In this weather we were willing to sacrifice fashion for warmth. We had seen several vendors selling these hats, but had liked one particular fellow. Our attraction to this one vendor was probably because he had a reasonable command of the English language. For whatever reason, we returned to his stand.

The man recognized us from our previous trip through and appeared anxious to serve us. Clearly on this very cold and snowy day, the foot traffic at this market was not too great and he was looking for a sale. We both let him know that we were interested in the rabbit fur hats. He assisted each of us in picking out the exact size we needed, and the right color. He began by asking us $30 US for each. I took the lead on the negotiations and said we were looking for a package deal and we would pay $20 for two. He continued to discuss a deal and we were at $13 apiece, and I was still trying to get him to come down a little further.

At the time, I was wearing a thin, cloth flat cap that I had bought a few years before in Scotland. He looked at me and asked which of these hats was going to be more effective in the Russian winter, and how much had I paid for the one I was wearing? I immediately reached into my pocket and fished out the $13 he wanted. He clearly was right. I had paid about $25 for the hat I had on and it was not at all suited for this extreme cold. Appearance be damned, we both without hesitation put on those hats and did not take them off until we returned home the next week.

We both had our eyes on another item, a blue, egg-shaped glass object with the symbol of Russia, a two-headed eagle etched in gold on the side. It was about the size of a goose egg and was very cool looking. A couple of different vendors had the item for sale and we could not get either of them to go below twenty dollars for their eggs. Buoyed by our earlier success in negotiating for the hats, we decided not to buy them. We were confident that we would seem them all over Russia during the next week.

Little did we know that we would not see them again on our trip? This gave rise to the circumstance my family and I refer to as the "Nancy Fleetwood rule." My mother, Nancy Fleetwood, was a world traveler who has done so extensively, visiting scores of countries. In fact, she stepped foot on all seven continents during her travels. Well, one of her fundamental travel rules pertained to shopping and that was, if you see something and you like it, buy it.

You can never count on finding the same item later on, irrespective of price. I have found this axiom to be true over time and we now attempt to follow it wherever we travel. Invariably, you see something at the beginning of your stay in a new country, believe that it will be available throughout your trip, and you will find it at a better price later. I don't know how many times it has taken me to fully appreciate this bit of wisdom my mom imparted on me years ago, but I have now become an advocate for this position myself.

After our minor shopping spree, we strolled around Nevsky Prospect window shopping and checking out the sights. After a short while we decided to duck into a bar, have a libation and shake off the cold. We found this place that was tucked away down in a basement. It was a large space, with a poolroom and was lit by orange, blue and purple neon lights. It was now mid-afternoon and, much to our surprise, the place was hopping. We ordered the now standard Baltikas, and watched the urban mating ritual that seems quite similar the world around.

After a couple of beers we decided it was time to return to the surface and try and figure out the public transportation system to return to our hotel for a short rest. We located the subway and with the help of a map that Warren had in a guidebook which was printed in English, we were able to find the stop closest to the Sovietskaya. We negotiated the subway to our station and reentered the cold of the day.

By now it was starting to get dark and the wind was blowing fiercely from the north. We had a several minute walk in this bitterly cold weather to reach our hotel. All I could think about was that good bottle of vodka on the ledge outside our room. It would certainly be very cold by now and it could help warm us after the cold walk.

We finally arrived back at the hotel and I remember the relief I felt when we entered the warm lobby. We went directly to the room and, after we removed our coats, I went looking for glasses while Warren retrieved the vodka bottle from outside on the window sill. Sure enough, the vodka could not have been colder if it had been in a freezer. We poured each of us a pretty stout glass and sat down on our beds to enjoy the nectar.

We reflected on the day and tried to understand the offerings on the television. The one thing that was clear to us was it was cold outside and the weather forecast called for more of the same, in fact, it appeared it was to get colder. As we enjoyed our drinks we began to consider our options for dinner that evening. We eliminated the hotel restaurants and pulled out Warren's guidebook and spread out a map to see where the recommendations were located. We determined that ethnic cuisine would seem to be the best option for that evening. Fortunately, a Korean barbeque restaurant was only a few blocks from the hotel and would be our target for that night.

We finished our drinks and pulled on our coats and fur hats and headed out into the cold. A thin layer of fresh snow had fallen while we were resting in our room and this provided a crunching sound as we walked toward our destination. The wind was blowing very hard and the evening was bitterly cold. Within a few minutes we spotted the sign for the Korean restaurant. We could not wait to get in out of the cold.

As we opened the door and felt the warm air rush towards us, we got our bearings. The restaurant was smallish, but had a very warm and stylish feel. The tables and chairs were black lacquer with red cushions. The place was very comfortable and the servers were very welcoming. We settled in to a nice table and ordered a couple of beers while we perused the menu. I had the pleasure of dining at a Korean barbeque in Osaka, Japan, and assured Warren that he was in for a treat. Warren is a very adventurous eater, so it took no persuasion to get him to try their offerings.

It quickly became apparent that, not unlike the restaurant I visited in Osaka, the tables were equipped with a small gas grill built into the table. Warren and I quickly decided that we would have an order of beef and one of pork ribs to prepare at our table. After we placed our order, we were served a cup of piping hot soup made from a beef stock which truly hit the spot on this cold night.

As our waiter was clearing away our soup bowls, the front door of the restaurant swung open and two very well-dressed men entered. Both were wearing dark, pinstriped suits with long leather coats and fedoras. They scanned the place, talked to the servers, and one of them stepped back outside. Shortly, the man reappeared accompanying a very stylish couple. The man was dressed in a similar fashion to the first two guys that had entered, and the gorgeous blonde woman on his arm was bedecked in fine furs and was dripping with diamonds. The couple were shown to a corner table while the two other men sat at a table near the front door.

Warren and I were amazed by this display. This had all the trappings of something out of _The Godfather._ We will never know exactly who these people were, but it appeared to be a mob boss, his moll, and two bodyguards. The restaurant was nearly empty, but gauging from the few other patrons, their take was the same as ours. I must confess that it felt like that at any minute someone could barge in the door and open fire with a machine gun. All we knew was we didn't want to take a stray bullet intended for another patron.

Our meat orders arrived accompanied with rice and vegetables. We immediately began to grill our meats, thin strips of steak and small pork ribs. We did our best to pay attention to our meals and enjoy our food, but all we could think about was finishing our food and getting out of there. The food was absolutely delicious and we devoured every last morsel.

When the waiter returned we declined the opportunity for dessert and asked for the check. When he reappeared we hurriedly paid the man and began to pull on our coats to leave. Sensing, and probably sharing, our apprehension, our waiter helped us with our wraps and showed us to the door.

As we made our retreat toward the hotel, we said little to each other until the restaurant was well out of sight. Finally, when we turned the last corner and the Sovietskaya was in full view, we began to share with each other the fears we had, given our fellow dinner guests. We entered the hotel and went directly to our room. Locking the door behind us we finally felt secure. Warren fetched the bottle of vodka from the ledge and poured a couple of stiff ones. As we recapped the evening's activities we drank our spirits and gave thanks that our worst fears were not realized. We looked forward to the next day's adventures.

We awoke the next morning after a great night's sleep and were now firmly planted in the proper time zone. Since we had no organized activities that day we looked forward to setting our own agenda and following it. We showered and went downstairs for breakfast, interested in seeing what might be offered that morning. As it turned out it was more of the same. I settled from some bread and jam, runny yogurt and an ample amount of strong coffee. Over breakfast Warren and I worked on the day's plan which started with trying to figure out how to get to Peter's Summer Palace, Peterhoff, via public transportation.

We finished up our meal and pulled on our outerwear to head to Baltiysky train station, the starting point of our journey to Peterhoff. Baltiysky station was about a ten minute walk from our hotel and features multimodal transportation with trains, subways and buses all originating, or terminating, at the site. In one of Warren's guidebooks they discussed catching a train to the town of Peterhof from Baltiysky station followed by a local bus from the town to the Summer Palace. Additionally, there was a conversation of catching a double-decker bus from in front of the station directly to the palace.

For some reason that currently escapes me, Warren and I had decided to try and catch a train to Peterhof and bus the rest of the journey to the palace. When we arrived at the station we located two different train boards posting schedules. Unfortunately neither had any English or western script, only Cyrillic. I had taken the two years of Russian in high school and we were hoping some of it would come back to me. I finally decided that one board was for major lines and the other was for local trains. We focused in on the local board and were unable to unlock the key to understanding our way to Peterhof. As we stood in this unheated room that had a dirt floor, we couldn't locate someone to translate for us.

After about thirty minutes of frustration and nearly complete dejection, we remembered that an alternative route to Peterhof was by double-decker bus. We went back outside to the bus station area immediately in front of the train station. There we spotted only one double-decker bus. Summoning up some courage and what little Russian I commanded, we boarded the bus and tried to ask the driver if it went to Peterhof. The driver's hasty retort was a firm, "nyet." Our hearts sank as we thought that this task of finding our way to the Summer Palace might be beyond our means. Just as we started to step back off the train, this large Russian woman who served as a matron and ticket taker on the bus stopped us.

The matron began to quiz us, speaking rapidly in Russian. It seemed she wanted to be helpful and I tried my best to remember the appropriate words in her language. Finally, Warren fished into his pocket and thumbed through his guide until he found a picture of the Summer Palace. Soon the matron was booming, "Da, da!" and telling us what the fare was. We pulled out some rubles, she took what she needed and gave us our tickets. We thanked her profusely and climbed the stairs to the upper deck and found some seats.

As we settled into our seats, the bus lurched forward and our trip was beginning. We felt some level of comfort and satisfaction in finally getting on a public conveyance headed toward our destination. As we moved through the streets of St. Petersburg we enjoyed the ride which soon gave way to a more rural setting. Suddenly a thought struck me, we had no idea where we were going! The only person who knew where we wanted to end up was the matron and she was downstairs. Warren and I quickly repositioned ourselves to the lower level within sight of the matron. She saw us and nodded to us approvingly, as if she knew why we were now downstairs.

After about a half hour ride, we came to the town of Peterhof, whose sign I could read as we entered. I told Warren that I thought we should get off here and we arose. The matron spotted us and barked, "Nyet," at us once again. She said something else that led me to believe that we needed to go one more stop. Sure enough in a couple of minutes we pulled up to a stop directly in front of the Summer Palace grounds. With a big smile, revealing several missing teeth, the matron affirmed that we should get off here. By now all the other patrons on the bus seemed to understand where we wanted to go and they, too, wished us well. As we were leaving the bus the matron grabbed me and pointed across the road to the bus stop so we knew where to catch our return bus. This kind lady, and about eighty cents for a fare, had gotten us to Peter's summer residence.

Peterhof sits back off the road probably a good quarter of a mile. Started by Peter the Great as his summer home, Peterhof backs up on the Baltic Sea and symbolizes the completion of the Russian struggle to establish a port on the sea. The mammoth three-story, yellow structure was built to rival the French summer palace at Versailles. The grounds contain several other palatial structures and, possibly most impressively, huge fountains, pools, and canals leading to the Baltic.

Warren and I entered the gates and strolled back down the gravel path toward the Grand Palace. As we reached the entrance we could hear the lovely sounds of a string quartet. They were dressed in rather ragged, period costumes and performing in the courtyard. We stopped to listen for a minute and a woman approached us and asked if we were interested in her services as a guide. She informed us that for about an hour tour it would cost the equivalent of six dollars for the two of us. She spoke English well and it seemed like a real deal to us, so we quickly agreed.

She led us into the Grand Palace and we purchased admission tickets for very little cost. As it turns out, the structure had taken a great deal of damage from Nazi bombings during World War II, and over fifty years later its renovation was far from complete. Our guide led us through the areas that were open for touring. First, we had to put on shoe covers so we would not mar the parquet wood floors found throughout the palace. My recollection is the most impressive interior sights were the heavily gilded Ballroom and the turquoise and white Throne Room. The Throne Room had a particularly noteworthy, intricate parquet floor.

Our guide then led us outside to show us part of the grounds. She took us toward the Baltic entrance to the palace, where we viewed the

Grand Cascade. The Grand Cascade is a series of 64 fountains that lead from the north side of the palace to the Maritime Canal which flows into the Baltic Sea. The only drawbacks we faced were the early onset of the Russian winter which made it particularly unpleasant that day, and the fact that the fountains were shut down for the winter months. However, it was plain to see that these gardens, fountains, statues, and canal were a definite high point for any visit to Peterhof.

Unable to endure the cold very long, we shortened our tour of the gardens and fountains and returned to the palace to warm ourselves. We decided to visit the small gift shop which was off the back of the palace. Both Warren and I made purchases there, I selected a particularly interesting Christmas ornament which was a handmade, small stuffed figure of a babushka. Warren and I picked up some nice scarves for the women in our lives, and we said our good-byes to our guide and thanked her for her service.

As we were retracing our steps, we decided to go into the little town of Peterhof which was nearby the palace. We had seen a very interesting Russian orthodox church from the bus that we wanted to see if we could gain access to. The place of worship, Saints Peter and Paul Cathedral, is a classic example of Russian revival architecture. Its red and green façade, topped with a golden onion dome with crosses, is eye-popping. We ventured inside to find a rather plain wooden interior, clearly another example of the parish deciding to spend the money on the exterior of the church.

After a brief look about we decided to find the bus stop and return to St. Petersburg. Not far from the church and the center of the town, we found the placard for the bus stop. There were times posted for the buses returning to the city and we discovered that we had over an hour until the next bus was scheduled for pick up. Given it was now snowing and there was no shelter to block the wind and cold, we decided to find a place that might provide us with some warmth and a quick bite to eat.

It was now well past noon and we were getting hungry. It did not appear that there were many restaurant options in this small town, but we did spot one sign for a tavern. We walked to the entrance of the basement establishment and literally ducked in as it had a low ceiling. There were about a dozen young Russians seated at low, wooden tables and chairs with a pool table in one corner. From the looks we received when we entered, we might have been the first Americans to grace the inn. Our quick scan determined that this might not be the place to eat, but they clearly had alcohol to drink.

We walked up to the rickety, wooden bar and I asked the comely, young bartender for two beers in my best Russian. She asked what variety, I believe, and I answered Baltika Number 9. She turned and grabbed our order off a wooden shelf behind her and blew the dust off the bottles. It seems that refrigeration was not in service in the bar, but given that we could detect no visible source of heat in the room, a beer directly from the shelf was not too bad.

Feeling somewhat like intruders, we took seats at a table around the corner in the "L" shaped room so we didn't interfere with any of the local activities. As we sat and sipped on our beers, we noticed that a litter of young kittens were roaming free in the room. Soon we were both picking clingy, little cats from our pants legs. It was cold in the room, little improvement from the outdoors, but the wind was at least blocked. We finished our beers and visited the restroom, an interesting experience in and of itself. By now, we decided that we needed to get back to the bus stop to insure we caught our bus, because the next one was not to arrive for two more hours.

When we got back to the bus stop, a few other people were huddled near the sign also waiting for a bus. We took this as a good omen because we calculated that meant we had not missed it. As we all stood around in a fairly tight circle for a group of strangers, we could see the bus arriving from down the road. It roared to a stop in front of the group and we all boarded and paid our fares. The bus was well-heated, which was a great relief, and we slumped into a couple of seats for our nearly hour-long ride back to the Baltiysky station.

As we were riding, Warren and I calculated that it had cost us a total of eleven dollars to visit the Summer Palace including all bus fees, admission and guide. Katarina had asked for two hundred dollars for the same trip, but it would not have been nearly as much an adventure. We would not have seen the church in Peterhof, nor had the beer with the kittens crawling on us. We think we made a very wise decision.

I think we both dozed off on the ride back to St. Petersburg which made the trip go by very quickly. When we returned we left the bus and headed up the street for our hotel. Along the way we passed a little meat market and decided to stop in to see if anything looked appealing. We were by now very hungry and everything looked good to us. We bought some sliced salami and cheese, and a loaf of bread and hurriedly returned to our room. Fortunately, our travel company had made arrangements for us to keep our room until our evening departure.

We fetched our key from the matron and entered the room. Warren went for the vodka on the outside window sill and I started to set out our food on the small table in the middle of the room. Soon we were enjoying an indoor picnic with slices of salami and cheese, hunks of the fresh bread, washed down with shots of ice cold vodka. I really enjoyed the meal and my family and I will often replicate this as a late afternoon snack prior to, or simply in place of, dinner.

Given we were in for an overnight train journey that evening to Moscow, we decided to relax in the room for a couple of hours before heading out again. We turned on the television and watched an American movie with Russian subtitles and drank the remainder of the bottle of vodka. It was now fully dark and we decided that we should head out to dinner to ensure we had ample time to return for our prearranged pick-up to the train station.

We had done some research and decided to sample some Armenian cuisine at a small place recommended in one of Warren's guides. Although it was not too far away from our hotel, given the inclement weather, we decided to make the short trip by the tram that stopped directly in front of the hotel. We soon arrived at the small restaurant and were greeted by the kind, aging woman who ran the place. She spoke no English and we had to rely on a combination of pointing and my pathetic Russian. It actually all worked out quite well.

As if to know exactly what we wanted, or needed, the proprietor disappeared after seating us. She returned shortly with a chilled bottle of vodka and pointed to the glasses neatly arranged on our table. Warren and I both selected the one that about the size of a juice glass and she filled them up. She presented us with menus in Russian and we pulled out a photocopied sheet we had of Russian food terms. With the kind lady's direction, we ordered a chicken based soup and some sort of grilled fowl.

Before we could finish our drinks, she returned with the soup and placed it in front of us. In a shallow bowl, the steaming soup was a translucent mixture of heavy broth with chunks of chicken with a few vegetables. We both began to eat the concoction along with lavash, the traditional flat bread which was served with the soup, and enjoyed it immensely. We had barely finished when our wonderful host and chef return with our main courses. On large plates, pieces of grilled fowl, presumably chicken, were arranged around the edges with home fried potatoes filling the center. We had no idea what a feast we would have when we arrived, but it was terrific.

We devoured our delicious entrees. We sat back in our chairs and our marvelous cook and waitress returned to clean our table. She inquired about the possibility of dessert and we both declined. After a short while she came back with a brown bottle in her hand and, before we could wave her off, she poured us large snifters of Armenian brandy. I had heard about this wonderful beverage from friends who had travelled to Russia before and had admonished me to be on the lookout for it. I had almost forgotten their advice until she was pouring the nectar.

We thoroughly enjoyed the after dinner drink and asked for our check. The owner returned with the bill and we couldn't believe our eyes, this sumptuous repast was less than ten dollars, all in, for the two us. I believe in all probability this was the best value of any meal I have had in my life. We gladly paid the woman, left a nice tip, thanked her from the bottom of our hearts and started to leave.

As we pushed back from the table three Russian men dressed in fatigues sitting at a nearby table said something to us in a loud voice. I turned and told them in Russian that we did not understand. One of the men in clear English invited us to join them for a drink. We had noticed them during dinner drinking vodka like water from large carafes, while they munched on beef jerky. I politely told him that we had a train to catch, but they would have none of it. We would have a drink with them.

They pushed out chairs from their table and asked us to sit with them. I tried to explain our limited timeframe, but they insisted we have one quick one with them. Grabbing a couple of glasses that we would use for water, they filled two to the rim and handed them to us. The man who spoke the best English began to quiz us about ourselves and why we were there. When we told him we were from Indiana he bellowed out, "I studied in your Michigan." They turned out to be delightful drinking companions and, if we didn't have to catch a train, we probably would have stayed out very late with them. But, slugging down our drinks we were now in a real time crunch. We thanked them for the hospitality and headed for the door.

We had no more than hit the cold when we saw a tram rumbling down the street. On a dead run we thought we could not catch it, but luckily it was stopped by a traffic light. The driver opened the rear door for us and we jumped in. We soon realized, even in our diminished state, it was now snowing hard. We got to the hotel in a couple of minutes and ran in the door where Katarina, Frank, and another man were waiting for us.

Hurriedly, we ran to the restroom, gathered up our bags and headed out toward the van. I took one step out the door on the stoop and the freshly laid snow caused my feet to fly directly out from under me. I fell flat on my back. Thank goodness that I landed on my soft-sided suitcase or I might have been in real trouble. My reduced capacity because of all the vodka probably also helped me absorb the fall. I got up, checked everything out and piled into the van for the Moscow Train Station.

Once we were in the van, Katarina introduced us to the new person who was with her. His name was Ed and he was a retiree from Columbus, Ohio, and he was actually the fourth member of our tour. He told us that he had taken the tour package to come visit friends in St. Petersburg and had stayed in an apartment in the building where his friends lived. He was now joining us for the Moscow leg of the journey and the trip home.

MOSCOW

We soon arrived at Moscow Station, a far more ornate and functional facility than the Baltiysky we had visited earlier in the day. We entered the attractive building and joined the congregation of travelers in front of the train board. Katarina pointed out to us a convenience store where Warren and I stocked up on a few Baltikas and some snacks for the trip. Shortly, our train was posted and we followed Katarina to the proper car. She helped us board the train, engaged the conductor and made certain that all our reservations were in order. Making sure we were set, Katarina bade us adieu and we thanked her and gave her a gratuity.

We had a nice, big compartment which was intended for four passengers, but Warren and I had paid, literally, a few extra dollars to have the whole compartment to ourselves. I didn't relish the thought of sleeping with strangers and had read of robberies on this route. Also, the thought of a drunk Russian stepping on me as he alit from the upper berth on the way to the bathroom in the middle of the night was not a pleasant one.

We soon departed and Warren and I opened our beers. We talked and laughed until our beers were finished and then decided to call it a night. I fell quickly asleep, but awoke in about an hour because the compartment was too hot. Warren was also awake and we tried our best to figure out how to turn down the heat, to no avail. Finally, we resorted to calling the conductor. Of course, he did not speak English, but somewhere in the dark recesses of my brain I came up with the Russian word for "hot." The conductor understood and turned a lever that reduced the temperature. He also took the pillows on our berths and switched them to the other end so our heads were not directly above the heat source. When he left we both felt like complete imbeciles. We were, however, able to get a pretty good night's sleep.

We awoke early the next morning as our train was arriving in the outskirts of Moscow. Our window was nearly completely frosted over making it almost impossible to see outside. We soon arrived at the station where we were met by our new guide, Anna. Anna was an attractive, thirty-something woman that had a great command of the English language. She led us to a waiting van. There a large, bald-headed driver in a black leather coat, who looked like he should be a bouncer at a biker bar, was keeping the vehicle warm. He loaded our bags in the back and the four of us and Anna piled in for the ride to our hotel.

Anna pointed out sights along our route to our hotel, the Izmailovo Alpha. The city was just coming alive as we made our way through town. The Izmailovo Alpha is located outside the Garden Ring in a northeast suburban area. The hotel is part of a huge complex of four hotel buildings that were completed to house visitors for the 1980 Moscow Olympic Games. It is reputed to be the largest hotel complex in the world with over 8,000 rooms. The 28-story buildings are very Soviet looking with stark concrete, upright rectangular facades and little architectural appeal.

After about a half hour we arrived at the Alpha and Anna ushered us into the massive lobby and assisted us with check-in. The garishly appointed public space was occupied by a number of Eastern European businessmen, or at least they were dressed to look the part. After checking our passport information we were assigned rooms and led to the elevators. We arrived at our floor and, again, the matrons were there to meet us and present us with our room keys. Anna made sure we got to our rooms and then arranged a time to meet us for breakfast downstairs.

Warren and I opened the door to our concrete block room to find a clean, but Spartan space. It contained two beds, a desk, a couple of red, molded plastic chairs and a television. The bathroom was spotless and functional, if not aesthetically pleasing. We hastily unpacked and took turns showering, getting ready, and preparing for the day of sightseeing ahead. Before we went downstairs for breakfast we inquired with one of the matrons about having some laundry done. She instructed us to leave it with her and one of them would take it home and return it to us the next day.

We met Anna and our two fellow travelers downstairs in the vast dining room where we were seated at a large, round table. Unlike our hotel in St. Petersburg, we had wait service and no buffet. Our server came to our table and asked if we wanted tea or coffee. She soon returned with our drink orders and plates containing our breakfast, plain omelets with a side of canned peas. The newest member of the group, Ed, offered that this was common in Russia. You would be served whatever they had at the time. Anna concurred, stating that the hotel had probably gotten a deal on canned peas and that was why we received them as part of our breakfast.

We were hungry and it didn't taste too bad to us. We were also served some bread and butter and we made the most of the meal. In short order, we were done and Anna led us out into the parking lot where we were met by our oversized driver. It turns out his name was Ivan. All we knew about him was he was a mean-looking dude, who was an excellent chauffeur and a chain smoker. I figured that since he was our driver, no one would mess with us as long as we were with him.

We headed out for our day of sightseeing. Our first stop was the Kremlin, the historic seat of the Russian government. As we passed through the gate in the huge red-brick walls you couldn't help but feel a sense of awe. The power that had been wielded from this collection of buildings ruling this vast country over the centuries is impressive. There we walked around much of the grounds, entering few buildings. We saw the Kremlin Palace, the 700-room structure that was home to the czars and seat of the Soviet government. We walked past the Armory Museum which is Russian oldest museum, which was unfortunately closed that day.

We then strolled to the Cathedral Square of the Kremlin. The Kremlin houses seven distinct orthodox churches that were erected during the 15th and 16th centuries. The onion domed structures are well worth the visit, both outside and inside. The Church of the Assumption is not to be missed. The white limestone structure has a spacious interior and was the sight of the coronation of many czars and the inauguration and burial of many Patriarchs of the Russian Orthodox Church.

Nearby you can view a couple of real oddities, the Czar Cannon and the Czar Bell. The cannon was designed in 1586 to defend the Kremlin and has a 40 ton barrel. The enormous cannonballs beside give you a distinct idea of the sheer size of the weapon, which was never fired. The Czar Bell is the largest bell in the world weighing an amazing 20 tons. The bell stands 20 feet high and is 21 feet in diameter, but was unfortunately cracked before it could be rung. The two unusual items stand today as a testament to Russian ambition.

By now we were freezing, and we piled back into the van with Ivan for a short ride to the other side of the Kremlin wall to Red Square. Red Square is the main public space in the city and one of the most famous addresses in the world. The Kremlin and Lenin's tomb border one side, St. Basil's Cathedral another and the world famous GUM Department Store, yet another. I remember standing in the middle of the square shooting pictures of all the sights I had seen numerous times on television, thinking that this was a very surreal experience for me. Growing up in a small town in Indiana during the Cold War, I would never have dreamt of standing in the middle of the most famous square in the Communist World. Life is good.

We walked around the square taking note of each of the important structures and paid particular attention to the beautiful St. Basil's Cathedral. I inquired of Anna about going in to visit, but it like many other things that day it was closed. I also remember Anna saying that from her perspective it was a far more impressive structure from the outside and she recommended leaving your observations to the exterior.

We then walked across the Red Square and entered GUM. GUM is actually not a department store, but rather a shopping arcade or mall. The building itself is a magnificent structure with its glass enclosed atrium and multi-level shopping. When we visited it was transitioning into a very high-end shopping center with some of the top retailers in the world in residence. As we entered the atrium, Anna pointed out to us a small liquor store on the main level. She informed us that if we were interested in purchasing any Stolichnaya Cristall, reputed to be the best vodka in the world, this was the place to do so. She explained that it might cost more here than in some other places, but you would be sure of its authenticity. It seems that there was a real problem in Russian at that time with unscrupulous persons rebottling lesser vodka in the Cristall bottles and selling the counterfeit for the genuine article.

St. Basil's on Red Square

Taking her advice we entered the store and quickly selected a couple of bottles of the Cristall along with our new favorite Armenian cognac, Ararat. Expecting to be hit with a big bill we were shocked when the Cristall was selling for the equivalent of two dollars a bottle. No doubt we had picked the ideal time to visit Russian from an exchange rate standpoint. We walked through the atrium to the other end and decided we had seen enough.

By now we were getting hungry and Anna took us to a small Russian restaurant not far from Red Square. The front window of the place was nearly steamed over as the warmth from inside collided with the cold exterior nearly freezing on the window pane. Anna was a huge help in ordering lunch and I had beef stroganoff and a cold beer. Our pretty, blond waitress brought out our high plates of food in very short order. The stroganoff was delicious and I ate it like I had not eaten in days.

After lunch, Anna and Ivan took us on a largely driving tour of Moscow. They drove us along the river and past a very large Russian Orthodox, the Cathedral of Christ the Saviour. The bright white church with enormous copper domes is the tallest Orthodox Church in the world. Originally built in the middle of the nineteenth century, the building was destroyed by the Soviet government in the 1930s. After the fall of communism the church was rebuilt with donations from over a million Muscovites. The reconstruction was very nearly completed when we visited Moscow.

As we continued our driving tour, Ivan drove us up a hill to view Moscow State University. The largest edifice of the university complex is a gigantic Stalinist structure. The 5,000 room building is one of the so-called Seven Sisters that dominate the Moscow skyline. These huge structures are part Russian church, gothic cathedral and American skyscraper. We descended the hill partially to a parking area where we had a view of the Moscow State University behemoth above us and two or three of the other sisters below us. It was a very impressive view from this vantage point.

As we got back into the van, Anna informed us that we had an opportunity to go the New Moscow circus that evening and wanted to know who wanted to attend. All four of us leapt at the opportunity and she decided we should return to the Alpha for a short rest before the performance. We wound our way back through the snarled Moscow traffic to Izmailovo and soon were reclining on our beds taking a short nap before our big evening.

We all gathered in the lobby to meet prior to leaving for the circus. Anna took us outside to the parking lot where Ivan was waiting with a warm van. We trekked across the city to the south side where the Moscow Big State Circus, or New Circus, is located. After nearly an hour of driving in heavy traffic we arrived at the permanent structure that houses the circus.

The Big State Circus is located is an impressive auditorium that appears to have been built specifically to host the circus. The modern venue has a capacity of nearly 3,500 with all patrons seated on comfortable, padded theater-style seats. The lobby houses large refreshment and souvenirs stands. In fact, we had our dinner at the event, arriving well before the start of the performance. I sampled some sort of sausage sandwich with popcorn and a beer.

The circus itself is quite a spectacle and well worth the visit. Unlike circuses you may have seen in the United States, the Big State Circus does not focus on large animal acts. Rather, it consists of spectacular acrobatic displays, small animal tricks (think dogs and monkeys), daring horse riding featuring a beautiful woman standing on a horse at full gallop and other cunning acts. There is a lot of music and lovely costumes. One of the final acts of the evening features a motorcycle in a cage doing loops at a high rate of speed all the while avoiding a patron standing at the bottom center of the orb. Overall, I would rate the experience as a must see and, if I ever return to Moscow, I will try my best to attend this circus again. Hank we need to get you there. I know you would enjoy it.

The performance lasted a couple of hours and afterward we all climbed back into the van and headed back to the Alpha. Initially, there was a good deal of chatter among us about the wonderful event we had just seen. But, soon the van grew quite as the events of the day caught up with us and we realized how tiring it all had been. Frank and Ed both fell asleep snoring loudly, while Warren and I enjoyed the near peace and the views of Moscow at night.

Arriving back at the hotel we went directly to our room. Warren had the foresight to stick one of the bottles of Cristall we had purchased on the ledge outside our room. By now, it was very cold and ready for drinking.

We opened the bottle and poured a couple of good glasses of this premium alcohol as a nightcap. This was the first taste either of us had of the Cristall and it was as good as advertised. We flipped on the television and watched an American show that was subtitled, finished our drinks and went to sleep.

We slept in a bit the next morning which was no real problem because we had no organized activities that day. However once we awoke, we hustled and got ready because we had a big agenda we were going to pursue on our own that day. We went down to the big restaurant for breakfast and, surprise, we had an omelet with peas again. I guess they still had an ample supply of peas. I will say the coffee at the Alpha was a vast improvement over what we had in St. Petersburg, it was actually almost tasty.

After breakfast we returned to our room to gather our things to leave for a day on our own. As we returned to the floor, the matron hailed us and we went to see what she wanted. As we approached she handed us a couple of bundles of clean clothes that she had done for us overnight. We paid her what she asked, I think around three dollars for what amounted to two loads, and returned to our room. We began to sort out the clean clothes and discovered that all were neatly folded and even our t shirts and underwear had been pressed before they were returned. What an incredible job for next to nothing!

There is a lesson here, don't pack for an entire trip, have laundry done, and you can save a great deal of space and wear and tear from handling excess baggage. We generally do not have it done in the hotel because they want to charge by the piece and this can get rather expensive. Besides it can be a real experience finding a drop off laundry that will do a great job on your clothes while you are out sightseeing. In most cities you can find a location near your hotel without much effort, where you can drop off in the morning and pick up in the afternoon. We have done this now on six continents and it can be a real savings to you.

One of the biggest advantages of the Izmailov Alpha is its proximity to the Moscow subway, there is a stop about fifty yards out the front door. The Moscow subway system is one of the finest in the world and it will whisk you around the city to very convenient locations, very quickly. Not only is the subway system one of the most efficient in the world, each of the stations are unique and can be an attraction, in and of, themselves.

From the Alpha you can take the subway to the center of the city in about fifteen minutes in reasonable comfort. Although we had little say in the choice of the Alpha as our hotel because it was a part of our package, I firmly believe that in choosing a hotel, proximity to public transportation should be high on the list of criteria in the selection process.

Warren and I departed the hotel on that cold, snow-covered morning and we could barely see in front of ourselves for the condensation from our own breath. We walked through the little handicraft and sundry market that surrounded the subway stop and descended into the station. Our destination that morning was Red Square and a visit to Lenin's Tomb. We no more than got to the bottom of the escalators than our train arrived and we hopped aboard. In about fifteen minutes we had made it around six stops and arrived at the Red Square station.

As we got off the train and got on the up bound escalator, I noticed a strange man following me. Warren soon noticed and, in fact, the man came up to me and jostled me. We decided to try and shake him and rapidly ducked back on the down escalator and he followed hastily. He passed several people on the stairs and approached me and asked me a question. I told him in Russian that I didn't understand his question and the man standing on the step behind me said something to him in Russian. He fled rapidly down the stairs.

The man on the step behind me then turned to me and said in English the man wanted to know what time it was. He told me to beware. When we reached the bottom of the escalator, the strange man was waiting there. At that moment a new train arrived, Warren and I stood at the door and jumped aboard just as the doors were closing. The strange man tried to do the same, but the doors closed too rapidly and he was left standing on the platform. We went one stop, turned around and came back to the Red Square station. To our relief, the strange man was no longer there. To this day I have no idea what to make of this incident, but I know it "creeped" both Warren and me out.

We hustled out of the station and moved across Red Square to the Lenin Mausoleum that lies on the west side of the square next to the Kremlin wall. We had come envisioning queuing in the cold in a long line that had constantly existed during the Communist era. Instead, we walked directly into the red granite structure with no one in front, or behind, us. It was a very solemn experience as we descended the stairs upon entering.

As we were about halfway down the embankment, Warren complained to me in a voice not much more than a whisper that it was difficult to see because of the dim lighting. All at once a loud "shush" startles us from behind. We thought we were alone, but turned to see a giant of a man in a Russian army uniform insisting on silence. He followed a few paces behind us as we turned and came back up some stairs where we could see Lenin's body. We started to pause for a few moments to take a better view of his remains, but the huge soldier scurried us along and out the door. The whole experience did not last but a few minutes, but it was definitely an interesting one.

We poked around Red Square for a while, checking our St. Basil's in a little more detail. We decided to reenter GUM to warm up and consult a map to plot our next steps. We determined that our next area to explore would be the shopping sector around Arbat Street. Old Arbat Street, the pedestrian shopping street, sits on the west side of the Kremlin. Although there was a subway stop nearby, we decided to hoof it to the area.

Old Arbat was once the main western artery running from the Kremlin. In the 1960s a new parallel street was built, New Arbat, to handle this traffic flow and eventually the "old" Arbat was designated as the Soviet Union's first pedestrian-only street. What has evolved is a haven for street performers, souvenir shops, cafes and pubs.

We trudged through the snow covered streets and finally arrived at the Arbat. Given the extremely cold weather we decided to duck into some souvenir shops to keep warm. Soon, we realized it was past lunch time and we found a nice, little café to enjoy a bite to eat. Warren and I sat down at a table along the far wall that provided us with a great view of the street scene outside the nearly floor to ceiling windows.

Our pretty, young waitress brought us a couple of beers and an English menu to decide on lunch. She also spoke some English, a welcomed addition. We both decided on a meat stew our server strongly suggested. In a few minutes, enough time to finish a beer, the meal appeared and proved to be an outstanding choice. The stew was served in a crock and was thick, well-seasoned and delicious. It was perfect for a frigid day. The stew consisted of a brown broth, beef, potatoes, carrots, onions and mushrooms and was quite filling.

About the time we were finishing our lunches, the café door swung open and two of the most beautiful women either of us had seen in our lives entered. The gorgeous young, long blond-haired women were dressed in long fur coats and tall leather boots. They looked like they had just stepped away from a photo shoot for Russian *Vogue.* Probably since we were the only other patrons in the establishment, they smiled at us as they sat down and ordered a couple of beers.

Deciding not to rush out hastily, we signaled our server for another round. After a short time it became apparent to me that they either did not speak English, did not have an interest in us, or most likely both. I vividly recall Warren berating me for being a poor student in my high school Russian class, otherwise I could be sweet talking these young ladies for us. It was a shame, but nothing I could do that day would change the circumstance. We sat and enjoyed looking at their beautiful forms for a while longer, but soon decided to pay up and hit the streets.

We spent about another hour ducking in and out of the various shops along Arbat Street looking for the perfect gifts for our loved ones back home. We both bought some more nice scarves for some friends and I found a Christmas matryoshka. As it turns out this was the beginning of a collection of the nesting dolls that my family and I enjoy. We display several of these year round in a den in our home and they all come out of their boxes for the holidays.

Tired, we decided to return to the Alpha. We set out for the nearest metro stop and discovered the Arbatskaya station was not only nearby, but on the same line needed to get to the Izmailovo. We entered the ornate station with its large vaulted ceilings and lovely chandeliers and purchased our tickets. As we walked to our platform we both wished we had an entire day to travel through the subway system and check out this beautiful, unique stations. We had no such luck, though, as we were leaving Russia the next morning.

We arrived back at the Alpha and went directly to our room to relax. We kicked off our shoes and fished the bottle of Cristall from the ledge. I poured us a couple of nice drinks and we sat back on our beds and recapped the day. By now the early nightfall had begun and we decided to get a jump on our packing so we had little to do in the morning.

The television was blaring another American-made movie which we were paying little attention to. We were now trying to decide what to do for our last night's dinner in Russia. We had both hoped to have a small taste of the Russian winter before we left, but neither of us desired the full brunt of it that we were experiencing. We checked the guidebooks and decided it was too cold to venture too far. The literature in our room made a pizzeria in one of the nearby sister hotels sound appetizing. We determined this would make a fitting place for the last night's dinner.

We could hear the wind howling through our room window. We put on all the outerwear we could find, even though we only had a short walk of about a block to the next hotel tower. We went down the elevator, through the lobby and out the front doors. It was unbelievable cold and the wind was worse than it sounded in our room. The pizzeria was in the hotel building to the north of ours, across a large concrete plaza. We rounded the corner of our building only to be met with a blast of full force Russian winter. The wind was so strong we were almost knocked off our feet. And we are not small people with both of us over six feet tall and in excess of two hundred pounds.

We quickly retreated back around the corner to regroup. We seriously did not know if we could make it to the pizzeria. Just then we spotted a small, convenience-style store about twenty yards away. We decided to make a run for it and see if there was something shelved there we could make do for dinner. We braved the wind and made it to the store. We finally settled on some very fatty looking salami, more fat than meat, some cheese and six beers.

We paid the cashier and ran back to our hotel, nearly freezing to death in the process. We returned to the relative comfort of our room and devoured our purchases with the rest of our Cristall and the beers. The meal may not have been the most pleasing to the palate I have ever eaten, but given the circumstances it was just fine. We sat around and drank our beers and laughed about the weather. Shortly after finishing our beers we turned out the light and went to sleep.

We awoke early the next morning, showered, finished packing and went downstairs to meet Anna and our fellow travelers. We sat down for breakfast, and we could not believe what happened. We were served a cheese omelet with toast and no peas. I guess they had finally run out of the peas. After the quick breakfast we all checked out and piled our suitcases in the back of the van and headed for Sheremetyevo Airport to catch our Finnair flight to Helsinki. Ivan safely piloted us to the airport and Anna helped us through the check-in process and the rather complicated immigration and customs exit procedure.

We thanked Anna for all her help and soon our flight to the Finnish capital was boarding. The short flight of a little over an hour was uneventful. As we deplaned in Helsinki, Warren and I said good bye to Frank and Ed and left the airport to catch the Finnair bus into the city. We spent the next three days exploring Helsinki and threw in a side trip to Tallinn, Estonia, for good measure. We had a terrific time and Warren and I have taken several subsequent trips to Europe together. We are good friends and really enjoy traveling together.

When we arrived back in Indianapolis we got off the plane wearing our new Russian rabbit fur hats. This caused a bit of a stir at the gate and our girlfriends got a good laugh over our new purchases. I still have the darn thing up on a closet shelf and have not worn it since.

CHAPTER 5

CENTRAL EUROPE

HANK, IN THE FALL OF 1999 change, again, was in the air in my life. Secretly the love of my life and your future mother, Jenny Medisch, and I were planning to get married the next spring. In preparation for this blessed event we had decided that we should buy a new home for us to share together, not the house that I had lived in as a bachelor the past fourteen years. We had barely begun to look around when the home of our dreams, about two blocks from where I lived went on the market. In short order, we put in an offer and had it accepted and, within a matter of weeks, I was the proud owner of a new home in which we still live today.

The only catch was to sell the home that I was currently living in. This turned out to be a little more difficult than I had originally anticipated, so for a few months I owned two homes. The only down side of this was I had two mortgage payments to make for an unforeseen period of time. If you have been through this before, you know that this can be a rather stressful period of time. After closing on the new home, and continuing to live in the old one on the advice of my realtor, I decided it was time to get away to Europe to relieve the anxiety before moving into my new abode.

Jenny and I had taken a couple trips together before and we had been quite compatible, but we had not gone to Europe yet. We discussed where we would like to go and it was decided that one of the cities we would visit would be Prague. Her maternal grandmother had emigrated from Czechoslovakia in the early part of the twentieth century and, Jenny, was a first generation American because her uncle was born on the ship in route to Ellis Island. I had the pleasure of visiting Prague on an earlier trip with my friend, Bill Schreiber. It was one of my favorite places I had traveled to and, consequently, it was not a hard sell to convince me to return.

We spent some time planning other potential countries to visit and determined that some of that would be driven by where we could enter and exit Europe. Since I was blessed with two mortgages, I decided to look in to cashing in air miles to cover our airfares. I had traveled a great deal on US Airways, particularly because my hometown, Indianapolis, had served as a mini-hub for them for several years. I had a decent stockpile of miles and decided this was an opportune time to use some of them.

I contacted the airline and determined that US Airways could accommodate our needs. In using free tickets you are often saddled with less than perfect routes and this trip would be no exception. We were to fly to Boston via Pittsburgh and change to Sabena, the now defunct Belgian carrier. Sabena would fly us to Brussels and we would then fly on to Warsaw. We would return from Prague, retracing our steps through Brussels, Boston and then back home. Although this was a less direct route than we would have liked, it was after all, free.

We began to play around with various itineraries and decided we would spend time in Warsaw, Krakow (which had come highly recommended from several of our friends who had recently visited there), Vienna, Bratislava and finish in Prague. I researched the various travel options on moving from city to city and determined that a Eurail pass made the most sense for this trip.

Today there is myriad competition to the rail services from low fare airlines and emerging bus services. It is wise to spend a little time in online investigation of your options if you are putting together a multi-country trip like this one. You might be surprised at how easy it truly is to unearth your options and decide which makes the most sense for you given your budget and time constraints.

Specifically, if you are looking at rail travel there are numerous alternatives including various regional, country particular, and travel companion deals that likely make more sense than a standard Eurail pass in most cases. Additionally, if you are not going to travel to many locations, a point-to-point ticket could be the proper choice for you. If you are concerned about purchasing these when you are overseas, and rail passes must be purchased here before traveling in Europe, they can be readily obtained prior to your departure from the United States. The bottom line is that options abound and are easily determined with a little internet work. To me, planning the vacation and determining your best course is part of the fun of your trip.

POLAND

Finally all the preparation was over, the middle of November rolled around and it was time to go. Our flights to Brussels went well and we cleared customs and awaited our connecting flight to Warsaw. The flight was delayed an hour or so because of weather. Eventually, we boarded our plane and set off for Warsaw. As we approached to land in Poland turbulence began to toss our plane and Jenny and I were ready to arrive. As we broke through the clouds tossing and turning we could see the reason for our delay and rough ride. There was a massive, first snowstorm of the season blanketing the Polish countryside.

As we neared our touchdown, the pilot pulled the plane back upward and we circled the airport careening about. I must confess that I was getting a little anxious and I could see the beginnings of fear creep into Jenny's face. After what seemed to be an eternity, we broke through the clouds once again and we could see the runway ahead of us. As we neared we could see that the airport authorities were frantically working to clear our path for a safe landing. We ultimately touched down without event and taxied to our gate. It was snowing hard, but it soon became apparent to us that the Polish crew working outside was experienced in these matters and our fears were for naught. I guess that if I had thought more clearly, I would have realized that this was commonplace in this climate and if we were going to fly into these conditions we were better off here that in most places in the world.

We passed through Okecie International Airport, a nice modern facility and bought a few Polish zlotys to get us into town. We caught a cab into the city, and as we traveled the fifteen or so minutes to our hotel, you could see the effects of their first major snowstorm of the year. Thank goodness that we had arrived in the early afternoon and traffic was light.

Our driver plowed through the streets and we were soon at our home for the next couple of days, the Hotel Harenda.

The Hotel Harenda is located in the center of Warsaw very near to the University of Warsaw and a short walk into the Old Town. This clean, modestly-priced property suited our needs well because it was so well situated within walking distance of nearly all the sights. We checked in and found our room and, much to our surprise it contained two single beds, not a double. Unable to push the beds together we checked back with the front desk and were told that no double rooms were available. We resigned ourselves to this fact and settled in, showered, changed and hit the street to see the sights.

As we slogged down the snow covered sidewalks we were pleased with our decision to wear our new Gore-Tex boots we had bought earlier that year. **Let me tell you that your choice of footwear can have a huge impact on the quality of your travels.** I firmly recommend that you wear comfortable walking shoes wherever you go unless you are going to be dealing with snow and ice then switch to boots. A sturdy pair of walking shoes is necessary because of the cobblestone and uneven pavements you encounter around the world. Additionally, I would recommend that you waterproof your shoes. This is a simple process to apply waterproofing liquids to your shoes. These products are widely available, but particularly can be found at shoe repair stores. Dry feet can go a long way toward improving your disposition on a rainy day.

We took a quick walk around the immediate neighborhood and decided it was not a great day to venture very far because of the inclement conditions. But, we noticed an inviting bar on the corner next door to the Herenda. We poked our heads in, found a well-placed vacant table and ordered a couple of beers. The tavern quickly filled up with young people, probably students from the nearby university and well-dressed young professionals. The place had a nice vibe, good, inexpensive beer and we settled in to people watch and relax from our travels.

After a couple of hours of sipping beers and making a couple of new friends with the young Poles who were fellow patrons, hunger set in. We returned to our room, freshened up and consulted our Frommer's guidebook for a dinner suggestion. We settled on a place around the corner from the hotel, Uniwersytecki Milk Bar. The milk bar is a uniquely Polish dining experience that clearly harkens back to the Communist era. Known for their inexpensive and tasty food, the milk bar has been a staple of the Polish dining scene for decades.

After a short walk through the snow we entered the Uniwersytecki. The diner was very Spartan, but warm and inviting. It was crowded and appeared to contain many of the same faces we had seen at the bar around the corner earlier. We found a table and discovered this was a mistake because we needed to order our food at the counter. We ascertained that the only menu was posted on the wall and was, of course, written in Polish. The establishment was run by a group of large, middle-aged women that looked like they were remnants of the Soviet regime. They did not speak English, we did not speak Polish. However, we were saved by a young woman patron who spoke our language and could see our dilemma. She interpreted the menu for us, helped us order and pay for our meal. Thank goodness for the kindness of strangers.

Returning to our table, one to the ladies quickly arrived with our orders; cabbage soup and pierogis. What a terrific meal. The cabbage soup, recommended by the young woman who came to our aide, really hit the spot on this cold, snowy night. And this was our first sampling of a pierogi. Pierogis are steamed dumplings filled with various foodstuffs, in this case I believe it was pork. This was the beginning of a search for the perfect pierogi the rest of our stay in Poland. What a treat and all for around two dollars for both of us.

As we left our little find, we determined that since it had finally stopped snowing we should take a short walk. We turned right out of the milk bar and walked a few blocks and passed the Presidential Palace which was brightly lit and looked lovely in its flocked state. As we walked on we noticed a liquor store across the street and decided to explore their offerings. The friendly clerk saw that I was perusing their supply of Polish vodkas. Although she didn't speak English she was able to assist me in picking out a bottle to take with me as a souvenir. This bottle would come in very handy before the end of our trip.

As we trudged back to our hotel, we once again passed the bar we had enjoyed that afternoon. It was still hopping and we decided to duck in for a nightcap. Settling in again for another couple of beers we really enjoyed this little place. Soon fatigue set in and we decided to call it a night.

Although we had not accomplished a great deal our first day in Warsaw, we had a culturally enriching day and we off to a great start of our trip.

We awoke after a great night of sleep to one bit of bad news. Jenny's back was hurting and it was limiting her mobility, at least initially, that morning. In fact, she was having trouble bending over to tie her boots and I gladly assisted in this task. After showering and preparing for the day we went downstairs to breakfast. Breakfast was served in a dining room on the second floor and was not the usual buffet, rather we were provided with menu options. We both scanned the menu and each chose a dish called the farmer's eggs. Their particular version was a dish of eggs scrambled with ham, onion, and cheese. It was delicious and a great start to our day.

After breakfast our first order of business was to have our rail passes validated for travel which must be done prior to their first usage. We ventured out into the winter wonderland that was Warsaw, armed with a map that was supplied by the hotel. We set out for the central train station, Warszawa Centralna. The station was only about a mile away from our hotel and although it was crisp it was a pleasant walk. By now, the city was awakening and as we neared the station we could see a street market beginning to take shape.

We soon entered the main hall of this rather modern, Soviet era structure. With the help of our Frommer's guidebook we were able to locate the rail office and got our passes validated. Along the way we checked out the train schedules to make certain we knew what track would be utilized, and our departure time for the next day for Krakow. Confident that we were set with the necessary knowledge to make our exit the next day we set out on our next task.

We had decided that it might be important to get seat reservations for our trip. European rail passes entitle you to travel on a train, but it does not avail you a specific seat. Often times this is not an issue as many seats are likely to be free. However, if you are traveling on a popular route and fear that all seats may be reserved, it is advisable to spend a little extra money and pay for a seat reservation. I learned this lesson the hard way a few years before when traveling from Rome to Florence and I had to stand up nearly the whole way. That is not a pleasant prospect for a journey of a few hours.

We followed our guide's advice and sought out an Orbis Travel office to most easily accomplish this task. If the guide was correct the nearest branch was in the vicinity of the Old Town, one of our primary destinations that day. As we departed the station the street market was in full bloom and we decide to browse. Appropriately, some of the big sellers were cold weather clothing and accessories and, Jenny, feeling the chill, purchased a black, woolen scarf that looked great with her green and black coat. The scarf would serve her well throughout the trip, and beyond, as she still uses it today. These types of markets are worth looking through as they can be a source for finding locally made goods that can serve as a useful souvenir of your trip.

The sun was now shining and the city looked attractive, flocked from the previous day's snowfall. We decided to walk the mile or so to the Old Town because it was so beautiful and we could get our bearings for the rest of the day. During our trek it was apparent that Warsaw had been greatly scarred by the Nazis in World War II, with a major portion of the city being leveled. Unfortunately, after the war Poland had fallen into the Communist Bloc and the rebuilding efforts had been led by the Soviets. As such, some of the dominant architecture in the city reflects these efforts and is not as attractive as it might otherwise have been.

In short order we were able to locate the Orbis office and, as we prepared to enter, a huge mound of heavy snow fell from the rooftop above us. This avalanche narrowly missed us. If it had hit us the consequences could have been great as a several hundred pound projectile of snow could have caused serious injury to anyone that was beneath its path. Believe me, this near miss caused us to pay a great deal of attention to what was overhead the remainder of our stay in Warsaw.

Once inside, the kind folks at Orbis were able to assist us in reserving seats for our trip the next day. They could not have been more helpful and it only took a few minutes and cost us a few zlotys to have the peace of mind that we would have prime seats on the train. After we departed, we began to explore the Old Town of Warsaw. Completely destroyed by the Germans in 1944 during the Warsaw uprising, the Old Town area was painstakingly rebuilt through the efforts of the citizens. The designs for the reconstruction largely come from old photographs and paintings. This remarkable effort culminated when UNESCO declared the Old Town a World Heritage Site in 1980.

The beautifully restored area makes for a great walking tour. You can stop and visit such sites as the Royal Palace, Cathedral of St. John, the Old Town Marketplace and the Barbakan, or old city walls which include turrets and a moat. It appears that this area is the soul of the city and a must for any traveler to Warsaw. There are numerous shops and restaurants worth your attention. We took our midday meal in a little Italian bistro on a beautiful square in the Old Town. The food was delicious and the sights were equal to the meal.

In the afternoon, we continued our tour of the city by visiting the neighboring New Town. Just to the north of the Old Town, New Town is another interesting area to visit. Home to several lovely churches and a few palaces, the area also has a nice mix of shopping and restaurants. Tiring and, not wanting to deal with the depressing aspects of the Warsaw ghetto and the fate of the Jewish Poles, we decided to head back to the hotel.

As we returned to the Herenda, we walked the Royal Way and got a daytime view of the Presidential Palace and Potocki Palace which resides across the street. We passed by Warsaw University and once again found ourselves standing outside our favorite pub next door to our hotel. We could not pass up the opportunity to soak up some more of its atmosphere, not to speak of a couple of beers. Wearily we retreated to our room where I helped Jenny remove her boots and we relaxed for a while.

That evening we were tired and decided to try a restaurant next door to the hotel. The main bill of fare was steak, and being red meat eaters we found it to our liking. Our steaks were well prepared and filling. Jenny was able to persuade me to go to the bar on the corner and have one last drink to end our evening. The next day we would be off to Krakow, the Polish city we most wanted to see. We ended up in Warsaw because it was the only point of entry into Poland we could get using my frequent flier miles. It turned out to be an interesting destination and one I would return to if the proper circumstances present themselves.

Awaking at a reasonable hour because our train did not depart until 9:15, we cleaned up and went back downstairs for our morning fortifications. It took us no time to order those delicious farmer's eggs we had eaten the day before and they did not disappoint. Returning to our room we finished packing, checked out and hailed a cab for the train station for the next leg of our journey. Arriving at the station quickly, we located our track and our train soon was ready for boarding. We found our car, located our assigned seats and stowed our luggage.

As we chugged away from Warsaw we were comfortably ensconced in our wide, first-class seats. Our particular rail pass entitled us to ride in first and, although second class travel on most European trains is quite comfortable, first can be almost cushy. This figured to be a pleasant three hour ride to Krakow. Indeed it was a very nice journey through the snow covered Polish countryside. After a short time a server came through the car and we selected some beverages, tea for Jenny and coffee for me.

While we were enjoying our tour and the beverages, Jenny asked me what we were going to do about her relatives when we reached Prague at the end of our trip. I guess I was aware that her Aunt Liz occasionally corresponded with some relations that were still in the Czech Republic, but this was the first I had heard of any expectation we would possibly meet them. I asked Jenny for more information and she fished into her bag and produced some three by five cards with the names and addresses of the folks her Aunt Liz had exchanged letters with in the past. It seems that all the exchanges had been in Czech and were translated by a woman Liz knew that wrote and spoke the language.

Aunt Liz had not informed any of these folks that we were coming, so we had to devise a way to contact them and, hopefully, arrange a way for us to meet. I thumbed through the half dozen or so cards and was able to ascertain that only one of them had a Prague address. I had been in Prague several years before and knew where the tourist information center was located, unless it had moved. We decided that our best tack was to go to the tourist information center when we arrived and see if someone could place a call to them and explain our situation. The prospect of meeting Jenny's relatives who still lived in the old country excited both of us. This topic was the major source of conversation the rest of the way to Krakow.

It seemed like no time had passed before we arrived in Krakow's main train station, Dworzec Gowny. The station serves as a transportation hub for the region and, knowing that we had a couple of side trips planned out of the city, we had made reservations at a hotel nearby. As we exited the station we looked to the left and there was our home for the next three days, the Hotel Europejski.

The Europejski is located at the south end of the train station and across the street. We took the two minute walk to the front door and upon entering, we stepped back in time. We soon learned its interesting history. The hotel was built in 1884 and was not only well situated, but a comfortable accommodation. During a period of years under the communist regime, the hotel was confiscated from its owners and fell into horrible disrepair. Finally in 1991 with the restoration of a democratic government, the hotel was returned to its rightful owners. The owners set about resurrecting the hotel and returning it to its place as a viable, cozy lodging. They succeeded. In fact, Jenny, our son, Hank and I returned to the Europejski a few years ago and it is an even finer establishment.

We received a warm welcome from the staff when we arrived. Although it was only a little past noon they assured us our room was ready and showed us to our place on the second floor. The room was quite large and well appointed. I would venture to say the bathroom was even quite elegant. We unpacked, settled in and rested for a few minutes before setting out to see the city. It was becoming apparent that our first order of business was to find someplace for lunch.

We set out toward the Old City being cautious because of the ice-packed sidewalks. We crossed under a main thoroughfare and entered into a park-like areas. Soon we could see the structure of the old city wall and found our way to the Florian Gate, the last remaining of seven original gates into the city. The Florian Gate is the opening onto the street that is known as the Royal Route that runs from north to south through the Old City ending at the Wawel Castle.

As we moved toward the center of town our thoughts returned to our hunger and we began to search for a place to appease this need. Soon we were downwind of a wonderful and familiar aroma, pizza. We spotted the source and quickly entered a warm, cozy Italian restaurant. We were greeted by a lovely, young Polish girl who showed us to a table. We wasted no time in ordering a pizza and beer. As we waited for our food we began to plot out the remainder of the day. We settled on touring the city on foot, starting with the Wawel Castle.

Our piping hot pizza and cold beers arrived in short order and we quickly dispatched of the tasty lunch. As we were finishing our beverages we noticed that the snow had begun to fall again. We settled our bill and set out on our tour. To reach the castle we had to walk through the Rynek Glowny, or the Main Market Square. On one side of the square is the grand Gothic cathedral of St. Mary's. Being a good Catholic girl, Jenny had to go in, light a candle and say a prayer for some family members. The large structure was built in the 13ᵗʰ and 14ᵗʰ centuries and is quite impressive. The massive wooden alter is worth the visit inside itself.

The huge square is bisected by the Cloth Hall, an arcade which was built in the 13ᵗʰ century as a commercial center. It is still used as a merchandizing center today and we decided to take another detour from our mission to take a look inside. The Cloth Hall is a large, covered structure that is open on the ends. Inside, there are rows of small shops selling handicrafts that are all produced in Poland. You can find anything from fine crystal ware, to hand-woven baskets, clothing, foodstuffs, works of art and other souvenirs. We were impressed by the fine workmanship displayed by many of the vendors. We decided to just browse at this time, but we knew we would be back later because the wares were impressive and the prices were very reasonable.

As we continued on the Royal Route we passed interesting shops and eateries. You don't have to travel too far before you realize that Krakow did not suffer the same fate as Warsaw had at the hands of the Germans in World War II. We had been told by several friends who had visited the city that is was beautiful and they had not steered us wrong. After a while we began to ascend the hill on which the Wawel Castle and Wawel Cathedral reside. The imposing structures cut an impressive figure perched atop the rise.

The Wawel Castle was begun in the Middle Ages and brought to greatness by Polish kings during the Renaissance. The structure, which served as home to Polish royalty for several centuries, was largely untouched by the world wars and is revered by the locals as a symbol of Polish pride. We toured the various aspects of the castle, the treasury, armory, and the Royal Castle rooms. The rooms contain a collection of Flemish tapestries that were kept in safekeeping during World War II in Canada.

After visiting the castle we poked our heads into the Wawel Cathedral. The cathedral was started in the 14ᵗʰ century and has seen several additions and revisions in succeeding centuries. We visited several chapels contained within the cathedral and saw the crypts of numerous famous Poles, but the prize for us was the bell tower. The tower houses the Zygmunt bell which was cast from a captured cannon in the 16ᵗʰ century. Although it is a bit of a hike, the view from the bell tower is breathtaking.

We soon began our descent back toward the city and eventually our hotel. As we passed into the Main Market Square we decided to nose around the shops that lined the south side of the square. Soon we happened upon a shop that we were in search of finding. The small space displayed the Christmas ornaments produced by an American who had set up production in Krakow, Christopher Radko. Jenny had learned about Radko from her friends, Mary Downs and Joe Kernan, who had discovered his works on an earlier trip to Krakow.

We are collectors of Christmas ornaments. It is a journey my mother, Nancy Fleetwood, who is a world traveler, started me on year's earlier by bringing me back ornaments from her travels. I began to reciprocate and, when Jenny and I got together, she joined me in this practice. This was not a difficult sell to get Jenny involved in collecting Christmas ornaments. She is a holiday maven, with Christmas at the top of the list. I have always said that if I didn't discourage her, she would decorate our house for Ground Hog's Day, which is how big a holiday girl she is.

Well, if you are unaware of Christopher Radko, he produces arguably some of the finest hand-blown glass ornaments in the world. According to the Christopher Radko Company website, the whole venture began when Christopher's family tree toppled over smashing over a thousand mouth-blown glass ornaments. Christopher began a search across the United States and Poland to find replacements. Unable to do so, he hooked up with a Polish glass blower and together they began to recreate the family heirlooms.

On that cold, snowy afternoon we fell in love with the works of this duo. Deciding not to wait, we picked out and purchased a few of these fine ornaments and they continue to adorn our tree each holiday season. We have acquired several other Radko's in subsequent years and they all are very special to us. They are positioned prominently on our tree with Jenny taking great care to insure each is very visible.

Spent from the day's activities and with darkness fast approaching, we decided it was time to return to our hotel and rest before going out to dinner. As we trudged through the snow packed streets the snow began to fall and the temperature seemed to drop. Entering the warmth of the Europejski we ambled to our room, pulled off our boots and laid down on the bed for a rest. Soon we were introduced to a pleasant aroma as the restaurant downstairs began to prepare dinner. Weary from the day we decided to just stay in and eat at the hotel.

After our rest, we descended the stairs and decided to position ourselves at a table in the bar for dinner. The pleasant, young server brought us large mugs of fine Polish beer as we began to study the menu. We soon discovered our choice for that evening's meal, pork filled pierogis. These piping hot dumplings soon arrived and I was quickly satisfied. As we devoured our meal, Jenny noticed that there was a familiar looking show on the television over the bar. As she watched for a while she realized it was the Polish version of the Millionaire. It was a reasonably new show at home which I had not seen yet, so my first experience with the program was in Polish. As the Millionaire ended, so did our meal. Weary from our travels we decided it was time to head to bed knowing that tomorrow would be another full day.

We awoke to a sunny, but cold, morning in Krakow. We cleaned up and went downstairs for a delicious breakfast. After filling up on the diverse offerings on the buffet and several cups of coffee, we decided to brave the cold and set out on our day. We bundled up and made our way to the train station to put our rail passes to use again. We had decided to catch an early train to Auschwitz.

There are two interesting side trips to be taken from Krakow and we decided to tackle the most compelling one first, Auschwitz. About an hour train ride west from the main railway station in Krakow, the industrial city of Auschwitz is home to one of the most stark examples of man's inhumanity to man, the Nazi concentration camps of Auschwitz I and Auschwitz II, or Birkenau. The ride through the Polish snow-covered countryside was pleasant enough, but it was filled with anticipation of what lie ahead. How do you react to such atrocities?

When we arrived at the station in Auschwitz we decided to look for the local bus that would take us to the concentration camp. Not knowing exactly where we were going, it soon became obvious as several fellow travelers were heading to the bus stop which turned out to be clearly marked. As a rule, when traveling to destinations such as this, don't worry too much about knowing exactly how to make your way. There are nearly always fellow tourists, or locals, that will gladly assist in helping you with logistics. After all, in a community like Auschwitz, visitors are probably coming to see one thing.

Shortly, the bus arrived and took us to the Auschwitz Museum. As we departed the bus and approached the gate, you could feel the level of anxiety rising inside of you, as well as your fellow travelers. As you pass through the gate with the words ARBEIT MACHT FREI (work leads to freedom) inscribed above, the chill of the day could be felt very clearly. You soon are ushered into a visitor's center where you watch a short film produced by the Soviet Army upon liberating the camp. These graphic pictures have a wrenching effect and bring the heinous nature of the atrocities that occurred here into clearer focus.

We next took a tour of the facility. The main buildings at Auschwitz I, or the original camp, are surprisingly substantial structures made of brick with tiled roofs. Originally built a Polish army barracks, the camp was opened by the Germans in 1940. As you walk through the various buildings you see displays of articles that were confiscated from the prisoners including luggage, eyeglasses and hair shorn from them to be used by German industry. The most sickening to me was a large glass enclosed room filled with prosthetic limbs that had been taken from prisoners as they were put to death. In most all cases, these were removed from people that had lost their arms or legs fighting for the German army in WWI. What a twisted fate!

As we moved from one building to the next you are shown a pond that was built as a small reservoir for fire protection purposes. We were told that during an International Red Cross inspection of the facility during WWII, this pond was presented to the inspectors as a swimming pool, as an example of the humane treatment of the detainees. Elsewhere there were exhibits of photographs of political prisoners with their dates of arrival and death.

Finally, we were taken to view the gas chambers and crematoriums. Over a million prisoners, mostly Jews, were put to death at these camps, making them the largest extermination camps in the Nazi killing machine. Most of these deaths occurred at Birkenau which is a couple of miles away and accessible by bus from Auschwitz. We decided that we had seen enough and did not need to see what remained of that camp.

We caught the bus back to the Auschwitz train station and hopped on the first return train to Krakow. As we took the hour ride back, we spent a great deal of the time in silence trying to process what it was we had just seen. It is nearly unfathomable to comprehend the type of hate that lead to these horrendous slaughters. One can only hope that bringing this issue to light by allowing visitors to see exactly these conditions and processes employed will lead to this never happening again.

We arrived back in Krakow in the early afternoon and decided that lunch would be our first order of business. We ventured back into the Old Town and located a café. Here we ordered a hearty plate full of sausages, sauerkraut and potatoes accompanied by a cold Polish brew. We plotted the rest of our day over lunch and decided there was time to take another short side trip out of the city that afternoon.

Again, acting on the advice of our friend, Joe Kernan, who happened to be the Lieutenant Governor of Indiana at that time and was Jenny's boss, we decided to visit the village of Wieliczka. Wieliczka is home to salt mines that functioned for over seven hundred years. We caught a minibus from the train station for the twenty minute run to the pretty, little city. The bus let us off almost in front of the entrance to the salt mines. We entered the property and reserved a spot on the next English speaking tour which was to begin in 45 minutes. We spent the next half hour walking around the pleasant village of Wieliczka. We window shopped and nosed around a couple of quaint stores until time for the start of our tour.

The salt mines are impressive, not only because of their sheer size, but the fact that over 500 years ago a miner began sculpting in the salt. This tradition has continued and there are now dozens of sculptures of various historical figures and scenes on display throughout the tour. Many of these figures are of religious leaders and entire chapels have been created hundreds of feet below the surface. There is one area that is large enough for big gathering and could, in fact, host a regulation basketball game with seating for hundreds. Unlike many other mediums used in sculpting, salt is translucent and can be backlit to present an even more impressive view. The mine is so unique that it has been designated as a UNESCO World Heritage site.

Concluding our hour long tour, we decided it was time to return to the Europejski for a rest from our travels. We were able to quickly catch a return minibus and soon arrived back at the station area. We retired to our room for a brief rest catching up on the events of the world on CNN in our room. After an hour, or so, regenerated we decided it was time to find some dinner. Although we had a delicious meal at the hotel the night before, we determined that we should venture out and find a suitable restaurant.

Earlier in our stay, we had spied a place that looked inviting from its menu posted outside. Near the Radko shop on the south side of the main square was the Italian establishment, Da Pietro. It turns out that the restaurant is in the basement of the building occupying several vaulted ceilinged rooms. As it was a very cold and snowy night, this atmosphere was particularly appealing to us. A warm hostess greeted us and ushered us to a table in the back of one of the rooms. Here we ordered a nice bottle of Italian wine and two orders of homemade pasta. Soon our server returned with two piping hot plates of delicious pasta. The wine, the pasta, the very reasonable price, oh what a fitting ending to a long day of sightseeing.

After dinner we walked back through the main square and up the Royal Route toward our hotel. As a light snow fell, the Old Town looked magnificent. We agreed with our friends who had recommended Krakow so highly to us that it was indeed a special place. As we walked and talked we planned our activities for our final day in the city. Since we were leaving on a night train departing at about nine-thirty the next evening, we decided to sleep in as late as possible the next morning. Arriving at our room, we were suddenly overcome by the day's events so we peeled off our clothes and quickly fell into a deep sleep.

The next morning we awoke late and had to hustle to make breakfast before they stopped serving. Over another yummy breakfast we decided that our plan of attack for the day was to shop for souvenirs, and our first stop would be the Cloth Hall. Finished with our meal we arranged for a late checkout time and were assured that they had a locked storage room for stowing our bags prior to our evening departure. We returned to our room, packed up our things so we could quickly vacate our room when we returned.

We departed the hotel and ventured forth with all deliberate speed for the Cloth Hall. We had both spotted some beautiful crystal stemware when we walked through the arcade the first day of our trip to Krakow. We had not investigated it thoroughly, but it had certainly piqued our interest. As we walked pass the shops we discovered that several locations offered the exquisitely crafted crystal. We also learned that it was very reasonable priced, as was everything in Poland at that time. Our decision was now which particular pieces did we want and how would we get them home? We narrowed down to a couple of patterns and enquired with each of the vendors if they could ship our wares to the United States. The answer in both cases was a firm "no." We broadened our search and in all cases we got the same answer. We even asked at a crystal shop across the square and they, too, would not ship to the States.

Realizing that we were confronting a problem, we simply decided to buy what we liked and figure out how to get it home after we purchased it. We went back to our favorite shop in the Cloth Hall and bought 12 high ball glasses, 18 white wine glasses, 12 small brandy snifters and a beautiful vase. The shopkeeper boxed them up, not too well, and we decided to try the Polish postal service to see if they could send them home for us.

We had noticed that the main post office was located by the train station across from the Europejski, so we set out on foot for our destination. I don't know if you have ever tried to lug a box containing 42 lead crystal glasses and a large vase, but it is heavy. With both of us putting forth a great deal of effort we were able to barely make it to the post office. Well, when we got inside another story ensued. The Polish women who were running the place were clearly a through back to the not consumer-friendly, Communist era, did not speak English, and had no intention of helping a couple of very needy Americans. All we could get from these women was, nyet, nyet, nyet! Finally, from out of the back of the room came our savior.

A much younger woman, smartly dressed in a woolen suit approached and, in perfect English, asked if she could be of assistance. What a relief! We explained to her that we had just purchased the crystal and would like to ship it home. She politely informed us that they were not able to ship glassware, but *could* ship souvenirs for us. She then looked at our packing job and said it was substandard and that it would not work. They did not have any packing materials at the Polish postal service. She suggested that we go somewhere, repack our souvenirs and return. She gave us the hours she would be working and wished us well.

At a loss for a moment, Jenny suggested that we try the nice folks at the Europejski. It was just across the street and they had been most helpful in all matters during our stay. So, we hoisted the box and made our way to the hotel. When we entered we were greeted by the front desk manager and we explained to him our predicament. Jenny was right, before you knew it boxes and old newspapers appeared and the manager, his assistant, Jenny and I were repacking all our wares. Soon they brought out hot beverages for all and they made a bad situation into a nice experience. When we finished the souvenirs were as well packed as our materials would allow. We truly appreciated this extraordinary customer service and they have two customers for life. We returned to stay there with our son several years later and I hope to repeat again one day.

Taking a deep breath, we headed back across the street for the post office. When we arrived all we could see were the grumpy, old women who wanted nothing to do with us. We nearly panicked, but soon out of a back room our angel appeared. She took our boxes, weighed them, made us attest to the fact that they contained souvenirs, not crystal, and promised that she would do her best to provide a safe arrival for them. We paid her and thanked her profusely. She then informed us that she did not work there on a regular basis, but was merely there that day on a special assignment. We could not believe it, it was like she was sent to help us. I don't know what we would have done without her kind assistance. We may not have been able to get our crystal home without her help. As it turned out, even though the packing job was not great, all but two of the glasses arrived safely to us at home.

By now it was well past noon. We had checked out of the hotel earlier and stowed our bags for pick up later before we were to catch our overnight train. Our first order of business was to find a spot for lunch. We went back to the Old Town and found a café that served some hearty soups and enjoyed them thoroughly. After lunch we spent the rest of the day roaming around the Old Town exploring streets we had yet to walk. It was a cold day and we stopped a few times for refreshments and to warm ourselves.

Tired and hungry we decided that it was time to find a place for our last meal in Krakow. Again, we consulted the guidebook and settled on Gospoda C. K. Dezerterzy. The tavern is located on a side street very near the south entrance to the Main Square. As we entered on this cold, snowy evening we were overcome by the wonderful aromas emanating from the kitchen. The atmosphere was inviting with a very casual, old Poland feel. It was adorned with white linen table cloths, exposed, wooden-beamed ceilings and antiques placed around the room and hanging on the walls. A quick look at the English menu and we were convinced this was the place.

Our server was efficient and soon fetched us a couple of beers as we decide on our choice. As we sipped our beverages we couldn't help but notice that several fellow diners were being served large plates of ribs. Being fans of ribs going way back, we both decided to follow their lead and placed our orders. We both started with a bowl of soup, Jenny had mushroom, and I had bean. Both of these starters were delicious and warmed your cockles on a freezing night. We followed it up with the ribs made in sweet sauce of honey prunes served with potatoes. It was succulent, so tender the meat was nearly falling off the bones, and the portion was huge. It was so good neither of us left a morsel on our plates. Clearly, this was our favorite meal in Poland. **(See Appendix 11 for the recipe)**

We finished our third tankard of beer and declined desert. We were just too full to attempt a final course and had enjoyed our meal so much we were afraid something else might spoil the moment. We called for our check and couldn't believe that this fine meal had been under twenty dollars for the two of us. We thanked our waiter and vowed to return one day. About a decade later we brought our young son here on his first night in Poland and he devoured a plate of these savory ribs. This is a meal not to be missed.

We departed, warmed by the atmosphere and fine meal and made our way through the cold night back to the Europejski. We gathered our luggage and took the short walk to the train station to catch our train to Katowice. We settled into our seats for the ride to Katowice where we were to change for an overnight train to our destination, Vienna. The uneventful trip to Katowice took about an hour and a half and we arrived on time. This gave us about an hour to kill between trains so we set out to explore the train station and locate the correct track for our connecting train. We decided to spend the few remaining Polish zlotys we had and purchased some snacks and a couple of beers.

By now we had less than a half an hour before our train was to depart so we decided to venture into the cold and wait at the track for our train.

We located a bench, opened our beers and waited. We had reserved a sleeping compartment, or berth with two beds, and were looking forward to crawling into those beds and having the rocking motion of the train put us fast to sleep. This was to be Jenny's first overnight train ride and we were anticipating sharing the experience together.

The train was to depart at 12:05 a.m. and we assumed it would arrive about five to ten minutes in advance of that time. As we sat in the cold and waited, midnight passed and we began to worry. After a couple of minutes I dashed downstairs to catch another look at the train board to make sure that the track had not changed. Running back up to join Jenny there still was no train. Soon a train arrived, but it was a local one, not an international which contained sleepers. The local train boarded its passengers and I checked with the conductor and he assured me that this was not our train. As this local train departed and no other was in sight, panic began to set in.

It was now 12:30 a.m. and we did not know what to do. I hurried back downstairs and the train to Vienna did not appear on the board. I rushed back, got Jenny and went to the main part of the terminal to try and figure out what was going on. Nearing one in the morning the station had thinned out, all that remained were a few undesirables. I approached the ticket counter and it was unoccupied. I banged on the glass repeatedly and finally an elderly woman came to the window. We could not speak each other's language, but I finally received the message: there were no more trains that night.

We will never know what happened. Had we missed the train? Had it been cancelled? We don't know but, first and foremost, we needed to find a place to stay that night. We exited the station and began walking, hoping we would run into a hotel. The neighborhood was commercial, but little activity was going on and I fear what was, was illegal. A few people offered to help, but we declined fearing the worst.

We walked a couple of blocks and spied a high-rise hotel in the not too far distance. It appeared to be within a simple walk, but we couldn't figure out how to get there. Suddenly a taxi appeared and we asked him to take us to the hotel. We piled our luggage into the trunk and sped off. We appeared to be headed in the wrong direction and soon we were going through a tunnel that had the feel of something out of the movie,

A Clockwork Orange. Jenny became very scared and thought it might all end that night in Katowice. We soon emerged from the tunnel and right in front of us was the gleaming hotel. Our driver had delivered us safely and, except for a minor "freak out," we were fine.

The cab driver told me what we owed him and I fished in my pocket and found that I had only a couple of zlotys left. We had decided to rid ourselves of them earlier because they would be of little use to us in Austria. Speaking little English we attempted to remedy the situation. I offered to pay him what I had left in zlotys and the remainder in U.S. dollars. I am confident that by now he realized that we were stressed, so he simply took the meager amount of zlotys, helped us with our bags, smiled broadly and bid us a good night. He had been another angel sent to help us and we had not recognized that until the end. Jenny later cried that night out of her frustration about our ordeal, but also for not trusting this kind taxi driver and fearing the worst in this situation.

The Silesia Orbis Hotel is a ten-story structure, rather stark concrete structure built in the Communist era by the same travel company we had used to get seat reservations in Warsaw. It clearly had been updated, was quite attractive and most certainly a very safe place to spend our short night. We entered the large lobby area and immediately moved to the front desk which was staffed by a young man and woman. To our delight they greeted us in English, a language we had not heard in the last several hours. We told them our tale of woe, and they could sense our exasperation and deep seated tiredness, and took pity on us. Yes, of course, they had a room for us and it would be sixty dollars for the night including breakfast. The young man from the front desk grabbed up our bags and insisted on escorting us to our room.

He showed us to the elevator and pressed one of the upper floors. When the door opened he led us to the far end of the hall and, using the room key, opened the door. They had not only assigned us a nice room, but we had a suite that stretched the entire width of one side of the building. There was a large sitting room, a dining/conference room, a kitchen area and a large king-bedded sleeping room. Jenny then located the bathroom which was one of the largest and nicest ones I had seen. We thanked our host abundantly.

I left Jenny in the room and returned to the lobby with the front desk person. I then huddled with these two kind folks that had taken care of us and explained our situation in great detail. I picked their brains about what they might know about train schedules, and took advantage of the fact that they had a good command of English. It turned out that they possessed some train schedules and they confirmed that an international train to Vienna departed around ten the next morning. They persuaded me that I should join Jenny and take a rest. They would call at seven in the morning and I could walk over to the station and take care of our passage.

Once again, I thanked these wonderfully helpful people and went upstairs to the room. By the time I arrived Jenny was in bed and watching an English language movie. I shared with her the plan that I would get up at seven, go to the station and figure out when we could continue on to Vienna. It took some persuading, but she agreed to stay behind while I went to the station in the morning and took care of the business. Within a matter of minutes the television was clicked off and we were both fast asleep.

My internal clock woke me just a little before seven. I slipped into the other room to call the front desk and cancel our wakeup call so Jenny could get some more needed sleep. I looked out the window of our suite and in the early morning light I could see the train station. Also, I was able to clearly see a simple path to reach it. I hurriedly showered, shaved, dressed and departed for the station.

Katowice was awakening as I strode toward the station. Not looking nearly as seedy or foreboding as it had a few hours before, it really was a short, pleasant walk. I entered the station and searched out the international train's desk. Luckily there was no one in line ahead of me, and even luckier for me the clerk was a man that spoke some English. I explained our circumstance to him and he could shed no light on what had occurred the night before. What he did do was issue us seat reservations on the next train to Vienna which departed in about two hours. I thanked him and retraced my steps to the Silesia.

Returning to the room I discovered that Jenny awoke when I had left and had been luxuriating in the beautiful bathroom. I laid out what I had discovered at the station as she finished bathing. Soon she was ready and we went downstairs for breakfast. We entered what appeared to be a small ballroom where an incredible breakfast buffet was set up. They had almost anything you could want or imagine. I chose a made-to-order omelet to start with, while Jenny went in another direction. We leisurely enjoyed the wonderful meal, sampling all sorts of delicacies and enjoying some good coffee and tea. Given the circumstances of the last twelve hours, this was one of my favorite breakfasts ever.

Finishing our meal, we returned to the room and packed up our things. Taking one final look around at this amazing suite and wishing we were staying longer, we went downstairs and checked out. As we took the short walk to the station we reflected on what an adventure the night before had been and how several very kind Poles had turned a nightmare into something more than bearable.

As we entered the station we checked, and double checked, the train board to be certain that we knew the exact track for our train to Vienna. We had about fifteen minutes until our departure, but decided to position ourselves at the trackside. Soon our international train roared into the station and we located our car. Shortly our bags were stowed and we were ensconced in our seats. We were both relieved to finally be headed toward Vienna, but realized that the events of the night before would be a good story to tell our friends and family when we got home.

AUSTRIA

The trip from Katowice to Vienna took a little over 5 hours. The first class car was not very full so we were able to stretch out and enjoy the ride. After a while of watching the Polish terrain pass, the rocking motion of the train and the short night before got the best of both of us, and we fell asleep. We were awakened by a Slavic customs agent, as we had now passed from Poland into Slovakia. She checked our papers and quickly moved to the next passengers.

It was now around midday and we were beginning to get hungry. I decided to venture forth and try and locate a dining car that might accept a credit card or U.S. currency, as that is all that I had. We were in luck in that a couple cars away was a dining car and that accepted a VISA card. We talked to a nice German-speaking couple sitting a few rows from us and asked if they would mind watching our things while we went to eat.

They kindly agreed and we retreated to grab some lunch. We both ordered sandwiches and enjoyed the passing view as we grew nearer to Vienna. It seemed that we had no sooner finished and returned to our seats than we were pulling into the Westbahn Hof in Vienna. It was our luck that our train's terminus in Vienna was at this station, because our lodgings for the next two nights was about five minute walking, or one subway stop away.

The Pension Hargita is surely nothing fancy, but it is clean, centrally located and well-suited for our needs. I had stayed there about five years before with my friend, Bill Schreiber. We had arrived in Vienna without a reservation and in a cold, driving rain storm. After we had struck out at three locations in trying to find a room, the kind proprietor of a fully occupied bed and breakfast called the Hargita for us, and luckily they had a room available. Since my previous stay had been pleasant, we decided to try it again and were not disappointed.

We hopped the U bahn from the train station and quickly arrived at our destination. One downfall of the Hargita is there is a bit of a climb up a couple of stories on a spiral staircase to reach the pension. We lugged our bags up the steps and reached the reception. The owner greeted us and showed us to our room up another flight. By now, it was after four o'clock and the sun was nearly faded. Tired from all the travel of the past couple of days, we kicked off our boots, turned on the television and relaxed for a couple of hours.

After getting filled in on all the world's events, we decided it was time to venture out for dinner. Not knowing exactly where to turn we headed down the main street, Mariahilfer Strasse, which ran directly in front of the Hargita. This busy shopping street runs from the Westbahn Hof to the central part of the city. After walking a few blocks we spotted a lively Greek restaurant, Der Grieche. We poked our heads in and were overwhelmed by hospitality in true Greek fashion.

Before we could even size up the place, we were whisked away to a fine table. The smells in the place were overpowering. I knew that I must be really hungry. The very attractive, young woman that greeted us, appeared to be of Greek extraction and spoke English well. It turns out that she was the owner's daughter and she attached herself to us for the evening. Before we knew it wine was flowing and large plates of food were headed out of the kitchen toward our table. We enjoyed a terrific meal of a salad followed by lamb chops and Greek potatoes. It was accompanied by some good, local red wine.

Thoroughly sated, we asked for our check. The young lady soon returned with a large piece of baklava for us to share and a glass of ouzo for each of us, compliments of the house. What a sweet ending to a truly fine meal. All the ingredients for an excellent evening were present; great company, excellent atmosphere and tasty food. Hank, you may recall that we returned to eat at this fine restaurant when we visited Vienna in the fall of 2013.

We settled our very modest bill and headed out into the cold. We had decided to hit the bed early that night and have a full day the next. The walk back to the Hargita was an agreeable one with a gentle snow falling. We were truly moving into the winter season in Austria and that would make the next day's activities even more redeeming. Shortly we were back at the pension and in no time were in bed asleep.

We slept well and awoke refreshed, ready for a big day tackling Vienna. Since we had the snafu with the overnight train from Krakow, we really only had the one full day here and we were determined to make the most of it. We cleaned up and went down a flight of stairs to grab some breakfast. The morning's fare consisted on a hardboiled egg, sliced ham and cheese and fresh breads. After all I had eaten the night before I needed little, but it really hit the spot. I finished my third cup of coffee and Jenny her tea and we thanked the kind folks and headed out for the day.

We went out the front door into a cold, blustery day. We descended into the subway which runs beneath the Mariahilfer Strasse determining that our first destination should be the core of the city and St. Stephan's Cathedral. The subway stop for the cathedral is practically out the front door, making it quite convenient to visit. The cathedral dominates a lovely square in the center of Vienna. When you ascend from the subway you are struck by the size of the Gothic structure. To me, the most impressive feature of the church is its roof. The colorful tiles that cover the building form mosaics. On one side the double-headed eagle which was the symbol of the Hapsburg Empire is visible. On another side the coat of arms of Vienna and of Austria are impressively depicted.

When you enter the cathedral you are struck by the High Alter, one of several alters that adorn the property. As we wandered through the church, Jenny lit a candle for her relatives and said her prayers. As with many European cathedrals, many famous political and religious leaders have found their final resting places here. Overall, the church is quite notable, not just for its imposing dimension, but also for the fine detail in the construction of its various features.

The area surrounding the St. Stephan's contains many interesting shops and eateries. We window shopped some of the surrounding cobblestoned streets and decided to stop in a café for a hot beverage and a superb pastry. As we warmed ourselves, we plotted our next move. We determined that it was time to explore the Hofburg Palace complex and its many attractions and museums. As we read our guidebook we discovered if we hustled we might be able to catch a practice session of the Royal Lipizzaner stallions.

The massive Hofburg Palace complex was the winter home of the Hapsburgs. It is located in the central part of the city and within walking distance of St. Stephan's. We set out to discover the wonders of the area and locate the Spanish Riding School which is part of the complex. Attempting to get to the daily training session of these talented horses that started at 10 a.m., we walked briskly and were able to locate the school in only about five minutes.

We presented ourselves at the ticket office and requested admission. We discovered that they offered a combination ticket that was good for both the training session and a tour of the Royal Treasury, a nearby museum. As the stallions were set to begin their exercises, we snapped up the combo tickets and went inside. As it turns out, the Lipizzaner stallions get their title of Royal quite honestly, they literally perform in a palace. The setting is really quite amazing. These magnificent equine beauties prance about on an earthen floor in an otherwise opulent showplace.

The practice lasts about two hours as their handlers put these beautiful large, white animals through their paces. With classical music playing the horses train for their routines in a room filled with huge crystal chandeliers. As you might expect during a training session, perfection is being sought. So when the horses are less than ideal, the trainers stop the session, huddle discussing the situation and then redirect the efforts. Even though this was just a practice, it was quite impressive to watch the precision of these amazing creatures.

As the training session wound down, we decided to move on to visit the nearby Royal Treasury. Housed in the Imperial Palace, the treasury is a testament to the power and wealth of the Hapsburg Empire. The museum is divided into and famous for two distinct areas: the crown jewels and its religious artifacts. The crown jewels are reputed to be the finest collection in the world. They include the largest emerald cut in the world, to the imperial crown. The crown dates from the 10th century, and is an awe-inspiring with its collection of diamonds, sapphires, emeralds and rubies. The size of the crown leads one to question if it was ever actually worn for any period of time by a Hapsburg ruler because of its sheer weight.

The religious relics included in the collection reminds one of the ability of ruling empires to gather up priceless works from the lands they conquered. The two most striking pieces in this collection are the nail removed from the right hand of Christ when he was crucified and the Holy Lance which is reputed to have been stuck in Christ's side while on the cross. Additional pieces include an agate bowl thought by some to be the Holy Grail, a tooth of John the Baptist and a unicorn horn. A curious collection indeed, but certainly worth and hour or two of your time to see what the Hapsburgs amassed.

By now it was well past noon and we decided it was time to find a spot for lunch. We referred to the guide and determined that an interesting place was located very nearby. The Augustinerkeller is housed in a cellar under the Albertina Museum in the Hofburg Palace and has been functioning as a restaurant since the 1920s. The vaulted brick ceilings and worn wooden floors make for a cozy, warm atmosphere in which to dine. We were pleased that we were shown to a nice table and presented with an English menu.

Surveying the menu we were presented with an array of Viennese options and were struck by the pleasing smells that filled the dining room. We settled on a couple of locally crafted beers and an order of beef goulash. Soon our servers brought us out huge plates of perfectly prepared goulash with a potato dumpling. The dish, a staple of the Austrian menu since the days of Hungarian inclusion in the Hapsburg domain, included big hunks of cubed beef, carrots, onions, a dill pickle and a frankfurter in a thick gravy heavily spiced with paprika. It was delicious. We devoured our servings as if we had not eaten in days. As we washed this scrumptious lunch with the tasty cold beer, we determined that this place was not to be missed and looked forward to returning in the future.

I am pleased to report that the restaurant is still serving delicious beef goulash, as Jenny, Hank, and I recently returned to Vienna and dined at this wonderful spot. Jenny and I both could not pass on the opportunity to sample the goulash once again. Hank went for the Wiener schnitzel served with fried, cubed potatoes and absolutely loved it. In fact, he became a huge aficionado of the entrée and has eaten it several times since, but proclaims that the Augustinerkeller has the best. **(See Appendix 12 for the recipe)**

We called for our bill and determined it was time to set back out into the cold and snowy day to continue our whirlwind tour of Vienna. We agreed that our next stop should be the Schonbrunn Palace, the summer home of the Hapsburgs. Our travel guide led us to a tram for the journey to the palace. Our first ride above ground provided us with a refreshing view of the city and after about twenty minutes we arrived at our destination.

The Schonbrunn Palace is an imposing baroque structure that is ochre in hue. The palace contains over 1400 rooms and was originally conceived to surpass the Palace of Versailles in grandeur. The building falls short of this goal, but is very impressive none the less. Various tours of the palace and grounds are offered. Given the time of year, amount of time we had and the gardens lying largely dormant, we opted for a tour of the Imperial Apartments. This tour takes you through over twenty rooms including the private apartment of Emperor Franz Joseph and his wife, Elisabeth. It also includes a viewing of the Rocco staterooms in the Palace. I have had the pleasure of visiting numerous palaces around the world and I believe this is one of the most inviting I have viewed.

We had begun to grow weary and decided it was time to start heading back to the Hargita to get some rest before we set out for the evening. We hopped on the tram and headed back into the city and I decided on a small detour was in order before returning to the pension. In Vienna there is a circular series of streets called the ring. There is tram that traverses the ring and many of the major attractions in the city line this route. We jumped on the ring tram and took the half hour tour that passes such sights as the State Opera House, the Radhaus (City Hall), the Imperial Palace and the Parliament Building. This is a great way to get your bearings and see many of the famous public structures from the climate controlled comfort of a tram.

It was now growing dark and we returned to our lodging to rest for a time before setting out to have dinner and to achieve our real purpose for visiting Vienna; going to the Christmas market. After an hour or so, we felt rested and decided it was time to set forth for the Radhaus, sight of the main Christmas market in Vienna. We took the U bahn to the center and soon were standing just outside the Radhausplatz.

If you are a fan of the holiday season, and can possibly see your way to going to Europe at that time of year, the Christmas markets are well worth a visit. They are prevalent in the Northern, Central and Eastern European countries and generally run from around Thanksgiving to Christmas Eve. You can check the internet sites for the tourist information centers in areas you might be visiting to find exact dates and locations. In many major European cities there are often times multiple locations hosting markets that are worth checking out. This time of year is also a great time to travel because it is way off peak and the lines you face at attractions are nonexistent, yet another reason to travel in the late fall, early winter.

The Vienna Radhaus bedecked for the Christmas Market

Jenny is a huge holiday aficionado, and when we started to plan this trip I knew we needed to come to Vienna for this market. A few years earlier my friend, Bill Schreiber, and I had happened upon this celebration quite by accident. He and I were riding the ring tram around sundown and passed the Radhaus. We saw the commotion, decided to investigate, hopped off at the next stop and walked back to the market. We both commented at the time that we would like to return with a woman we were in love with to make the experience a better one.

Well, this was my night. A gentle snow was falling. The whole square was awash in Christmas decorations and music was playing, the ambiance was perfect for the occasion. Just as we arrived a ceremony was starting. It appeared to be the kickoff of the market, with speeches by local politicians, bands playing and trumpeters popping out of the windows of the City Hall hailing the start of the season. This was followed by children's choirs singing and, soon, fireworks. This was an amazingly festive sight.

Every tree, post and structure was decorated for the holidays. Your sense of smell was overwhelmed by roasted nuts, candies, hot mulled wine, sausages and other foodstuffs that filled the air. The entire square in front of the Radhaus was filled with small, temporary huts selling all kinds of wares. There were shops stuffed with locally produced handicrafts, perfect for small Christmas gifts. Other vendors were selling ornaments, many traditional and others that depicted scenes of Vienna and Austria. Couples were strolling arm-in-arm with gluhwein and beers in their free hands. It was a terrific party!

Jenny and I made not one, but two laps around the grounds sipping on the hot mulled wine and enjoying the sights, sounds and smells. We made a couple of purchases of special Christmas ornaments that yet today grace our tree. We nibbled on some roasted almonds and surveyed the other food offerings as we began to grow hungry. We decided that rather than nosh on an appealing looking sausage as we walked around, we would return to our neighborhood and seek out a decent last meal in Vienna.

Feeling the cold and a growing desire to eat, be left the Vienna Christmas Market hoping that one day we would return. We caught a subway back to our neighborhood and scouted out a place for dinner. After walking around the area we settled on the Goldene Glocke not far from the Hargita. The restaurant was warm, dimly lit and welcoming. We were greeted by a pleasant server who showed us to a table next to the front window. An English menu soon arrived and we were pleased to see that Austrian specialties filled the pages.

We both decided to have the Weiner schnitzel with potato salad. I also ordered some sauerkraut, which I thoroughly enjoy, but Jenny has no taste for. Our server brought us both a large stein of Austrian beer and a basket of breads and soft pretzels. We dove into the bread basket as we sipped our beers and waited for our entrees. Soon our plates arrived with the schnitzels so large they were hanging over the sides of the plates. It was all delicious and we polished off everything that was served to us. Wisely we passed on some very appealing looking desserts and settled our bill.

Thoroughly satisfied we took that short walk back to our pension. As this was our last night in Vienna we considered going out for a night cap, but decided instead to call it a night. The cold of being outside for a great deal of time had caught up with us and the warmth of our room felt terrific. We were soon ready for bed and had a brilliant night's sleep.

Our train for Bratislava, our next destination, was not until after 10 o'clock so we were in no rush the next morning. We ambled down a flight of stairs to the main entrance of the Hargita which was the site of the breakfast room. We again enjoyed their offering and lingered for a while over our hot beverages. After breakfast we settled our account and returned to our room to finish packing. We loaded up our belongings and dropped our room key at the office on our way out.

SLOVAKIA

It was a bright, sunny day as we were leaving Vienna and we decided to just walk up the street to the Westbahn Hof to catch our train for Bratislava, the capitol of Slovakia. We arrived at the station, located the track for our departing train and went to the platform. Soon our train was ready for loading and we found our seats and settled in for the short ride of a little over an hour to our destination. The brief trip was uneventful and we were soon pulling into the main station in Bratislava.

Upon arrival we changed some money at the train station and decided that we would just catch a cab to our hotel. Instead of trying to figure out the public transit system at that time, we would wait until we were settled into our hotel and do it when we were ready to go sightseeing. As we left the station we spotted the taxi cab line and joined it. When our turn came, we were assigned a cab with a driver who spoke no English. We were able to communicate to him that we were going to the Hotel Dukla and he acknowledged that he knew where we wanted to go.

I had an uneasy feeling about our driver. I don't know if it was the large scar that ran the length of one side of his face or the shiftiness in his demeanor. All I know is that soon we were on our way and the meter in the cab was whirling with great rapidity. After about five minutes we pulled up in front of the Dukla and got out of the cab. As we were collecting our belongings, he showed me what the amount of our fare was, it was over ten dollars. Instinctively, I knew that this was way too much. I had read about prices in Slovakia and believed that this was way out of line. Sensing no recourse, I paid him and he quickly sped off.

As we entered the Dukla, I located the front desk and we checked in. I asked the woman at the reception if she could tell me how much a cab ride from the train station should be. She informed me that it should be about the equivalent of two dollars. I told how much I had paid and she was outraged. She told me that he had obviously run a "fast meter" scam on us and that we should have come on into the hotel and verified the rate before we paid. I was upset with myself that I had been taken. I have subsequently had this happen to me a couple of more times around the world. I should have taken the Dukla front desk clerk's advice and checked in with someone more knowledgeable in these circumstances, too. I only bring this up because this happens all too often I fear, so check with someone before you overpay for taxi services.

Having said that, the Hotel Dukla is a little bit to the east of the Old Town, but still well located. A modern, Soviet era structure, the Dukla had a feel of the Eastern bloc architecture, but with warm hospitality. We were shown to our room by the front desk personnel and were surprised by how appealing it was. A large room with a king bed, everything was stark white and spotlessly clean. There was a small sitting area, a desk, and a television with international channels. The attached bathroom was very large, equally spotless and was equipped with all the amenities one could want.

We took a few minutes to settle in before we decided to explore the city on the only day we were going to be visiting. We checked with the front desk folks before departing and they supplied us with a very useful map of the city, with tickets and instructions on how to use the bus that stopped almost in front of the hotel, and directions to the Old City. Armed with everything we needed we left the hotel and went to the bus stop. Soon our bus came along and delivered us to the center of the Old Town in about five minutes.

Bratislava reminds me of a smaller version of Prague. There is a castle that dominates the skyline sitting on a hill high above the city. A beautiful river bisects the town, in this case it is one of the world's great rivers, the Danube. In fact, Bratislava is one of four European capitals that are situated on the Danube. The Old Town is compact and filled with pastel colored buildings that reflect various periods of architecture. In all, our first impressions of the city were quite positive, and remain so to today.

Our bus dropped us off right in the heart of the city. We were a few short steps from St. Michael's Tower and the main entrance into the Old Town. The Old Town is filled with pedestrian only streets and is easily navigated by foot. We soon arrived at the main town square, Hlavne namestie, lined on one side by the Old Town Hall. Much to our surprise and pleasure, the square was abuzz with workers setting up for a Christmas Market. Some of the vendors were putting out their wares and we thought we were in luck and would be able to return that night to view it in its full glory.

We struck up a conversation with one of the exhibitors who was arranging his ornaments meticulously throughout his booth. He spoke excellent English and informed us that the market would not officially open until Friday evening, or the next night. We were crestfallen, but browsed the area as the set up continued. We were able to get a good feel of how the square was going to look the next evening and only wished we had one more day in Bratislava so we could more thoroughly enjoy the event. As we passed by the shop of the first vendor we had spoken to, we saw he now had a lovely arrangement of small, hand-blown glass birds. We were able to persuade him to sell a couple and we got our pick of the flock. The precious little creatures made it back with us safely and every Christmas remind us of our visit to this lovely little city.

We decided to move on and take the twenty minute, or so, hike to the top of the castle. It was a bit of a strenuous uphill climb and when we got to the top we discovered the castle was closed, a bit of a disappointment. However, the views back down the hill onto the Old Town and the Danube below were well worth the effort. We took in the vistas for a while and realized that it was early afternoon and we had not yet eaten lunch. This needed to be remedied.

We soon began our descent and our search for an appropriate luncheon location. As we made our way down the hill we decided that our midday repast could wait a few more minutes to allow us to duck into the nearby Cathedral of St. Martin. The cathedral, the main church in the city, is an imposing structure with a long history. It was the site of the coronation of numerous Hungarian kings and queens during the Turkish occupation of Hungary when Bratislava served as the Hungarian capital. The communist treated the building with less respect constructing a major freeway right outside its front door. We peeked inside and Jenny dutifully lit a candle and said her prayers.

We exited St. Martin's and began to get more serious about taking care of our hunger. I had once again consulted our guide and decided that a beer hall on the other side of the Old Town looked intriguing. As we began our walk across town, I started to feel like I was coming down with something. I began to cough and have chills, this was not a good sign. As we made our way toward Stara Sladovna, I realized that I had miscalculated the distance and we should have taken a bus or grabbed a cab.

After what seemed to be forever, we found our luncheon destination. The Stara Sladovna was a large, multi-level establishment with a traditional Slovak beer hall on the first floor and an Italian restaurant of the second level. We settled in to the main level and ordered large steins of the local pilsners. By now, I knew that I was definitely feeling poorly and my immediate solution was to try and drown it in alcohol and some good soup. Our half-liters of beer quickly arrived with menus that contained some clues in English. I scanned the room and saw a hearty, stew looking dish and decided to place my order.

Our server returned and we ordered, Jenny a chicken dish and I, the beef stew. It didn't take long before our meals arrived and we made quick work of them. I was really feeling flu-like symptoms now and so we finished up, paid our bill and departed. We decided that the next move would be to return to the Dukla and rest up. We caught a return bus and soon were back at our hotel.

We arrived back in our room and decided that I should try and take a nap. I quickly undressed and slid under the comfy duvet that covered our king bed. In no time I was asleep and only awoke when I suffered from chills related to my illness. After a couple of hours I awoke and felt somewhat better, although not entirely myself. Jenny and I began to discuss what we were going to do that evening. I suggested that I did not know if I wanted anything else to eat and might just try to go back to sleep.

Jenny then gently reminded me that it was Thursday, not just any Thursday, but Thanksgiving! I had completely forgotten and felt badly because I know how important holidays are for her. She then offered that maybe we should just try the dining room in our hotel. A few minutes later after we had spruced up a little we stepped off the elevator and into the Dukla's restaurant. We had not been in the dining area yet, and were pleasantly surprised to see how nice it was. Clearly, the whole hotel had undergone some renovation since the communist days, but the restaurant was nicely upgraded.

We were met upon our arrival by an attractive young woman who seated us at a very nice table. The large room was about half filled with patrons seemingly enjoying good food and quiet conversation. I decided that an orange juice would be appropriate given my condition and Jenny ordered a glass of red wine. The server provided us with English menus, of which we perused. I think we were a little disappointed, but not surprised, that turkey and all the trimmings did not appear as an offering. Despite this fact the options did, however, look promising.

By the time our drinks had arrived, Jenny had convinced me that I needed a small glass of vodka to go with the orange juice to further ward off the flu. We placed our orders; Jenny would have Chicken Kiev and I, hunter steak. Our waitress returned shortly with a glass of vodka that had just been removed from a freezer and we enjoyed the drinks and the surroundings. After a short wait our dinner appeared and we were anything but disappointed. I remember enjoying that hunter steak like it was yesterday. Jenny enjoyed her chicken dish, also. This turned out to be one of the most memorable Thanksgiving dinners of my life, thus far. Although I have only had a few meals in Slovakia, I think I would be hard pressed to top this one. The atmosphere, the company and the food were all of the highest quality. **(See Appendix 13 for the recipe)**

We lingered for a while sipping after dinner drinks and enjoying the moment. We paid our very modest bill and retired upstairs for the night. The rigors of travel and my illness were catching up with us and we went straight to bed. We awakened the next morning and I was feeling somewhat improved. We cleaned up and went back down to the restaurant for our last meal in Slovakia. It turned out that the restaurant was equally as appealing in the daylight and the breakfast offerings were up to the quality we had experienced the night before. We finished our meal, returned to our room and made final preparations to depart. We checked out and bade the Dukla a fond adieu.

The hotel had a cab waiting for us to take us back to the train station to catch our mid-morning train for Prague. Our taxi driver was a very pleasant man who provided us with a nice ride to the station. I watched the cab's meter gently inch forward during our ride and when we got to the station the cabby told us we owed him the equivalent of two dollars, with a decent tip included. Life was better on the way out of Bratislava than it was on our arrival.

CZECH REPUBLIC

We easily located our train and found our assigned car. Packing away our belongings we settled in for the trip that took a little over four hours. We enjoyed the scenic views of the rolling Slovak and Czech countryside as we made our way toward Prague. I could tell that Jenny was a little anxious to find out about a potential meeting with her relatives. We discussed our plan which was to first check into our hotel and then make our way to the Tourist Information Center to see if they could assist us in locating her cousins.

We arrived at the main train station in Prague, Praha Hlavni Nadrazi. The Art Nouveau structure is a bustling place that is connected to the Prague public transit system by subway and tram. We exited the station and found the subway headed the direction of our home for the next few days, the Hotel Balkan. The hotel was only a couple of stops from the station and about a three blocks walk from there. It is in the Smichov district west of the river, between the Old Town and Prague Castle. The working-class neighborhood is not a touristy area, but is safe and convenient. We entered into the small lobby area and were greeted by a young woman who spoke great English. They indeed had our reservation and she showed us to our blue-toned room. Certainly not the Ritz, but our room was spacious, clean and met our needs.

We unpacked and relaxed for a few minutes before venturing out to find the Tourist Information Office. The young lady at the front desk supplied us with a good map and directions to the tourist office which was still located where it had been when I had visited Prague a few years before. We set back out to the subway and rode to our stop. We emerged from the underground and only had a couple block walk to our destination.

We quickly located the Tourist Information Office and entered to a warm reception. The woman who greeted us spoke English quite well and Jenny began to explain her story to the kind person. She showed the woman the 3 x 5 card that had the name and address of her father's first cousin printed on it. The clerk located a Prague telephone book and began to search for Jenny's kin, Jaroslav Novotny. It turns out that the name Jaroslav Novotny is about as common as Jim Smith is in the United States, making the task slightly more difficult. Finally, she was able to locate their phone number and we asked her to place the call since she spoke Czech.

The clerk had a lengthy conversation with Jaroslav's wife, Vlasta. No one in the household spoke English and they were not aware of Jenny, but they would try to locate a translator who could assist with a visit. We were to check back in an hour. We thanked the kind lady and decided to go do some quick sightseeing to kill the time. Since we were in the center of the Old Town I thought that we might take a short visit to the Old Town Square, Staromestske nam. We set out to see the sights.

Let me say that Prague is one of my favorite cities to visit. It was fortunately spared the ravages of the world wars and has a beautiful historic center. The city is filled with wonderful architecture and the spires from the multitude of churches that abound create a lovely silhouette. Many of the buildings that line the cobblestone streets are pastel colored. There are a number of streets that are pedestrian only making for a great walking environment. Many of the main sights are within walking distance of each other, those that are not are generally easily reached by public transportation.

The public transit system in Prague is another reason to like the city. The metro area is well served by multi-modal transit; subways, trams and buses, all efficiently move people around. It seems to me that the old Eastern bloc made a number of serious mistakes, but one thing they consistently invested in and got right was public transportation. The subways are convenient and the stations are well placed, so you do not have a long walk from them to the top attractions. One word of caution, the subways in Prague tend to be deep underground and the escalators that take you to the surface are very fast. So, when you prepare to enter or exit, jump on and hold on.

As we walked the streets and narrow passageways toward the Old Town Square you could feel the excitement of a Friday afternoon as the weekend was approaching. As we neared the square I was looking forward to seeing Jenny's reaction to this lovely square. When I had visited a few years before I was struck by the openness of the space and the beautiful churches, buildings and shops. I knew she would have a special kinship with the area because of her family roots in the Czech Republic.

As we entered the square I was dumbstruck by what we saw. The beautiful open space was now filled to capacity with a huge Christmas market and this was its opening day. I couldn't believe it, rows and rows of temporary wooden chalets now stood in neat alignment with vendors preparing to sell Christmas gifts, ornaments, local foods and, of course, hot mulled wine, hot chocolate, and beer. There was also a large stage for performances and what may have been the world's largest Christmas tree, meticulously decorated. Jenny's eyes were bigger than saucers as she surveyed the sight. I knew now that we were going to be spending additional time in this area over the next few days.

We spent some time strolling around the market watching final preparations take place for that evening's opening. In no time our hour was up and we started back to the Tourist Information Office. As we entered the office, the clerk who had assisted us hailed our return. She quickly placed another call to the Novotnys and discovered that their efforts to locate a translator had gone for naught. They had gone to the nearby school in hopes of finding someone there to assist us. However, by the time they arrived on that Friday afternoon it was closed for the weekend. Since we were leaving early on Monday morning, the school was of no benefit. They had no other suggestions, but told the clerk that if we were able to come up with a solution they would be home all weekend.

We discussed the matter with the kind folks at the Tourist Office, but they had no ready fix for our problem. Disappointed, we thanked the people at the tourist bureau for all their assistance and headed out into the cold. It was now growing dark and a gentle snow was falling. We determined our best course of action was to return to the Balkan, rest for a while and contemplate our dilemma. The subway was nearby and soon we were back in our hotel.

We stopped to chat with the very pleasant young lady, Sylvia, who was working the front desk. She gave us some tips on the transit system, largely that the tram stopped a lot closer to the hotel than the subway station. She believed it was quicker and more convenient to use the tram to get most places than the subway. In the future we followed her advice and used the tram more extensively, which was easier and also provided us with a great view of the city as we moved about. Additionally, Sylvia gave us a tip on a restaurant a couple of blocks away, in case we did not want to venture back into the Old Town one night.

We got to our room and kicked off our boots for a rest period. Jenny fell asleep for a while and I checked out the English language channel on the television. When she awoke we began to discuss our options for the evening. We were thoroughly warmed being in our room and the thought to venturing out into the night was a little daunting. We determined that we basically had three options; stay and dine in at the small restaurant in the hotel, venture out into the city and visit the Christmas market eating somewhere nearby it, or try the neighborhood place Sylvia recommended.

We decided that the third option was the most attractive to us that evening. As we left we informed Sylvia of our plan and got solid directions from her. We poked our heads out the door and realized it had gotten very cold while we rested. The snow was still falling and a stiff wind was blowing as we trudged toward our destination which was only a couple of blocks away. Shortly we arrived at the spot and peered through the lace curtains that covered the windows. It looked inviting serving traditional Czech food, and we decided to give it a try.

As we entered we were greeted by a very pretty, blond woman in her 30s, dressed in a traditional Czech costume. The restaurant, U Matouse, was packed with what appeared to be locals that were out for a Friday night of food and fun. She soon figured out that we weren't from there and was very accommodating. It seemed every table in this small dining room was taken, but shortly she had cleared a table for us. The place was bright, well-appointed with antiques throughout the room with linen cloths covering all the tables. It was warm and the patrons were obviously enjoying their meals and libations.

We settled into our table and soon realized that we were probably the only native English speakers in the place and possibly the first in quite a while. It soon became apparent that the pretty lady that greeted us and her equally handsome, dark-haired husband were the proprietors. Much as you would expect, there were no English menus, but the couple spoke some English and were most willing to explain the bill of fare, as best they could.

One thing we could easily order was a nice cold Czech beer, some of the best in the world. The blond quickly returned with two brimming steins of Budvar, the original Budweiser, and one great beer. After attending to other tables for a while which allowed us to consume some of our beers, the couple came to our table in tandem. Between the two of them, with some help of gestures, we were able to understand all the offerings. As I recall, we both ordered pork medallions with dumplings and vegetables.

Our waitress returned in short order with our brimming plates of food. The presentation was very appealing and the food was outstanding. Our pork dishes were prepared in a white wine sauce that was delicious and the veggies and dumplings were also equally good. As we enjoyed our meal, we began to discuss how to connect with the Novotnys. Under the circumstances, Jenny came up with a brilliant idea. She decided to compose a letter of introduction and ask Sylvia to translate it for us. We would then ask her to call the Novotnys and find an appropriate time we could go to their home to present the letter and, at least, meet them. Perfect!

We finished off our entrees as we drank a couple of more of those fine beers. After a time, the owners appeared with apple dumpling deserts which we had not ordered. They insisted we try them, as best we could tell they were a house specialty. Although the simultaneously sweet and tart treats would not fit into hardly anyone's diet, they were out of this world. What a fitting ending to a truly wonderful meal. We settled our ridiculously small bill and said goodnight to the nice couple that ran the fine establishment. As we strolled back to the Balkan we were filled with the warmth of the fine meal and hospitality.

We soon arrived back at the room and decided it was time to go to bed, we knew we had a big day tomorrow. We slept well and awakened refreshed with the last lingering effects of my flu now gone. We cleaned up and went downstairs for breakfast. The a la carte breakfast featured several options and we both went for the cheese omelet, which proved to be a tasty and filling choice.

As we were departing breakfast we noticed that Sylvia was once again staffing the front desk. Jenny asked her to assist with translating the letter of introduction. Sylvia graciously agreed and Jenny began to write the letter. After a short while it became obvious to Sylvia what the letter was about. She stopped Jenny and proposed an alternative, why didn't we invite Jaroslav and Vlasta to the Balkan and she would serve as our translator. Jenny suggested that we would not want to impose on her, but she would hear none of it. Further, she explained that tomorrow afternoon or evening would be the perfect time. The Balkan only had two of its 26 rooms reserved (one by us), the restaurant and bar would be open, and she would not be busy. She said she would call them and invite them over for the next day. We thanked her profusely and went upstairs to prepare for a day of sightseeing.

We came back downstairs to leave in about a half hour, and Sylvia greeted us with a very warm smile. She had talked to the Novotnys and they had accepted our offer and were coming to visit the next day at around four. Jenny was brimming with excitement as we headed out the door to catch the tram. She could hardly wait to meet her dad's first cousin, Jaroslav, and his wife, Vlasta. This would be the first meeting between the two parts of the family in over 80 years, pretty heady stuff.

Our first order of business was to catch the tram in the direction of the Prague Castle. There are various ways to get to the castle, primarily by tram or subway. I have found it easiest to catch the tram which, if you stay on it long enough, will take you to the top of the hill instead of climbing to the top from the subway station. You can then walk through the castle seeing all the sights and depart by walking down the hill and either catch the subway or tram at the bottom of the hill. There are also numerous vendors selling unique souvenirs on the side of the hill. You can make any purchases on the way down, so you don't need to carry them up the hill.

We caught the tram almost outside our hotel and rode it to the top of the hill near the entrance to the castle. We took the short walk toward the castle and entered the large cobblestone square that lies just outside of the castle. Just as we were arriving we could tell some activity was about to occur. Soldiers in dress uniform were amassing on the far side of the square. I then looked at my watch and realized that it was approaching noon and we were about to witness the changing of the guard.

We entered the castle grounds through a gate and were in another cobbled courtyard. Here people were beginning to line up to watch the ceremony. We fell into the line at what we believed to be the most advantageous location to view the goings on. Soon castle guards were marching into the courtyard and others were queuing, readying to be replaced. Shortly the palace windows opened to reveal uniformed trumpeters and drummers that produced music that called the marching soldiers to action. After about fifteen minutes the procedure was over, with the new guard taking over and old retreating out of the courtyard from whence the their replacements had arrived. We felt very fortunate to witness the ceremony and the serendipitous occurrence that had lead us to be there at the proper time to be part of it.

We now moved on further into the castle grounds and reached the point where we needed to purchase tickets. We located the ticket office and purchased the appropriate ducats for the portions of the grounds we wished to visit. After moving through the impressive Mathias Gateway we entered into a second courtyard. Here you begin to see why the castle is listed as a UNESCO World Heritage site. You can easily spent several hours visiting the various sites, both political and religious. We spent a couple hours and only scratched the surface.

There are numerous impressive structures to visit. One of the first buildings you encounter is St. Vitus Cathedral which is an imposing Gothic structure. Inside its walls are several chapels including the St. Wenceslas, which holds the Bohemian Crown Jewels and the remains of the "Good King." The Royal Crypt contains the worldly remains of several

Czech kings and the church has numerous stained glass windows that are well worth viewing.

A short stroll leads you to the Old Royal Palace. Dating from the 12th century, the palace was home to royalty for centuries. In the center of the building, Vlatislav Hall, is a huge space used for coronations, banquets, and other official functions. Moving on you come to the Convent of St. George, which as the name implies was once used as a convent, but now houses the National Gallery which holds an impressive collection of Czech art.

The oldest religious structure, the Basilica of St. George, is further into the grounds. An excellent example of Romanesque architecture the church dates for the 10th century and contains the crypts of several early Czech rulers. Further into the castle area you encounter the Golden Lane toward the back of the property which is not to be missed. Named for the gold merchants who called the area home in the 17th century, the colorfully painted houses are tiny and built into the arches in the wall. Several notable persons have occupied these homes including the noted author, Franz Kafka.

As you move to the rear of the castle you come upon the ramparts with their sweeping vistas of the Vltava River and the Old Town beyond. The views here are truly stunning so be sure to have plenty of battery in your camera for this photo opportunity. From here we began our decent toward the city below. The long climb down the hill is a pleasant one because of its beautiful sights, but also the browsing one can do at the various vendor locations, many selling unusual souvenirs.

As you reach the bottom of the hill, subway and tram transportation awaits you. However, on this sunny day we decided to walk back toward the city with our first order of business finding a place to stop for lunch. As we ambled along toward the Charles Bridge we happened upon an inviting looking establishment that was in the tip of a flatiron building. We entered and discovered that they served Czech food and had an English menu, we were in luck.

Even though it was a sunny day, it remained cold and there was still snow on the ground. I decided that a warm goulash would hit the spot with me. Jenny chose a bowl of potato soup and we each ordered a large draft Pilsner Urquell. Our young server returned with our cold beers that were perfect for the occasion. The restaurant had a very rustic, Old World feel, was filled with antiques, and the patrons seemed to be enjoying their lunches. Ours soon arrived and we made quick work of our orders. We sucked down another beer and settled our bill.

We ventured back out into the day and walked a couple of blocks when we arrived at one of the most famous landmarks in Prague, the Charles Bridge. The pedestrian-only structure is over six hundred years old and lined with statues on both sides of the bridge. The dark coloring, due likely to years of soot build-up, adds to the ambiance. As we crossed the bridge a veritable party was taking place. Lined from one end to the other by tourists, vendors, and artists, the atmosphere is akin to Bourbon Street in New Orleans, less the open containers of alcohol.

Jenny and I sitting on the Charles Bridge with Castle in background.

When you reach the far, or Old Town, side of the river the bridge has a tower that can be climbed up for a fee. The hike up is a bit of work, but the views down on to the bridge and across the river at the Prague Castle make it well worth the trek. Climbing down we continued toward the Old Town Square along the pedestrian filled streets. If you are in the mood to shop for souvenirs, or the local semi-precious stones, garnet and amber, you are in an excellent place. As we wound our way toward the center of the Old Town we came across a building crowd. We once again had arrived at a destination quite by accident at a fortuitous time.

It turns out that we were now standing in front of Prague's Old Town Hall and its famous astronomical clock. Crowds gather here daily on the hour from eight to eight to see the show that the glockenspiel performs. The clock was built in the 15th Century and every hour a bell strikes and two doors open and figures parade out. I am not certain what all is represented, but there is most certainly a religious connotation. There are several of the little people, the only one recognizable to me is the caricature of death. In all, it is very interesting sight to observe and to think it has been performing for over six hundred years is mind boggling.

It is only by a stroke of good fortune and poor marksmanship that the clock is still intact. If you move to the east side of the rose colored building (the side that faces the Old Town Square) you can see how close the clock came to meeting its fate. Prague was spared by the Nazis in World War II save for one bombing that was aimed at taking out the glockenspiel. However, the bomb dropped on an adjoining building causing significant damage. The building was reconstructed to functionality, but the jagged outer wall was left intact as a reminder of the incident.

After watching the miniature figures perform, we moved on to take in the Old Town Square. The Christmas Market was in full swing and it was difficult to keep Jenny's attention away from its various attractions. I was successful in getting her to walk the perimeter of the square and take in the main sights before diving headlong into the market. The square is a wonderful blending of Gothic, Renaissance, Baroque and Rococo architectural styles. There are two very impressive churches that we visited, the Tyn and St. Nicholas.

The Tyn Church is on the west side of the square and is probably the most photographed church in Prague because of its Gothic nature and its impressive spires. The St. Nicholas Church is a very handsome Baroque structure and it is equally beautiful on the interior. The impressive Kinsky Palace with its lovely Rococo façade sits near the Tyn Church and was once a residence and later a government building.

We finished our lap around the square and visited the churches. It was now snowing and the large stage built near the Jan Hus Monument in the middle of the square was now in full swing. A large children's choir was performing Christmas carols and any thoughts of further sightseeing were now a thing of the past. We bought a cup of hot mulled wine and set out to thoroughly explore the Christmas market and its offerings. It was a wonderful day for this activity and we spent the remaining daylight and into the early darkness enjoying the various choral groups, nibbling on freshly roasted nuts and buying small, handmade Christmas gifts for family and friends. And, of course, more ornaments that still adorn our tree.

Finally, the cold of the day began to set in and we decided it was time to return to the Balkan. We caught the tram back to Smichov and were soon ensconced in our room. We rested and warmed ourselves and planned our evening's activities. We decided our best course of action was to return to the little neighborhood restaurant, U Matouse, we had visited the night before. Mustering what little energy we still had we went back out into the snowy, cold evening.

The walk to the café seemed even shorter that the night before. We pushed our way in and the proprietors greeted us as if we were long lost friends. They quickly prepared a table for us and brought us a couple of cold beers. I had noticed that they had hunter steak on the menu the night before, and decided to see how it compared to my wonderful Thanksgiving dinner at the Dukla a few nights before. Jenny, fearing she might miss out on something special, ordered the same. The tender steak was prepared in a thick, tomato-based sauce that was filled with vegetables and accompanied by broiled potatoes, and was outstanding. I am not prepared to say it was better than the Dukla's, but it was at least its equal. We finished off our meal with some local plum brandy that the owner's recommended.

That evening's dining experience was even better than the night before and I did not believe that was possible. When we travel we occasionally return to restaurants we had eaten in before on a trip and are often disappointed that we did. They never seem to hold up to our original dining experience, but in this case it did. We rue the fact that U Matouse no longer exists. On a return trip to Prague with Jenny's brother, Leo Medisch, a noted chef and major foodie, we tried to reprise our earlier dinners. I knew where the café was, but when we arrived at the location, it was no longer there. This was a major disappointment for us and we will have to wait for a subsequent writing for me to chronicle my favorite Czech meal because of this stroke of bad luck.

We said our good byes to our hosts and struck back into the cold enjoying our return walk to our hotel. These kinds of evenings is why we seek the small, out of the way, local establishments. We experienced wonderful hospitality, terrific food and made new friends with the proprietors. I don't think this is possible when you stick to the franchise joints that so many travelers only want to experience. Traveling is about venturing out, trying new things and learning from those opportunities.

We awoke the next morning rested and filled with anticipation of the day's activities. After finishing a tasty breakfast, we stopped at the little office to confer with Sylvia. She suggested we go out for the day, but return around three o'clock to be safely back before our guests were to arrive at four. She also confirmed that there was only one other room reserved that night and, barring something unforeseen, she could spend all her time translating for us. She also had notified the kitchen and bar folks that we would be in the house and likely in need of service.

Sylvia was so kind to assist in so many ways. Her confidence and ease in this matter put us at rest that all would go well if the Novotnys did arrive. We decided to venture out into the Old Town and see more sights that we had not been able to see, thus far. We caught the tram towards the city and it was very serene on this Sunday morning. Few people seemed about and a fresh blanket of snow had fallen overnight making for some beautiful street scenes.

We jumped off the tram and decided to explore the area around Wenceslas Square. The square, which is the commercial center of Prague, was rather quiet that morning. I am sure this was in sharp contrast to the when this square had been the epicenter of massive political demonstrations in the country. These gatherings have occurred on the square at important times in Czech history, like the Soviet invasion of the late 60s, and the Velvet Revolution of November and December of 1989, which led to the fall of communism in Czechoslovakia. We walked through the snow covered sidewalks and took in the beautiful buildings that surround the square. The area had its origins as a horse market decades ago, but now has given way to impressive department stores, commercial buildings, hotels and the National Museum.

We soon wandered toward the Old Town Square and came upon the Powder Tower, the imposing 15th century structure that once served as one of the city's gates. We knew that if we continued on we would be back at the Christmas Market. Jenny was wanting to do a little more shopping and the stores were now opening and greater activity was starting to take place.

We arrived back in the Old Town Square and the area was filled with the sounds of a grand choir performing on the large stage. The Christmas Market was awake again and wide open for business. We decided to peruse the offerings that the market had in hopes of finding a proper gift to give to Vlasta and Jaroslav. Finding none we decided to begin to look through the shops on the adjoining streets.

Soon we realized that hunger was about to overtake us and decided to check out an Italian restaurant we had passed earlier near the Powder Tower. Ambiente Pasta Fresca is a bistro that is situated in the several rooms in the basement of a building not far from the square. The ambience is delightful, exposed stone wall with candlelit tables with white linen cloths. The trattoria features a variety of homemade pasta dishes that are fresh and delicious. We were seated at a great table in the back corner of a room and ordered a bottle of still water and a glass of Chianti.

Our waiter soon arrived with our drinks and an English menu. Jenny quickly decided on a risotto with bacon and mushrooms and I went for the rigatoni all' arrabbiata. They left us some freshly baked bread and olive oil to munch on while we waited. Our main courses arrived and we were extremely well satisfied with our choices. We made quick work of our pastas and finished our glasses of wine.

When our waiter returned with our check, Jenny asked if he knew of any nearby flower shops, thinking fresh flowers would make a nice gift for the Novotnys. He pointed us in the direction of a very nice little shop which was only about a block away. Luckily when we arrived they were open and Jenny, with the assistance of the owner, picked out a nice bouquet for the gift. It was now about two o'clock and we decided it was time to return to the Balkan and ready ourselves for the big occasion.

We hopped the tram back to our hotel. When we arrived Sylvia was on the ready at the front desk and gave Jenny her full approval of the bouquet she had selected for our guests. You could tell that Sylvia was looking forward to the encounter, and so were we. Jenny was truly pumped as she spruced herself in our room. It got to be about three-thirty and she decided it was time for us to go sit in the cramped lobby and wait for her cousins.

Jaroslav Novotny was first cousin to Jenny's father, Joe Medisch. Joe's mother, Anna, had come to America in 1909 and was the sister of Jaroslav's father, Rudolph. Anna was a member of a large family having 8 siblings and once she arrived in America she never returned to her home country. In fact, there is only one known meeting of family members since Anna's arrival in the United States. One of Anna's sisters, Rose, came to the United States in the 1960s to visit her for a month, an event that was newsworthy enough that it was featured in an article in the local paper. Jenny's aunt, Liz Medisch, was able to keep in touch with some of the Czech relatives by writing letters to them and having them translated into Czech by a woman she knows in Dayton, Ohio, where she lives.

After a short while Jaroslav and Vlasta arrived on the cold, snowy afternoon. Dressed in their Sunday best, the elderly couple now well into their 70s had taken the tram across town to meet with us. Shaking off the snow and cold, they quickly realized who Jenny was, and kisses, and embraces abounded, and soon tears began to flow. A wonderfully warm and touching experience had ensued. Sylvia sprang into action acting not only as a translator, but as host, and she began to facilitate the dialogue. She ran into the little bar and fetches us some drinks.

As we sank into the couches in the lobby, Jenny presented Vlasta with the beautiful bouquet we had purchased for her and the Novotnys gave us a couple of wonderful gifts; lovely, delicate bone china tea cups and saucers for Jenny and a large, hinged top beer stein for me. We realized that we didn't really have anything for Jaroslav and I asked him if he drank vodka. At first he thought I was asking him if we wanted a glass of vodka and said he was fine with a beer. Sylvia soon corrected the misunderstanding and he offered that he did, on occasion, enjoy vodka. So, I excused myself and ran upstairs and found the bottle of good Polish vodka I had purchased in Warsaw and presented it to him. He seemed very grateful and said he would drink it over the Christmas holidays.

The Novotnys appeared as excited to meet us as we were to meet them. Vlasta said she did not know what to make of the phone call she had received on Friday afternoon. They did not know that Jenny existed. They knew of her father and aunt, but not Jenny. She told us that the woman who had placed the call for us from the Tourist Information Office said that everything seemed to be on the "up and up." She told Vlasta that, "I know this young woman is from the United States, but she looks 100 per cent Czech to me." We found this particularly amusing because soon after I met Jenny I told her that I though she looked Czech to me, which is home to some of the most beautiful women in the world in my book.

Jenny explained to them how they were related and they offered that they had concluded that she must have been Joseph's daughter. But then, Vlasta pulled out an old photo of Jenny's family in which she did not appear. Jenny is the baby of six and is nearly seven years younger than her closet sibling. She explained to them that she had not yet been born when the picture had been taken. With that, any apprehension on the part of Jaroslav and Vlasta melted away.

The next several hours were spent learning about the lives of their families. Vlasta had come armed with numerous family photos starting with their wedding and moving forward. It seems that Jaroslav had spent his working career with the electric company and Vlasta had raised their two kids. They also brought along lots of old pictures of the extended family so Jenny could learn a bit more about what had happened to her grandmother's kin. Jenny filled them in on all of Anna's family in America.

After a couple of hours we moved into the restaurant and ordered another round of drinks and a good Czech meal. As we talked I asked Jaroslav how life was different now that they lived in a democratic society, rather than under communism. I thought it a harmless question, but Jenny asked Sylvia not to interpret it thinking it might be going to a sensitive place. Sylvia, bless her heart, was by now totally invested in the experience and told Jenny she wanted to ask it because she was curious what the response might be. They offered that it was tougher is some respects now because their pensions had been cut, but that a free economy offered far more choices for them. There was no more queuing for everything and waiting sometimes for months if something like a refrigerator broke.

A couple of things that stands out to me about that evening. Jaroslav Novotny and Joe Medisch were first cousins and were only a few months apart in age. They had grown up in far different circumstances, separated by thousands of miles and never met. But, having a conversation and dinner with Jaroslav was eerily like being with Joe. They had very similar mannerism, expressions, and gestures. I thought the case for genetics was made strongly that evening.

Additionally, this family was clearly cut from the same cloth on both sides of the Atlantic. Shortly before they departed, Jenny complimented Vlasta on the sweater she was wearing. Her response was to begin to remove the sweater in attempt to give it to Jenny as a gift. Jenny quickly and artfully defused the situation, but it shows the lengths that kindness runs in this family. It was a truly humbling moment.

The hour was now growing late for the Novotnys to trek back across Prague to their apartment on the other side of the city. Sylvia offered to get them a taxi home, but they would hear nothing of it, the tram was fine with them. We said our tearful good byes and walked them out into the snow to the tram stop. There after another round of hugs and a few more tears we put them on the tram and closed off one of the most special moments I have experienced in travel and my life.

We went back to the Balkan and talked about the evening's events with Sylvia. She was so helpful in making everything right that we could never properly thank her for all she did. However, it was obvious from talking to her she wanted nothing in exchange for her services. She had a clear understanding of how special the event had been and how pivotal her role was, that she gained total satisfaction from her good deeds. We said thanks one last time and went to bed.

Sylvia did us one last favor before we left. She had arranged for a friend that drove a taxi to pick us up the next morning and take us to the airport. She had also prearranged a very favorable price for us. After breakfast we piled into that cab and headed to the airport. We had a nice experience on the way to the airport. We caught our Sabena flight to Brussels and onward to Boston. USAir got us home the next day from Boston.

Hank, if I had any doubt that your mom was the one for me, it was all dispelled on that trip. We had a great time together on this journey, enjoyed each other's company and got married the next May. We have been happily traveling together since.

Jenny and I with her cousins, Vlasta and Jaroslav Novotny

Chapter 6

SWEDEN, THE BALTIC'S AND FINLAND

HANK, AS YOU PROBABLY ARE aware by now, I am intrigued by the countries which used to be situated behind the "Iron Curtin." In the summer of 2001 your mom and I began to shop around for a place to take our yearly, late fall vacation. My gaze fell squarely on Northern Europe because I had done little traveling to the region and your mother had not been there at all. We shopped around for flights on Northwest Airlines, our carrier of choice at the time, and ended up booking a reasonably priced, open-jawed trip into Stockholm, Sweden, with a return from Helsinki, Finland.

A couple of years before while on a trip to Russia with my friend, Warren Mathies, we had stopped off in Helsinki for a few days on our return from Moscow. I had a favorable impression of the Finnish capital, but one day of our stay we took a boat trip to visit Tallin, the capital of Estonia. I was thoroughly intrigued by this lovely Baltic city and could not wait to return. I was also curious about how it compared to the other capitals of the Baltic countries, so we decided to wedge these three nations into our visit between Stockholm and Helsinki. We found that this trip was not too difficult to put together logistically, and we made the necessary arrangements.

So, in late October, early November 2001, Jenny and I traveled to Stockholm and onward to tour the Baltic countries, ending our journey in Helsinki. What a trip! This was a time when many Americans were very reluctant to travel because of the terrorist attack that had occurred less than two months before in New York and Washington. As you may recall, domestic and international air travel ground to a near halt in the weeks that followed the attacks of 9/11 on New York and Washington.

These times were filled with a great deal of uncertainty, would there be more terriorist activity? When? Where? We decided to adopt the attitude that if we just sat home, the perpetrators of these heinous deeds would, indeed, be the victors. We were determined to carry on with our plans to travel and hope for the best.

I think that some of our family members thought we were a little daft and were potentially moving into harms way by venturing out of the country. They were quite wrong. Indeed, we felt a general outpouring of warmth and affection from people we encountered in each of the five countries we visited. It was almost paternalistic in nature. I am quite sorry that those feelings toward Americans have diminished because of various foreign policy gaffs, but we certainly enjoyed the attention and kindness we received from numerous hosts during our trip.

SWEDEN

Upon our afternoon arrival into Stockholm we boarded the Airport bus for the forty-five minute journey to the Central Station. Conveniently located at the Central Station is the hub for their subway, or T- Bana, and we hopped on the Green Line. After a few stops we arrived in the Kungsholmen neighborhood of central Stockholm. We exited the subway and found the entrance to the Hotel Aldoria which was literally a few steps from the station. Located on the fourth and fifth floors of a commercial building, the hotel a small, clean establishment in a business strip bordering a residential neighborhood about ten minutes from the center by subway. The Aldoria is certainly nothing fancy, but it met our needs and was an affordable property in a very expensive city for lodging.

After settling in and taking the obligatory shower to remove the stale airplane film, we decided to have a drink. We procured some ice from the small front desk operation, fished bottles of liquor from our suitcases and proceeded to have a couple of cocktails. I think that the convergence of transatlantic travel and the libations began to reduce our expectations for that evening's activity. We had originally planned to venture forth and find a nice meal at a restaurant recommended by a guidebook we had in tow. Now, it was painfully obvious to us that we needed to find something that was within a reasonably short walking distance and nothing in our notes pointed us to anything in our immediate neighborhood.

Once again, we marched to the diminutive front desk area to seek their assistance. They sent us packing down the street about three blocks to an Italian restaurant that they highly recommended. As we neared our presumed destination, the building looked very dimly lit. By now, we were very hungry and our worst fears were realized when we donned the stoop of the restaurant and discovered that it was not functioning that evening. What to do now? Based on the lights we could see, the street which intersected our main drag seemed to contain some promise of dining opportunities. We headed up the street and within a block our destination for dinner became apparent, an Asian joint called the Hot Wok Café.

We could see through the window a small dining room filled to capacity with a lively crowd of young people swilling beer and munching down large plates of Chinese food. This looked like our kind of place, and it was. Our only question now was, could we find a place to sit as it was truly packed. As we opened the door any doubts that we wanted to eat here were dispelled by the smell of garlic and other hot spices which filled the steamy air.

We pushed through the crowd to a counter that separated us from a couple of chefs toiling over, oddly enough, hot woks. As we watched the flames leap and ingested the tantalizing aroma, a young server noticed us and approached. After she greeted us with some Swedish phrase that she could see blew right past us, she quickly switched to English in hopes that would be more recognizable to us. Thank god. We expressed to her our keen desire to dine at the establishment and she assured us that a table would be available momentarily.

After we stood awkwardly for a few minutes in the center of the room, she showed us to a cozy table and took our order of a couple of Carlsberg's. Leaving us with menus, she hustled off to fetch our cold beers. As we perused the offerings we realized the menu matched the funky, rock-and -roll vibe that permeated the place and the music blaring from their speakers. Our waitress assisted us in choosing our entries explaining in perfect English all the ingredients. I do not remember what Jenny ordered, but I settled on the Original Hot Wok Thundering Chicken.

As we waited for our order, our server returned with another round of beers. Just what we needed, as by now the effects of the alcohol and of sleep depravation were taking a firm foothold. In fairly short order, our entries arrived. As promised, my chicken was stir fried with numerous vegetables and copious quantities of spices and came with brown rice. It was spicy hot and delicious. Jenny was equally satisfied with her selection and we truly enjoyed our meal. From our prospective, this little place is one the guidebooks missed. **(See Appendix 14 for the recipe)**

After dinner, fully sated, we stumbled back to our little hotel to sleep "the sleep of the angels." The "sleep of the angels" occurs for me when I have traveled overseas and pushed through the entire day of arrival without taking a nap. Then if I am fortunate, after a great meal, like the one at the Hot Wok Café, I am able to sleep through the night getting ten to twelve hours of uninterrupted sleep and awake not only refreshed, but in sync with your new time zone. I find it a huge mistake to take a long nap upon arrival, rather I just try to gut it out that first day making it through dinner and hope I can sleep through the night.

Jenny and I really enjoyed our stay in Stockholm and, in fact, it is one of our favorite cities. There are numerous sights to see including two truly outstanding museums that should not be missed; Vasamuseet and Skansen. There is a wonderful old town, Gamla Stan, a beautiful waterfront where you can take a boat ride and a great pedestrian-only, shopping street, Kungsgatan, which seems to be a requirement for all great European cities.

After awakening the first morning and feeling refreshed, we ate a continental breakfast at the hotel, and then we set out to visit the museums. A subway and tram ride later, we were in the near downtown area on the waterfront at the Vasamuseet. This museum is dedicated solely to the oldest surviving warship in the world. Built for war with neighboring Poland, the warship was a large vessel for its time with over sixty cannons and 300 sailors prepared to fight. The Vasa sailed on its maiden voyage from Stockholm in 1628 in front of thousands of curious onlookers, and immediately sank in the harbor.

In 1961 the ship was salvaged from those cold, dark waters amid great fanfare. It was an engineering and archeological feat of major proportions. The Vasa was painstakingly restored using as much of the original materials as possible. In fact, over 95 percent of the original timbers were utilized in the reconstruction. The museum was built specifically to house the vessel and its contents, and gives the appearance of a maritime structure from the exterior. An amazing number of original artifacts were recovered and are on display including clothes, tools, coins and even decorative sculptures. It is a very unique experience and well worth the time.

After nosing around the old ship and its artifacts, we again hopped aboard the number seven tram which continues on to the Skansen Museum. Skansen is the world's first open-air museum. It continues to serve its original mission of bringing traditional, rural culture to the capitol city. This has been accomplished by relocating entire farmsteads, structures and dwellings brought from all over Sweden to display typical Swedish lifestyles around the country. Additionally, garden plots are cultivated in an effort to further demonstrate farm life. There is also a small zoo largely consisting of both domesticated and wild animals which are indigenous to the northern part of Sweden.

At some point the museum's mission was expanded to include an urban theme as well. Typical homes from the ninetheenth and early twentieth century's were added along with factories, windmills, craftsmen's shops and more. In this area you can view various artisans plying their trades including glassblowing, blacksmithing, baking, and weaving to name a view. The museum employees who demonstrate these arts are dressed in period costumes to further illustrate the era they are depicting.

The nude models being painted. We are not in Kansas anymore.

If you go, and you should if you visit Stockholm, be sure to wear some comfortable shoes because you will do a lot of walking. Skansen is really part museum, and a leafy, green park, with a little theme park thrown in for good measure. You can spend an entire day viewing its various offerings and learning about the proud history of this Scandanavian country.

We have since discovered that these types of museums exist in several Northern European countries. If you have an interest in the history and culture of a country, these open-air museums are definitely worth your time. You can learn a lot about numerous aspects of a country by visiting these displays.

After spending several hours at Skansen our stomachs told us it was time to move on. Although there are several food options on the property, we decided we had seen enough and wanted to return to the center of the city to find our midday meal. We hopped back on the number seven and began to thumb through our guide in search of a restaurant. We quickly settled on a café in the Ahrens City, a large downtown department store.

We hopped off the tram nearly at the front door of Ahrens City. As we entered the building we had no idea that we were about to witness an event in Stockholm which we have not seen before, or since, and are not likely to see in the United States anytime soon. It was really quite a sight!

When we walked in the main entrance of the store we were surprised to see two young, beautiful female models standing totally nude in front of us. Of course, we couldn't help but stop and try to figure out what was going on and take in this rather breathtaking sight. These two nubile women were preparing to be painted by an artist and a crowd was gathered to watch. And so we did, too.

After a time, and the taking of several pictures, we wondered upstairs and to have lunch. We entered the comfortably decorated dining room and were promptly seated at a table by the side window. Our waitress promptly arrived with menus and we both chose Ceasar salads topped with grilled tuna. We stuck with water to drink, as we try to consume a great deal of it to replenish any lost to dehydration on the transatlantic flight. The crisp greens turned out to be coated in a tasty, garlicky dressing and the large tuna steak was quite fresh and flavorful. We made quick work of this healthy lunch and decided to further explore the city.

When we had finished our meal we prepared to leave and retraced our steps only to find the models still standing on the stage, now about three quarters covered in paint. Again, we watched the show for several minutes, snapped some more pictures, but were unable to comprehend what was going on as we was moved back out into the cold. We may never understand exactly what prompted this artistic display, but we certainly enjoyed it none the less.

After our lunch we decided to explore the immediate downtown area. We window shopped our way through the streets until we stumbled onto the pedestrian-only, Kungsgatan, or Kings Street. We spent the remainder of the afternoon exploring all the street had to offer. We bought some small souvenirs from shops along the way and stopped into a couple of cafes for warm beverages to knock off the chill from the cold, windy day.

Tiring and with daylight dimming, we decided to make our way back to our hotel to rest a while before heading out for our evening meal. We found the green line and soon the swift subway had returned us to our neighborhood. When we stepped off the elevator into the Aldoria's lobby, we were greeted by the same front desk clerk who had checked us in the day before. Before we could ask, he inquired if we needed any ice that evening. We quickly accepted his offer and were soon back in our room with our boots off sipping a fresh cocktail.

As were were finishing our drink and beginning to think about where to dine that evening, we looked out the window to see a very steady snow falling. We decided that we should have another quick drink and stay in the neighborhood for dinner that evening. I slipped down to the front desk to consult the clerk for another nearby restaurant suggestion. He marked down a spot on the map of a small, locally owned tavern that had been in business for years. It sounded perfect to me.

I returned to the room and Jenny and I bundled up bracing for the cold we knew we were going to encounter. We exited the hotel and made the short walk down the street to our destination. When we arrived we swung open the door into a room dominated by a large bar on one end and a room filled with patrons drinking and eating appetizing food. A large boned, middle-aged waitress met and ushered us through the bar area to a knotty pine paneled dining room in the back. The cozy room was nearly full of families enjoying a weekend night out.

Our waitress assisted us in working through the menu and taking drink orders. She returned with a couple of Carlsbergs and we both ordered the meatball dinners. Why not, that is the dish most associated with Sweden by Americans and since we were here... Soon our waitress returned with teeming plates of meatballs in a brown gravy atop a bed of homemade buttered noodles. They were served with a side dish of fresh vegetables and we could hardly wait to dig in. It was delicious and filling, a truly enjoyable meal.

After washing down this ample meal with a good Swedish beer, we paid our tab and made our way back through the snow-covered streets to our hotel. In no time we were in bed and asleep after our full day of exploring Stockholm. We awoke rested, and after cleaning up, we fortifided ourselves with a breakfast of yogurt, museli and freshly baked bread. We packed up our things and checked out of our room leaving our bags for safekeeping with the clerk at the front desk.

Since our departure was not until early that evening we had nearly a full day to further explore the city. We set out to explore the old town, or Gamla Stan, area of the city. We took the subway back toward the center of the city and were fortunate that the green line would take us all the way to the Gamla Stan neighborhood. Exiting the underground we were impressed with the well preserved and vibrant area we were entering.

We spent the remainder of the morning exploring the narrow, cobblestone streets of this the medieval core of the city. We walked by several beautiful structures including cathedrals and palaces in the area, but spent the majority of our time ducking in and out of shops and coffehouses that populate these streets. We picked up a few more momentos of our trip and warmed ourselves on hot beverages.

We finally decided to stop for lunch in one of the area eateries. We chose a little Italian place near the Royal Palace and ducked into the cozy café. The aroma of garlic was the first thing that hit our noses as we waited to be seated. We were directed to a small table in the center of the crowded dining area. We quickly perused the menu and both decided that a pizza being eaten by some folks at the next table would be our choice for lunch.

Our waiter took our orders, two individual sized pizzas topped with ham and mushrooms and a glass of the house Chianti for each of us. The service was quick and within a few minutes our hot, gooey pizzas arrived.

We both enjoyed our selections and the red wine was pleasing to our palates. After we had finished our meal we paid our bill and noticed it was now after two o'clock and time for us to head to the airport.

We made our way back to the Aldoria and collected our bags and thanked the clerk for all he had done for us during our stay. We grabbed the green line to the Central Station and made our way to the loading area for the Airport Bus. Soon we were enroute to the airport filled with anticipation of the next leg of our journey. Stockholm is a great city to visit. We enjoyed our stay and have been back for another visit since that time. Hank, we clearly need to get you there, as I am confident you would enjoy this fabulous city.

LITHUANIA

We were sorry to leave Stockholm, but it was time to move on to the capital of Lithuanian, Vilnius. We returned to Arlanda Airport via public transportation using the same route on which we had arrived. We checked in to our $99 flight arranged through the useful EuropeByAir. EuropeByAir was founded by a group of airline executives whose aim was to make air travel in Europe affordable and to compete with the rail passes. They utilize capacity on smaller regional airlines and sell the service for $99 per route. The only hitch with EuropeByAir is that you have to pay the taxes on your ticket at the departure airport. This is not a big deal, but sometimes it can be time consuming, finding the proper counter in an already strange airport, and getting them to understand your need to pay these taxes and expecting payment. I enjoy traveling by rail, but this enables you to cover a lot more ground in far less time and at a comparable cost.

We arrived early enough that during our wait we found a lounge near our gate and had a beer to make the time pass. Our carrier to Vilnius was the now defunct Lithuanian Airlines. We boarded our Russian-made aircraft. It was quite nice for a regional-type aircraft with seating for two on one side of the aisle and for one person on the other. When airborne, our attractive and efficient young flight attendants sprung into action. We quickly were given drink service followed by a hot meal. Given that the flight was only a little over an hour I was impressed and surprised. Many

American airlines would have a difficult time getting you a drink and a bag of peanuts in that timeframe.

After the trays were cleared, we heard the pilot make an announcement from the cockpit. It was unusual in that the pilot spoke in Lithuanian and not English, the language used by most pilots on these occasions. Because our knowledge of Lithuanian is lacking, we were unable to understand what the pilot said. One thing became abundantly clear however, it had to do with something going on out the left, or north side on the airplane. There was a dramatic shift of the passengers to the empty seats on that side of the aircraft. They stared intently out the window.

After several minutes had passed, one of the flight attendants passed by and I stopped her to see if she could tell us what was up. She hesitated searching for words and finally said, "I don't know how you say it in English, but it has something to do with the lights in the north." By now several of the passengers had shifted back to their original seats and we quickly moved to the other side of the plane. Sure enough she was right; on that evening we were able to see the aurora borealis in its full glory. Jenny and I sat for several minutes with noses pressed to the glass watching one of nature's greatest displays. The wavy green lines moved and shimmered across the horizon. It was truly impressive and a moment not to be forgotten soon.

An interesting footnote to this story is that Steve Rogers, a colleague of mine at work, had asked me prior to our departure if there was anything that I had not seen in my travels that I would like to see. After thinking for a while I responded with the aurora borealis. Little did I know that in a few short days I would have a front row seat from thirty thousand feet to this sight? That moment was worth the journey in and of itself.

We soon arrived at the Vilnius airport, a dark, dank Soviet era structure in need of remodeling. We pressed through an unusually large crowd of people welcoming passengers, particularly for a late night arrival. We hailed a taxi that sped us to the Old Town where our hotel was located. The Rinno was to be our home the next two days and was a welcomed sight for a pair of weary travelers. The small hotel is really quite nice and has a very helpful staff. In fact, our room was so nice we could have spent more time in it just lounging.

The check-in to the hotel was quite efficient and the staff directed us up the stairs to our room on the second floor at the back. We entered to find a very nice room, done in earth tones with a comfortable seating area, a big king-sized bed and very large bathroom filled with amenities. The main attraction for us that evening was a large television which we flipped on while we unwound preparing for bed. Soon the day's travels caught up with us and we turned off the television and fell asleep.

The next morning I awoke from a great night's sleep in our comfortable bed. I cleaned up and prepared to make the most of our one full day in Vilnius. Jenny, however, preferred to take her time and enjoy the room, even taking a long, hot bath and wrapping herself in the soft towels that were draped on the heated towel racks. So, I decided to go on to breakfast.

The breakfast room was just off the lobby and included a sumptuous buffet filled with assorted cold and hot dishes. I filled my plate with cold meats, cheeses and whole grain bread in preparation to enjoy a Northern European style meal. As soon as I returned to my table an aging Lithuanian woman approached and brought me coffee and freshly squeezed orange juice. She soon tried to communicate with me and it was quite obvious that a language barrier existed. My two years of high school Russian were a little helpful and I was able to order an omelet. She returned shortly with a ham and cheese omelet which was delicious.

I thought that Jenny was going to join me, but that didn't happen. I lingered and let this fine server/cook pamper me, bringing me more coffee and delicious pastries. She seemed very concerned that my wife had not come down, but when it came time to close the breakfast I decide to find out what was up with Jenny.

By the time that I reached the room, Jenny was refreshed, dressed, looking fabulous, and ready to explore the city. As we departed for the day we passed through the lobby and, out of the breakfast room, bolted the woman who had just finished pampering me. She immediately accosted Jenny, pulling her by the arm into the dining area and insisting that she have breakfast before she could leave. All at once the breakfast room that was closed was reopened and fresh eggs over easy, hot tea, juice, and toast with homemade jams appeared, and Jenny enjoyed an excellent breakfast. This was our first real taste of the overt Lithuanian hospitality we enjoyed during our stay.

After Jenny and the kind woman decided that she had enough fortification for the morning, we stopped by the front desk to drop our key. The clerk supplied us with a nice map of the city and as we were preparing to leave, we noticed a copy of an <u>IN YOUR POCKET</u> guide for Vilnius for sale. On a previous trip to Eastern Europe we had discovered these handy little guides and for only about a dollar how could I pass it up? These paperback treasures will assist you in finding great local sites, lodging, eateries and more.

Armed with our map and new guide we headed out for the day. We spent the day roaming the Old Town of Vilnius. Not as impressive as many Old Town areas of some European cities and a little down in the mouth from years of Soviet dominance, it nonetheless has a certain charm. Compact and very walkable, it has numerous sites worth visiting including the requisite number of old churches and government buildings.

Our first stop was to be the Gates of Dawn, the last remaining city gate from its original fortifications. The <u>IN YOUR POCKET</u> guide insisted it was a "can't miss" attraction and we decided to find out for ourselves. We followed our map closely and after a several block walk on a cold, snowy morning we arrived at our destination. We walked through the portal and once we passed through, we discovered an entrance for the chapel that rests atop the gate.

We climbed the stairs to the second floor entrance to the area of worship. We pushed open the door to find the stunning, little chapel devoted to the Mother Mary. The small, dark wood paneled room is partially covered in a frieze of hammered metal sculpting which has been coated in silver. On one of the long walls of the retangluar room there is a small alter over which there is hung an incredible painting of the Virgin Mary.

On either side of the painting there are Corinthian style columns in marble. Next to the columns on each side there are gilded statues of Mary's parents, St. Anne and St. John. On the opposite wall there is a large, leaded glass window which looks out on the pastel colored building on the Old Town street below. After Jenny finished saying her prayers we decided it was time to head on back into the cold day.

We decided to stick with the religious theme and head through the Old Town in search of the Vilnius Cathedral. Our route would take us through the heart of the city. We passed by the Town Hall, an impressive neo-classical structure and made a way through the major university in the city, oddly enough named after the city.

As we plyed these streets we could not help but be reminded that it had only been a short decade since the country had gained its independence from the Soviet Union, the first Baltic country to do so. The fiercely independent Lithuanians had long struggled against the Soviet oppression, and in 1990 elected a reform-minded parliament which would proclaim their sovereignty from the Soviet Union.

Initially, the Soviets concurred with the independence action, but early the following year the Red Army moved on the new government seizing, several public buildings including the television tower. The Lithuanians stood strong, and dispite some bloodshed and loss of life on the very streets we were walking, prevailed in the quest for freedom.

Another interesting aspect of the Old Town is there are a number of small markets that line the main pedestrian streets. Here you can buy wares from kiosk operators that appear to be handmade, and not mass produced. We bought a few trinkets here including a pair of leather gloves with rabbit fur linings, that the vendor claimed that she made and I have no reason to doubt her. These gloves kept my hands warm the remainder of the trip and they still come in very handy on a cold winter's day. We also found an ideal Christmas ornament, a handmade and painted bell which made it home in one piece.

We finally reached the Vilnius Cathedral, another neoclassical structure which was designed by the same person who had done the Town Hall. The current cathedral dates from the early fifteenth century although it has seen several renovations and additions. We were immediately drawn to its eleven chapels, but most particularly to one devoted to St. Casimir, the patron saint of the country. Done in High Baroque style, the chapel is built of Swedish sandstone and is ornately decorated in stunning frescos and impressive stuccowork.

The Cathedral has had an interesting history. The building was seized from the Catholic Church by the Soviets in 1950. During their reign, the structure was used as a warehouse, an art gallery, a concert hall, and even an auto workshop. The cathedral was returned to the Catholic Church in 1988 and was returned to a house of worship.

We finished our exploration of the cathedral and exited the building. We were immediately drawn to the Cathedral Belltower across the plaza. The tower was originally part of one of the city's gates in its wall, but is now a freestanding structure. The building is currently a popular meeting point for the citizens. We attempted to gain access, but it was closed. It is probably a good thing because a hike to the top of the nearly two hundred foot structure was most likely not going to happen for us.

By now we were becoming hungry and cold, so we went in search of a spot for lunch. We didn't have to venture too far before we located a bustling, little café which looked good to us. We entered the restaurant and were pointed to a table for two in the front window by a busy waitress. In a couple of minutes the server freed herself and brought us menus and took drink orders.

As we fumbled with the offerings, she returned with large steins of a local brew and explained their offerings. She recommended a daily special which was a hearty, chicken soup with vegetables. Jenny and I both went with her choice which sounded particularly good on a cold day. Before we barely had time to take a sip of our beer she returned with the entrees and a basket of dense, dark bread. The thick, stew-like soup was filled with white chicken meat and potatoes, carrots, onions, celery and corn. The tasty concoction really hit the spot and was quite filling with the brown bread.

We perused our guide as we finished our lunches. We determined there were a couple of very unusual sites we wanted to visit before calling an end to our sightseeing that day. The first was the Genocide Victim's Museum. After settling our bill, we headed back out into a now sunny, crisp afternoon. The museum is not a long walk and soon we were standing in front of a government looking building.

The museum is located in a former KGB, or Soviet intelligence organization, headquarters and is dedicated to those who were tortured or murdered during the Soviet period. We were able to join an English speaking tour and were first ushered into the basement of the building. Here we were shown the prison used by the KGB which served as a detention center for persons who were not loyal to the Soviet Union.

During the post WWII period thousands of Lithuanians were interrogated and tortured in these rooms. Many, including entire families were deported to forced labor camps in Siberia after these detentions. We were shown through cells, explained the processing centers interworkings including photographing and fingerprinting of all the prisoners. We were also shown various methods the detainees were to extreme forms of punishment.

We next were led to the ground and upper floors which is dedicated to the Lithuanian struggle for independence. Here you can learn about the structure of the freedom fighters and their valiant efforts to resist the Soviet oppression. Armed resistance was carried out from 1944 until it was finally suppressed in 1953. After that time various forms of civil disobedience occurred until the Soviets were finally dispelled for good in 1991.

The Frank Zappa Memorial in Vilnius, an oddity!

The museum is at once both depressing and inspiring. Clearly, the torture and depravity suffered by the Lithuianian people gives one cause to sink to the depths of human emotion. But, at the same time one cannot help but feel uplifted by the efforts of these brave people to resist the oppression they were confronting. Their independent spirit is one to be admired.

It was finally time to move on to the next unusual memorial. We walked several blocks in the direction of our hotel where we came across our next destination. The second site is a monument to the late rocker, Frank Zappa. By all accounts there is no real reason for this memorial. Zappa had no real connection to the city. He never performed there and I don't believe he was of Lithuanian extraction. Nonetheless, in the corner of a small park in downtown Vilnius, there on a steel post is a small, bronze statue to Mr. Zappa. Go figure?

After a full day of sightseeing and shopping we retired to our room to rest and select a location for dinner. We kicked off our boots and soaked up the warmth of our pleasant hotel. As we caught up with the news of the world on our television we began to think about dinner. Armed with our reflections of the day, we relaxed and perused the <u>IN YOUR POCKET</u> and landed on what we hoped would be the ideal spot for us that evening, Lokys.

We had decided that since this was likely to be our only trip to Lithuania we should try the local fare. Lokys is a located within walking distance of our hotel in the Old Town and came highly recommended for its authentic Lithuanian offerings. What seemed like a perfect match for our needs and desires was indeed so.

Finally, about six o'clock we decided it was time to seek out this interesting sounding restaurant. We pulled on our boots and warm coats and headed out into a steady snowfall. Lokys is located in the Old Town about a ten minute walk from our hotel. The time passed quickly as we kept a good pace in an effort to outrace the snow and cold. We soon spotted the restaurant and headed for the door.

Upon entering the old building which dates back to the 15th century, we were ushered to the arched grotto rooms. The environment was very warm and hospitable. The rustic tones provided an excellent setting for a wonderful meal. Our young waiter appeared with menus and soon reappeared with large, earthenware mugs filled with delicious beer. We started off our meals with soup to help with the distinct chill that permeated the night air. I selected mushroom and soon discovered that it was the best I had ever tasted. Filled with large chunks of mushroom and in an appealing broth, this really hit the spot. Jenny had an equally appetizing onion soup and after another crock of beer we were ready for our entree.

We both selected the national dish of Lithuania, cepelinai, or zeppelins as they are commonly known. Zeppelins, which are named for the inventor of the dirigible balloon, are sort of a very large potato dumpling stuffed with meats, gravy, onions, sour cream, and are truly delicious. They probably are taxing on the waistline and your cardiovascular system, but they are a treat going down and are unique in my experience. **(See Appendix 15 for the recipe)**

After the soup and zeppelin, we were so full that the thought of dessert was not a pleasant one. So we polished off our last large beers and strode back to the Rinno. There was one distinct difference between our arrivals at our hotel this night and the previous one, the sounds of revelry. It seems that the lower level of our hotel is the home of a "gentlemen's club" which had not been open the night before. That night we were lulled to sleep by the thumping base emanating from the basement.

LATVIA

We awoke the next morning and ambled down for another sumptuous breakfast. This time Jenny was right beside me because she had learned that this experience was not to be missed. Our same Lithuanian babushka doted over us in spades. Jenny was able to feel the full effect of the pampering this wonderful woman dishes out. What a positive memory this caring woman has left on me and created a terrific impression of the warmth and hospitality of the Lithuanian people. This impression would be further amplified by our next encounter.

After breakfast I inquired at the front desk about the proximity of the hotel to the downtown Avis office and what would be the easiest method to get there. The front desk clerk suggested there was no need to travel to Avis; rather they would be glad to bring the car to us. Promptly he called Avis and confirmed that they would bring the car to us shortly. We scurried upstairs, finished what little packing that needed to be done and returned to the lobby.

When we arrived back in the lobby we were greeted by an attractive, young blond woman wearing a red Avis jacket. She informed us that our car was waiting outside and there was some paperwork that needed to be completed. We sat down in overstuffed chairs that adorned the small lobby and began to fill out the necessary documents. Soon the Avis representative discovered that we are Americans.

Immediately, our conversation turned to the terrorist attacks that had occurred less than two months prior. This young lady was describing how she had watched the horrific coverage of the events of 9-11 for days. The next thing we new the three people working at the front desk of the hotel had entered into the discussion and there was an inspiring outpouring of condolence and support for the United States. At that moment we were very proud to be Americans.

We finally had to break up the conversation about the attack on the World Trade Center and hit the road north to Latvia. After receiving assistance loading the car and directions on how to get out of Vilnius, including three people standing by the car pointing out the route, we departed in our little, red Avis rental car. After we wound our way through the streets in Old Vilnius we found the A2 Highway, our route north toward Riga.

The highway is quite nice; in fact, it is four lanes, divided with limited access for more than half the way to the Latvian border. Eventually, we merge on to the E67 which is the main north-south highway through the Baltic countries. This would become our main route throughout our trip and is well-paved and sign posted. We made our way through thousands of acres of flat, to gently-rolling, fertile-looking farm ground, some planted in winter wheat. We passed through, or near, well-kept little villages and towns. In a few hours we reached the Latvian border and, after a short interruption, we are allowed to enter the country and proceed to our destination, the capital city of Riga.

Riga is the largest of the Baltic capitals and an interesting mix of a well-preserved old town and Soviet modern. As we entered the city you are taken with the working nature of this industrial city. We passed numerous factories belching smoke and steam from their stacks. We wound our way through the city without the benefit of a good map or directions, but were able to successfully negotiate our way, dodging the ubiquitous street cars, to the Laine Hotel, our home in Riga. The hotel is now known as the Art Hotel Laine and has had an interesting history including once being the home to American Peace Corps workers during the Soviet era.

The hotel is tucked back on a side street near the Old Town. We pulled our rental car up to the hotel entrance while Jenny ran in to find out where we were to park. She quickly returned and pointed me to a narrow entrance for the courtyard which contains several parking spaces for guests. We picked out a good spot, parked, grabbed our bags from the trunk and entered the art nouveau building.

We took the elevator to the third floor reception desk and were greeted by an attractive, young woman who spoke English well. She quickly checked us in, supplied us with a map of Riga, and showed us to our room on the next level up. The hotel was interestingly appointed with the common areas having a fresh coat of kelly green and yellow paint. Our light blue room turned out to be a large space with a queen bed, sitting area, television, refrigerator, and a large bathroom with nice amenities.

After settling into our room, we headed out walking to the Old Town area of Riga that was only a short five minutes away from the Laine. We soon discovered that the Old Town is a well-preserved medieval area filled with many interesting sites and buildings. We cut through a nice park and soon stumbled upon the Freedom Monument.

This monument is a national treasure to the Latvian people which commemorates their war of independence against the fledgling Soviet Union following World War I. The towering travertine column is topped by copper figure of liberty in female form holding three stars representing the districts of Latvia. The monument is protected by a Latvian Army Guard that changes hourly during good weather. Since snow was falling and the wind was howling, the ceremony did not take place during our visit.

Venturing further into the Old Town we decided to visit the St. Peter's Church. The church is an impressive old structure dating from the sixteenth century, but for us the attraction was the church's tower. We were told at our hotel to ascend the wooden tower for a view of the city to get our bearings, and we thought it sounded like an excellent idea. Once the highest tower in Europe, the elevator ride to the top lets you out on a platform that provides you with a spectacular view of the area. Given that our visit was in early November and snow was falling, it was also very cold up there on that platform and we questioned the wisdom of our visit. After a couple of minutes we decided to abbreviate our viewing from the tower and beat a hasty retreat.

We determined it was time to find a place to warm up. We spotted the Visitor's Information Center and ducked in to see if any exciting events were going on while in Riga, specifically was there a professional basketball game, hockey match, or rock concert taking place in the next two nights. Sure enough, we were in luck and there was a basketball game that night that we decided to attend.

As we were exiting the tourist office we noticed an inviting little café across the street and we decided to pop in for a late lunch. Given it was now past two o'clock there were few patrons in the small, rustically decorated diner. A nice, young woman who spoke excellent English directed us to a table in the front window from which we could watch the pedestrian traffic on the busy street outside.

We were told that the special of the day was a potato-mushroom soup and the waitress highly recommended it to us. We both eagerly agreed to give it a try along with a couple of hot beverages. The waitress returned in a few minutes with our soup and drinks. The thick, creamy soup was filled with potatoes, mushrooms, onions and bacon and was delicious. The hearty bowl made for a good lunch and prepared us for the rest of the afternoon.

We finished our lunch and headed back out to visit a few more sights before departing in search of the basketball game. Our first stop was the House of Blackheads, a building which dates from the 1300s, but was destroyed during WWII. The structure was rebuilt a few years before our visit and the Gothic structure with a Dutch renaissance façade is quite impressive. To me, the building would fit in along a canal in Amsterdam.

Originally, the House of Blackheads served as a lodging for single German traders who were doing business in Riga. Later its purpose became a meeting place for various local activities. Located on the Town Hall square we were able to enter the building and tour its various rooms which were equally ornate as the exterior. We were quite impressed and pleased we had the opportunity to view the lovely facility.

The light of day was beginning to fade and we decided to relax before we headed to the basketball game. We checked the time and determined we did not have time to return to the room so we went in search of a bar to have a beverage and sit for a little while. Given that we were in the center of the city and a highly pedestrian area, it did not take us long before we identified a suitable place to light.

We settled into an inviting Old Town tavern, found a table next to the bar, and ordered a tankard of the local brew and a snack. The engaging server spoke excellent English and helped us with directions to the gymnasium that was hosting the ballgame that evening. After polishing off a couple more beers and the plate of cheese, cold meats and assorted breads the bartender pointed us in the proper direction for the street car to take to the game.

Traveling north by street car about 15-20 minutes we arrived at the gym. The facility was about what we would expect for a high school in Indiana, but a near capacity crowd was gathered for the event. The teams were warming up and game time was nearing when we arrived. We felt lucky to find two good seats near center court in the balcony. It was obvious to us that we were not at a high level professional game, rather probably a contest between teams in their late teens, or early twenties, maybe a college game. At any event, the caliber of competition was good and we settled in to enjoy the game.

During the first half of the game I began to feel ill. I started to have chills and felt feverish. I thought this can't be happening. I tried to ignore it but by the end of the third quarter, Jenny and I decided to leave. We had not eaten any dinner, but I felt rotten and we decided to just head back to the room. We caught the street car back south and were soon hopping off the vechicle a couple of blocks from the hotel.

We made our way back through the snow and cold to the Laine. We went straight to our room and I immediately prepared for bed. Before I knew it we were snuggled up together and I was fast asleep. Surprisingly, I slept well through the night and awoke the next morning feeling much better. Whatever bug I had caught seemingly left me a quickly as I had caught it.

The next morning we arose to discover more snow had fallen and welcomed the nice, hot breakfast provided to us at our hotel. The buffet which included scrambled eggs and sausages (think small hot dogs), cheeses and breads. The meal made us feel much better because we had not eaten anything since our snack prior to the basketball game.

I was excited about today because we were visiting the Central Market. You should understand that I enjoy going to markets because I believe that you learn a great deal about the culture by seeing what the locals are buying and selling. However, I was even more excited about this market because I had seen references that it was the mother of all markets, at least in the Baltics.

The market area is located on the banks of the Daugava River in a seemingly industrial area a little south of the Old Town. In looking on the map we decided it was a little too far to walk and caught public transportation most of the way. We walked the last few blocks through the snow in the cold, but now sunny morning.

The advance notices did not really do the market justice. I am confident that if you want something, you can get it at the Central Market in Riga. The place is huge. The market is centered on five main buildings that during WWI served as dirigible hangars, so you can imagine the size. The market spills out of these five buildings into outbuildings and open-air stands. Anything from meats, fish, and vegetables to washing machines and autos are available. In fact, I am quite certain that you could purchase nearly anything your heart would desire, legal or otherwise. It is quite a sight and well worth your time if you are in Riga.

After slogging through the Central Market all morning, we moved on by foot to explore the Old Town area once more. Our appetites were whetted by our trek through the Market and all the wonderful, and some not so wonderful, smells. As we were walking we stumbled upon an interesting, little Italian restaurant in Old Town and took a table in the front window. Our view was out on to a plaza across a narrow street. There must have been a college nearby because, as we sucked down our plates of pasta Bolognese with a glass of red wine, we watched students cavorting in the snow and engaging in a snowball fight. It was a beautiful break, good food, satisfying wine and the stage was filled with the exuberance of youth.

After our satisfying lunch, we spent the rest of the afternoon seeing the street sights of Riga's Old Town. We strolled past the Three Brothers, the oldest stone residential structures in the city which are interesting architectural examples, from medieval to Baroque. The oldest dates from the 15th century with the other two built during the 17th and 18th centuries.

We next headed for the Old City Wall and the Swedish Gate, the oldest remaining portion of the city's original fortifications. This rather short section of the wall was built between the 13th and 16th centuries and ran between two castles. The Swedish Gate was built in 1698 to commemorate the occupation of Latvia by the Swedes. The small portal allowed access to barracks which were built outside the city wall.

Our final stop that afternoon was at the monument to the Latvian Riflemen. This controversial memorial was built in 1970 to honor the Latvian Red Riflemen who sided with the Bolsheviks during and after WWI. Many of these riflemen went on to be Lenin's personal bodyguards after the conflict. Some Latvians think the impressive red statue, done in social realism style, should be removed because it harkens back to an era of oppression under the Soviet Union.

Finally tiring and cold, we returned to our hotel room to rest and select our dinner location for the evening. As is often the case, we laid on the bed in our room perusing our trusty travel guide for dining options while comparing potential candidates to the city map. We knew one thing, our destination would not be too far from the Laine because it was becoming bitterly cold outside and there were several inches of snow on the ground. Soon our search revealed our choice for the night, an Armenian restaurant, Arba, which was only a few short blocks from the hotel.

I had the pleasure of dining on Armenian food a few years before in St. Petersburg, Russia. It had been a delightful experience with great food, stout drink and excellent companionship with my friend, Warren Mathies, and I could not wait to try this cuisine again. My wife, Jenny, is a wonderful woman who is not averse to adventure and this certainly holds true for eating. So, it was not a hard sell to convince her to try Armenian food that night. Little did we know, we would not be disappointed?

We bundled back up and set out to find the eatery. In a few blocks we located the Arba, which sits atop a downtown building with an entrance on the backside of the structure. The entire restaurant is a glass enclosed atrium and with touches of Armenia everywhere. The dim lighting and dark wood furniture provides for a warm atmosphere. You are immediately engulfed by the aroma of hearty food and the welcoming staff that are very attentive.

Our waiter quickly appeared at our table after we were seated and offered us a libation. I quizzed him about what their selection of vodka entailed and he informed me that they served several varieties including Stolichnaya Cristall which I promptly ordered. Cristall is considered by many to be the finest vodka in the world. I watched our waiter go to a nearby deep freeze, open the top and grab a bottle of Cristall and return to our table to pour me a healthy glass of this fine vodka. I knew then that this evening was going to be a special one.

After sipping on our drinks for a few minutes and ordering refills, it was time to address our dinner desires. Given it was a very cold evening, we both ordered soups to begin our meal. Jenny had clear broth with meat balls and vegetables and I had a hearty beef soup strongly resembling a stew. We thoroughly enjoyed these starters and they were perfect for this cold night.

We both settled on a skewered meat for our main entrees. The kabobs came with large chunks of grilled lamb and chicken and were accompanied with rice, vegetables and lavash, a delicious Armenian flat bread. Copious quantities of garlic were used to flavor our dinner which we absolutely found to be a very pleasurable experience. We washed all this down with a dry, red Armenian wine which we thought was very complimentary of the dishes we had ordered.

After dinner, Jenny decided to try a baked delicacy somewhat akin to the Greek baklava. The sweet layered dough made for a perfect ending to a great meal for her. I, however, turned my attention to a true Armenian specialty I had discovered a few years earlier on my trip to Russia, brandy. Ararat brandy is very similar to cognac and is possibly the best after dinner drink I have consumed.

I am not the only one who has enjoyed the pleasures of Armenian brandy. It has been reported that during World War II Josef Stalin introduced this beverage to Winston Churchill and he became a big aficionado. In fact, apparently 400 bottles were shipped to him annually. It was reported that during the blitz, or nightly bombings of London, Churchill would sit on the roof of the War Rooms smoking cigars and drinking his Armenian cognac. Needless to say, a glass of this brandy went a long way to ensuring that this was my favorite meal in Riga. (**See Apendix 16 for the recipe**)

ESTONIA

The next morning we awoke, enjoyed our last breakfast at the Laine and we checked out of the hotel. Before we departed, we walked down the street to a liquor store we had passed the previous day. To my delight they were open, and to my greater pleasure they had Ararat brandy in stock. I bought a couple of bottles as souvenirs to bring home and we headed for the car to make our retreat.

We packed up our little Avis rental and pointed it toward the E67 heading north and our final stop on the Baltic capital tour, Tallinn. I had the pleasure of visiting Tallinn for a day a few years before. I had been in Helsinki and had taken a high speed catamaran over to Tallinn. I was very impressed with the city and could not wait to share the experience with Jenny because she had not been with me on the previous trip.

As we wound our way north on the E67 we enjoyed the heavily wooded countryside. The four hour drive was a simple and enjoyable one. The border crossing from Latvia into Estonia was painless and as we moved closer to Tallinn my anxiety rose as we were attempting to figure out where the Avis office is located so we could drop off our rental. We stopped at a gas station and filled up the tank and thankfully the attendant spoke decent English and was able to give us directions to our drop off point.

We arrived at the Avis office unscathed and returned our car. Upon our arrival, the kind folks at the office contacted the people at our accommodations to arrange for our pick up. We had no sooner conclude the paper work associated with our rental return than our host arrived to drive us to our lodging.

We had reserved a room at a small bed and breakfast in the Old Town called the Romeo Hotel. In my email exchange with the owners while making the reservations, they had offered to pick us up and take us to their lodging. We gladly accepted their offer and the owner met us at the Avis office in his big sedan.

He drove to the nearby Old Town and before we got to his hotel, he took us by a couple of their apartments to see if we might prefer renting one of them instead of a room at the hotel. We were very impressed with these spacious units, for appearance, functionality and location, but ultimately decided for our short stay we would stick with the hotel. Hank, I will tell you that if you had been with us then it would have been a no-brainer. We would have rented one of the apartments, and if we take you there someday we just might do so.

The Romeo is a very nice, cozy three-room inn that is well-situated for all the main attractions in Tallinn. Our room was large with a king-bed, a sitting area, and a television with satellite reception and a large bathroom with nice amenities. We were quite pleased with our selection. The proprietors of the Romeo were extremely helpful to us and it made a terrific choice for us for our stay.

After stowing our bags in our ample room we set out exploring. Tallinn is a beautiful old city with a well preserved medieval core. In fact, most of the original city walls are intact along with several of the guard towers. This UNESCO World Heritage site is filled with winding, cobblestone streets that pass beautiful, pastel colored buildings. As you ascend to the top of the hill you pass a myriad of shops, small galleries, eateries and pubs. This is truly a great city to wander and take in the sights and culture.

Additionally, Estonia was long considered the most western of the former Soviet republics. This was likely due to its exposure to western media via the Finnish airwaves which were a short distance away across the Gulf of Finland. This availability of Finnish television and radio also probably led to Estonia's relatively easy transition to the post-Soviet era.

We started our exploration by venturing into the city's town square and checked out the old Town Hall. The Gothic structure was built in the 14th Century and dominates the square. You are able to visit the interior and, if you are feeling spry, you can even climb to the top of its tower for a bit of a view of the Old Town.

From the square we headed up the hill toward the castle. Along the way we looked in the numerous shops and paid particular attention to the amber pieces available. Apparently, the Baltic region has one of the earliest known and most abundant supplies of amber in the world. As I understand, it literally washes up on the shores of the Baltic Sea in these three countries. At any event, there are lovely jewelry pieces and other object de art readily available and reasonably priced. The most highly prized pieces of amber include insects trapped inside the fossilized tree resin.

Shopping for Russian souvenirs is good, as well, in Tallinn. You can find loads of matryoshkas, the nesting dolls, and old Soviet Red Army artifacts. I was able to buy Jenny a beautiful Faberge egg pendant at a shop on top of the hill near the Castle. These replicas of the handiwork of Carl Faberge are a great gift and are easily concealed so they can be saved for that special occasion when you return home.

Finished with our minor shopping spree, we made our way to the top of Toompea hill were we visited three of the major sights in Tallinn; Toomkirik, Toompea Castle and Alexander Nevsky Cathedral. Toomkirik is probably the oldest church in Tallinn. From its commanding position on top of Toompea hill it provides an excellent view of the Old Town and the harbor. It is also the burial ground for many famous people in Estonian history.

Toompea Castle is the traditional home to Estonia's government. The parliament of Estonia meets in the large pink, baroque style building on the grounds. Across the street from the Castle sits Alexander Nevsky Cathedral. As with many traditional Russian Orthodox churches, the Nevsky Cathedral has a very ornate exterior crowned by the traditional onion domes. In the Soviet era, the Cathedral fell into disrepair and has undergone extensive renovation since Estonia gained its independence.

As we began our descent, snow was falling at a rapid pace and the wind was howling. It was cold and I remembered the perfect antidote for this condition. A few years prior when my friend, Warren Mathies, and I had visited Tallinn it was a similar day. Some how in the middle of the snow and cold we stumbled upon a warm, cozy tavern built in one of the remaining towers in the City Wall. So, we went in search of this pub.

Sure enough, we were able to find the café. The square tower, Neitsitorn, or the Virgin Tower, was originally built in the 14th Century and served as a prison for prostitutes. Now, they are more famous for their hot, mulled wine. We entered through the heavy wooden door and ascended to the second level where we could enjoy a commanding view of the Old Town. We ordered a mug of gulhwein which was served with a bowl of nuts. We sat in the warmth near an open fire sipping this delicious nectar, enjoying its Christmas spice aroma, and snacking on peanuts. I had fond memories of my first visit here, but this moment surpassed those very quickly. This type of experience is the reason to travel.

After a couple of cups of the grog we decided it was time to return to the Romeo to rest before going out to dinner. On the way back to our room we stopped in a liquor store to buy a couple of local beers, Saku, to enjoy as we relaxed in our room. The store was staffed by a very attractive, tall brunette woman who noticed I was eyeing the vodka supply. I was thinking of buying a decent Russian vodka to take home as a souvenir.

She approached me and impressed me with her command of the English language and her apparent knowledge of vodka. She talked me into purchasing a bottle of Estonian vodka and a Russian Standard, which she said was recently acclaimed the best in the world. Nearly ten years later I was shopping in my corner liquor store and there in the middle of the vodka section was a display of Russian Standard. I could not believe my eyes that this treat was now becoming my house brand. This seems to me to be further proof that the world is truly shrinking and we are becoming more global in nature.

We returned to the Romeo and rested for a few hours and wished we did not have to leave the warmth and comfort of our cozy room to seek an evening repast. But, that was not the case and after consulting our trusty In Your Pocket we bundled up and ventured out into the snowy evening in search of an Italian dinner at a restaurant named Cassanova. (We were staying at Romeo's and dining at Cassanova's, maybe there is a theme here?) As we ambled through the cobblestone streets we arrived at the Town Square and were pleasantly surprised by how pretty it looked with the snow falling through the evening illuminations.

We continued up the hill a short way from the Town Hall and arrived at our destination. The smell of garlic filled the warm, dark interior of the restaurant. We both settled on plates of penne pasta smothered in a think Bolognese sauce. We split an inexpensive, but tasty, bottle of Italian red wine which really complimented the pasta. This was a great, hardy meal which warmed us as we prepared to walk back down the hill for our night's slumber.

We awoke the next morning after a solid night's sleep and could smell the aroma of freshly made coffee wafting into our room from the breakfast area just outside our door. After getting ready for the day we emerged from our room at a prearranged time for our morning meal. Breakfast is served in a well-appointed room that doubles as a sitting room for the guests the remainder of the day. The Romeo serves a delicious breakfast with made to order eggs, cereals, breads, meats and cheeses. They also will not let your coffee cup get empty. It is a very enjoyable experience.

Well fortified, we set out on our days activities. Our first order of business was to walk down to the harbor and ensure that our reservations for our trip the next day to Helsinki were in order. It's a pretty good hoof from the Romeo to the harbor side offices of the ferry services, enough so that we vowed to grab a cab the next morning for our departure. We entered the offices and boarding area of the Helsinki ferry lines and confirmed that our reservation on a catamaran the next day was valid. With our business done, it was now time to set about exploring Tallinn again.

As we entered into the Old Town through a city gate near the McDonald's, we encountered another great local institution, the Wall of Sweaters. In the lower end of the Old Town is a row of outdoor shops built into the old city wall selling primarily hand-knit sweaters made by local women. Warren and I had happened upon these shops by accident in my earlier trip to Tallinn. Jenny and I located these shops and could not help ourselves and purchased a couple of these lovely sweaters. These beautiful garments come in all shapes, sizes and colors and are priced right for our wallets.

Given the bulky nature of our new treasures, and that we prefer to travel lightly, this gave rise to a trip to the Estonian postal service to ship our purchase home. Thankfully, one of the proprietors of a sweater shop gave us directions to a post office within a few blocks. Unlike some previous visits to post offices in foreign countries, we were able to communicate with the clerk and the transaction went smoothly. We have shipped articles home on several occasions and firmly believe this is a good idea. Dealing with the local postal service can be challenging and time consuming, but it is an interesting experience.

By now we had worked up a hearty appetite and set out to find a location for lunch. Following the narrow cobblestone streets we were soon back to the Town Hall Square. We spied a stylish little café right on the square that appeared inviting on this cold, grey day. Once inside we felt confident we had made the right decision. We were seated at a window table with a fine view of the square and it was indeed nice and warm inside. After a quick perusal of the menu we both decided on soups and they delivered them quickly. My goulash soup hit the spot and prepared me for an afternoon of exploring the byways of the Old Town.

We spent the next couple of hours exploring the side streets of the Old Town. We did some shopping for gifts for family members for the upcoming holidays. After a couple of hours of directionless meandering we decided to call it a day.

The cold of the day took its toll on us and we returned to the Romeo. We took a short nap; fixed a pre-dinner drink of the Estonian vodka we had picked up the day before and consulted our guide to find a location for our last evening meal in Tallinn. We quickly decided that Eeslitall, or Donkey Stable, would suit our needs.

We set back out into the cold night and after about a five minute walk we arrived at our destination. The Donkey Stable was a somewhat rustic restaurant, candlelit and a romantic place. Our waiter seemed attentive, quickly taking a drink order and returning to the table with said. We ordered our dinner and he strongly recommended a bottle of Georgian wine to accompany our meal. Not knowing anything about Georgian wine, we explained to him that we prefer big, dry reds and certainly nothing fruity or sweet. He proffered a recommendation and disappeared to place our order.

Upon his return to our table he brought our starters, cups of hot, thick soup and a bottle of the wine he recommended. The bottle was open and he left us glasses, but did not offer us a taste before leaving. So, I poured some in our glasses which in due course we both tried. Our immediate consensus was that the wine was very fruity and sweet and in no way resembled what had been billed. I hailed down our waiter and tried to explain to him that the bottle of wine did not meet our needs and we would like to try something else. He began to debate the subject with me rather strenuously. I tried further to get him to understand our position to little avail. Finally, for some unknown reason I summoned up a few words of Russian, and barked those at him and the debate ended. It was like my few words in Russian had a chilling effect on him. I guess that the years of Soviet occupation still had a lingering effect on the Estonians.

At any event, he quickly removed the bottle and glasses and replaced it with a full-bodied, dry red wine from Georgia. It was very much to our liking, as was our meal. He brought out our entrees in short order and they were delicious. I had a hunter steak which was extremely tender and the sauce was to die for. We had a very lovely evening and received great service from our waiter the remainder of the evening. However, the most memorable part of the dinner was our encounter over the wine and how it was resolved. **(See Appendix 17 for the recipe)**

FINLAND

The next morning we awoke to another cold, snowy day in Tallinn. We savored our last meal in Estonia at the Romeo, gazing out the window of our breakfast room onto an Old Town square. We were both a little melancholy because of our pending departure from Tallinn, a city we enjoy immensely. Our time in the Baltics had been a wonderful experience, but it was now time to move on to our last leg of the journey, Helsinki.

After breakfast we ducked back into our room and finished packing. I then asked the proprietor of the Romeo to call us a cab for the ferry port. Being the very hospitable folks they are, they would have none of it and insisted on taking us themselves. So, we piled into the owner's sedan and were transported to the harbor. Thanking the owner of the Romeo profusely for his kindness we bade him adieu and entered the staging area for our fast ferry ride to Finland.

The trip across the Gulf of Finland to Helsinki is only 43 nautical miles. This can be accomplished by various types of ships, but the quickest and our preference was by hydrofoil. Given the time of year that we were making the crossing, the seas can be rough and the hydrofoils may not be running for the winter. However, we were very lucky that these speedy vessels were still going and we were able to make the crossing in about an hour and a half. The much slower large ferry boats that make the journey year round cover this expanse in three to four hours.

The jaunt on the hydrofoil is actually a pleasant one. The cabin is bedecked with airplane type seats that are roomy and comfortable. Even though the sea is beginning to turn ugly for the winter the ride is smooth. There is a small restaurant onboard serving a range of snacks to full meals and the full compliment of beverages. Our arrival port was smack dab in the middle of downtown Helsinki and any customs and immigrations issues were very easy to navigate. Thus, when you disembarked the ship you are ready to tackle the city.

Our first order of business was to locate and check in to our hotel. The Hotel Finn is perfectly situated in the center of town. I had stayed at the hotel with my friend, Warren, on an earlier trip to Russia a few years before. The accommodations are located on the fifth and sixth floors of a downtown office building. Although the walk from the port to the hotel was a little further than I had remembered (probably because I wasn't lugging a suitcase last time I made the trip) it is certainly doable.

After about a ten minute walk we arrived at the Finn. The establishment is very functional, if Spartan. The front desk personnel showed us to our room, which to my pleasant surprise was larger and better appointed than the room I had stayed in before. It had a king-sized bed, ample closet and dresser space, a television and a nice bathroom. We stowed our belongings and rested for a few minutes and decided it was time to hit the streets and find some lunch.

We largely retraced our steps as we returned through the downtown area toward the port. Our route took us along an esplanade which is lined with largely upscale shops and eateries. This is the heart of the shopping district of Helsinki. Our destination was at the end of the esplanade at the waterfront, Kauppatori, the Market Square and Market Hall.

The Kauppatori is an interesting mix of an outdoor market with a nearby indoor (heated in winter) hall selling a myriad of items. Fresh fish, meats including wild game, cheeses, produce and other foodstuffs, as well as, furs, handicrafts and souvenirs are available. We came not to shop, but rather to eat at one of the restaurants that are in the Market Hall. There are several savory offerings in the Hall, but we quickly settled on a couple of large sandwiches made to order before our eyes.

On long slices of thick, whole wheat bread the counterperson slathered a thick layer of freshly prepared tuna salad followed with mayonnaise, tomatoes, onions and pickels. He handed us the sandwiches in white waxed paper along with a couple of big bottles of local beer. We found a table nearby and sat down to enjoy our delicious sandwiches. In my mind, it was a meal fit for a king.

After devouring our lunch, we continued to brose around the market area. As we departed the Market Hall we could not help but notice the imposing Uspenski Cathedral across the small harbor. Being suckers for old, imposing churches we walked around the harbor to the red brick structure. The Russian Orthodox Church was built in the 1860s and is topped by onion-domes. The interior of the structure is more ornate than many I visited in Russian where more attention seems to be paid to the exterior than the interior of their churches.

Continuing with our religious theme we decided to take the short walk and visit the other church that dominates the skyline of the Finnish capitol, the Helsinki Cathedral. The chalk white structure is capped with a green dome and sits atop the Senate Square, a few blocks from the waterfront. The neoclassical church rises high above the surrounding buildings and it cannot be missed. The interior of the church is rather plain, but does contain statues of early leaders of the Protestant movement.

Beginning to tire after our travels and sightseeing we headed back to the Finn for a rest before venturing out to dinner. When we got back I decided it would be a perfect time to try some more of the Estonian vodka the helpful clerk at the Tallinn liquor store had highly recommended to me. So, I checked with the front desk at the hotel and, to little surprise, there was no ice to be found at the Finn. Often times the small hotels where I stay around the world do not offer ice as a service.

Undeterred I was forced to resort to Plan B. We decided to try and find a supermarket where we could purchase a small bag of ice. The gentleman at the front desk directed us down the street about a block and a half to what he described as a large grocery. So we bundled up and set out to acquire some ice. We found the very nice store and searched high and low, but there was no ice. We even inquired at the service desk about our interest in acquiring ice and they looked at us like we had two heads.

It was now time to resort to what has been a foolproof plan for us. We have discovered that when we want clean ice to fix a cocktail we simply go to the Golden Arches. I had noticed a McDonald's location down the street from our hotel. So we exited the grocery and were soon at the counter of the fast food joint. Generally, we will offer to purchase a couple of large soft drinks, but we don't want the soda, simply the ice. More often than not, and this was the case that evening, after checking with the manager the counter person will just give you the cups of ice for free.

Problem solved and a sufficient supply of ice is procured to have a couple of vodkas on the rocks prior to dinner. After our pre dinner cocktails we ventured out to a local Greek restaurant for dinner. We had picked up an <u>IN YOUR POCKET</u> guide for Helsinki and the Athanasios Taverna had come recommended.

We walked a few short blocks and found the homey, little restaurant in a courtyard just off a main street. The small restaurant was decorated in the Greek colors, blue and white. Here we supped on the house specialty, moussaka, sort of the Greek version of lasagna, which hit the spot on a cold and snowy Finnish evening. Fully sated we trudged back to our room to call it a night.

One small draw back of the Hotel Finn is that no breakfast is served. However, this allows you to extend out into the city and find what the area has to offer. Consulting our travel guide we decided to try the Café Engel. What a great decision! This would turn out to be our favorite meal while in Finland.

The Café Engel is a few blocks walk from the Finn. Located in one of the oldest buildings in Helsinki, it is directly across the street from the Senate Square and the aforementioned Helsinki Cathedral. The quaint café is very comfortable and the odors emanating from kitchen were either very pleasing, or we were quite hungry, or both.

After close inspection of the menu and watching the plates delivered to nearby tables, we both settled on their Bacon and Eggs breakfast. Jenny order black tea and I selected coffee. The drinks quickly arrived at our table and we were very pleased. In fact, I am quite confident that these were the two best breakfast beverages we had on this trip. Soon the plates of scrambled eggs, bacon, orange juice, fresh fruit, along with pastries and freshly baked bread, toasted to perfection, and homemade jams were delivered. This was a meal made in heaven, extremely fresh and pleasing to the palate. We could not have been happier. **(See Appendix 18 for the recipe)**

After lingering over our tea and coffee, we finally decided it was time to venture forth and spend our last day of this vacation as fruitfully as possible. Our first stop was at a small shop very near to Café Engle that had very cool, Russian-made Christmas ornaments. Being shooed away by Jenny, I could tell that she had found something that would end up under our Christmas tree with my name on it. As it turns out she found a number of items we could not live without. They included an ornament, a Christmas matryoshka nesting doll set, a Father Christmas carving and a really neat wooden, Christmas figurine that contains a bell inside. This was quite a haul of ethnic holiday decorations.

Down the street from our shop was the tourist information office. We decided to pop in and see if there were any activities going on in town that we might like to attend. Specifically, I was interested to see if one of the local professional hockey teams were playing. When I had visited Helsinki before, Warren and I had gone to a hockey game at an arena near downtown and it had been a very pleasurable experience.

It turns out that we are in luck. Not only is there a professional hockey game that late afternoon, but it is an international match with a Finnish team scheduled to play one from Sweden. The tickets for the game were being sold at the largest department store in Helsinki, Stockmann's. We thanked the clerk at the tourist information center and headed back out into the cold. We had no problem finding the department store. Stockmann's is an imposing structure almost across the street from the Hotel Finn and is an interesting place to stroll through. We located the ticket office and discovered that there were in fact some good seats still available at a reasonable price and we snatched them up.

After drinking in the sights, smells and sounds of Stockmann's we realized that we had some time to kill before we set out for the hockey game. We decided to return to the Finn and consult our travel book for suggestions on a sight to visit before we had to leave for the game. After a brief scan of the book we decided that a visit to the Mannerheim Museum was in order.

The Mannerheim was reached after a ten minute walk from our hotel through a beautiful neighborhood that includes a number of foreign embassies. Upon our arrival the warmth that was emanating for the building was a welcome relief as the day had gotten colder and the snow was now flying about at a good pace. The villa was the home to Baron Carl Gustav Mannerheim, a great Finnish military leader, politician and the Marshal of Finland. Mannerheim served in both the Russian and Finnish armies and was the President of Finland from 1946-48.

His home is preserved largely as it was when he lived in it from 1924 until his death in 1951. The home is filled with personal mementos and military artifacts from his years of service in the Imperial Russian army and the newly established Republic of Finland. Additionally, there are numerous antiques and gifts from admirers collected from around the world. In all, if you are a student of history, war, or the early foundation of the Republic of Finland, this museum is well worth your time.

A quickly empty hockey rink after the game was called.

As we walked back toward the downtown area we admired the beauty of the neighborhood with its stately homes. During this stroll it became clear that many Finns had acquired wealth around the turn of the last century, and many others remain so today.

Reaching the center we hopped on a tram nearly in front of Stockmann's for the Ice Arena located just a little north of downtown, but still well within the city. As the tram rattled its way toward the game we picked up more fans and the excitement began to mount. As we passed the Olympic Stadium, site of the 1952 track and field events for the Helsinki Games, I knew we were getting close to our destination.

As we entered the building the buzz of pregame activity was mounting. We found our seats which turned out to be quite good and watched the players warm up. Since we had some time we decided to grab a beer and also bought a couple of T-shirts to commemorate the occasion. Returning to the seats we realized that the players had left the ice and a new message appeared on the scoreboard. Unable to read Finnish, a couple of fellows sitting in front of us informed us that the arena was having trouble with its ice-making equipment and they were working to repair the situation.

Sure enough, about fifteen minutes later an announcement came over the P.A. that the game had been called for lack of proper ice. Bummed out, we along with the other 8,000 patrons began to file out of the building. We decided our best strategy was to try to get back to Stockmann's before they closed to get a refund since we were leaving in the morning. We squeezed onto the first tram that arrived and we able to return to the department store just before it closed. The clerk at the ticket office in Stockmann's was very sympathetic and forked over a refund in cash.

Our new dilemma was what to do with this cash on a Saturday evening as all stores were closing. We returned to our room after stopping at the McDonald's for ice and fixed a before dinner cocktail. Consulting our guide we decided to try an Italian restaurant for our last meal in Helsinki.

We bundled back up and trudged through the snowy streets to our destination. Entering the building we descended to the lower level to the restaurant, Al Viale. As we entered the trattoria, we were surprised to see a truly lovely atrium filled with plants, patrons at linen clad tables and wonderful aromas. A very welcoming host met us and took us to table along the back wall.

An attractive young waitress soon appeared with a large, multipage menu written in English. Flush with cash we decided to begin by ordering a nice bottle of Italian red wine. We were informed that all the pasta was made on the premises, so we knew which direction we would go. We both ordered plates of rigatoni Bolognese along with Caeser salads.

Our waitress left for a few moments and returned with the wine, salads, and freshly baked garlic bread. The salads were very crisp and fresh, the garlic bread nearly melted in your mouth and the wine was full-bodied and very pleasing to our palates. As we finished our salads, our waitress arrived with our brimming plates of pasta. We enjoyed a delicious dinner which turned out to be an affordable meal in a very expensive city.

Since it was still early we decided to stop for a nightcap at a bar along our route back to the hotel. We had seen a news piece on the television just before we left about how the Finish people were not too social. This aledged inability to mix was a purported source of alcoholism and an impingement on their ability to meet their life partners. Based on what we saw that evening in the bar, the report might have been correct. Although the place was crowded, it seemed dead to us. So, after one drink we headed back to the Finn and were soon in bed.

The next morning we boarded the Finnair bus which picks up a several locations and is the best transit option for the airport. After check-in we had one final task before we departed for home; spend our remaining Finnish markka. Thankfully, the Helsinki airport has a nice duty free area that sells all the usual items, plus Finnish handicrafts. We used our final local currency to purchase some hand-blown glassware which still rests on my nightstand. We boarded the plane and returned home with great memories of the beautiful countries, their great food, and kind people who were so welcoming particularly in the aftermath of the World Trade disaster.

Hank, I hope one day that you get to experience these countries. I am sure you will find them welcoming and their histories will be of interest to you. My only regret about our time in the Baltics was I wish we had a longer stay. As I would tell anyone, we need to get you there before they become too westernized. I hope they do not allow themselves to become too overrun with American franchise fast-food outlets and they maintain their native charm and cuisine.

CHAPTER 7

SCANDINAVIA

JENNY AND I HAD A tradition of celebrating our wedding anniversaries by taking a large, international trip to mark the occasion. Hank, you may recall that we continued this tradition until you started school and your schedule began to interfere. Although your entering school did not stop us from pulling you out for international travel, it became more difficult the older you became. We continue to take you on these wonderful trips, but we do so with less incursion on your school time.

We actually began this tradition by getting married barefoot on the beach in Ambergris Caye, Belize, on May 6, 2000. In May of 2003, this custom continued for our third anniversary. We decided to travel the continental Scandinavian countries of Norway, Denmark and Sweden. We had both been to Stockholm a few years before, really liked it and had a strong desire to return. I had been to Copenhagen with a friend, Mike Price, a few years before and had thoroughly enjoyed the city. My mother and others had traveled to Norway and were glowing in the reviews of the natural beauty of the country and, so, we decided to give the area a try.

Once again, I did my research and determined that the best way to traverse the area, at that time, was by rail. I investigated further and discovered that we could purchase a Scandinavian rail pass that would enable us to travel throughout these three countries, our required number of days, at a very affordable price. We ordered up two of the passes that allowed us to travel four days in a two month period which would work perfectly for us.

We booked our flights through Northwest Airlines and their partner, KLM, the Dutch airlines. We booked an open-jawed trip, into Bergen, Norway, with a return from Stockholm, Sweden. Arranging to travel by starting your journey at one point and concluding it from another can save you a great deal of time retracing your steps. Thus, you are able to cover more ground on your vacation. Also, I have found that this generally does not cost more money to do an open-jawed trip, in fact, there have been times it has actually been cheaper to enter and exit continents from different locales.

We decided to start our journey in Norway, first visiting the city of Bergen and then on to the capitol, Oslo. We would next travel to Copenhagen and environs and finish the trip by revisiting the beautiful city of Stockholm. We had done all the research and chosen our hotels and train schedules. We were ready.

NORWAY

The day of our departure in mid-May had finally arrived and we were excited for our trip. We went to the Indianapolis International Airport and checked-in the requisite two hours before hand. We killed some time eating a late lunch at the Budweiser Brewhouse and finally boarded our flight for Detroit where we were to make our connection for Amsterdam. We had been upgraded to first class because of our status with the airline and we crawled into seats 1A and 1B still swirling with anticipation. We had a couple of drinks and a smooth flight to the Motor City.

We arrived a few minutes early and started to proceed to the concourse where most of the international flights departed from the old Detroit terminal. When we arrived in the large circular boarding area that serviced several gates, it appeared that something was amiss. Our flight was delayed, as were some others. We found a couple of open seats and stretched out for a wait which we hoped would not be an extended one. We were scheduled to depart on the next flight out to Amsterdam, which was the first of three that evening. Our plane, a DC-10, was the workhorse of Northwest's international fleet, and we had seats 10A and 10B reserved which were exit row seats with ample legroom.

After our flight was delayed again for another hour, I decided it was time to have a conversation with a gate agent to explore our options. I noticed a pleasant-looking woman at a nearby gate working away, but with no customer bothering her. I thought she appeared to be our best option at the time. I approached her and asked for information and told her about our concern that our connecting flight the next morning from Amsterdam to Bergen might be in jeopardy. She said our plane was experiencing a mechanical issue and we would have a further update in about a half an hour.

Then, she looked at our tickets and notice that we were both elite fliers with the airline. She informed me that there might be an opportunity to get on the next flight to Amsterdam, she would see what she could do. She asked about baggage and I told her we were only traveling with carry-on luggage and she indicated that was a help to our cause. In those days before you came along Hank, we always only took the maximum allowable carry-on bags designated by the airline. This made for easier passage through customs and immigration and allowed us to be more nimble in situations such as we were confronting that evening. Although it was somewhat of an adjustment, checking bags after you came along was a small trade-off to having you with us Hank.

I thought I would push the envelope even further and ask about seats, since we had good ones reserved and I did not want to sit in a regular coach seat given my size. She informed me that there were a couple of seats available in first class on the next flight that she would try to procure for us. Now, I was to leave her alone and check back with her in about thirty minutes. I returned to Jenny and filled her in on the news. Even though we were now tiring because of a nearly two hour delay, we both were excited about the prospects of the possibility of an upgrade.

The report came in a half hour that our flight was going to be further delayed. The boarding process for the next flight to Amsterdam was set to begin and the kind gate agent caught my eye and motioned us to come over and see her. She was standing by the boarding gate for the next flight out and was holding two boarding passes with our names on them, seats 1G and 1H. She told us to run get our bags and we could board immediately. She said we might miss our connecting flight to Bergen, but she would take care of us. We thanked the kind soul profusely.

The moral of this story to me is that **airlines reward customer loyalty.** If you are going to fly much, try to figure out which carrier makes the most sense to you for where you live and where you are going to travel. You truly need to maximize the opportunity with an airline, if you are going to be a frequent flier. We certainly were not selected for this upgrade for just my charm or my wife's good looks, rather it was because we were elite travelers with Northwest. For whatever reasons, we greatly appreciated the opportunity to fly up front where the experience is far more special.

Thrilled, we both grabbed our things and bolted to the plane and took our seats in the front row. As we were stowing our bags in the overhead bins, the flight attendant brought us each a glass of champagne. We knew then that it was going to be a wonderful flight, and it was. We dined on filet mignon, drank excellent wine and enjoyed delicious ice cream sundaes to top off our meals. After a glass of cognac we stretched out in our comfortable, reclining seats and slept for a few hours which made our arrival in Amsterdam much more pleasant.

When we got to Amsterdam, we had indeed missed our flight to Bergen. But, true to her word, the gate agent in Detroit had taken care of us. She had moved us to great seats on the next flight out and we made it safely to Bergen by late morning. Upon arriving in Bergen we changed some money at a currency exchange at the airport and hopped the airport bus into the city. You couldn't help but be struck by the natural beauty of the Bergen area on the ride in from the airport. Like Rome, Bergen is reputed to being built on seven hills and the lush spring colors were beginning to awake.

The bus station where we arrived was in the central part of the city. It was a comfortable walk from the station to our accommodations, the Bergen Gjestehus. I had read about this small hotel on the internet and decided that the price and location were a good match for us. Located on a side street a couple of blocks from the main square in Bergen, Torgalmenneningen, it was within walking distance of all the major attractions, as well as a variety of restaurants, bars and shops.

After a few minutes stroll on this brisk, spring morning we arrived at the door of our hotel. We entered the smallish lobby and were greeted by a friendly young man working the front desk. He quickly retrieved our reservation and dispatched us to our room up a couple of small flights of stairs, but really on the second floor above the lobby with a full street view. The room turned out to be quite large with a king bed and a sitting area with a black leather couch and chair and a television with international stations.

As we settled in we showered and prepared to venture out for the day. It was then we discovered one of the most impressive facets of our room, the bathroom floor was heated. The large grey tiles in the bathroom were heated to a very nice temperature making for a very pleasant feel on your feet as you padded about in the room. This was particularly true as our stay continued and the exterior temperature dropped in a typical spring cool down.

It was now well afternoon. But, before we left to find some lunch, I called back to the office for my customary check in with my assistant, Elyse Rumely. She reported that she had everything under control and said that she would call our aging parents to let them know we had made it to Norway safely. I thanked her for all her help and we departed to begin to explore the virtues of Bergen.

As we set out we retraced our steps across Torgalmenneingen Square and headed for the old part of the city down near the waterfront. But first, we needed to find a place for lunch as the small breakfast we received on the plane several hours before had worn off. As we neared the waterfront, we came across a casual-looking Thai food establishment that appeared inviting. We perused the English menu in the window and noticed that they had several luncheon specials that could satisfy our needs.

We entered the cozy eatery and were welcomed by a very attractive, young Asian woman who showed us to a table with a view out the front window. Being very hungry and overcome by the wonderful aromas emanating from the kitchen, we both decided quickly on plates of spicy chicken Pad Thai with hot tea to drink. In very short order our dishes arrived and the Pad Thai did indeed turn out to be quite spicy, as I like it. We devoured our very enjoyable lunches, sipped our tea and enjoyed each other's company.

After paying the bill we began to wonder around the Old Town of Bergen. The area along the eastern side of the waterfront is known as Bryggen. This series of colorfully painted, timbered structures are Hanseatic commercial buildings dating back ages. This is the oldest part of Bergen and has suffered several fires, only to be rebuilt. Today the area is on the UNESCO World Heritage site list. The buildings are now filled with shops, bars, and eateries. We spent the rest of the afternoon browsing through the shops and stopping for a beer, or two, in one of the pubs. This very cool, picturesque area is well worth the visit.

Tiring from a long day of travel, we returned to our hotel to get some rest before heading out to dinner later that evening. When we entered the hotel the young man at the front desk stopped us and asked that I call my office as soon as possible. We knew that this could not be good news because Elyse is very competent and would be able to handle almost anything that she confronted and would not bother us with trivial matters. We hustled to our room and I immediately called Elyse back. It turns out that Jenny's father, Joe Medisch, had been hospitalized with chest pains and she needed to call her mother.

Elyse and I hung up and Jenny called the number at the hospital that Elyse had provided us. As it turns out her father answered the phone in the hospital room. He had undergone a series of tests and there was nothing to be alarmed about, probably just some acid reflux. Once Jenny talked to her dad and realized that everything was okay she felt profoundly relieved. We decided to go downstairs to the little pub in our hotel and have a beer to celebrate the good news.

Our hotel was certainly no showplace and the pub, as you might expect, was rather Spartan but welcoming. We both ordered a pint of the local brew, coiffed it down, and reorder another. As we finished our second one we decided it was time to consult our guide upstairs in our room for a dining spot. I asked for the bill for the four pints of beer and was informed that I owed them the equivalent to $44, or $11 a piece. I almost choked when I heard this.

I had read before we left that Bergen was, at that time, the most expensive city in the world, apparently having something to do with the North Sea oil industry situated nearby. The lunch we had was far from cheap, nor were the beers in the pub earlier. But, I had figured that in those cases we were buying some atmosphere given the location of each of those establishments. Clearly, that was not the case for the pub at the Bergen Gjesthus. I now was beginning to get the feeling that Bergen was indeed a very expensive place to visit.

We returned to our room for a brief consultation with the travel book we had assembled, and decided to try a highly recommended pizzeria for dinner that evening. We bundled up as it was now getting rather chilly and headed out in search of the eating establishment. Our destination, it turns out, was only a few blocks away. We entered the lively place which was packed and were lucky to be shown to the only vacant table in the joint. Our waiter came by directly supplying us with English menus and taking our drink order, a pitcher of local beer.

Jenny is very close with her family and was very relieved that there was nothing seriously wrong with her father. She clearly felt like having a good time and this bright, upbeat restaurant seemed to be a good match for her mood. We order a large pizza with sausage, onion and mushrooms and poured ourselves a glass of beer from the pitcher. We swigged on the beers and talked about our very positive first impressions of the natural beauty of Bergen as we waited for our pizza to arrive.

Before too long our piping hot, large pizza was delivered. The reviews were correct, the cheesy, tomato-saucy concoction was very pleasing. We downed every morsel of the pizza and ordered another pitcher of beer. We had a great time enjoying the evening, the music playing in the background, and the rest of the second pitcher. We polished off our beer and decided it was time to get to bed since it had been a very long day of travel and trauma. I hailed our waiter and he brought us the bill. I can remember I nearly fainted when I saw it, **over one hundred dollars for a pizza and two pitchers of beer!** I needed no further confirmation, we were indeed in a very expensive place to visit.

As we left the pizza place and began our walk back to our hotel I remember thinking it was very light outside for that time of night. As we crossed Torgalmenneingen Square I looked up at the large clock that adorns the top of the local newspaper building, the Bergens Tidende, and it read 9:50. Although not fully light, it was still bright enough that you could have read a copy of that newspaper. I am sure we were not far enough north for midnight sun, but it was a real reminder that we were not too far away from that point.

Jenny and I soon returned to the hotel and went straight to bed. It did not take a lullaby for us to go to sleep that night and I remember sleeping like a rock. However, we made one fairly serious mistake, we did not pull the curtains tightly closed before going to bed and the morning light awoke us earlier than we would have liked. But that was okay, we had a big day of touring ahead and needed to make an early start.

We both showered up and went downstairs for breakfast which was served in the pub. Breakfast consisted of sliced ham and cheese, some muesli, yogurt, bread, juice and coffee. We really enjoy these types of Northern European breakfasts and ate to our hearts content. I am almost embarrassed to admit the next thing we did, but not quite.

I had seen an episode of a Rick Steves journey through Scandinavia on PBS where he had suggested that you might want to make an extra sandwich at breakfast and take it with you to have for lunch, given how expensive it is in that part of the world. Well, Jenny and I decided that after paying over a hundred dollars for pizza and beer the night before, we would follow this bit of advice. So we grabbed some bread, ham and cheese, and made a sandwich and wrapped it in a napkin and shoved it into Jenny's bag to eat later that day. I am not necessarily proud of this, but it is a practical solution to a real problem.

One of the real enticements for coming to the Bergen area was to experience the Norwegian fjords. Fjords are an impressive natural phenomena that were created when glacial activity formed a long narrow inlet with steep cliffs bounding its sides. We had read about the best way to experience them in a day was to take a trip called Norway in a Nutshell. I did some research prior to our arrival and discovered you could take this journey as a full-day trip from Bergen. This was to be that day and our multi-modal adventure awaited us.

Soon after breakfast we took the pleasant walk from our hotel to the Bergen Train Station. Shortly after 8 o'clock we arrived at the station where our first order of business was to have our Scandinavian rail pass validated. Utilizing our passes helped to defray the transportation costs of the tour. After we finished this minor ministerial function, we next turned to locating our train for our first destination, the Norwegian village of Voss. We quickly found our train in this efficient, small station and filled some comfortable seats.

The Bergen Train is a terrific experience as, in short order from leaving the city, you climb up the mountainous spine that runs through the center of this beautiful country. This one-hour ride was punctuated with beautiful vistas and snow-covered peaks. Upon arrival at the Voss station we alit into a hard snowfall. We had a bit of a wait before we transferred to a bus for an hour-long ride to Gundvangen, a tiny village that is the point of embarkation for our fjord cruise. We stood shivering in the cold huddled outside the station waiting for the bus, but man was it beautiful. The mountains and the fresh snow flocking everything, almost made you forget that we were underdressed for the temperature. Again, this bus ride is a very scenic natural including waterfalls and mountain vistas and delivers us to the true highlight of the day, sailing of the fjords.

After arriving in Gundvangen, we were deposited at ferry terminal to await boarding our ship. With scarcely enough time to take a restroom break, we were called to depart for our fjord cruise. Jenny and I took seats on the forward deck in order to experience the trip al fresco. We were run inside on a couple of occasions by pop-up showers including one that featured some pelting frozen rain. These brief storms gave rise to a couple of beautiful rainbows that punctuated our trip.

A stunningly beautiful fjord in Norway!

As we steamed for two hours through the series of fjords, we were met with constant natural beauty and wildlife. Various species of birds soar overhead and marine mammals play in the wake of the vessel. The sheer rock cliffs give way to numerous waterfalls and you can wear yourself out clicking picture after picture. It is truly a sight to behold and it is little wonder these fjords are listed as a UNESCO World Heritage site.

At the end of the spectacular trip we arrived in the quaint little town of Flam. In Flam we had a break for over an hour where we browsed around a few little shops. We bought something to drink and ate our ham and cheese sandwiches we had purloined at breakfast. They were mighty tasty, but were not enough to satisfy our appetites so we augmented them with some bread and cheese we were able to purchase in a small shop.

All in all, Flam was a good break to the trip. After our respite ended, we next got on the Flam Railroad, yet another interesting aspect of Norway in a Nutshell. The Flam Railroad runs about twelve and a half miles from Flam up to Myrdal where you can connect with the Bergen Railroad. The train ascends nearly three thousand feet over its length and is one of the steepest trains in the world. The vista are magnificent as you chug along through tunnels past raging streams, waterfalls and snow-capped mountains. It is a very beautiful ride lasting about an hour.

When we arrived in Myrdal we again confronted a cold, snowy afternoon with knee deep snow covering the ground and more falling. There was little for us to do but stand on the platform in the cold before we transferred to the Bergen Railroad for the two-hour ride back to the city. The worst part of the journey was this last leg. Somehow we were given seats in a smoking car that was very crowded and thick with smoke. There was a number of young people in the car and they were having a good time drinking and smoking, smoking and drinking. By the time we got to Bergen, I would venture to say that over three quarters of the passengers in our car were inebriated. I guess it is always more fun to be part of the party than to be merely an observer.

By the time our train got back to Bergen we had been gone nearly twelve hours and we were spent. We trudged back to our little hotel and stopped into the pub off the lobby for a light meal and a few beers. We munched on tuna salad sandwiches on brown bread and thoroughly enjoyed the quiet surroundings that evening. Almost falling asleep at the table, we decided to call it an evening. We settled our bill and went upstairs to bed.

We awoke the next morning feeling refreshed after our first truly good night's sleep since arriving in Norway. It was a bright, sunny day and we were looking forward to our opportunity to wander about Bergen and find out what it has to offer. We showered and dressed and went downstairs for breakfast. We enjoyed a leisurely start to our day enjoying our Northern European breakfast and lingering over several cups of coffee and tea.

We set out that morning intent on seeing as much of Bergen as our time would allow. We decided that the best way to gain an overview of the city was to take the funicular up to the top of the most famous of Bergen's seven hills. The Floibanen funicular is very near to the waterfront and the ride to the top is well worth the time. The car ascends over a thousand feet up the side of the hill, taking over five minutes to do so. Once you arrive on the top of the hill there are paths to walk to various vantage points with great views of not only the City of Bergen, but mountains, fjords, and lakes in the distance.

We wandered around on top of the hill for quite some time taking in the remarkable views. After a time we decided to descend and further check out the area around the waterfront. First, we went to Det Hanseatiske Museum which is located in one of old wooden buildings in Bryggen. The museum chronicles the commercial activities of the area from centuries ago. The Norwegians would trade fish, grain, and salt to German merchants in the summer months driving the economy of the area. The museum contains authentic articles dating back to the seventeenth century.

We next visited the nearby St. Mary's Church, which is the oldest structure in Bergen. The Romanesque structure is quite beautiful and worthy of a quick peek. After these two stops we were beginning to get hungry and happened to stroll by the Bergen Market which further whetted our appetites. The Market is located on the harbor front in the center of Bergen and is a delight to your senses. Here you can buy handicrafts, fruits and vegetables, but the main attraction is the fish. You can purchase everything from salmon, to caviar, to whale. The merchants will give a free sample prior to deciding on your purchase.

After examining all the wares we decide to make a purchase and have lunch. One vendor was selling fried halibut which looked too good to resist, so we bought some and a couple of beers. We sat down at a nearby picnic table and enjoyed the incredibly fresh fish, the sunshine and, of course, the beers. It was an extremely pleasant lunch.

We reveled in the beauty of the day and the environment of Bergen, but decided there was one more stop we wanted to make before calling our sightseeing to an end, the Bergen Aquarium. I had read that the Aquarium was a nice one and we are both a fan of aquatic life. We struck out walking in the direction of the Aquarium which sits at the tip of a peninsula that overlooks the entrance to Bergen Harbor. On the map the distance from the Market to the Aquarium looks short, but in reality it has to be a fifteen to twenty minute walk. Somewhat more than we originally bargained for.

When we finally arrived at the Aquarium we were pleasantly surprised. In fact, we did not believe that the favorable reviews we had read did it justice. The setting of the Aquarium is exceptional with its views of the fjord, but the marine life is outstanding. There are large tanks housing seals, penguins, and various fish that are indigenous to the area. Additionally, there are numerous aquariums with colorful tropical fish from all over the world. It is really a delightful experience and one we had not expected to experience in Bergen, Norway. I believe that it is the highlight of our experience in Bergen.

After spending a good deal of time at the Aquarium, we tired, and decided it was time to return to the Bergen Gjesthus for a rest. We hiked the length of the peninsula back to the center of the city and to our accommodation. We took off our shoes and threw ourselves onto the bed and were soon fast asleep. We awakened a few hours later and decided it was time to pull ourselves together and go out for our last meal in Bergen.

As we ventured out into the evening it was still very light after eight o'clock. We decided to return to the waterfront and take our chance on finding a reasonably priced meal there. This proved to be a difficult task, but we finally found a pub a block off the water that had prices that were fairly reasonable. We ordered beers and both settled on fish and chips. Before long the waiter returned with mounded plates containing three large pieces of cod and more fries than any one human should eat. But eat we did. The cod was delicious and well-prepared and the fries hit the spot. We drank another beer as we finished off our massive meals and discussed our day's activities. We both really liked Bergen, but only wished it was a more affordable destination.

We finished our beers and paid the waiter for our supper. As we strolled back to the hotel for the last time we surveyed the cityscape and enjoyed the views of the seven hills for one last evening. We returned to our room and made preparations to leave the next morning. We had an early departure of around eight and the trip would take over six and a half hours. As we finished what packing we could do that evening, we turned out the lights and fell asleep.

We got another great night of sleep and awoke fresh that morning. We went through our morning routine and headed down for breakfast. Once again we dined on ham, cheese, wheat bread and beverages. We hurried through breakfast wanting to allow ample time to finish our light packing and head out to the train station. But, before we left breakfast we again fixed a couple of ham and cheese sandwiches each to make it through the day and our long train ride to Oslo.

We checked out of the hotel and headed the few blocks toward the Bergen Train Station. We arrived about a half hour before our scheduled departure and our train was already waiting on the track. We found our seats and settled in to our comfortable surroundings, this time in a nonsmoking car. Thank goodness.

We departed Bergen on schedule and soon were gaining altitude as we rose to cross the mountainous spine of Norway. The Norwegian travel authorities proclaim that this journey is the world's best train ride. I am not sure I would dispute this claim. The trip takes you through beautiful mountainous terrain with views of lush valleys, waterfalls, streams, mountain lakes, as well as, snow-capped peaks. You pass through numerous, quaint villages and towns that you wish you had time to get out and explore.

In a couple of the towns I spotted an unusual looking church with which I was not familiar. I would find out the next day while visiting a museum in Oslo that these churches are called stave churches. These unique structures were built in medieval times, the thirty or so that continue to exist in Norway were generally erected between 1000 and 1300 A.D. The distinctive wooden design is created as a blossoming of the Viking tradition of combining art with woodworking. These houses of worship with their steeply pitched roofs are indeed of extraordinary design and are truly noteworthy.

We enjoyed the scenery, read our books, ate our ham and cheese sandwiches and drank in the experience. After nearly seven hours we arrived in Oslo Sentralstasjon, which is a modern structure that contains a shopping center and sits at the foot of Karl Johans Gate, the main thoroughfare through downtown Oslo. This major shopping, entertainment, and strolling boulevard begins at the station and stretches to the Royal Palace on the other end.

Knowing that we were only spending two nights in Oslo, we had made reservations at a small hotel near the train station. The City Hotel was only a couple of blocks from the train station and was within walking distance of many of the major attractions. We felt this would help us maximize our time by being close to everything we wanted to do. The only downside to the hotel was speculation that the neighborhood was a little sketchy, but this did not deter us.

We rolled our bags out of the Sentalstasjon onto the plaza out front into a bright, sunny afternoon. We walked a couple of blocks to our hotel, entered the building and took the elevator to the fourth floor reception area. We entered into a well-appointed reception area with antique furniture and a large grandfather clock. The gentleman behind the front desk greeted us, found our reservation, showed us around the common areas, and directed us to our room down the hall.

We entered our room and were pleasantly surprised to find a large space that appeared to have been updated recently. It included a small sitting area, a king-size bed, television with international channels and a very nice, clean bathroom. We unpacked a bit and rested a while from the rigors of sitting on a train the better part of the day.

As we were resting we decided what to do next. We determined it was too late to venture out to a museum, so we went for a walk to get our bearings. But first, we retraced our steps to the station and found a tourist information office. There we armed ourselves with maps and pamphlets and also bought a 24 hour Oslo Card, good for the next day. The Oslo Card would enable us use of the public transportation system and gave us free admission to all the museums we wished to see. It was a particularly good buy for someone in our circumstance, who were preparing to jam as much as possible into one day.

We departed the station and headed down Karl Johans Gate in the direction of the Royal Palace. This main street was exceptional for strolling as it is lined with upscale and local shops, and many eateries and pubs. We window shopped and people watched, and before we knew it we were within sight of the Royal Palace. Downtown Oslo has many attractive buildings and a great deal of green space lending it to an appealing cityscape.

We turned back around and headed toward our hotel. We realized that the ham and cheese sandwiches we had taken from our hotel in Bergen and eaten on the train, had now officially worn off. We began our search for a restaurant as we retraced our steps. We found an inviting little pub around the corner from our hotel and popped in for a beer. As we drank our beer and talked, we realized how hungry we were and we needed to eat.

We paid the bartender and went back out in search of dinner. We settled on an Italian place we had seen earlier which was in our guidebook, Mama Rosa. They were located on the second floor of a building right off Karl Johans Gate. Although we could not see the restaurant clearly from the street below there was an English menu which looked good to us and the prices were right.

We mounted the stairs to the second floor eatery and were pleased with the feel of the place when we entered. A woman of Italian decent met us at the door and whisked us off to a table overlooking the street below. The restaurant was pleasantly decorated with a Mediterranean feel with peach colored walls and was very airy feeling with large windows. The waiter came to our table and we decided to order a bottle of red wine for the occasion. However, the server informed us that for some inexplicable reason they could serve no alcohol that evening.

Greatly disappointed, we both ordered water and perused the menu. Jenny ordered a plate of fettuccini Alfredo and I went for a penne alla Bolognese. The waiter returned shortly with crisp Romaine lettuce salads with Italian dressing and some warm homemade bread. We ate our salads and bread and watched the activity on the street below. Before too long, our entrees arrived and we were both pleased with our choices. We both believe that our pastas were homemade and the sauces were prepared to our liking. We finished off our tasty meals and paid our waiter.

We decided to go looking for a nightcap before turning in for the night. We returned to the little pub around the corner from our hotel thinking this would be a great place for our drink. When we arrived the place was packed, in fact, there was no room for us. Disappointed, we just decided it was time for bed since we had a big day tomorrow. We returned to the City Hotel, put on an English movie subtitled in Norwegian and before I knew it I was asleep.

Having gone to bed reasonable early the night before, we awoke early. Given all we were trying to accomplish that day this was a good result. We showered and went down the hall to the breakfast room. Here we found a larger array than in Bergen, with a nice buffet laid out. There were the standard meats and cheeses with various breads, but also several cereals, eggs, yogurts, fruit and juices. We had some muesli with yogurt, soft boiled eggs and some bread and jam. Their coffee was delicious and the orange juice appeared to be freshly squeezed. We thoroughly enjoyed this meal and ate to our hearts content.

As we were finishing our breakfast we noticed a sign that couldn't help but make us chuckle. It read something to the effect that you were welcome to eat all you like for breakfast, but taking sandwiches away would require a separate charge and see the front desk before doing so. I guess that previous patrons had read, or seen, Rick Steves advice on making a sandwich for lunch and the owners had caught on to the trick. Although we had not contemplated it that morning, we decided that given the warning we certainly would not be fixing any sandwiches for take away that day.

After we finished our breakfast we headed out for a day of sightseeing. The day was overcast and cool as we headed to the waterfront to catch a ferry over to the Bygdoy Peninsula to visit some of Oslo's major attractions. The ferry port is near the Radhus, or city hall, a pleasant walk from our hotel. The short ride across Oslofjord to Bygdoy Peninsula takes you to a concentrated area of great museums, all worth a visit. We decided to try and take in all five of these attractions that were all within walking distance of each other and all admission were covered on our Oslo Card.

The Stave Church at the Norwegian Folk Museum. Interesting architecture.

Our first stop was the Norwegian Folk Museum. The Scandinavian countries all seem to have these types of wonderful museums where they collect typical, indigenous structures and locate them in one area for visitors to see. We had visited a similar museum in Stockholm, Skansen, and were mesmerized by it. We could not wait to see what the Norwegians had to offer in this area.

The Norwegian Folk Museum is one of the world's largest open-air museums with a collection of 150 plus buildings, gathered from throughout Norway including an impressive Stave Church. These structures, which in some cases date back to medieval times, are excellent examples of traditional Norwegian design over a number of centuries. The park spreads over a large number of acres and docents in traditional Norwegian garb are positioned throughout the structures to provide you with further information about the buildings. Representations from all parts of Norway are present including rural and urban, which are grouped by region and type.

A visit to this museum is like strolling through the country of Norway in a couple of hours. The place is a living, breathing testament to the country. Not only are the structures available to visit, but there are craftsman such as blacksmith, potters and candle makers, plying their trades with their finished products available for purchase. Additionally, there are horse and buggy rides available, folk music and men and women in traditional costumes performing local dances. It is a very neat experience.

Desirous of packing in a lot that day, we decided to move on to the next museum, the Viking Ship Museum. Very near to the Folk Museum, the Viking Ship Museum features, among other things, three Viking ships that were discovered in Oslofjord late in the 19th century. The three were buried in blue clay which had a preservative effect on the boats. They were burial ships for Viking nobility and some of the effects of the dead were recovered with the boats and are also on display.

The three boats are probably the finest examples of Viking ships available anywhere today. These vessels could accommodate thirty, or more, oarsmen and move swiftly through the water. It is presumed that similar boats were used to cross the Atlantic Ocean and explore North America.

From the Viking Museum we moved to three maritime museums that are clustered together. They are located a pleasant walk across the Bygdoy Peninsula from the Viking Ship Museum. The first of these we visited was the Kon-Tiki Museum. This edifice is home to the world famous balsa wood raft, Kon-Tiki, which Norwegian scientist Thor Heyerdahl sailed from Peru to Polynesia. The journey, made in 1947, was an effort by Heyerdahl to prove that the original peoples of Polynesia had come from South America and how they could have made the journey. In addition to the raft, there are other articles from Heyerdahl's trips and experiences.

Then, we moved next door from the Kon-Tiki to the Fram Museum. The Fram was the strongest wooden sailing vessel ever built and the most famous of the polar exploration ships. It was captained by Fridjtof Nanse across the Artic from 1893 to 1896. Later the boat was used by Roald Amundsen to explore Antarctica. Amundsen subsequently became the first explorer to reach the South Pole.

The Fram is wonderfully preserved as it was when it plied the waters of the polar cap regions. Visitors can tour the vessel thoroughly and are able to envision what life was like for the crew of the ship. I remember having a sense of the chill the crew must have felt in the difficult conditions under which they worked. This is truly a highlight of Oslo. Hank, I know how much you want to visit Antartica, but a visit to the Fram would only further whet your appetite.

Our final stop on the peninsula was the Norwegian Maritime Museum which is next door to the Fram. I remember we were nearing our fill of nautical museums and had a ferry to catch and, thus, did not give this museum our all. The Norwegians have a proud seafaring history and this museum chronicles that history. I recall from our quick pop-in that there were a number of small craft housed in the museum and one section oddly focused on shipwrecks. I think the museum deserved more time than we lent it, and if I have the pleasure of returning to Oslo, I plan to devote more time to this museum.

As we were thinking of leaving the Maritime Museum, we could see the ferry back to central Oslo approaching the nearby dock. It was either make a dash for it, or wait an hour for another. We decided to cut our visit short and try to catch the boat. We jogged nearly the whole way to the dock and made it with a couple of minutes to spare. Pleased with our effort we slumped into the first two available seats and caught our breath.

By now it was well past noon and we were becoming hungry. As we arrived at the ferry port it started to rain pretty hard, so we needed to make a quick decision on finding a place to eat. We ran off the boat and under a nearby awning to figure out our next move. We consulted our map and realized that Aker Brygge was nearly across the street.

Aker Brygge was an old shipyard that has been converted into a shopping, eating and entertainment center by the harbor side. Surely we could find something suitable there. We waited a minute for the rain to slow down, then made a mad dash across the street. Staying under shelter we came upon a nice-looking, little bar that appeared to be serving good food. We made our way in from the elements and were immediately seated at a table with a view of the harbor through the large windows. This was just what the doctor ordered.

We asked the waiter to bring us a couple of pints and he returned shortly with frosty glasses of beer and English menus. We both decided that we should have the fish and chips, given our close proximity to the fjord. Our young waiter returned and we placed our order. By the time we had finished our beers, our fish and chips arrived. We reordered beers and set about sampling our entrees. The white fish of some variety was delicious, lightly battered and not at all greasy, and the fries were freshly cut, and thick. We enjoyed the lunch and washed it down with the second beers.

The place had been a real find and an excellent break from our day of museum hopping. We had one more museum we wanted to take in before we called it a day. We settled our bill and headed out in search of the Nasjonalgalleriet, or National Gallery. By now the rain had stopped and we decided to just walk to the Gallery which was not too far from our location.

Our ten minute, or so, walk took us by a number of Oslo's landmark buildings including the Oslo Concert Hall, the City Hall, the National Theater and Oslo University. We arrived at the National Gallery which is housed in an attractive, brick building which has a distinctive government feel to it. The museum houses the largest collection of art in the country and is focused heavily on the works of Norwegian artists. There is a particularly impressive collection of paintings by Edvard Munch, perhaps Norway's most famous artist.

The Munch collection is in excess of fifty pieces and includes one of four versions of his masterpiece, *the Scream*. Several of Munch's other famous paintings are on display along with some fine Norwegian landscape artists. The National Gallery version of Munch's *Scream* had been stolen in 1994 on the first day of the Winter Olympics in Lillehammer. Their copy was recovered a few months later unharmed. Ironically, another copy of *the Scream* was stolen from the Munch Museum a little over a year after our visit to Oslo. It, too, was eventually recovered.

A number of big name European artists works are also part of the collection, Rubens, Picasso, Van Gogh and Cezanne, to name a few. Their works are impressive, but the primary purpose of a visit here is to appreciate the Norwegian art on display. Posters of the Scream are on sale in the museum shop, I know this because Jenny bought one, had it nicely framed, and it has hung on our wall ever since. It is a great little reminder of our trip and how much we liked Oslo and the National Gallery.

Totally exhausted, we decided to head back to the City Hotel to get some rest before going out to dinner. Once we got back to our room we kicked off our shoes, flipped on the television and watched some international news in English. We fought off the temptation to fall asleep and decided to start packing because we had another fairly early train to catch in the morning. When we had our fill of preparing for our departure, we decide it was time to go out to dinner.

We departed the hotel and walked purposefully toward our dining choice for the evening, Brasserie 45. We had noticed this restaurant the night before and almost chose it, but decided that Italian seemed more to our tastes that evening. So, we made a pact that we would return to Brasserie 45 for our last dinner in Norway. The eatery was on the second floor of a building right on Karl Johans Gate and the menu looked good to us when we perused it the night before.

As we approached the substantial brick structure that housed the restaurant, we could see that the menu was still posted outside and we decided to give it one more look before entering. We both saw several options that were appealing to us and the price was good by Norwegian standards. We entered the building and climbed up the stairs to the second floor. The large open room had a number of huge windows which made for an airy atmosphere. The décor was quite nice with starched white linen table cloths and the walls and furnishings in warm earth tones throughout the room.

I can tell you that our initial impression was very positive and the atmosphere exceeded our expectations, particularly given the menu prices. Our attractive blond-haired, blue-eyed server arrived promptly and provided us with menus. We ordered a bottle of the house red wine and began to decide on our dinner choice. The wine arrived and we were pleased with how it tasted. Our waitress took our dinner orders, Jenny had a pork dish and I went for the pepper steak.

In an appropriate amount of time our entrees were delivered and they looked outstanding. Jenny's pork fillet was covered with an appetizing mushroom sauce and was accompanied by fried potatoes and a salad. My beef tenderloin was smothering in a green pepper sauce and was served with grilled mushrooms, vegetables and a baked potato. We could barely wait for the first bite because it looked so good. The appearance did not belie the taste. Both our meals were scrumptious.

We both savored every bite. Clearly this was our favorite meal in Norway and my pepper steak was as good as I have had anywhere. We finished our meals and sipped on the remaining wine. We both agreed that this meal had all the proper ingredients, pleasant surroundings, excellent company and delicious food. This was a true highlight. (**See Appendix 19 for the recipe**)

We paid our bill and departed into the sunny evening. We strolled down Karl Johans Gate and reflected on the day. We had seen some outstanding museums, eaten great food and had thoroughly enjoyed Oslo. Our expectations for the Norwegian capital had not been too high for some reason, but we felt very good about our time there. If given the opportunity we certainly would return.

Soon we were back at the City Hotel. We were both very tired from the day's activities and it did not take too long before we were off to sleep. The next morning came early as we had to catch a train to Copenhagen around seven in the morning. We rose, showered, finished what little packing we had to do, and went to breakfast. The morning meal was equal to the day before and we ate a healthy amount knowing that we had a long train ride ahead of us.

We checked out of the hotel and headed for the Oslo train station. It was a clear, crisp morning and the short walk felt good. When we arrived at the station we quickly located our train, but before boarding we decided to spend down what few Norwegian kroners we had left. The Oslo train station was the perfect place for this task because it contains a shopping center.

We decided the best use of our money was to buy some food for the train ride. We didn't know for certain what food and beverage would be available on the train, but we did know that in an over eight-hour trip we would be hungry. We found a little shop that was preparing sandwiches to order and they looked good. We both ordered tuna salad on thick whole wheat bread, with lettuce, tomato and mayo. We shoved them into a brown paper bag and headed for the train.

DENMARK

We found our car and reserved seats and settled in for the long journey. As we chugged out of the station we bade adieu to Oslo, a city we had come to enjoy. Soon we were rolling through the countryside headed for the Swedish frontier. I got up and roamed around the car a little and discovered that there was a snack shop located at the rear of the car. I ordered a tea for Jenny and got a coffee for myself and returned to our seats. Jenny was a happy camper when she saw the tea as she could drink it all day.

We enjoyed the Norwegian and, then, Swedish countryside, verdant and rolling. I don't remember making too many stops, nor seeing very many cities, just a whole lot of farms and trees. After several hours we got hungry and decided that we should break out the tuna sandwiches. I went back to the snack shop and got us some beverages and chocolate for dessert, and we began to eat our lunch. I will tell you that sandwich was one of the best I have ever eaten. I don't know if it was the ingredients, or if I was just so hungry, but it was great. Certainly it was the best tuna sandwich I have ever had, and one of the best sandwiches overall. If you ask Jenny where she had her favorite tuna sandwich, she would quickly agree with me. Even though they were very nice size my only regret was that I hadn't bought two more. They surely would have been eaten.

Not long after we had eaten our lunch we arrived in the Swedish city of Goteburg. Sweden's second largest city, Goteburg, looked very pleasant from the train, but we were here merely to change trains to continue on the Copenhagen. Our train pulled into the station on time and we hopped off the train and scurried to find a train board. We needed to confirm which track our train to Copenhagen would be departing on. We discovered that the train was ready to board on an adjacent track so we found our car, seats, and soon we were on our way again.

When I had visited Copenhagen previously with my friend, Mike Price, we had taken a ferry from Copenhagen into the Swedish city of Malmo. Malmo is located on the southwestern tip of Sweden which is separated from Denmark by the Oresund Strait. Since Mike and I visited Malmo in April of 1998 the two countries had connected each other by a massive bridge and tunnel project. So we would not need to leave the train in Malmo and cross the strait by ferry to Copenhagen.

The Oresund Bridge was opened in 2000 and is dual level, one carrying rail traffic and the other vehicular. The bridge is five miles long and connects to an artificial island in the strait, which in turn connects to Denmark by a two and a half mile tunnel. A few hours from Goteburg we hit the bridge after a brief stop in Malmo. It is a very impressive sight. The cable-stayed bridge allows for a very swift and uneventful crossing from Sweden into Denmark.

Only a few minutes after arriving on Danish soil, we were pulling into the Copenhagen Central Station. We grabbed our things and made our way through the bustling, brown brick terminal. We excited the building and crossed the street to the Copenhagen Visitors Information, just making it before it closed for the day. We stocked up on free maps and pamphlets and, most importantly we bought a three-day Copenhagen Card.

The Copenhagen Card entitled us to free use of all public transportation for the next 72 hours and enabled us to visit numerous museums and attractions for free, or greatly reduced prices. We have found that often times these purchases are prudent. We had calculated that it certainly made sense for our visit here because of what we wanted to do, and the presumed amount of traveling that would be required.

After buying our cards we crossed the street to where the city buses originate outside the train station. We were heading to check into our hotel, a small accommodation a little northwest of the center called Hotel 9 Smaa Hjem. We needed to catch the number 40 bus and get to our hotel before 5 o'clock when the front desk operation closed. Otherwise, they would leave the key for us in a proscribed location. Our chance of arrival before the front desk closed was slim.

The 9 Small Homes is a unique property, probably best suited for long-term stays. The little hotel consists of nine rooms on the top floor of an apartment building in a largely residential area. The rooms are tidy with two sofas that convert into beds, a table and chairs, a lounging chair, cable television and a private bathroom. There is a kitchen at your disposal, and a private laundry with washer and drier. You get daily maid service and the breakfast of your choice is delivered to your room each morning.

We really didn't know where we were going for sure, but the kind bus driver told us where to get off the bus and pointed out the hotel. Sure enough, we were too late to meet the office personnel, but they did leave the keys and a greeting packet in a box for us. We now faced the most significant drawback to staying at 9 Small Homes, the room was on the fifth floor and there was no elevator. This meant that the rooms were actually on the sixth floor, as most times in Europe the first floor is the one above the ground floor. We struggled with getting our bags up the stairs, but we finally made it.

We entered the room and were pleasantly surprised how nice and efficient the space was. We took a little while to settle in and decided that, given it was now after 5:00 p.m., we would do no sightseeing that day. Instead, we decided to get our laundry done that evening. The greeting documents informed us where the washer and drier were located, in a small building in the rear of the property.

We gathered up our dirty clothes and headed down to start the process. We found the equipment available and started the washer. It was a very pleasant early evening and there was a table and chairs in the backyard near the laundry, so we decided to stay outside and enjoy the weather. I had noticed that a Spar Grocery Store was only a few steps away and ran out to get us a couple of beers. We sat out in the yard behind the apartment building and drank Carlsberg's and waited for our laundry to finish. It really was a pleasant experience for us, enough so that I had to run back to the Spar for more beer.

Once our laundry was finished we climbed the stairs back up to our room. We folded and packed up our clean clothes, and thought about what to do with our evening. We finished off our beers and decide we were really tired from the long train ride, and we were starting to get hungry. We determined that our best course of action was to find a nearby restaurant, eat and call it a night.

We headed out into the still, light evening in search of a place to eat. We walked by the Spar and headed down the street in the direction of some neon lighting that we could not make out from that distance. As we neared the signage it became clear that it was a Chinese restaurant and it was open. We had found our spot for dinner. We entered the cozy, neighborhood diner and were greeted in Danish by a host who was clearly of Asian descent. He quickly changed to English when he found out that we were Americans.

We were seated at a table upfront with a view out the window onto the street. Our host provided us with English menus and took our drink orders, beers for both of us. We soon discovered that the restaurant specialized in Hunan cuisine, which was perfect with us as we preferred the spicy offerings from that region. He came back shortly and we both placed our orders, Jenny, Hunan pork and I had the Hunan chicken.

Our server brought out to us a plate of eggrolls with the appropriate sauces. I doused mine in the hot mustard sauce and enjoyed them immensely as the spicy condiment cleared my sinuses. It had been quite a while since we had our last meal, the tuna sandwiches on the train somewhere in Sweden. We had no more than eaten our eggrolls when our entrees arrived. Piping hot, they smelled delicious and were. We took little time in finishing off our spicy offerings which were served with brown rice. The meal was nicely filling, but I was not stuffed.

We finished our second beers and paid our bill. We strolled back down the street, saving energy for the long climb to the top of the apartment building. As we made our way to the top, we both gave thanks that this was the last time that day we had to make that ascent. We entered the room and quickly prepared for bed. We watched a few minutes of television and decided that it was time to shut off the light and go to sleep. It had been a long, but good day, and we needed to sleep.

We slept late for us that morning. Even with the sun streaming in the window early that day we awoke after 8 o'clock. I guess the long train ride and the pace we had been keeping thus far was taking its toll. When we had gotten to our room the previous day there was a breakfast menu on the table for us to fill out. We must have been hungry and checked everything on the list. When the hotel worker arrived with our breakfast trays that morning, waking us up, they were teeming.

We had ham, cheese, soft-boiled eggs, cereal and milk, toast and assorted breads, yogurt, orange juice, tea and coffee. The small table in our room could barely hold it all. I guess the Chinese food from the night before wore off quickly because we ate every scrap on the trays. It really hit the spot. On the bottom of the tray was a menu for the next day and we ordered the exact same thing for delivery at the same time the next day.

We were pretty slow to move that day and sat around enjoying our breakfast beverages trying to understand what was being presented on the Copenhagen morning news program on the television. Finally, we began to move and clean up to set out for the day. I had consulted the map and decided that a nice walk might be the best thing to get us started. We plotted out a plan to walk to see possibly the most famous landmark in the city, the Little Mermaid.

We finished dressing and decided it was time to head out for the day. We raced down the stairs for fun, Jenny of course was the winner, and when we hit the street she asked me if I had the camera. I checked my pockets and did not. Darn the luck, this meant that I had to climb all the way back up to the apartment to get it. We learned a lesson that morning, make a list before leaving the room and double check it to avoid having to go back up those stairs.

We decided that the first stop should actually be the hotel office to let them know we had made it safely. We entered the building next door where the office is housed and were warmly greeted by the very attractive, blond-haired woman who was working the front desk. We attended to what little business was needed with the hotel and headed out into the sunny day. We trekked through our neighborhood which housed a number of embassies for various nations including the United States, which was only a few blocks from our hotel.

To get to the Little Mermaid we had to walk through a large park, the Kastellet, which bounded the harbor on one side. The lovely park was not only a pleasant green space but contained a number of structures including a former citadel used as early naval defense for Copenhagen, and a large, old-fashioned windmill. The citadel is still used by the Danish military, but the surrounding park is available to enjoy.

We finally reached the other side of the park and there, at the water's edge is the Little Mermaid. The character in the story by Hans Christian Anderson, Den Lille Havfrue, is sculpted in bronze and is slightly smaller than life size. This lovely, but somewhat overrated, landmark has been the target of several attacks including multiple decapitations. She was sitting so close to the shore that Jenny was able to stand next to her for a picture.

We took in the view for several minutes until an Asian tour group overran the site and we decided it was time to go. Our next destination was to view the Changing of the Guard at Amalienborg Palace which occurs daily at noon. We had plenty of time for the ten to fifteen minute walk from the Little Mermaid and were looking to kill some time. Just as we were discussing what to do we spotted the Danish Resistance Museum about a hundred yards away.

The museum was included in the Copenhagen Card list of free entrance, so we decided to take a quick walk through. It turned out to be a very wise use of this extra half an hour. The museum is dedicated to the Danish efforts to resist the Nazi incursion during World War II. The museum depicts various efforts undertaken by the Danish Underground during the war to undermine the Nazi machine on every turn. We found it quite interesting and would recommend it to others with a few minutes to spare.

After our brief visit we hoofed it down the street to the Amaleinborg Palace, home of the Royal Family of Denmark. When I had visited Copenhagen a few years before with my pal, Mike Price, we had rented a room from a very nice lady about a block from the palace. We had seen the Changing of the Guard and, being a sucker for these types of ceremonies, I wanted Jenny to see it. We arrived just in time and the ritual was pulled off without a hitch. The best part of it was that Jenny enjoyed it as much as I did.

After the ceremony was over we decided to put our free access to the Copenhagen public transportation system to work. By now we had walked a great deal and we decided to catch a bus to the Christianshavn neighborhood on the other side of the harbor. We walked a couple of blocks and caught a bus which let us out in the middle of Christianhavn.

We decided to come to this neighborhood to visit three things: Christiania, Von Felskers Kirk and have lunch at a wonderful little spot

I had discovered on my previous visit, the Café Wilder. Our first move was to explore Christiania, a totally unique neighborhood. Christiania is a former Danish military base that was abandoned, and in 1971, it was occupied by a group of hippies that have proclaimed the area a "free city." The move was unsanctioned by the government and has been a source of controversy ever since. The squatters have developed their own society and claim independent status as a nation. The neighborhood is most famous for its open sales of "soft drugs," marijuana and hashish.

We entered the area off a city street where an archway sign proclaims the territory. The area is home to over 800 people and the occupants have colorfully painted the former barracks and other buildings. There are murals on most exposed walls and there are artisans' workshops and stores selling their wares. A few eateries and bars exist, but the main attraction for most visitors is Pusher Street. This street is home to an open bizarre featuring scores of stands selling soft drugs and paraphilia. It is truly like nothing you have seen before.

We walked around the hippie commune for about an hour and decided it was time for lunch. We exited Christiania and walked about four or five blocks to the Café Wilder. This great little bistro has a warm bohemian feel and serves up some fine food. We entered and were ushered to a table by the window by our pretty, young blonde server. We ordered a couple of large Carlsberg's and began to eye the English menu that we had been supplied.

Our waitress returned and took our order. Jenny selected what is probably their signature dish for lunch, cheeseburger and fries and I went for the chicken salad. The large window next to our table provided us with a great view of the street activity as we sipped our beers and waited for our lunch to arrive. In good time our orders arrived and we were both very pleased with our choices. Jenny's burger was cooked to perfection and the fries could have pleased a Parisian. My chicken salad contained the distinct flavor of bacon as one of its ingredients, which I think makes any dish a winner.

We finished our entrees and drank another large beer while continuing to look out the window. There is just something special about the Café Wilder, a place I have returned to every time I have the good fortune to be in Copenhagen. Finishing our beers we decided to move on, so we paid our bill and left. We decided to stop by the Von Freslers Kirk while we were still in Christianhavn.

Just down the street from the Café Wilder a couple of blocks is Von Freslers Kirk, or Our Savior's Church. This house of worship was built late in the seventeenth century and this impressive baroque structure is most noted for its corkscrew tower that tops the building. Visitors can climb to the top of this spiral staircase by mounting 400 steps. From the top there is a wonderful view of Copenhagen that can help you get oriented for your stay in the city. We were very fortunate that during our visit a musician was practicing on its huge organ that contains over 400 pipes. It is clearly capable of making beautiful music.

We were now ready to move on from Christianhavn, so we caught a bus back to Radhuspladsen, or City Hall Square, near the center of the city. From here we headed north to explore the Stroget, for my money one of the best walking and shopping streets in the world. The pedestrian-only thoroughfare is the longest of its kind in Europe and is an ideal place for people watching, as well as, shopping.

We browsed the windows of various shops, some high end, while others are souvenir oriented. We enjoyed the walk and particularly focused on the wonderful porcelain that the Danes are famous for producing. We wound past the various shops, museums, and eateries ending up at Kongens Nytorv, another lovely square where the Stroget terminates. By now we were tired and, as it turns out, we could catch a bus from Kongens Nytorv back to 9 Small Homes, so we grabbed it.

We slumped into a couple of front seats on the bus. We had walked a great deal, it was late afternoon, and it felt very good to sit down. We determined our best course of action was to return to our room and relax before we ventured out to dinner. Soon the bus turned down our street and we were let out almost at our front door. We decided to drop by the Spar, a few steps away, and grab a couple of beers to enjoy while resting in the room.

We successfully climbed the six flights of stairs without having a cardiac, and entered our room. We kicked off our shoes and turned on the television to see if we could find some programming that was in a language we understood. We were not successful, but we left the television on as a challenge to sharpen our Danish, to no avail.

The rest was good for us and the beers tasted great, but after a couple of hours we decided it was time to venture out for dinner. We thought it best to extend out a little further than we had last night, so we consulted our book for possible locations. We chose a delightful little café I had eaten at on my previous trip to Denmark, the Kobenhavner Cafeen.

We set out to grab a bus back down to Kongens Nytorv, as our choice for dinner was on a side street just off the Stroget. We were in luck because a bus toward the center was coming down the street as we were exiting our building. We hopped on and in a matter of minutes we were walking down the Stroget and were soon in front of the restaurant.

We entered the café, which is very cozy, almost clubby. The dining room is small with dark wood paneling and starched white linens on the tables. We were pleased to see that there were a couple of available tables. The kindly, aging server showed us to a small table in the corner on the back wall. I must say that this candle lit little place was very romantic that evening.

I think the ambiance was the reason we decided to order a bottle of red wine to drink when our waitress returned. She provided us menus and left to grab our wine. When she came back we sampled our wine which was to our liking and we placed our orders. Jenny chose pork tenderloin in a mushroom cream sauce with boiled potatoes and I selected the Danish meatballs with red cabbage, potatoes and gravy.

We sipped our pleasant wine and talked about the day until our dinners arrived. When it appeared, we were favorably impressed with the presentation and aromas. The taste matched, and we thoroughly enjoyed a fine meal. In fact, this could have easily have been my favorite meal in Denmark, but we had another day. I will say that the Kobenhavner Cafeen is our kind of place and I would recommend it to my friends who travel to Copenhagen.

We finished our servings and the wine. The waitress tempted us with some fabulous looking desserts, but we passed, and paid our bill. We ventured back out into the gloaming and searched for a bus to return us to the hotel. One came along soon, and a few minutes later we were back in the room and preparing for bed. It had been another long day, and our final day in Copenhagen was ahead of us.

We awoke the next morning with the delivery of our sumptuous breakfast. Again, we must have been very tired because we slept over ten hours. The hot beverages and food got us going as we once more ate all that the hotel provided us for our morning meal. We showered and prepared for the day. Before we left we checked our list, not once but twice, to be certain we had everything we needed before going downstairs.

Our first stop that day was to be the Nationalmuseet, or National Museum of Denmark. We caught the appropriate bus from our hotel to the former palace that houses the museum. We used our Copenhagen Cards for free admission and began to wonder the collections. The primary focus is its repository of anthropological artifacts which represent different cultures, but as you might expect the Danish collection is the most impressive.

The museum covers over 14,000 years of Danish history from the hunters of the Ice Age to present day Denmark. To me, the most impressive part of the collection is the Viking era which includes stones, helmets and battle gear. There seems to be a fascination with burial gear in the museum, but it is certainly well worth a visit.

After browsing the artifacts for a couple of hours we decided it was time to get out into the fresh air of the day. The sun was shining brightly and the temperature was now in the high 50s and an alfresco destination was in order. We took the public transportation to Kongens Nytorv where we began our exploration of the Nyhavn area.

Nyhavn, or "New Harbor," is a canal inlet off the harbor which originally provided a protected area in which to load and unload cargo from the rough waters of the sea. Today, the area is home to colorfully painted, seventeenth century buildings that mainly house restaurants, bars, shops and entertainment venues. It is very touristy, but hip and a must stop in Copenhagen. We wandered the canal, looking at the old boats moored along its sides and window shopped its businesses. Finally the aroma of several of the restaurants overtook us and we began to search for a place for lunch.

We finally settled on Nyhavns Faergekko which is located directly on Nyhavn near Kongens Nytorv. The nautically themed restaurant is housed in the building that was once the home of the White Star steamship line. The cozy establishment specializes in Danish fare and at lunch serves a herring buffet with ten different preparations of the fish.

Not being a herring fan, we were drawn in by the location, quirky décor and a lunch special of fried plaice and fries. We chose to be seated at a table on the lower, think half-basement, level and ordered a couple of Carlsberg's. Once our server returned with our beers we requested the luncheon specials and began surveying the accumulated articles in the room. Most of the decorations in the room would have been comfortable in the stateroom of a captain for the White Star Line.

In no time our heaping plates of fish and chips arrived served with mayonnaise and a very dense brown bread. We really liked our food and looking out on the street which was vibrant with pedestrian activity. We finished our entrees and decided we really needed to get out into this nice day. So, we settled our bill and ventured out for the main tourist attraction, and one of the primary reasons we came to Copenhagen, Tivoli Gardens.

Tivoli Gardens is an amusement park smack dab in the middle of Copenhagen, literally across the street from the Central Train Station. Founded in 1843 as a garden oasis in an urban area, the park has evolved over time, and is considered to be the original theme park. Walt Disney used it as the inspiration for his parks and attempted to buy Tivoli. Apparently, Michael Jackson was so taken with the place when he performed here, he also tried to purchase it. The park is such a Danish institution the mere thought of a sale to foreign interests is repugnant to the locals.

We had been reading about the wonders of the park for years and really wanted to go see it. When I had visited Copenhagen a few years before, Tivoli had not yet opened for the season. So, this was our opportunity and it was a fine spring day and we were not going to miss the chance. We decided to walk the Stroget from Nyhavn to Tivoli. As we made our way enjoying the sights and sounds of the city we were anxious in anticipation.

We arrived at the park after about a twenty minute walk and, again, our Copenhagen Cards did the trick in getting us in for free. We strolled around the park taking in what it had to offer. As you might expect, there are lovely flower gardens, amusement rides for all ages, ample shopping opportunities, bars and restaurants, and games of chance geared for adults to children.

We drank a beer and I had an inspirational moment for me, to fully experience the place we had to ride the rides. I located the ticket office and bought each of us an all-day pass for the amusements and we took off. For the next several hours we rode every ride that looked interesting to us, and had a blast. We particularly loved the 1914 wooden roller coaster which we rode over and over. One of our major travel regrets was not buying a candid photo taken by the Tivoli folks of us on the coaster. We had expressions of sheer joy on faces, but I was too big a tight wad to pay the inflated price they wanted for the picture. Please do not make this mistake if you are one day in my shoes. You will regret it.

As evening was setting in we were still not ready to leave, so we began to look around for our dining options. There are all kinds of choices at Tivoli, from hot dogs, to prime steak and seafood, and everything in between. We walked the park surveying our options and settled on Faergekroen. The restaurant is located on the edge of the lake and is a replica of a Danish fisherman's house. The inviting bistro featured Danish specialties: meat balls, fried plaice, pork chops with red cabbage, and something we had not encountered yet, labskovs.

We were seated at a table overlooking the small lake at Tivoli and ordered a couple of beers. It felt good to sit down and rest because we had been acting like a couple of teenagers all afternoon and evening riding the amusements. Our young waiter came around with our beer and we both decided to order the labskovs. Labskovs, or ship captain's beef stew, is a hearty, Danish concoction that is primarily cubed beef and potatoes. Our waiter recommended it very highly so we decided to give it a try.

As we drank our beers we enjoyed the view of Tivoli Gardens afforded from our vantage point at our table overlooking the lake. The sun was just beginning to set and the thousands of lights that illuminate Tivoli at night were just coming on. It was a gorgeous sight and our seats were the perfect setting to view the changeover. It truly is a sight to behold.

Our dinner arrived as we were draining our beers, so we ordered a couple of more large ones, and prepared to eat. Our waiter set a large bottle of Lea & Perrins Worcestershire Sauce on the table along with our large plates of food. We were quite familiar with the condiment, but I felt compelled to ask him why he brought it to us. He informed us that the proper way to eat labskovs was to thoroughly douse it with the sauce. This sounded good to us so we complied.

The dish had a very thick consistency almost like very stout mashed potatoes with large chunks of lean, cubed beef. There had been some diced green onion tops sprinkle on, but the Worcestershire sauce lent it the little zip it needed. It was incredible! I cannot begin to tell you how much we enjoyed this meal. I have had the good fortune to return to Copenhagen and each time I have sought out this dish. **(See Appendix 20 for recipe)**

Jenny and I finished dinner and our beers and set off to take a couple of last rides in the now moonlit night. As we exited Tivoli we vowed that if we were ever blessed with a child, and that child wanted to go to Disney World, we would bring him to Tivoli first. A few years later we were very fortunate to have Hank come into our lives. Although he has yet to ask to travel to a Disney property, we have fulfilled our commitment to each other, and brought him to Tivoli first. And, Hank, you will recall riding all the rides until you were too tired to ride anymore. We are incredibly fortunate for these experiences.

It was now getting late and we had a morning train to catch to Stockholm. We discovered that our Copenhagen Cards were good for all trains that run frequently from the Central Station to Osterport Station, which is a couple of blocks from 9 Small Homes. We left Tivoli, walked across the street to the Central Station, and immediately caught a train to Osterport. It was even quicker than taking the bus.

My beautiful wife, Jenny, and I sitting on a lion
statue outside our hotel in Stockholm.

Before we left the Osterport Station we checked to see what times the trains were running to the Central Station in the morning. We wanted to know when the optimal time for us to arrive back there in the morning to catch a train to the center, where our international train would originate. We follow this practice when travelling routinely. If we are relying on public transit we will double check time schedules for public conveyances to ensure we will arrive at our destination with ample time to board our train or plane. We think this is a key to successful travel.

We finally arrived back at the hotel and immediately began to pack our things for our morning departure. We had to be at the Central Station before eight o'clock so we had to hustle in the morning. Once we got everything done we could possibly do that night we shut off the light and went to sleep.

The next day our travel alarm went off early. We began to get ready when the morning knock on the door occurred indicating that our breakfast had arrived. We ate as we showered and dressed. After breakfast we descended the six floors of stairs for one final time. We had stopped by the office the previous day and had paid our bill, so all we had to do was drop our keys at the office on the way out.

SWEDEN

We dropped the key in a box and retraced our steps to the Osterport Station. We arrived a couple of minutes early and caught an earlier train to the Central Station. We arrived at the Central in good shape with over a half hour before our train to Stockholm was to depart. We had some extra Danish krones and bought some foodstuffs for the ride at a store in the station.

We located our train for Stockholm and settled in for the long ride. We enjoyed the Swedish countryside and each other's company on the over six hour journey. When we arrived we made the short walk from the railway station to our hotel, The Bentley. The Bentley is centrally located on the main shopping street in Stockholm, Drottninggatan.

The very pleasant hotel would probably have been too expensive for our tastes except we were able to procure a weekend special. Since I have covered Stockholm in a previous chapter I will be brief. We really liked the city on our first visit, but probably liked it even more this time through. It is clearly a world-class place to visit and our hotel was very much to our liking. If we have the opportunity to return to Stockholm we would leap at the opportunity and would gladly stay at the ideally located Bentley again.

CHAPTER 8

THE PRINCIPALITIES

HANK, AS YOU KNOW BY now your mother is a special woman. One of her attributes is her appreciation for life. She is particularly attuned to celebrating holidays and milestones. In the summer of 2003, after our return from Scandinavia, she asked me where we were going for our annual fall trip around Thanksgiving holiday. She suggested that since I was to be celebrating my 50th birthday in October of that year, we should make it a special trip. I threw out a couple of suggestions like Viet Nam, or Australia, and she replied that she was hoping for a return to Europe.

She asked me where I had not been in Europe that I would like to see. Since I had traveled throughout the continent by that time, my options were somewhat limited. Some thought was given to further exploring some countries in the old Communist bloc that I had not yet been to see. Then I suggested to her that I had always had the desire to see the five tiny countries that somehow still exist in Europe: Andorra, Liechtenstein, Monaco, San Marino, and the Vatican.

Jenny was intrigued by this notion, and so, we set out to plan our best path to visit these countries. Since I had already been to the Vatican, we eliminated that destination from our itinerary. Ultimately, we decided that Andorra was a little too far removed from the other three countries and we would reach it on a future trip. Monaco, San Marino and Liechtenstein would be the stated objective of this 50th birthday celebration.

Fearful that these tiny countries would lack enough to keep our interest for an extended period of time, they would be done in conjunction with visits to nearby cities in neighboring countries we were interested in exploring. We began perusing maps and determined that Nice in the south of France would be a great location from which to day trip to Monaco. Bologna, Italy, would serve as a very suitable locale from which to reach San Marino. And the Swiss city of Zurich is very near to Liechtenstein and held great deal of interest to us.

Hank, about the same time we were planning our trip for that fall we visited your uncle, your mother's brother, Leo Medisch, in Lewes, Delaware. Leo was a fabulous chef and was part-owner of the best restaurant in the state, the Back Porch Café in Rehoboth Beach. His love of cooking extended to his wonderful home where he was a terrific host, always had a room for guests and lived literally within a stone's throw of the beach. Jenny and Leo were very close and he became a very good friend of mine. We would go visit him almost every 4th of July weekend and over the Labor Day Holiday. Leo had a real zest for life and loved to travel.

One evening during our visit in July we were sitting on his screened-in back porch which wraps around two sides of the house. Hank, you remember this fabulous porch, the sight of many fine evenings. We had just finished a fabulous meal of the world's best crab cakes, one of Leo's specialties, accompanied by fresh Delaware corn on the cob. As we were sipping a nice cabernet, eating some dark chocolate, and listening to the waves in the background, we began to discuss our proposed trip to Europe that November. Before you know it, we were asking Leo to join us on the journey.

We had traveled with Leo prior to this and found him easy to be with and we very much enjoyed his company. He immediately indicated he was very interested, but he needed to confer with his business partner. The Back Porch is a seasonal restaurant, given its location in a major East Coast resort community, and it closes in November, reopening the next May. Leo and one of his partners, Keith Fitzgerald, would take an annual trip after closing the restaurant to celebrate the conclusion of a successful year. So Leo wanted to make certain the trip would not interfere with this annual event.

By the time we returned for Labor Day, the trip was all worked out. Leo and Keith were going to make their annual trip this time to Europe, spending several days in Amsterdam, with a stopover in Paris, and then meet up with us in Nice. Keith would join us for a few days and then return home from Nice in time to spend Thanksgiving at home with his wife and three daughters. It was a plan, and we were all excited.

I continued to work on the logistics of the trip. We had determined that we would start the journey in Nice followed by Bologna, Zurich, and end our trip in Prague so Leo could meet the Czech relatives that Jenny and I had visited with a few of years before. We arranged for open-jawed tickets to Nice with a return from Prague, thus enabling us to cover more ground and preventing us from retracing our steps.

As with other trips in this timeframe, the most effective and cost efficient way for us to travel was by rail. In working with the good folks at Railpass, we determined that our lowest cost alternative was to buy point-to-point tickets for all our trips. We also decided to reserve couchettes and travel at night on the three big legs of the trip: Nice to Bologna, Bologna to Zurich and Zurich to Prague. This decision was based on our ability to maximize our time and still get some decent rest. We, in fact, rather enjoy overnight travel by rail which we find adds a little excitement and romance to the journey.

NICE, FRANCE

The time had finally come for us to depart for our journey. We were flying on Northwest through Minneapolis to Amsterdam and on to Nice with their partner, KLM. Our flight did not depart Indianapolis until a little after 5 o'clock so we both did some last minute things in the office in the morning and got to the airport in ample time for the two hour advance check-in. We got upgraded to first class so we boarded the plane first and took our seats in the front row of the plane. It was a particularly nice flight and we each had a couple of drinks and enjoyed some snacks.

Upon our arrival in Minneapolis we had a nearly three hour layover before our flight was to depart, so we were able to try out one of my birthday gifts, a membership in the Northwest Airlines Club. Jenny is one of the most thoughtful and generous people you will ever meet and she had purchased for me a three-year membership in WorldClubs because I traveled a great deal on business and she thought I might enjoy it. She had gotten me the three-year subscription to give me ample time to decide if

I thought it was worthwhile. I assure you, that for my money it is a great perk to have, and I would highly recommend it if you travel a good deal and can afford it.

We settled into the comfortable, overstuffed chairs in the club and whiled away our layover enjoying the snacks and open bar that comes with membership. It seemed like no time until the announcement came that our plane was about to board. Our plane that evening was a DC-10 which was the workhorse of Northwest's international fleet. We had procured my favorite coach seats on the plane, 10 A&B, which were on the emergency exit. These seats had terrific legroom so I could stretch out and get a little rest on the flight.

One of the oddities of sitting in these seats was that two flight attendants sat directly opposite you in jump seats on takeoff and landing. After boarding concluded and we were about to take off, two very nice attendants strapped into the seats across from us and we began to have a conversation. They told us about making this trip from Minneapolis to Amsterdam several times a month and how they enjoyed the journey.

Once airborne one of the flight attendants, an attractive and personable woman probably in her late forties began to express some concern about the way she was feeling. She appeared flushed and complained of nausea. As soon as the plane reached ten thousand feet, she unbuckled her seat belt and went to the forward cabin. A few minutes later the pilot came on the public address system and announced that we were going to have to return to Minneapolis for a medical emergency. We would be circling for a while as we dumped fuel so we could make a proper weight to land.

Only one of the two flight attendants returned to the jump seat area when we were preparing to land. It seems as though her colleague, that only minutes before was seated across from us, was having a heart attack and that is why we were forced to turn around. As we landed we looked out the window and saw an ambulance parked by a gate with its red lights on. We stopped next to the emergency vehicle and paramedics swiftly boarded the plane and carried the stricken, flight attendant off to the awaiting ambulance.

What a bummer of a start to a much anticipated vacation! We sat helplessly as she sped off with sirens blaring. The captain came back on the p.a. and told us what he knew. She was conscious and comfortable and a doctor onboard the plane had been attending to her. We would be waiting for a few minutes while another crew member was located to take her place and the plane was refueled. About a half hour later we were back underway and, I am pleased to note, that on our return trip we found out that the flight attendant had suffered only a mild heart attack, and was well on her way to a total recovery.

Thank goodness the rest of the flight was uneventful. We had a very close turn in Amsterdam with only a little over an hour scheduled between our flights. We thought for sure that we would miss our flight and be forced to catch a later one, but a strong tail wind enabled us to make up time and we made our regularly scheduled flight. We landed in Amsterdam, hustled through a customs checkpoint and quickly made our way to our gate. When we arrived they had just begun to board the flight and we walked right on the plane with perfect timing.

Our flight on the KLM CityHopper to Nice was a pleasant one. It was a bright, clear day and the only noteworthy events were the beautiful scenery and the bumps we experienced as we flew over part of the French Alps. By the time we arrived in Nice it was after three in the afternoon and, although we had gotten some sleep on our transatlantic flight, we were weary.

The Nice airport is situated right along the Mediterranean Sea, just west of the downtown. We gathered up our luggage and caught a bus from a stop right outside the terminal. A few stops later we hopped off in the center of the city into a sunny, bright afternoon. Our hotel was a short walk down a crowded, pedestrian-only street, not far from the sea. As we neared our hotel rolling our bags behind us, we heard someone holler out our names. We looked around to see Leo and Keith seated at an outdoor café drinking a beer and soaking up the sun. What a pleasant surprise.

Leo led us the few remaining steps to our lodging, the Hotel Canada. The well-located, small hotel came recommended by the Frommer's travel guides and, although not my favorite room ever, it proved to meet our needs. You enter the hotel up a set of winding marble stairs which leads you directly into a small lobby with an adjoining breakfast room. We checked-in and were directed to our room on the third floor, which opened directly on to a large terrace.

We quickly stowed our luggage and hustled back down to the café to join our friends in an afternoon libation. It was a truly glorious afternoon and the cold beer tasted good after the long journey. We listened to Leo and Keith regale us with stories of their time in Amsterdam, Paris, and their trip by high-speed rail to Nice. We sucked down a couple of beers and decided it was time to go get a shower. We agreed to meet in an hour, or so, at our rooftop terrace to continue the party.

Jenny and I showered quickly and put on some fresh clothes, making us feel more like members of the human race again. I was thoroughly worn out from the trip, but the shower and rush of adrenaline from the new city and old friends kept me going. Soon Leo and Keith arrived toting a couple of bottles of nouveau Beaujolais they had just picked up at a shop on the street.

As we would discover, it was the time of year for these new wines in France, and it was a big deal on the streets of Nice. Merchants from small shops to large department stores had set up displays selling the various vineyards wares. You could barely walk ten feet down the street without running into a table loaded with wine and a sales clerk hawking it. Actually, it was a very cool thing to encounter.

Keith, being a bit of a wine connoisseur and the partner in charge of the wine selection at a top-rate restaurant, had selected a couple of very nice bottles. We sat on the terrace around an old table and drank the wine, watched the pedestrian traffic below and had an enjoyable conversation. As time passed I noticed I was really feeling the effects of the alcohol on my system. I very much needed to eat, and soon.

I am certain the others realized my condition as well, so we decided to find a place for dinner. Once we exited the hotel and reached the street, I informed Leo that I need not go very far and we could seek out a finer dining experience another evening. We walked a couple of blocks and found a little Mediterranean restaurant (and why wouldn't we, we were only a few meters from that sea). We were seated at an outside table and were presented with English menus.

The smells emanating from the kitchen were nearly overwhelming to me. Jenny and I then realized that we had not really eaten a meal since the night before on the plane. We had a light snack on the plane from

Amsterdam, but that was hardly sustaining. No wonder I was hammered, no food and no sleep, a bad combination.

Our waiter soon appeared and we ordered. Leo and Keith decided to sample some seafood pasta and Jenny and I ordered a couple of pizzas. I stuck to water to drink. I didn't realize it, but we must have ordered salads, because in a couple of minutes the waiter returned with a large bowl of salad for the table. The traditional greens were joined by peppers, onion, olives and other goodies tossed in an oil and vinegar based dressing. It was delightful and certainly helped my disposition. We had barely finished the salads when our entrees arrived.

Our pizzas were lapping over the sides of their plates and were brimming with toppings and gooey, hot cheese. The other's pastas looked fresh and were filled with a variety of shellfish. All of us immediately dove into our dinners and hardly resumed our conversations until all had finished their food. I felt much better, but could barely hold my head up from the rigors of the past two days. I motioned the waiter for the check, which we paid, and headed back out into the night.

On the short walk to the hotel we devised our plan for the next day. We would meet for breakfast in the hotel around eight o'clock, and then head out to Monaco for the day. There were frequent trains from Nice's Ville Station to Monaco with a travel time of less than a half an hour. One train left shortly after 9:00 a.m. and only took about fifteen minutes to get there, this was our objective.

Arriving at the Canada, we parted company with the gents, and went directly to our room. I barely got my teeth brushed before I fell asleep. I don't think I moved all night and I awoke quite refreshed about ten hours later. Jenny was also just waking up when I slipped into the bathroom to begin cleaning up for the day. She fell in right behind me and we were soon ready to meet the fellows for breakfast at eight.

When we arrived at the breakfast room Keith and Leo were already there drinking their morning coffee. It turns out that breakfast was truly continental in nature; hard rolls, butter and jam, coffee and fresh squeezed orange juice. We sat around and ate breakfast and drank coffee until it was time to start our walk to the train station to catch the 9:18 train to Monaco.

A view of Monaco.

MONACO

The walk to the main train station, Gare de Nice Ville, was a pleasant one, almost due north of the Hotel Canada about a mile away. It was a very bright, sunny morning probably already in the low sixties, and we covered the ground in seemingly no time. We arrived early and were able to catch a train departing about ten minutes earlier. There was some manner of warning message that we were unable to interpret, but we found out on board the train that there was work being done on the tracks because of a rock slide that had closed the track prior to our arrival in Monaco. We would be forced to disembark the train at a station just short of the Principality and we would be bussed the rest of the way.

The train ride to Monaco was a very beautiful journey indeed. The car traveled along the side on the mountain while the azure waters of the Mediterranean Sea lay below on the other side. There is an occasional village perched on the side of the mountain with an undeniably tremendous view. We were tempted to hop off at a couple of stops, but we resisted and made it to Monte Carlo. The change to the bus proved to be only a slight inconvenience which stretched the travel time to a whopping half an hour.

We arrived at the Gare de Monaco-Monte Carlo which is near the center of this tiny nation, second only to the Vatican as the smallest country in geographic area in Europe. The modern station is built underground and the view when you exit the station is breathtaking. The city-state clings to the side of the mountain and seems to virtually cascade down the mountainside to the sea below. We stood on a platform outside the station for several minutes drinking in this glorious scene and snapping photos. We procured a map of the city, and headed out to explore what it had to offer.

It seems that Leo had visited Monte Carlo on a previous trip with his life partner, Tom Wilson, several years before and had some recognition of the surroundings. So, we followed Leo's lead and we began by descending the hillside and exploring the old city. We wandered down through the cobblestone streets and window-shopped its stores. Not too far into the city, we spotted a shop selling, among other things, Christmas ornaments and Jenny and I ducked in and selected an exquisite little, hand-blown and painted Santa carrying a knapsack. For us, it is the perfect souvenir from this lovely little country and takes me back there every holiday when we place it on our tree.

Soon we wandered into the area known as "the Rock," which houses among other things the Palace of the ruling Grimaldi family. The Grimaldi's have ruled this nation-state since the thirteenth century and their residence dominates the skyline from its commanding position in the elevated fortress. Our timing was not good, but I understand that there is an impressive changing of the guard each day at precisely 11:55 a.m.

We opted not to visit any of the areas open to the public or museums contained therein. Rather, we continued our walking tour which next lead us to the area around the port and marina. I am not sure I have ever encountered such an ostentatious display of wealth as I saw in the marina at Monte Carlo. The amazing sailing vessels that were moored in that harbor that day spoke volumes about the tremendous affluence that is attracted to this tax-free haven. A walk around the marina with its nearby toney hotels, restaurants and shops is truly something out of the _Lifestyles of the Rich and Famous._

Continuing on our walk, the sunshine had given way to gray skies and finally a steady rain had begun to fall. We were now approaching the famous Monte Carlo Grand Casino, which lies along the coastline just to the north of the port. Setting up on a terrace above the Mediterranean Sea, the Grand Casino is an architectural gem. Designed by the famous French architect, Charles Garnier, the designer of the Paris Opera House, the magnificent structure was completed in 1893. All you have to do is view the structure from afar to realize that the house has to be the winner, not the patrons.

As we neared the casino, the rain began to really pick up and we needed to find a place to get in out of the rain. It was now well past noon, and we were all quite hungry. Just then Leo realized we were standing in front of a restaurant where he and Tom had eaten on his previous trip to Monte Carlo, the Café de Paris. The brasserie resides across a garden from the casino and I am quite certain that in good weather one could be seated on their terrace, and have a wonderful vantage point from which to people watch.

However, it was not to be for us that rainy day. Looking akin to four drowned rats, we entered this nice establishment and were, much to my surprise, offered a fine table. The dining room was a large open space with tall windows and is very light and airy. The tables were covered in white linen and the waiters were dressed in tuxedo shirts and ties. The floors were marble and the whole place reeked of class. One of my first thoughts was that this was going to be a very expensive lunch.

The waiter arrived at our table and brought us menus. My first glance at the offerings confirmed my suspicions, it was indeed a pricy establishment. I am by admission a pretty frugal guy, I really prefer to think of myself as value-conscious, and this place did not fit my idea of value for the expenditure. I had the feeling we were about to spend a whole lot of money for a decent meal, but in large measure we were paying for the view of the casino and the atmosphere of the establishment.

If it was up to me I think I would have found a different spot for lunch, less pretentious and less costly. However, I could tell rather quickly that this place held special meaning to Leo. I imagine he had some romantic thoughts about the last time he had eaten here with his partner, Tom. Tom had passed away several years before and, understandably, this loss had left a deep hole in Leo's soul. If eating here gave Leo pleasure, I was all for that notion. I would just suck it up and pay the tariff, whatever that may be.

The waiter returned shortly and asked for our drink orders. Jenny and I ordered beers and Leo and Keith ordered some white wine with an eye towards a seafood platter they were about to select for their lunch. The waiter came back with our drinks and Leo ordered a rather large, chilled shellfish arrangements that he and Keith were going to split. Jenny decided on the Penne Arrabbiata and I selected the Spaghetti Bolognese, not surprisingly one of the least expensive items on the menu.

We people watched and chatted as we waited for our food. In a few minutes it arrived. The seafood platter the guys were splitting looked absolutely smashing, and our pasta dishes were also well presented. Soon we were all deeply engaged in our lunches, which were all very tasty. I guess we had all gotten very hungry because the lively conversation slowed greatly as we turned to our stomachs.

As you know by now, one of my objectives in writing this book is to recount my favorite meal that I had in each country and try to provide you with a recipe from that dish. Since this was the only meal I had in Monaco, it has to be my favorite. I will tell you however, it is not difficult to recommend this restaurant, or the Spaghetti Bolognese, from the Café de Paris in Monte Carlo. The pasta was a little al dente and the sauce meaty with some zip to it, just how I like it.

In my opinion three ingredients go into making a really good dining experience. First, the companionship must be enjoyable. Second, the atmosphere must be to your liking. And, finally the food must be of good quality. The lunch that day in Monaco fit all those criteria many times over. The company could not be any better, the surroundings were most pleasant, and the food was great. Leo and Keith are serious foodies, being in the business, and raved about their seafood. Although they offered to share, and I declined, it did appear to be first-rate.

We asked for another round of drinks and sat a while enjoying the conversation and the atmosphere. The rain began to slack off and we decided it was time to make our move. The waiter arrived with the bill and Leo, much to our chagrin, picked up the whole tab. He was much too generous, but he would hear nothing of us helping to pay. (See Appendix 21 for the recipe)

We left the delightful brasserie and decided to explore the casino area. The grounds surrounding the casino are exquisitely manicured and feature some restful gardens. We strolled to the entrance of the main casino building and debated whether we should try to enter, given our attire. Eventually, we decided to duck in to see what it looked like inside. We barely got inside and saw the marble floors and ornate columns crowned with gold leaf, before a polite security officer let us know that our blue jeans, walking shoes, and rain jackets were not proper clothing for admittance to the casino.

This outcome came as no shock to us and we were not greatly disappointed. None of us were big gamblers and didn't really have a great desire to play, we simply wanted to be able to say we had been to the casino in Monte Carlo. I guess that technically, we had now fulfilled that desire and it was time to move on.

We exited the building and spotted an interesting looking terrace and walked over to get a view of the sea below. It was very impressive, but as we stood there we decided our next move was to head back to the train station and return to Nice. We began to retrace our steps to the station, but discovered that several well positioned, public elevators existed which would make our return up the side of the hill much easier.

We picked our route to take advantage of the lifts and in no time we were back at the station. Since at least four trains travel to Nice each hour, we knew it would be no time before we were back in Nice. Sure enough a bus whisked us to the nearby train station on the other side on the construction where we boarded a train headed toward Nice.

This particular train seemed to be a local, making several stops along the route to Nice. Some friends of ours had told us about a particularly quaint village, perched atop the mountain overlooking the sea, called Eze. We had noticed the station for Eze on the trip to Monaco, and soon were upon it again, but this time we stopped. On a split second decision we decided to jump off the train and visit Eze.

The village had been described to us as picturesque locale, with its cobblestone streets filled with artist studios, craftsmen's workshops and perfumeries. We will probably never know, because when we got off the train we discovered that the station may be labeled Eze, but Eze was nowhere to be seen. The train station, what there was of it, was virtually devoid of life. Thank goodness, there was a small inn across the road from the station and we went in to find out what they could tell us about Eze.

It seems that Eze was indeed on top of the mountain above us, but certainly not within easy walking distance. They would be glad to call us a taxi, which they indicated would take a while to get there and would be quite expensive. There was some sort of local bus service, but they could not guarantee when it ran. So, we decided to cut our losses, have a drink and catch the next train that stopped in about half an hour.

We all had a glass of a pleasant local red wine and laughed about our mistake. We finished our drinks, thanked the proprietor for his assistance, and walked back across the road just as our train was pulling into the station. A few minutes later we were back in Nice, headed to the Hotel Canada to rest for a few minutes and decide what to do next.

The weather had turned back in our favor, and since we were all leaving Nice the next day we decided that we should do some exploring. I was now late afternoon and we decided to go visit the Old Town and do some shopping before the stores and the market closed for the evening. On our way to the Old Town we walked through the center of Nice and window-shopped stores there. We cruised into the Old Town and wandered around the Marche a la Brocante, the city's largest market. Nearby we bought a bottle of wine to drink back on our terrace before dinner. We were impressed with several items, but decided to wait until the next day to make any purchases.

Russian Orthodox Church in Nice, an anomaly.

We returned to the Canada and proceeded to our terrace where we cracked into the bottle of wine. The four of us drank the bottle as we watched the busy street activity below. After a time as we finished off our glasses of wine, we decided it was time to venture out for one last dinner in Nice. Leo had done some research and decided on a place back in the Old Town.

We headed out into the evening and took the short ten-minute walk to the restaurant of choice for the evening. The Old Town is replete with narrow, winding cobblestone streets. It would be a great place to get lost, but with the aid of his trusty map Leo was zeroing in on our destination. The place Leo chose was a rustic, Mediterranean place with a Spanish flair. We sat on brightly colored, overstuffed pillows and drank good red wine.

Leo took control of the dinner ordering process and we all shared a large vessel of a paella which was richly filled with various types of seafood. It was a truly delicious meal. Once again Leo had hit a home run with his restaurant choice. We topped off the meal with some very rich gelato. This time I grabbed the check before anyone could beat me to it and we headed out into the night.

We had the option of heading back to our hotel the way we had come, or working our way back along the beach. We choose to take the beach route. By now, it had cooled down, probably slipping below the 60 degree mark and a fresh wind was blowing. This did not stop several groups of young partiers from populating the gray, pebbly beach.

We strolled the strand, and tried to stay warm in only our long sleeve shirts. A bright moon helped light us back to our street which intersected with the beach a couple of blocks from our hotel. We said good night to Leo and Keith and agreed to meet again the next morning for breakfast. The following day Keith was headed home, and the other three of us would be leaving on a night train for Bologna. We needed a good night's sleep because a big day of travel lay ahead for all.

We met downstairs from breakfast in the morning. Jenny and I had both had an outstanding night of rest and felt like we were both now acclimated to the time zone. We ate our continental breakfast, drank coffee, and made our plans for the day. Keith was headed to the airport to catch a flight back to Philadelphia, and on home to Delaware to prepare for the Thanksgiving Holiday. Jenny, Leo and I were catching a night train to Bologna, Italy, so we had virtually the entire day to sightsee and shop in Nice.

After breakfast we all returned to our rooms to pack for our departures later that day. We checked out of our room and left our bags with the front desk folks for safekeeping until later that evening. By now, it was time for Keith to leave for the airport so we all said our goodbyes and put him in a taxi to head for home.

Jenny, Leo and I decided it was time to head out and see more of Nice. Our first stop was to head for the Gare de Ville to double check our departure arrangements. We made quick work of this and headed on north and west to visit our first sight of the day, St. Nicholas Orthodox Cathedral.

Only about a five-minute walk from the train station, this Russian Orthodox Cathedral is reputed to be the most impressive Orthodox structure outside the old Soviet Union. It seems very odd that this beautiful religious site would exist in Nice. However, in the middle of the nineteenth century the Russian royalty began to visit Nice following a precedent established by other European ruling monarchs. The railroad was completed to Nice in the 1860s, and Czar Alexander II visited the area by rail and became infatuated with the climate. This began a relationship between Russia and the French Riviera that continues to this day.

The church was a gift to the Russian religious community in the area by Czar Nicholas II and was completed in 1912. The structure was dedicated to Nicholas Alexanderovich, a member of the Russian royal family that died in Nice at the age of 20 following a bout with tuberculosis. The building still functions as a working Orthodox Cathedral with regular church services. The impressive, onion-domed structure can be seen from afar which is how we, in fact, came upon the sight.

Jenny, Leo and I walked down the street to the structure and snapped several photos of the cathedral as we approached. We took a few minutes to tour the structure and I would recommend it to anyone that is visiting the area. It is so incongruous to me that I think it is worth stopping by, even if only for the freak occurrence that it exists in this area, seemingly far removed from Russia.

As we left the church and were strolling down the street that runs in front of the cathedral, we came upon a little sundry shop that was run by some local Russians. The business clearly catered to the local Russian community selling a variety of products including foodstuffs from the motherland, particularly caviar and vodka. What caught our eye was, in the front window, they had displayed a small Christmas ornament version of the Cathedral. The little wooden decoration was nicely hand-painted, and it had to be mine. We popped in the store and I quickly purchased it and, to this day, I find it to be one of my favorite trimmings for our tree.

We wandered back down toward the center of the city and started to look for a place to eat lunch. It was another gorgeous day; clear, sunny and probably nearly seventy degrees. We decided to seek out another restaurant

Leo had read about, Auberge De Theo. The bistro was located in the Cimiez area of Nice, a toney locale on the hill overlooking the city and the sea beyond. We hopped a bus for the ride up the hill and were dropped off near the entrance to the restaurant.

We were fortunate to score a table on an outdoor patio in the bright sunlight. Our pleasant server arrived and took our drink orders. We all had a glass of a local red wine and placed our food orders. The menu reflected the area with a strong Italian flavor with a hint of France, not a bad combination at all. They settled on different pasta dishes, I went for an antipasti plate.

Our waiter returned with some fabulous bread and olives with oil. We munched on it until our entrees arrived, which were all quite delicious. We decided to have another glass of wine and sit in the sun and enjoy the fine weather. Our fear was that this could be the last day of warm sun we would experience for the rest of the trip. Our solution was to just have another glass of wine and drink in more sun.

After about an hour we finally became restless, and decided to visit the Matisse Museum which is perched on the same lovely hill overlooking the city. The museum is dedicated to the works of the French artist, Henri Matisse. We hopped a bus for the short ride around the hill and were soon dropped off in front of a large red and yellow villa.

A magnificent 17th century mansion has been the home to the museum since 1963, and houses a large permanent collection of colorful paintings, drawings and sculptures that were primarily donated by the artist and his heirs. Matisse lived and worked in the Nice area nearly all his adult life and was, as you might expect, very fond of it. The villa, and its setting, is a terrific home for that artist's works, and makes the whole experience more worthwhile.

We wandered through the mansion and its wings taking in all its considerable offerings. It was such a pleasant day that you did not want it to end. The grounds surrounding the villa provide a park-like setting that proved to be a very pleasant area to stroll after we had finished viewing the artworks. Nearby there are Roman ruins that are available to explore. The vistas from the hill overlooking city and further to the sea are quite captivating.

The time had come for us to return to the city and do some last minute shopping before we had to catch our overnight train to Italy. We took the bus back down the hill and were let out very near a large department store, Galerie Lafayette De Nice. They were selling nouveau Beaujolais and some tempting looking snacks. We bought a bottle and some food for our travels that night and continued with our shopping.

We returned to the street where the Hotel Canada is and shopped at several of the stores that lined its sides. One particular place we had walked by caught our eye, it was a perfumery. The area around Nice and the French Rivera produces a major portion of the world's perfume. The towns of Grasse and Eze (remember our attempt to visit Eze) are two of the largest areas and both contain several factories that produce the sweet essences.

This retail establishment on our street was associated with a factory in Grasse and somehow beckoned us to enter. The seemingly knowledgeable sales personnel were adept at explaining how the products were produced. They were also proficient at directing you to fragrances that mixed well with your metabolism, and could direct you to essentially generic equivalents of famous fragrance for purchase at a fraction of the price. We purchased some cologne for both Jenny and me.

There also was a shop that sold beautiful linens and tablecloths. The table coverings and napkins looked as if they could have been inspired by one of the many artists that have plied their trade in the sun-washed French Rivera. Jenny decided on some particularly fetching napkins that have been our favorites ever since. In our house Saturday night is steak night, if we are home. When it is steak night you can rest assured these napkins will be in use, thus at least weekly I am reminded of this beautiful city.

It was now growing toward evening and we were shopped out and running out of time in Nice. We had a little over an hour before we needed to gather our things and head for the train station. We were not really hungry because we had eaten a late lunch so we decided to collect our luggage from the Hotel Canada and begin rolling our bags toward the train station.

We thanked the kind folks at the Canada for securing our luggage and headed down the stairs to the street. We started walking north when Leo hollered out to us that there was an open table at the café where he had first spotted us on the day of our arrival. So, we sat down at the table and ordered a round of beers clinging to the last few minutes we had in France.

It was good to relax for a short while because we had a big evening of travel ahead. We knew that we had several changes of trains, further exacerbated by the train-bus-train we would face to get through the track outage getting to Monaco. We finished our beers and said good-bye to our waiter who had served us since we arrived in Nice and began rolling our bags toward the station.

Once we arrived at the station we quickly located our train for Italy. We really did not have time to settle in because we knew we would have to change for a bus shortly. We departed Nice and about a half hour later, after our changes, we arrived in Monte Carlo. We were able to board another train there that would take us on to Italy.

For some reason, which I don't fully remember, we stopped in the Italian city of Ventimiglia, just across the French border for nearly an hour. By now it was around eleven o'clock at night and the lack of dinner was catching up to us. We got off the train and in the station, to our surprise, there was a little bar/trattoria. We found a vacant table, seated ourselves and all placed an order of pasta with a Marinara sauce. Within minutes the waitress brought us our teeming bowls of pasta with spicy Marinara sauce and covered with Parmesan cheese. We were very pleased with our good fortune as the meal was terrific and we washed it all down with an inexpensive, red table wine. A very pleasant treat indeed.

BOLOGNA, ITALY

We returned to the train and boarded our car. Our compartment contained a three-tiered berth, and was very chummy to say the least. We finally were able to negotiate space for all our luggage (good thing we were traveling light) and as we pulled away from the station we all crawled into our beds. We chatted a while and played a word game before shutting out the lights. We knew the trip was to be a quick one, because we had to change trains in about five hours in Verona.

After what seemed to be a very brief night's sleep, we were awakened by a knock on the door. It was the train conductor informing us that we were about ten minutes outside Verona and we must prepare to leave the train. The three of us kicked it into high gear and, amazingly, were standing at the door with our bags when the train pulled to a stop at the station. We only had twenty-five minutes between trains in Verona, so by the time we located our train on its track we boarded it and we were off again.

We had a little over an hour and a half until we were to arrive in Bologna. We all settled into our compartment, of which we were the only occupants, and dowsed in and out of sleep the entire trip. We arrived in Bologna a little after seven in the morning, tired and slightly disoriented. We walked out of the train station into the dawn of a Sunday morning in Bologna.

It was a foggy morning and probably thirty degrees colder than the last time we had breathed fresh air. We pulled out our directions to the Hotel Arcoveggio, our home for the next two nights. The hotel was a little away from the center of the city, north of the train station which was just far enough we didn't care to walk it that morning. We waited for the number 27 bus to arrive which would take us three stops and we would be there.

Fairly early on a Sunday morning the bus took a while to arrive and we stood in a damp cold for several minutes before one arrived. Our nerves were a little frayed because of lack of sleep and the uncertainty of the new locale, and it was a blessing when the bus pulled into the stop. Sure enough in less than five minutes we came to our stop and the hotel was only a short walk from the bus stop.

We didn't know much about the Arcoveggio, but we knew it met our expense requirements and came recommended by some travel book. From the looks of things the hotel sits in a rather working-class neighborhood largely surrounded by residential buildings. We opened the door not knowing what to think, but stepped inside to find a rather chic décor. As you might expect when arriving at your lodging at around eight o'clock on a Sunday morning, our room was not ready. However, the man working at the front desk said that they would do their best to prepare our rooms and invited us to enjoy breakfast while we waited.

He showed us into the next room, where a buffet breakfast awaited us. The elegant breakfast room/lounge was not too busy, so we took a table and inspected the offerings. It was a veritable feast. They had most anything you could possibly want from eggs, meats and cheeses, numerous cereals, breads and rolls, jams and preserves, juices including freshly squeezed orange, and an espresso machine that made a mean latte. Jenny was also excited by the wonderful assortment of teas.

Suffice it to say we were impressed and it looked like the Arcoveggio was going to exceed our expectations. The three of us ate a fabulous breakfast and drank hot beverages to our heart's content. Finally, about an hour after we arrived the front desk person found us and told us our room was ready and Leo's room would be done in another hour. We finished our drinks and went to register and gather up our luggage to go to our room.

By the time we finished the check in process, someone had already moved our bags into our room, so the clerk handed us our key and directed us to the building next door where our rooms were located. We entered our room and found it to be spacious, and quite stylish. There was a king-size bed, sitting area and a large bathroom with all the amenities. Clearly, we had hit a home run on the value for the price ratio.

Jenny with her brother, Leo Medisch, under the portico in Bologna, Italy.

Jenny and I rested for a while and began to remove the travel grit when Leo rapped on the door. He had stayed back to drink more coffee and had just gotten his room which was directly across the hall from ours. He was equally as pleased with his lodging and wanted to meet in about an hour to begin exploring the city. We took our time cleaning up and enjoyed the moments in our pleasant surroundings.

We met Leo in the lobby at the prescribed time and received a map of the city from the kind folks at the front desk. We ventured forth into the late Sunday morning, a day cloaked in a pea soup fog. We decided that a walk was in order because we felt the exercise would do us some good and we could get oriented to the city. So, we set out for the center of the city, the Piazza Maggiore.

The walk from the hotel to the center was a pleasant one despite the fact that you could cut the air with a knife. It was cool and crisp, quite the change from Nice. Bologna gives you the feel of a very old city and it is one of the oldest university towns in the world. This abundance of students lends a certain vibrancy to the city and helps create one of the most liberal environments in Italy.

Bologna is noted as the culinary capital of the country, and in a nation that is noted for its fine cuisine, that is saying something. Leo could not wait to try a couple of the local delicacies, and we could not wait for him to lead us in the proper direction. Leo was clearly amped up to eat and I was in search of the Bolognese sauce. I am a huge fan of this Italian meat sauce and I figured that I was now at the source and surely I would find the very best in Bologna.

We arrived at the Piazza Maggiore, or the main town square, after about a half hour walk. The main sight to see there is the Basicilia de San Petronio. This huge church is unfinished and has been that way for centuries when a pope halted the construction fearing it would outpace St. Peter's in Rome. Mass was just letting out when we arrived and we entered the church to view its impressive frescos and simply take in its sheer size.

After our brief tour of the church and Jenny's ritual candle lighting for her ancestors, we exited the building in search of the leaning towers of Bologna. During Medieval times the wealthy families of Bologna constructed numerous towers for some largely unknown reason. At its peak it is believed that nearly 200 such towers existed. Today, around twenty of these tall, red-brick rectangular towers remain with the two leaning ones, the Asinelli which stand 97 meters high and the Garisenda which is half that size, are the two most prominent. The smaller tower leans more noticeably and, in fact, is closed for fear of toppling. The Asinelli is available to climb if you want to mount the nearly 500 steps to obtain a commanding view of the red-tile roofed city below.

We walked to the Two Towers and surveyed the situation, and ultimately decided that, given the dense fog of the day, the hike to the top was nearly pointless. We determined that since we could barely see the top of the tower from the ground, the view would be very minimal that day. We would try to mount it before we left on Tuesday, but as it turns out the fog did not lift while we were there and we were denied the apparently magnificent view from the top.

We did some light shopping and spent some time in a wonderful bookstore near to the Two Towers. We left the bookstore and, by now it was approaching two o'clock, we were ready for our first dining experience in Bologna. Leo had scoped out a lively little spot a couple of blocks from the Piazza Maggiore. The Bar IL Calise is located on a main street and upon entry you are in the midst of a crowded café, but if you ascend the steps there is a very nice dining room on the second floor.

We were escorted to a nice table that overlooked the street below. We ordered a nice glass of a local, red wine and began to peruse the menu. Leo immediately noticed that they had a cold appetizer plate that included cold cuts and cheeses. He insisted that we order it and what a blessing that decision was. The waitress returned and took our orders, Leo ordered the cold cut plate and we all went for a plate of freshly homemade pasta.

Shortly, the server returned with our appetizer platter. There were a number of interesting and tasty meats and cheeses served to us, but the most important thing about this dish was it contained a healthy serving of mortadella. In preparation for this trip, I had read about this deli meat, which had been revered by the reviewer. I had not eaten it before and did not know why the writer had such a fixation for the glorified meat, akin to what we Americans refer to as bologna.

Well, I was the first to sample this delicacy and soon understood why the author had effused about the meat. To compare mortadella to bologna is like comparing a Lamborghini to a Kia. It is incredible! The buttery flavor and rich texture of the meat is well worth seeking out, and I could hardly believe that I had been deprived of this delicacy for over fifty years of life. There was some wonderful prosciutto, salami and outstanding pungent cheeses on that plate, but give me the mortadella.

Whenever we travel through Europe, or visit an American city with a sizable Italian population, we go in search of mortadella as an appetizer to take back to our room to have with a pre-dinner drink. Hank, I know that you enjoy it too, but we have to make sure we get the olive variety, and not the mortadella which contains pastichios because of your nut allergy. We simply love the rich flavor of this cold cut and get excited when we find it on a menu, particularly when we spy it on a breakfast buffet at our hotel. The rating of that hotel jumps several notches in our estimate.

Not only did I try mortadella for the first time at the IL Calise, but I had my first real taste of a true Bolognese sauce. I had begun my search for the best Bolognese sauce in Bologna, by ordering the tortellini topped with this tomato, meaty concoction. I was not disappointed in the least, it was truly delicious and the others liked what they had ordered. Even though this was my first Bolognese experience, this sauce was clearly in the running for the best in class.

We finished our entrees and decided to linger over another glass of the house red. We finally determined it was time to move on and paid our bill. We spent what was left of the afternoon browsing around the core of the city. We ducked in and out of several trendy shops and enjoyed the sights.

I had read online that the top local professional basketball team, Fortitudo Bologna, had a home game early that evening. I am a big basketball fan and had attended games in Europe before and enjoyed the level of play exhibited. I had convinced Jenny that this was an experience she would enjoy (this was not a hard sell because she is a huge basketball fan) and we invited Leo to join us in this event. Leo was a fan, but decided not to go to the game. He had other areas of the city he wanted to explore. Consequently, Jenny and I parted company from Leo and headed toward the arena agreeing to meet up with Leo later at the hotel and go to dinner.

Armed with our trusty map from the Arcoveggio, we made our way toward the PalaDozza, the home venue for Fortitudo. The arena was a pleasant walk from the core of the city, probably a mile or so from where we parted company with Leo. We arrived at the building, which is often referred to as the Madison Square Garden of Bologna, to a definite pregame buzz of excitement. Because of the crowd assembling outside, we wondered if we would be able to get a ticket.

We approached the ticket office and were pleased to score a couple of tickets near the midcourt area. Once inside the place was alive with activity. We checked out the souvenir and concession stands, located the restrooms, bought a beer and found our seats. You couldn't help but be affected by the electric atmosphere. There was music blaring, laser lights flashing, cheerleaders tumbling and nearly 6,000 screaming fans.

The team's rosters were filled with players from throughout Europe with a few former American college stars on sprinkled in. The Bologna team was facing a team from Avellino, a city in southwestern Italy. Of particular interest to us was one of the players on Air Avellino, Nate Green, and a former standout at Indiana State, a university where I earned a master's degree and was a member of their Board of Trustees at that time.

The game was an exciting one with the home team pulling out the victory. We thoroughly enjoyed the evening and picked up a couple of Fortitudo t-shirts on the way out as souvenirs of the game, undoubtedly becoming the only kids on our block with the spiffy garments. I strongly recommend that if you are a sports fan you investigate attending a game while traveling abroad. I have attended several basketball, hockey and soccer games in Europe, as well as, baseball in Japan and these can be not only entertaining, but a peek into the culture of the area.

After the game we began the walk back to our hotel. The arena was only about a ten minute walk from the train station where we planned to catch a bus to our hotel. Sure enough, just as we got to the bus stop by the train station, our bus pulled up and we were home in no time.

Leo was at the hotel when we got back and ready to go to dinner. By now it was nearing nine o'clock and we needed to eat and get to bed because we had a big day planned for the next day. We asked the kind folks at the front desk for a recommendation of a nearby restaurant. The fellow immediately recommended a very local place just a couple of blocks away. I believe it was named Le Rose.

The establishment turned out to be a very cozy and inviting café run by a friendly family and filled with residents of the neighborhood. We were warmly received upon our arrival and shown to a table next to the exposed bar. I am not certain any English was spoken in the joint, but they had a good house red wine and the aroma wafting through the room was pleasing.

Leo's years of cooking and familiarity with menu terms came in handy in deciphering the Italian offerings. We ordered a prosciutto and buffalo mozzarella appetizer which turned out to be outstanding. Leo and Jenny had a wood-fired pizza and, I, continuing my search for the best Bolognese a la ragu, ordered their tortellini. We all enjoyed our meals which were fresh and tasty. The service was outstanding and the prices were very affordable. This is probably not the kind of place that will highlight many guidebooks, but they sure produce some very palatable food at affordable prices.

We finished off our carafe of wine, paid our bill, thanked the host family, and headed out into the night air. All we could talk about the couple of blocks back to the hotel was what an enjoyable meal we had just concluded, and how good food can come from many different places. We arrived back at the hotel, said goodnight to Leo and turned in for the evening. We were worn out after a short night on the train, and a long day of exploring Bologna. We needed some good rest because our second Principality, San Marino, lay ahead the next day.

SAN MARINO

We got a great night's sleep and cleaned up and met Leo for breakfast in the hotel dining room at eight o'clock. We enjoyed another excellent breakfast then set out to begin our trek to San Marino. We had reserved a car through Avis for pick up at 9 o'clock at a store just down the street from the train station. It was another gloomy, foggy day as we walked toward the Avis outlet. We had reserved the car for pick up at nine hoping any morning rush hour traffic might have cleared by the time we hit the road.

We arrived at the rental agency a few minutes before the appointed time and soon we were piling in to our little, white Opal Agila. We found our way through the city streets without event and, with Leo as my navigator, soon we were on the A14 headed in the direction of the Rimini on the Adriatic Sea. The Italian Autostrade, or superhighway system, is an excellent roadway with smooth, well-paved surfaces. If you drive on this highway system you must be prepared for one thing, speed.

Although I believe posted speed limits exist, some exceeding ninety miles per hour under certain conditions, no one seems to observe them. If you are traveling at less than a hundred miles per hour, you better stay out of the left lane or you may literally get run over. Our little Opel ran quite comfortably at around eighty, so we settled into the middle lane and let the fast cars blow past us.

The ride on the A14 was a pleasant one. The fog lifted after we were not far out of Bologna and the sun began to peek through. The countryside was green and rolling as we blew by a number of small towns and villages. Within an hour or so we reached our exit, the Rimini -San Marino Highway. We turned south on the highway which was closely akin to a good, two-lane state highway in the United States. Within about fifteen minutes we were entering this little anomaly of a country.

San Marino is the third-smallest country in Europe in geographic area. The country contains about thirty thousand resident citizens that live in an area that essential encompasses one mountain. Mount Titano, which rises over two thousand feet above the Adriatic Sea less than fifteen miles to the west, is the start of the Apennines. On a clear day, which we enjoyed, the Adriatic is easily visible from many parts of the country.

When you arrive in San Marino, essentially at the base of the mountain, you immediately encounter retail shopping outlets. With a far more favorable tax climate than surrounding Italy, San Marino has become a shopping mecca. Bargains abound on clothing, shoes, fragrances and cosmetics, and electronics, to name a few. These outlets were teeming with shoppers as we arrived.

Shopping was not our purpose that day. We were, instead, interested in exploring the capital of San Marino, a medieval town and fortification which commands the top of Mount Titano. To reach the Town of San Marino, all you have to do is follow the road that winds around the mountain until it reaches its conclusion near the top. There you will find a well-paved parking lot where you can stash your car, because it is all on foot from here.

The capital is essentially a pedestrian-only area. The extremely quaint town is a maze of cobblestone streets that ascend and descend the peak of

Mount Titano. The Old Town walls still protect the citizens and serve as a tourist destination. After we parked our car, we descended the elevation until we reached one of the city gates. Once inside you felt like you had effectively stepped back several hundred years into the Middle Ages.

The earth tone, stone and brick structures that comprise the City of San Marino look like something right out of a movie set. The gate we entered the capital leads you into the core of the city and up a grade to the Piazza della Liberita, the heart of the city and home to the seat of government. The Palazzo Vecchio, or old palace, dominates the square and has been the home to the democratic government of San Marino for centuries. We took a self-guided tour of the facilities which includes the meeting place of their parliamentarians. The building is a repository for a number of historical artifacts, documents, and statuary for the country.

We spent the next couple of hours wandering inside the old city walls. We visited the Three Towers which are the symbols of the country and part of the fortifications of the community. You are left with the clear feeling when walking around these towers that this small city is simply perched on the peak of this mountain. We strolled on top of the old city walls and enjoyed the vistas; a verdant, fertile valley below, the Apennine Mountains beyond, and the Adriatic Sea to the east.

We also spent time shopping in the small boutiques and souvenir shops that lined the streets of the town. We purchased a beautiful ornament for our Christmas tree, a clear, hand-blown orb with another scenic orb suspended within, truly a unique piece (unfortunately it was broken on the trip home). We also took home some delightful limoncello, the citrus after-dinner drink, and a crystal globe filled with the Italian beverage, grappa.

Between the sightseeing and the shopping, we had worked up a hunger and began to search for a suitable spot for lunch. We finally settled on a quaint little place near the gate we had entered called the Ristorante Pizzeria del Ghetto. The little café had some outside tables and we were able to grab one that was sitting directly in the bright sun. It was an extremely pleasant day by now and the feel of the warm sun on our faces felt good indeed.

Our young waitress came and took our order, we got a liter of the local red wine, sangiovese, and for lunch the others ordered pastas and I took a break and ordered a prosciutto and mushroom pizza. We sat around and ate some delicious bread with fresh olive oil and sipped the bold red wine we had ordered.

Promptly our lunches arrived and they looked and smelled delicious. Jenny had a delicious tortellini Bolognese, which I had to try, and must say it was quite good. Leo had received a huge portion of lasagna, the feature dish of the day, and he thought it to be delightful. My pizza was a perfect for me. It had a perfectly cooked thin crust with a hint of the wood taste from the oven. The toppings were plentiful and fresh with a gooey layer of mozzarella covering the pie. It might have been that I was extremely hungry, or the atmosphere, but at that moment it was one of the best pizzas I had ever eaten. (See Appendix 22 for the recipe)

It did not take us long to clean these three plates. We sat in the sun and finished our carafe of wine and made our plans for the remainder of the day. We decide to begin our return trip to Bologna. We paid our bill and began our descent to the parking lot. We reached our car, stowed our purchases in the trunk, and headed back down the mountain road. We stopped at a couple of random shops on the way out of San Marino, filled the car with cheap gas, and soon were on the A14 headed toward Bologna.

As we cruised along at eighty miles per hour, being passed by other vehicles several times a minute, we reflected on our second Principality. The place really makes no sense to us why it exists. It is surrounded on all sides by Italy, it is the land mass of one mountain, but it somehow it is able to maintain its independence and own identity. It is a pretty little place and we were all glad that we had spent the day visiting the tiny country.

Within minutes of finishing our conservation about San Marino, both of my passengers were fast asleep. I let them get in a good nap, but when we were entering Bologna I woke them both up to help me navigate our way back to the Avis agency. We had use of the rental car until the following day, but had decided that we had no real need for it so we decided to return the vehicle to Avis. My co-pilots were able to guide me back to Avis and we returned the car safely.

By now we were all whipped, so we took the ten minute walk back to the Arcoveggio to have a rest. Well, that rest turned into a nap that lasted for a few hours, and when we awoke it was well into the evening. We decided to take the easy route and just went back to our neighborhood café, Le Rose for dinner. It was close by, the food and service were good, and the price was right.

We entered the restaurant and the family who owned the place greeted us like long lost relatives. They whisked us to a table and brought us bread, olive oil and a carafe of red wine before we could say anything. I have no recollection what the others had, but I know that I kept to my word, and had another delicious plate of tortellini Bolognese.

It was at least as good as the night before and we all had a great time with our new Italian friends. Before we could leave they insisted we have some homemade spumoni with them, and they serve it with a glass of grappa for all. They were so nice, spoke virtually no English, but we were able to communicate through our mutual love of food. If I have the good fortune to return to Bologna one day I will definitely return to that welcoming little spot. I hope our friends are still there.

With full stomachs and warm hearts we made the short walk back to the hotel. This was to be our last night in Bologna, as we were leaving on an overnight train for Zurich the next day, so we decided to try and sleep in. We parted company with Leo and agreed to see each other the next morning in the breakfast room, whenever we got up. Jenny and I watched a subtitled American movie for a while, and fell asleep.

The next morning I think we didn't get to breakfast until about nine-thirty. We had caught up on some much needed sleep, and we took our time enjoying the wonderful offerings on the buffet. After breakfast we made arrangements with the front desk for our departure. We were not catching our train until after eleven o'clock that night, so we arranged to keep Leo's room until we departed to have a place to rest and store our bags.

We returned to our rooms and packed our bags, moved them to Leo's room, and checked out of our room. We were all a little slow that day, and our pace reflected it. We finally left the hotel at nearly noon and headed back toward the center of the city. It was another gloomy, foggy day with very low visibility, the kind of day you are glad you are not trying to fly out somewhere.

We decided to walk downtown and spent a great deal of time popping in and out of shops along the portico covered streets. Eventually, we wondered into the university area in search of the Pinacoteca Nazionale di Bologna. The National Picture Gallery is housed in a former monastery which dates back to the early 18th century. The gallery displays the works of famous Italian artists, with a special emphasis on paintings that flourished in Bologna. These works range from 14th to the 20th centuries. The collection is impressive and the building serves as an excellent host for these works of art.

After spending a couple of hours browsing the collection in the National Gallery, we determined that it was time for a late lunch. I had read in a guidebook about an interesting sounding restaurant which was only a few blocks from the museum. The Osteria dell'Orsa was billed as having some of the best Bolognese sauce in the city, and since I was on a quest to find my favorite sauce we needed to give the place a try.

We found the restaurant and entered to discover the atmosphere was electric. The café was crowded even at this late hour and filled with the noise and excitement that a young crowd can bring about. We were greeted by an attractive, young woman who led us to seats at a communal table toward the back of the room. We sat down to what I believe was a group of students at the nearby university and the vibe told us that we were going to be in for a good experience.

Our server brought us the Italian-only menu and took our drink orders, the house red wine. We were working on deciphering the menu when a young man seated at our table speaking excellent English offered to assist. We took him up on his generosity and he walked us through the menu and volunteered a couple of his personal favorites.

He opined that he was a university student and he and his friends were regulars at the dell'Orsa largely for three reasons: it was close to where they studied, it was inexpensive, and, most importantly, the food was very good. This all was music to our ears. Our waitress returned and we all ordered a pasta dish, I, of course was trying the tagliatelle Bolognese. We also ordered a plate of mortadella as an appetizer for the three of us to share.

The service was quick and the mortadella appeared in seemingly no time. It was so good that I wished I had another order right now. It was a wonderful consistency, almost creamy in texture with a wonderful flavor filled with olives and peppercorns. The three of us made quick work of the meat and bread which had accompanied it. Just as we were polishing of the last morsels of the mortadella, our pastas arrived.

Leo immediately testified to the homemade nature of all three pastas, and we couldn't wait to dive in to our heaping plates of food. Mine was truly outstanding and I will not take issue with the Frommer's guidebook that suggested that they had some of the best Bolognese sauce in the city, or for that matter the world. The house red wine went perfectly with these freshly-made egg noodles and sauce, so I was forced to order another to help me wash down this large serving of food.

After we finished our pasta, we sat around sipping beverages and watching the young crowd of patrons interact. Clearly, this place was another true find. We still had another meal to eat in Bologna, so I was not prepared to proclaim the sauce at the dell'Orsa the winner of the competition, but it certainly had to be a serious contender.

I spotted our waitress and asked for the check. When she returned and we saw the bill, we knew that the young man who had served as our interpreter for the menu was right, the food was excellent, and the price was very reasonable. This was truly my kind of place. I am confident that if we lived in Bologna we would become regular customers of this establishment also.

After lunch we spent the remainder of the day roaming the core of the city shopping. It was more of an exploratory mission than one with a purpose, but we did find some interesting stores. Jenny and I found a nice ornament for our Christmas tree, and we found some very intriguing shops selling food stuffs. We bought and immediately consumed some excellent dark chocolates, in fact, we kicked ourselves several times later in the trip for not buying more.

I grew tired and Jenny and I decided to return to the hotel and rest up before we went out to dinner. Leo had something else up his sleeve, so he stayed out while we returned to the room. Upon our arrival at the hotel we watched some television and took it easy knowing that we had a long night of travel on the train.

I think we dosed off about the time Leo arrived back at the room. He was carrying a bottle of red wine he had purchased on his route back and he announced that he had found the perfect place for dinner that evening. He offered few details, but told us he had made us reservations for eight o'clock which should give us ample time to come back, collect our luggage and get to the train station for our 11:30 p.m. departure. It sounded like a good plan to us.

We spent the next hour drinking the bottle of wine and watching Italian television in the room. About seven-thirty, as we were finishing the fine red, we decided to head for the restaurant with an intermediate stop at the train station to reconfirm all the details of our trip that night. We set out into the cool night and took the ten minute walk to the station. We were able to locate all the information we needed for our overnight train to Zurich, and departed for Leo's restaurant of choice for that evening.

Leo continued to be circumspect about the restaurant, only telling us that it was along our normal route to the Piazza Maggiore. After walking about half the way from the train station to the center of the city we stopped and walked up a stairway to the restaurant Leo had chosen. On a second floor up under the porticos was this small, warm café that looked divine.

Apparently, Leo had learned of it from one of his restaurant rating guides, and had stopped by earlier in the day to check it out. He was most excited because they had a rabbit-based Bolognese sauce, and he was a big fan of rabbit meat. The kitchen area was open to the small dining room, and we sat near the aperture so Leo could observe the chef's activities.

We sat down and ordered a bottle of wine and Leo took over from here. Leo began a dialogue with the chef, as if they had known each other for years. The chef first showed us a huge roll of mortadella that must have been nearly two feet in diameter. He then thinly sliced the meat onto a plate with some local ham, cheeses, and olives. Our waiter took the plate from the chef and served it to us along with some still warm bread.

The antipasto plate was simply amazing, the mortadella was the best we had tasted and the ham, cheese and olives were wonderful accompaniments. Leo ordered for all three of us and insisted that I continue my theme, but eat the rabbit Bolognese over the freshly-made fettuccini. I don't remember what Jenny had, but I know that Leo had a rabbit dish which he raved about. It was all good. My rabbit Bolognese was simply delicious, so much so that I made Jenny and Leo try it.

We absolutely sated ourselves, finishing the meal off with some homemade banana gelato and a glass of grappa. Unfortunately, I have no idea what the name of this fabulous little bistro is and really no way of finding out. It was a truly outstanding meal, a fitting end to our visit to the culinary capital of Italy.

As we walked out into the night to return to our hotel to gather our bags, and catch the night train, we unanimously agreed that Bologna deserved its reputation for wonderful dining. We had eaten in a wide variety of dining establishments, from neighborhood to rather high end, and had not had anything but a great meal. As for the winner of the best Bolognese sauce, I could not pick. They were all good, varied in their own way and deserving of an award. You could not go wrong with any of them. Hank, knowing what a fan you are of a good Italian meat sauce, you would love eating in this community. I hope you can one day.

We arrived back at the Arcoveggio, returned to the room and grabbed our luggage. We checked out of the hotel, but not before thanking the front desk manager for all his assistance during our stay. We headed to the bus stop just as the number 27 was arriving. We got to the train station about a half hour prior to our departure and bought a few snacks for the trip.

Our train arrived, we found our couchette, and we boarded and stowed our luggage. The sleeping compartment had space for four people, but we were pleased to find out from the conductor that no one had reserved the other berth. We would have the space to ourselves all the way to Zurich. Our train departed on time and we sat up discussing our impressions of Bologna. All three of us agreed that we had low expectations for the city, but we had been very surprised at how much it had to offer. I hope one day to return and settle the question as to who actually makes the best Bolognese sauce in Bologna. I am betting it is a grandma somewhere.

ZURICH, SWITZERLAND

The train ride to Zurich was an uneventful one, as you would like it. We all awoke in the morning about an hour before our scheduled arrival into Zurich, a little before nine o'clock. We were pleasantly surprised to peer out the window and see that we were now in the beautifully, snow-covered Alps. A steady snow was falling as our train made its way through the flocked evergreen forests and mountains above. It was truly a lovely sight.

A vendor with a food cart came clamoring down the hallway outside our compartment and we all took hot beverages and muffins to start our day. We had by now put up our berths and were seated on the cushioned chairs they convert into for daytime use. We enjoyed the scenery and the light breakfast until we arrived in Zurich a few minutes ahead of schedule.

We had no idea what we were about to see when we got off the train in Zurich's Hauptbanhof. As we disembarked from our train, we headed for station house and walked directly into a large indoor Christmas market that was under construction. Scheduled to open the next day, workers were decorating the centerpiece of the market, an enormous live Christmas tree covering it with Swarovski crystal ornaments. Shopkeepers were busily preparing to open their holiday kiosks which would sell small gifts, ornaments and various edible delicacies. It was a sight to behold, and provided a very positive impression of Zurich upon arrival.

The station was abuzz, not only because of the market set up, but commuters were flooding into the city as the work day was beginning. The station houses a large shopping center and is one of the nicest train facilities I have had the pleasure of visiting. Knowing that we were very early for check in at our hotel, we exchanged some money and bought another cup of coffee at a café. We sat for a while and enjoyed the hubbub of activity around us.

After finishing our coffees, we decided it was time to venture out to our hotel and attempt to check in. The Bristol Hotel is only about a five minute walk from the Hauptbanhof on the other side of the Limmat River. Upon exiting the station we walked across a tram-choked plaza, which serves as the mass transit hub for the city. We then crossed the river on a bridge immediately in front of us. Once we reached the other side of the river we turned left and the Bristol sits on a little hill a couple hundred yards or so ahead.

The hotel is stone structure with the upper floors painted a pale blue. As we entered the lobby a great deal of activity was going on as people were spilling out of the breakfast area and folks were lining up at the front desk to check out. We joined the queue and were soon greeted hospitably by a suited clerk. We were indeed early, but he took our bags and invited us to return in a couple of hours, assuring us that our rooms would be ready then.

We decided that our best course was to follow his instructions and go for a walk and begin to get our bearings. We retraced our steps to the train station to visit the Tourist Information Center we had spied when we were departing the station. There we met with a representative of the tourist office and she provided us with maps and brochures of Zurich and the area. She also gave us information about all the events that were taking place while we were in town.

We departed the train station and headed out across the Bahnhofplatz toward the main shopping street, Banhofstrasse. We strolled down Bahnhofstrasse, window shopping our way toward Lake Zurich on the other end of the street from the station. It was a clear, crisp morning with fairly fresh snow on the ground. As we walked we passed the headquarters on some of the world's largest banks and extremely high end retail outlets.

If you can think of a major designer, they probably have a location on this street. Additionally, an abundance of fashionable jewelers selling famous Swiss-made watches are housed in nearby shops. We made it several blocks passing the likes of Gucci, Burberry and Cartier before we were attracted to the Swiss chocolate shop, Sprungli. We peered through the window at the wondrous display of decadent-looking chocolates.

Being the huge foodie, Leo, had to go in, so we followed. Soon he discovered that the shop included a café and he decided it was time for a more filling breakfast than the coffee and muffin we had on the train as we arrived. He and Jenny were determined that an omelet, or some French toast swimming in Sprungli chocolate sauce sounded irresistible.

I, on the other hand, felt gross from not having showered and could not see myself eating in this pretentious looking establishment with an oily body. I decided it was time to go back to the Bristol and see if our rooms were ready, so I could do something about getting cleaned up. We parted company with them agreeing to meet me back at the hotel after they had breakfast.

On my way back to the hotel I stopped for another coffee and a ham and egg croissant at a little place in the train station shopping center. I wolfed down the sandwich and the coffee au lait and crossed the Limmat River back to the hotel. When I arrived at the Bristol, the hubbub of activity that we had encountered upon our arrival had subsided. The same desk clerk that had greeted us upon our arrival was on duty, and proudly announced to me that our room was ready. He also informed me that he had taken the liberty of having our bags delivered to our rooms. He handed me a key and directed me to the elevator on the other side of the lobby.

I took the lift to the third floor and moved down the hallway to the far end where our room was located. I opened the door and discovered a large corner room with a king bed, sofa, desk and chair, and plenty of room. Our bags had been stowed and all was in order. I flopped down on the light blue bed spread and just lay there for a minute. I soon began to undress and turned on the television to CNN to catch up on world events, and for some background noise as I cleaned up.

I hopped in the large bathtub and enjoyed a long, hot shower under a shower head with the perfect amount of pressure. It felt so good that I decided to just shave while in the shower. I finished cleaning up and was just putting on some fresh clothes when Jenny arrived at the room. She and Leo had a very pleasant breakfast and she was now ready for her turn in the bathroom. I laid on the bed and watched the news as she readied herself for the day.

We decided that our first order of business was to get some laundry done because I had just put on my last pair of clean underwear and socks. As Jenny was finishing up, I went back downstairs and asked at the front desk about any nearby laundries. They assured me that they could handle the task on a per piece basis, which I declined. They then offered that they did not know of any drop off or self-service laundries nearby.

I returned to the room to tell Jenny what I had found out. By now, Leo had joined her in our room and we let him know what we were planning to do. He was good with the scheme as he was running low on clean clothes, and he thought a slow day was in order after our overnight train trip had worn him out. All in agreement, I volunteered to go back to the Tourist Information Center to see if they could help us find a laundry not far from our hotel.

Leo offered to go along with me and we made a quick trip to the train station. It turns out that the good folks at the information center assured us that a very nice self-service laundry was just up the hill from our hotel about a block away. We returned to the hotel, gathered our dirty clothes and the three of us set out to find the laundromat. Sure enough, we exited the hotel, climbed up a set of stairs to the street that ran parallel to ours and the laundry was in sight a couple of businesses down.

We entered the clean, little building and discovered that they did not do drop off service, but there were several free washers and dryers at our disposal. We commandeered three of the washers and began our task of cleaning our clothes. Leo decided to scout the area and left for a walk. He returned about an hour later and told us he had found an interesting little café nearby that he thought might be a good bet for lunch.

We dried and folded our things and walked back down the hill to the Bristol to stow our now clean clothes. We met back in the lobby in a few minutes and Leo led us to the little Middle Eastern café he had discovered a couple of blocks from the hotel near the laundry. We walked into the warm, little place which was had the décor of a hookah bar. The walls were covered with colorful kilims, incents burned in brass fixtures, and the booths were covered with thick- cushioned pillows.

The friendly, mustachioed proprietor waved us to take any open table and we settled into a corner booth. Our swarthy looking waiter soon brought us an English menu and we all quickly decided to follow the lead of the guy at the next table. We all ordered a plate of shawarma and fries with a cup of the aromatic herbal tea that others were drinking. Our delicious tea was served as we watched the cook slice our shawarma from the vertical spit, it looked and smelled outstanding.

Our orders were delivered to our table very quickly, each of us with a heaping helping of the meat served with tahini sauce, tabbouleh, freshly cut French fries, and pita bread. To us, it was a true feast. I guess we were very hungry by now, but the combination of the hunger and the rich flavors of the food appealed to all three of us. We absolutely devoured our lunches washing it all down with the several cups of the tea.

It came time to leave and our waiter brought us the bill. We could not believe that this delightful culinary experience was only about twenty dollars for the three of us. I true bargain if I ever had one. We paid and decided to take a walk to help settle our stomachs from this hardy meal. We strolled down the street determined to explore the right bank of the river, the side on which our hotel resides and we had not explored yet.

We only walked a couple of blocks south from our hotel and entered the Altstadt, or Old Town, which exists on the right bank. The narrow cobblestone streets and alleys are home to medieval buildings and homes. The streets are lined with very unique shops, restaurants, bars and cafes. As we headed south we began to take notice of several restaurants which we had read about in our guidebooks, places where we might return for dinner.

As we entered the heart of the area we heard a bit of commotion down a side street off the main drag. We decided to investigate and discovered that a red-light district existed in the area. Here young men, apparently intoxicated in the mid-afternoon, were hollering up to women who were half-dressed, hanging out of windows above. I had seen this before in places like Amsterdam, but it is such a foreign notion from my Midwestern roots, I always am surprised by it.

We decided not to attract attention to ourselves, and not interfere with potential commerce, so we moved through this area of prostitution quickly. As we window shopped our way down the streets we discovered several stores that were selling truly local items. There were numerous shops that specialized in cuckoo clocks. We stopped in and looked at various ones of these timepieces. We debated the three days we were in Zurich if we wanted one of the interesting clocks, ultimately decided we did not need one at this time.

As we were walking I pulled Leo aside and told him of a plan of mine. I wanted to buy Jenny a decent, Swiss made watch while we were in Zurich. Years before, and in a period of a more preferential currency conversion, I had bought myself a good Omega watch while in Basil, Switzerland. I also purchased a Raymond Weil watch for myself in Zagreb, Croatia, on an impulse buy when the exchange rate was much skewed in favor of the U.S. dollar. I thought it was time that Jenny had a nicer watch, too.

I began to separate myself from the other two and duck in and out of several jewelry stores that were along our route on the right bank. It seemed to me that a better deal could be had on this side of the river rather than along Bahnhofstrasse because it seemed that the overhead was higher along that toney street. I came upon a very interesting jeweler near the south end of the right bank, close to the final bridge across the Limmat. Here the owner appeared to specialize in vintage, used watches. He had some pretty amazing timepieces and I fell for an Omega with a white face and gold case and bracelet. I decided to wait and check other store over the next two days. This would be a last day decision, after I had time to thoroughly investigate the situation and attempt to find the best possible deal.

It was now late afternoon and we decided it was time to have a drink before we returned to the hotel to freshen up before dinner. We had stumbled across an interesting looking establishment that I had read about in a guidebook before we arrived. We entered the Café Odeon as the light was fading and the place appeared to be picking up after work traffic.

The café had been in business for nearly one hundred years and is quite the place. You are immediately taken by its appearance; crystal chandeliers and sconces, marble topped tables and a long brass bar. The place has been frequented by the rich and famous and is noted as the place that Vladimir Lenin waited out World War I before his successful postwar efforts to establish Russia as a communist state.

We sat down on a red leather covered bar stool and ordered a beer. This was an outstanding place to people watch. It seemed to be a young professional crowd that afternoon, and the activity was very lively. We relaxed and sipped our beers as we discussed our dinner options. Finally, the place got too crowded for our tastes and we took our leave, making the trek back to the Bristol to relax for a few minutes before going to dinner.

On the way back we window shopped dining establishments attempting to decide on a locale for supper. We finally decided to try a regional Swiss restaurant on the right bank not far from our hotel, Le Dezaley. By the time we got back to the hotel we were all tired and hungry. We decided we better not stop for long, or we would never get started again. I threw a little water on my face and we went back out into the cold night air.

It began to spit snow as we walked to dinner. The stroll down the hill into the Old Town did not take long and soon we were entering the warm and smokey restaurant. The place was very crowded and we were seated in an earth-toned room with vaulted ceilings at a long table shared with several other diners, in European style.

The Le Dezaley specializes in Swiss cuisine from the Vaud area of Switzerland, a French speaking part of the country. One of their specialties is fondue, but we all decided to pass on that entrée, and turned to more traditional Swiss dishes. Our waiter arrived and took our drink orders, beers all around and returned with them along with a bread basket. We all placed our orders, Leo and Jenny went for a veal dish with fried potatoes and I selected the bratwurst dinner which also came with the hash browned potatoes.

We drank our beers and checked out the atmosphere of the very old establishment. The building dates from the 13th century and, although greatly updated, it maintained a rustic feel. The place was slammed that night and the acoustics made for a pretty loud crowd. But, people were having a great time and seemed to be enjoying their meals. We soon understood why as our entrees arrived and they looked and smelled delicious.

The veal "Zurich style" was is a cream sauce with mushrooms and was terrific. My bratwurst was equally good, but the star of the show was the side dish, rosti. This grated potato dish is similar to what we know as hash browns, but on steroids. It is clearly fried in butter and had a little onion and bacon added. I have come to find out that it is considered a national dish of Switzerland and finds its origins as a farmer's breakfast staple. Clearly, this would now be a side that I would seek out in the future.

We finished our tasty meal and drank another beer, washing down the remnants of our food. We asked the waiter for our check, paid the bill and headed back out into the cold, dark night. We were only five minutes from the hotel, but the snowy, windy evening made the walk seem longer. We arrived at the Bristol and headed directly to our rooms. We agreed to meet for breakfast and depart mid-morning for our final Principality of the trip, Liechtenstein.

We awoke after a good night's sleep, cleaned up, and went downstairs to join Leo for breakfast. The breakfast room was packed with fellow travelers and we were relieved to find Leo seated at a table large enough for all of us sipping his morning coffee. The offering was quite nice, cold cereals, fruits, meats, cheeses, juices, and an assortments of breads and jams. We soon filled our plates and enjoyed a hearty, continental meal.

LIECHTENSTEIN

After eating our fill and drinking several cups of coffee, we gathered our things and headed to the Hauptbanhof to catch a train to Liechtenstein. We had discovered in our research that we could take a Swiss train to the border town of Buchs, and there we could bus to Vaduz, the capital.

Then we could take a bus to, and catch a return train back from Sargans, another border town. By entering the country at one point and exiting from another we would be able to see a great deal of the little country.

The train to Buchs departed at 9:30 a.m., but we arrived in plenty of time to buy our tickets and find our track for departure. Having a little extra time, we looked around the impressive retail complex attached to the station. The Christmas market that was housed inside the terminal was fully prepared to function, but didn't open until later in the day. We determined then that this would be our first order of business upon our return from Liechtenstein.

The train arrived on time and we departed for Buchs. The trip took a little over an hour and was a very scenic ride. We followed the west, then south shores of Lake Zurich for its length riding just above the waters and below the snow-capped Alps on the other side. We chugged through several alpine villages stopping occasionally to exchange passengers. We passed by a couple of other mountain lakes and finally arrived at our destination.

We hopped off the train and walked into the small terminal area looking for the bus that would carry us to Vaduz. As we exited the train station, there on the opposite side of the tracks, a modern yellow bus awaited us. The driver sold us our tickets convincing us that our best course was to purchase a ducat that was good for the whole day, our cheapest option.

We boarded the comfortable coach and set off through the Liechtenstein countryside. This country was the largest geographically of the three small countries we were visiting, being two and a half times larger than San Marino. The country is a beautiful haven nestled entirely in the Alps with its western border with Switzerland being the mighty Rhine River. The infrastructure and buildings appeared very well-kept, underscoring the fact that the country has one of the highest per capita incomes in the world. There were signs of manufacturing as we drove along, which is coupled with their role as an international tax haven and banking center.

We cruised through the country's largest town, Schaan, and in about five minutes we were on into the capital city of Vaduz. Vaduz is a fairly quiet place, dominated by the impressive and imposing royal castle that looms above the town several hundred feet on the side of a mountain. The quaint buildings are all very neat, well-kept and Germanic-looking.

The bus station sits in the center of town with the Tourist Information Center about half a block away. We made the repository of travel info our first stop for a couple of reasons. First, we wanted to get a map of the area and to find what we need not miss while in the country for a few hours. Second, we wanted to get our passports stamped to prove we had been here and the Tourist Information Center is the only place in the country to accomplish this task.

We strode into the office and were greeted by a couple of friendly, aging women. They spoke English well, but with a heavy German accent, and were more than happy to tell us all about their splendid little country. Our first order of business was to get our passports stamped. The ladies informed us that there was a fee associated with receiving the emblem on our documents, as I recall it was a couple of dollars apiece. I attempted to sweet talk the women into giving us the stamp for free, but to no avail. We forked over the cash and they obliged us by supplying our passports with the official stamp.

The kind ladies supplied us with maps, but were short on suggestions for sights to see. It seems there were two major museums, one art and another dealing with postal stamps. The art museum was closed that day for some reason, and the stamp museum did not sound interesting to us. They tried to convince us that we should take a hike, literally, but the cold, snowy weather was a deterrent to us.

We decided just to walk the streets of the town and see what appealing shops were around. We happened upon a couple of very interesting souvenir-oriented stores and spent some time, and money, exploring their wares. We found a great Christmas ornament in one of the shops. It is a flat, round, hand-blown red disk with a likeness of the Vaduz Castle painted on one side. It was too good to pass up and it is clearly one of our favorites today.

Soon it was time for lunch and we began to survey our options. As I recall, there were only really a few choices and we narrowed them down quickly. One place looked like it really catered to tour groups that might be passing through and had a wide variety of cuisines on its menu including Asian, Italian and local fare. The other, which we chose, had more standard German fare and a great view of the castle above.

We entered the Old Castle Inn and sat at a table on one of the large front windows facing the castle. The smells inside were quite pleasant and the staff was friendly. There were not many patrons, and those who were there were huddled around a large bar drinking beer. We decided not to buck the trend of the establishment, so when the waitress came around we ordered a round of beers. We perused the menu and all decided it was time for some real German food, so we all ordered Weiner schnitzel and French fries.

As we waited for our orders we determined that the local beer we were drinking was quite good. The clouds parted for a few minutes and the warm sun shone through the picture window brightening our day. The schnitzel and fries arrived and we ordered another round of beer. The plates before us looked good, and the large schnitzel was cooked to perfection and the hand-cut fries were an excellent accompaniment. We enjoyed the meal, the beer and the beautiful view. Since this is my only meal in Liechtenstein, to date, it must go down as my favorite. **(See Apendix 23 for the recipe)**

Our lunch at the Old Castle Inn was a truly enjoyable experience. About the time we were preparing to get our bill and leave, another round of beers appeared at our table. It seems that one of the locals at the bar was the proprietor, and he decided to buy us another round. He came by our table to introduce himself and thanked us for coming in. He said it looked like we were having a good time so he thought another beer was in order. We thanked him profusely and, so as not to make him feel badly, we drank the brews.

We finished off our beverages and paid the check. We knew that we had a little time before catching the bus for Sargans and decided to walk a bit before we left. Energized for some unknown reason, Jenny decided we should walk up the mountain to the Vaduz Castle and see if the royals were home. Leo offered he was going back to the Old Castle for a beer, the hike looked far too strenuous for him. Reluctantly, I agreed to tag along.

We headed up the cobblestone street toward the path that leads toward the castle. I am not an expert on degrees of slope, but I can assure you that is was very steep. After a couple of blocks hiking what seemed to be at a forty-five degree angle, we aborted the mission. It was so steep that just coming back down the hill was difficult. We got to the bottom of the hill just as Leo was exiting the Old Castle Inn and the bus for Sargans was pulling into the station.

We rushed to catch the bus, climbing aboard just as the driver was exiting to take a couple minute break. We sank down into a few choice seats and soon the driver returned and we were underway. The winding route to Sargans took us by a couple of castles perched on outcroppings of rocks above us. The green valley contrasting with the snow-covered mountains made for a beautiful ride.

We arrived at the station in Sargans shortly before the train headed for Zurich arrived. Soon the westbound train pulled into the station and we hopped on and headed back to the Hauptbanhof. During the hour long ride back to the city we took in the wonderful vistas and discussed how much we had enjoyed our visit to Vaduz. We all agreed that our visits to the three Principalities had been very worthwhile, each offering a very different, but enjoyable day.

We rolled into the Zurich train station and departed the coach, alighting almost smack dab in the middle of the Christmas Market which was now in high gear. We wandered around the little kiosks shopping for ornaments, discovering fine Swiss chocolates, and drinking another beer. We marveled at how nice and how big the Christmas tree was, the centerpiece of the market, covered in all those crystal ornaments. If you are in the area at the holidays, you should drop by and see this market.

Somewhat tired from our day of travel, we decided to go back to the hotel and rest a while before venturing out again for dinner. We took the short walk back and the three of us huddled in our room for a while deciding where to go for dinner. Leo and I looked at our guidebook and determined that Zeughauskeller on the left bank would be our selection.

Our brief respite reenergized us and we decided to head in the direction on the restaurant on the Bahnhofstrasse and do a little shopping. Leo had agreed to assist me with diverting Jenny so I could check out a couple of more modestly priced jewelers we had spotted the day before. We hiked back across the river and crossed the plaza in front of the train station and headed down the Bahnhofstrasse.

It was another cold night and snow was spitting. As we passed the toney shops Jenny remembered a shoe store she had seen earlier and she and Leo decided to go look at their display. We agreed to rendezvous at the

Zeughauskeller, which was just up the street, in an hour. I set out to find a good, Swiss watch for Jenny's Christmas gift. I walked toward the lake and stopped in to a couple of the famous watch shops, Beyer and Bucherer, and walked away with sticker shock.

As I grew nearer to the water I noticed a nice little jewelry store about a half block down a side street. I entered the store and was greeted by a rather large, middle-aged man. He was most pleasant and willing to assist. I told what I was looking for; a women's round-faced, gold watch with a gold bracelet that was reasonable priced. He pulled out several including one that particularly caught my eye; a Raymond Weil which matched what I was looking for with a mother-of-pearl face. It was a little more than I wanted to spend, but it clearly was a finalist.

I stopped in a couple of other shops, but nothing caught my eye like the Omega I had seen at the shop on the right bank the day before, or the Weil I had just seen. I wanted to get Leo out with me the next day and solicit his opinion on the two timepieces. I was beginning to run out of time and headed back toward the restaurant. After a couple of blocks I spotted the siblings walking down the other side of the street a little ahead of me. I hollered at them to stop and we all proceeded to the restaurant together.

The Zeughauskeller is a venerable structure built shortly before Columbus discovered America. The building, as the German name suggests, was an arsenal for several centuries. The restaurant was established on the sight. The large dining area can seat a couple of hundred people and the walls are adorned with some of the former medieval armaments.

The restaurant is known for its hardy Swiss fare, and when we entered the smell of pork was heavy in the air. Fortunately, we were shown to a table in the far corner near a window. For as large a room as we were in, and as many patrons were there, it was surprisingly not too noisy. The servers were bringing out large steins of local beers which looked inviting. When our server arrived with English menus, we all ordered a large stein of the amber colored local beverage.

We surveyed the menu and the first thing I noticed was they had rosti on the menu. I was pleased by this and having this potato side dish would help drive my entrée decision. Ultimately, we all decided on different dishes. We had the advantage of watching people being served at nearby tables and used this knowledge in making our selections. Jenny ordered the roast pork, Leo had the Weiner schnitzel, and I went for the schweinshaxe, or pork knuckle.

Although some of the offerings were supposed to come with different side dishes, we all asked for and received our new favorite potato concoction, rosti. When our orders came out they were all fantastic. Leo, the top chef, tried each of our dishes and heartily approved of each preparation. We could not have been more pleased with our choices and the rosti was out of this world. We had thoroughly enjoyed it the night before, but this preparation took it to another level.

This meal stands out to me as my favorite I've had in Switzerland. We all had a great time, the ambience was quite good and the cuisine first rate. I have included a recipe for rosti, because this side dish made the meal extra special for me. **(See Apendix 24 for the recipe)**

We finished our meals and called for the check. We paid our waiter a very reasonable price for the quality of the meal, and headed back out into the cold night. We debated stopping somewhere for a nightcap, but decided that another long day awaited us tomorrow. We were again taking an overnight train the next day, this time to Prague, our final destination. We found our way back to the hotel and quickly made our way to bed. We agreed to sleep in as late as possible and meet for breakfast whenever we awoke.

Hank, I am sure you will recall our visit to Zurich in November of 2014. We had lunch at the Zeughauskeller on our last day of our stay. We enjoyed it so much that we made reservations for dinner that evening before we departed. We thoroughly enjoyed both our meals at the unique restaurant. We received excellent service and high quality food on both occasions.

Jenny and I awoke around eight and set about cleaning up. We called Leo and decided to meet in the breakfast area at nine. We went downstairs at the appointed time and found a table. We noticed a sign on the table that omelets were available for a nominal additional charge and we each ordered a ham and cheese.

The server returned shortly with three large omelets spilling off their plates. We enjoyed the breakfast greatly and sat around drinking hot beverages and planning out our day for quite a while. We decided on a fairly ambitious day. We wanted to go to a movie and take a cruise on the lake, or go to the circus. Additionally, I had to finish my shopping and decide on a watch for Jenny.

We quickly returned to our rooms and packed up our things. We had checked with the front desk and we needed to vacate our rooms before we went out for the day. We took our luggage downstairs and checked out. The Bristol would hold our bags until it was time for us to depart. We headed out the door for the bridge to cross over to the left bank to visit the Tourist Information Office again to gather specifics for lake cruises and the circus.

When we had been walking on the Bahnhofstrasse, you couldn't help but notice a big top tent set up near where the Limmat River meets Lake Zurich. It was also near where the Lake Zurich cruise boats dock and disembark. We had decided that one of the activities could be an interesting way to spend part of the day. The friendly people at the Tourist Information Office filled us in on the schedule for both, and the only potential for us was a cruise on the lake.

We found out that there was an hour and a half cruise on the lake leaving at one o'clock which sounded ideal to us. That meant that we had a couple of hours to do some shopping and for me to try and make a decision of the watch. We all headed toward the lake ostensibly to purchase our cruise tickets, but also to have Leo give me his opinion on the Weil watch.

As we approached the end of the street near the jewelry shop, we asked Jenny to give us a couple of minutes alone. She went into a nearby store while Leo and I went into the watch shop to view the women's watch I liked. The same gentleman who had waited on me the night before opened the door for us as we entered the shop. He remembered the exact watch I was interested in and produced it for us to look over. Leo approved of the selection and liked it better than the Omega we had seen at the other shop on our first day in Zurich.

Rather than procrastinate, I made the decision and bought the watch on the spot. The kind shopkeeper had it gift wrapped for me and I shoved it into one of the big pockets in my coat. We set out to find Jenny, which was easily accomplished, and then proceeded to the boat line office to purchase the cruise tickets.

We bought the tickets for the ride and set out to do some shopping for the next couple of hours until our cruise took off. We crossed the river on a bridge at the mouth of the river and entered the Altstadt on the right bank. We found the shopping on this side of the river to be more to our liking and spent the next couple of hours browsing the shops in the area. When it was about time to go to the boat we decided to pop in a little shop we had seen and pick up some sandwiches and drinks to take on the boat with us as sort of a picnic lunch.

With a sack of food in hand, we climbed aboard the boat for our lake journey. It was not a very nice day, gray and gloomy and the lake was choppy from a wind that had come up. Nonetheless, the trip was a pleasant one as we sat inside the cabin looking out on the Alps and villages that surround the lake. We ate our lunch and drank our sodas and were thankful to be off our feet for a while.

The hour and a half passed quickly and we were soon back at the dock. Our next move was to cross the river back to the right bank and head toward a movie theater we had spied on our first day. The first day when we did our laundry we saw this old theater down the street from our hotel. It had been divided into four or five screens and looked interesting to us, particularly when we saw that Quentin Tarantino's Kill Bill was playing.

We entered the modernized lobby of the old movie palace and purchased tickets for the show. We moved into the small theater and took seats toward the middle of the room, but we could have had whatever ones we wanted because no one else was in the house. The seating was highly pitched which provided good viewing and the velvet covered chairs were thickly cushioned. Perhaps most importantly for me there was a great amount of legroom.

We went back out to the concession stand and got some popcorn and cokes. We had no more settled back into our seats when the previews started. A couple of other people straggled in just before the feature began, or we would have had the place to ourselves. We enjoyed the film and the surroundings, chalk it up to another cultural experience in a foreign land.

After the movie we decided to head directly to dinner, as we were beginning to run out of time in Zurich. We made our way a couple of blocks further into the Altstadt to the Zunfthaus zur Zimmerleuten, our choice for dinner that evening. Located on the banks of the Limmat River, the restaurant found its start as a guild house for the carpenters dating from the 14th century.

We were shown to a nice table on a window overlooking the river from its second floor elevation. The dining room was well appointed with crisp white linen tablecloths and napkins. We decided to try a bottle of their house wine, a Swiss red. The waiter took our orders, Jenny had the veal "Zurich style," Leo the guinea fowl breast and I had the baked perch, all with our last chance at rosti as a side for a while.

The wine was poured and was much to our liking. The dinners came out and all looked delicious. Each of us enjoyed our entrees and the rosti. It turned out to be an excellent choice for our last night in Zurich. The ambiance was excellent, the food was quite good, and the company was unsurpassed.

Vlasta and Jaroslav Novotny, family friend,
Martina, Leo, Jenny, and I in Prague.

We finished our meals and paid our bill. It was now time to begin our trek to the train station. We walked the few blocks to the Bristol Hotel to gather our things and thank them for their hospitality. We rolled our bags toward the Hauptbahnhof and within five minutes we were standing in front of the train board figuring out which track our train was arriving on.

PRAGUE, CZECH REPUBLIC

We had almost an hour because of our early arrival and spent it taking one last lap around the Christmas Market and some adjacent shops that remained open. Jenny found a couple of more Christmas decorations she could not live without. We stopped by a sundry shop to spend our few remaining Swiss francs on some staples for the road including some fine Swiss chocolates.

Our train for Prague arrived and we found our compartment without any trouble. We discovered to our pleasure again, that the fourth berth in our room was to be unoccupied for the entire length of our journey. After the train got rolling we played some word games until we were too tired and turned in for the night.

We arrived in Prague late the next morning and headed immediately to our hotel. The Salvator Hotel, located in the heart of Old Town turned out to be a perfect base for our time in the city. Leo enjoyed his first visit to the city and we also enjoyed the terrific Christmas markets of Prague again on that trip.

Additionally, we had a nice dinner one evening with Juraslav and Vlasta Novotny and some other Czech relatives. Unfortunately, not long after our return to the States, we got word that Juraslav had passed away. Since I have already discussed the wonderful city of Prague in a previous chapter and I plan to revisit it briefly in a future offering, I will confine my remarks to the above.

Overall, this was an outstanding trip which we all enjoyed thoroughly. Each of the Principalities offered a truly unique travel experience, as did the nearby cities which we chose to serve as a base for our explorations into the little countries. I would highly recommend that if you find yourself near one of these small republics that you take the time to visit. I don't think you will be disappointed.

Again, Hank, I hope you don't overlook these destinations as you travel in the future. I know that you have been to Liechtenstein, but I hope that you are one day able to visit Monaco and San Marino. I am sure your mom and I would not mind returning with you.

CHAPTER 9

GREECE, MALTA AND ITALY

HANK, ON THE SATURDAY OF Memorial Day Weekend in 2004, we found out that your mom was pregnant with our first child, you my boy. This conception had not come easily as we had been trying for over three years, and had worked with a wonderful fertility doctor to finally achieve this success. We decided a few weeks later that we should plan a special vacation prior to the blessed event. Obviously, we did not want to do anything that might jeopardize your health, Hank, but we knew this would probably be our last opportunity to travel together as a couple for quite some time.

After discussion with Jenny's doctors it was decided that we could travel safely up to about six weeks prior to her due date. Since the projected birth day was in late January, we were good to take our usual trip around Thanksgiving time. After much thought and discussion, we decided that one of the stops on our trip should be Rome. Although I had been to the Eternal City a couple of times before, Jenny had not, and she thought a trip to the Vatican prior to the birth would be a great idea. Jenny is a good Catholic and thought the pilgrimage would be a positive strategy. Maybe there would be no Papal blessing, but just being in the Holy See could create an undeniable, clear energy going into the birth.

Further, we discovered that our friend, Louis Stergiopoulos, the patriarch of the fine family that runs the wonderful Greek Islands Restaurant in our hometown of Indianapolis, was going to be spending time in his home country about that time as well. Louis invited us to visit him in his native village near Corinth while in Europe. We decided that this was an opportunity we could not decline. We very much like Louis and having a local show us around would be a wonderful chance, not to be missed.

So we would travel to Greece and Italy, but I still wanted a visit a country new to me. I began to do some research on areas in that part of the world that I had not been to yet, and discovered that the island nation of Malta made the most sense. We could get a fairly attractive airfare from Athens to Malta and onward to Rome, and in reading, the locale seemed quite historical and interesting.

Hank, we began to make plans for the trip when we went for our annual visit to Delaware to see your uncle, Leo Medisch, over the Fourth of July. As we had the year before when we had toured the Principalities of Europe, we suggested to Leo that he would be welcome to join us on this trip. Again, he consulted with his business partner and friend, Keith Fitzgerald, to see if they wanted to make this journey as their end of year, restaurant closing trip.

Hank, you will recall that the two own the nicest eating establishment in the state of Delaware. It is located in the beach resort town of Rehoboth Beach, but it is a seasonal business that closes for the winter. Their custom had been to take a trip after the restaurant shuts down to celebrate the closing, and get some much needed rest and relaxation after their hectic season. Well, the upshot is that they decided to each join us for part of the trip and we were set.

I made airline reservations through our favorite carrier at the time, Northwest, and their partner KLM, the Dutch carrier. For the first time I used airline frequent flier miles to upgrade our service to first class, thinking that this would allow a higher level of comfort for Jenny given her condition. We had our arrival into Athens and departure from Rome established. We needed now to figure out an itinerary that would fill the sixteen days we were to be gone.

I had the pleasure of visiting Greece a few years before and thought that three nights in Athens was plenty of time to enjoy the sights. My opinion was that, although Athens is a great city, many of the most interesting parts of the country lie outside the capital. I had truly been impressed with the Aegean Islands I had visited on my previous trip, and wanted Jenny to experience some of that environment. Given we were going to visit in

November, it was a little chancy to visit the islands by ferry, the most common method of travel to the islands. Besides many of the businesses on the islands virtually closed by that time of year.

I began to focus on the island of Crete, a place I had not visited on my previous time in Greece. The largest of the Grecian Islands in the Aegean, it had come highly recommended by my friend, Bill Schreiber, who had visited on a honeymoon trip. It was large enough to have an economy other than tourism, so businesses would remain open. Also, there was routine air service linking a couple of different cities on Crete with Athens. Ultimately, we decided to pop down to the island for a couple of days visiting Chania, toward the western end the island. Chania has an interesting history and seemed quite appealing to us.

With a schedule in place I began to fill in the blanks by booking hotels in each of the areas that we were to visit. Leo and Keith were set to travel to Greece, arriving before us and keeping a separate itinerary part of the time. Leo would join us for Malta and some of the time in Rome, and it all would work. All that was left now was to wait until our November departure and hope that Jenny remained healthy.

GREECE

Veteran Day of 2004 finally rolled around and we were set to depart. We had a late afternoon departure, so we both worked that morning. We rendezvoused at home a little after lunch and headed to the airport. We checked-in and after a couple of hour wait, we climbed into our seats in the front row of the DC-9 heading for Detroit. Everything went smoothly and we arrived in Detroit with enough time to cool our heels in the Northwest World Club for a few minutes.

Shortly, our flight was called and we boarded our plane for Amsterdam. Again, we were seated in the first row and the flight attendants paid particular attention to Jenny, given her delicate situation. Just a little short of seven months along, Jenny was sporting a bit of a bump by now. My wife is a very beautiful woman, but she never looked better to me than when she was pregnant and showing as she was now.

The kind crew on this brand spanking, new Airbus 330-300 were extremely attentive to us. It was our maiden voyage on these big, new aircrafts. The seats were wide and comfortable, and capable of reclining to a nearly flat position. Each seat had an individual, large television screen with a wide variety of entertainment options. I had a glass of champagne, Jenny juice as we prepared for takeoff.

In a matter of minutes after settling in our plane was roaring down the runway and was aloft for our seven plus hour flight to the Dutch capital. Quickly our flight attendants sprang into action serving us beverages and taking our dinner orders. We both chose the filet mignon with mashed potatoes. But first, appetizers were served, followed by a salad course, and finally our entrees. It was all delicious and I washed mine down with a nice French Bordeaux.

The attendant had hardly taken away my cleaned entrée plate before the dessert cart was being wheeled down the aisle. The choices were all so tempting I just had a little of everything. That included a chocolate and strawberry sundae with all the toppings, some delicious cheeses and fruits, and a piece of dark chocolate. To ensure that I ingested all the calories possible, I also had a glass of aromatic port wine with my dessert.

Having finished my heavenly meal, I turned my full attention to finishing the movie I was watching. By the time it was over, I was ready for some rest and checked on Jenny who was now sound asleep in the next chair. I shut everything down and within a matter of minutes was fast asleep. I was the most comfortable I had ever been on a plane. The additional room was a godsend.

I was awakened by a gentle nudge from my wife who was informing me that it was time for breakfast to be served. I somehow managed to eat a cheese omelet with sausage, potatoes and a croissant. I drank several cups of decaffeinated coffee and tried to prepare for our landing. Before I knew it we were pulling up to our gate at Amsterdam's Schiphol Airport. We made our way through this well-organized and passenger-friendly terminal, stopping only briefly at a KLM Crown Lounge for another cup of coffee and to freshen up a little.

Our flight for Athens was on time and we once again were seated in the first row of the plane. The Dutch flight attendants were extremely attentive to Jenny and I think she enjoyed the pampering she was getting from the airline personnel on these flights. We were served a quick lunch and before you know it we were landing at the new Athens International

Airport. This lovely airport was part of the infrastructure improvements that came about as part of the Olympic Games held in Greece earlier that year.

We made our way through customs and immigration and found the new subway line that connected the new terminal to downtown Athens. We boarded a train for the last stop on the line, Monastiraki. We arrived at the Monastiraki Square subway stop in about a half hour. Our hotel, the Attalos, was a little over a block up the street from the subway. We took the short walk and arrived at the door in a couple of minutes.

I had visited Athens a few years before and had stayed at the Attalos on my previous trip. It is extremely well located and served my purposes well on my previous visit. However, I hardly recognized the place as we walked in the door. Clearly, we were once again the beneficiary of an upgrade that occurred because of the Olympics. The entire place was spruced up. An aging lobby area had been upgraded with sleek new, glossed wooden furniture. The front desk was now a highly polished mahogany, and everything seemed to be in shipshape.

Our check-in went smoothly and we rode a new elevator toward the top of the hotel to our room. We exited and moved down the hall to our abode and were pleasantly surprised that the updates had included the guest rooms as well. We entered a beautiful room with glossy wooden flooring, a king-sized bed with ample storage, a desk, a sitting area and a large screen television. The bathroom was also completely new and very modern.

The real selling point of the hotel is not just its location, but its view. We walked out on our balcony and looked to the right and the Acropolis was in there in all its glory. It seemed that you could nearly reach out and touch the Parthenon. Before we unpacked a single item, we sat on our balcony and took in the amazing vista.

I had told Jenny before we arrived about the view of the Acropolis, but the rest of the hotel might be lacking in some areas. With all the improvements that had occurred, there was no longer a need to apologize about anything in regard to the Attalos. We began the process of removing the road grime when our phone rang. Leo and Keith were back from a day of sightseeing and were wanting to get together. We told them we would meet them at the bar in an hour.

We finished cleaning up and went upstairs to the rooftop bar. If you are ever in Athens and do not stay at the Attalos Hotel, I would recommend that you come have a drink in their bar. Situated on the roof of the building, I find it hard to imagine that many locations have a more commanding view of the Acropolis than this tavern. By no means a fancy place, it is comfortable, has cold beer at a good price and this unbelievable sight. If you come be sure you bring your camera because you might want to capture the moment.

When we walked into the bar, Leo and Keith were waiting for us at the best table in the house. The attention in the room quickly shifted to my lovely wife, her radiant beauty, and the bump that in a couple of months would be you, Hank. We all had a beverage, enjoyed the surroundings and caught up with them on their travels, thus far. After the men had consumed a couple of beers, our thoughts turned to our stomachs, and we began to focus on finding some dinner.

We were all tired, us from a long day of travel and they from sightseeing. I recommended a place I had really enjoyed when I had been here a few years before, which was just down the street. They agreed with the idea and we headed out. We arrived at Monastiraki Square and there on the corner across from the subway station sits the Taverna Sigalas-Bairaktaris. When I pointed out the restaurant to Leo and Keith, they informed me that they had already eaten there and loved it.

We found a table outside the taverna in the fresh evening air. It was a beautiful night and we were greeted by a particularly friendly waiter. We ordered a round of drinks and began to study the menu. The waiter returned and, before I knew it, Leo had taken over and was ordering tons of food. Since I am a big fan of Greek food, it all sounded good to me. I did insist we try a dish I had never had before, stifado. This beef and onion stew sounded really good to me for some reason and I was not to be disappointed.

We were drinking our fine Greek beers when the first wave of food arrived. I don't remember what all appetizers were brought out in addition to a large Greek salad, but I focused squarely on the fried calamari. It was incredible, lightly breaded, fried to perfection, and not greasy. What a wonderful start to a magnificent meal. Our entrees arrived and I immediately went for the stifado. It was a thick, beefy stew comprised primarily of chunks of meat and baby onions. It was seasoned with several ingredients including garlic, rosemary, bay leaves, clove, and also nutmeg and cinnamon which gave it a truly unique flavor. I absolutely loved it.

We all enjoyed our meals. There were lamb chops, souvlaki, Kota (baked chicken dish) and numerous side dishes were served and consumed. Clearly, this was a true Greek feast and although I would go on to have numerous outstanding meals on this visit to Greece, this one stands out to me as my favorite meal in the country. The food was phenomenal, the company terrific, and the alfresco dining on the square was superb. This was truly one of the most memorable meals of my life. (**See Appendix 25 for the recipe**)

Jenny and I in front of the Parthenon in Athens.
Hank, notice your mom's bump. That's you.

Totally sated, I ordered a glass of ouzo as a nightcap. We all finished up, paid our bill, and thanked our outstanding server. We walked around the area for a few minutes until Jenny finally said she had enough. We all needed to return to the hotel and go to bed. We walked the few blocks back up to the Attalos and parted company. Jenny and I got back to our room, peeled our clothes off, and fell into bed. We were now overcome by the exhaustion from the long day of travel, the food, and lack of sleep. Within a matter of minutes we were both in deep sleep.

We both slept well and awoke after over ten hours of solid rest. We started our clean-up process and called Leo to find out when they would like to meet for breakfast. They were already to go and we met them in the dining room about a half hour later. Breakfast at the Attalos was a pleasant experience with a full range of choices from eggs to cereals, and meats to yogurt. The four of us had a nice meal, except Leo who was dealing with some stomach issues.

After we finished breakfast and lingered over our beverages for a while hoping Leo would feel better, we decided to go visit the signature attraction of Athens. The Acropolis is the hill that sits above the Old Town, or Plaka, and is home to among other things, the Parthenon. Leo was still not on top of his game when we decided to depart, so Jenny, Keith and I determined to head out without him.

We made the decision to walk up the hill, as I had done on my previous trip to Athens. The easiest way to do so is to walk down to Monistiraki Square, wind your way through part of the Plaka, past the Roman Agora, and ascend the hill up paths and pedestrian only streets. After passing around the Agora, the path gets rather steep and I had not taken into account the fact that Jenny was seven months pregnant, lugging you around Hank.

We climbed the hill and probably were three quarters of the way to the entrance when Jenny decided she could take no more climbing. We sat down at a little café which was nearby and had a coffee and rested for a moment. We then descended the hill back down past the Agora and hailed a cab in Monistiraki Square. The cab driver then drove us around the Plaka to the other side of the Acropolis where we could get up near the entrance.

He let us out on the street just short of the top of the hill where we were able to make our way from there to the entrance. We bought our tickets and pushed our way passed the throng of students congregated at the opening. As we moved passed, we could now see the various temples that populate the top of the hill, as well as, the fantastic Acropolis Archeological Museum. As we reached the crest, we could look down and see the ancient theater which hugs the southern side of the hill. The outdoor amphitheater has been renovated and is still used for performances.

Soon we encountered the first structure, the Temple of Athena Nike, a lovely little Ionic temple built in the fifth century B.C. However, you are immediately drawn to the Parthenon which is the crowning glory of the hill. The Parthenon was erected nearly 2500 years ago in honor of the goddess Athena, the patron deity of Athens. The finest surviving example of Greek architecture, the structure was designed and built in the simple Doric style.

The temple has performed many functions over the ages including serving as a mosque, a Christian Church and even a powder magazine. In 1687, during a clash with the then ruling Ottoman Empire, a Venetian shell exploded the magazine causing great damage to the Parthenon. Several of its statues were damaged, columns were destroyed, and the remains of the roof collapsed. The temple lay in ruins for over a century.

In the early nineteenth century, the Earl of Elgin, Britain's ambassador to the Ottoman Empire received permission to work on the archeological site. The extent of the Earl's authority is in doubt to this day, but the result is clear. The Earl removed several of the Parthenon's statues and they are today known as the Elgin Marbles. They are housed now in the British National Museum in London. The Greek Government has for many years been campaigning for the return of the Marbles, but thus far to no avail.

We took in the remains of the Parthenon and other surrounding temples, and then moved on to the impressive Acropolis Museum. The unassuming building in the back corner of the Acropolis houses a collection of antiquities that were found on the Acropolis. These objects of art came from the Parthenon and the other surrounding structures. We spent the next hour or so marveling at this wonderful collection. As an aside, it is my understanding that this museum has now been shuttered because of space issues. It has been replaced by a larger facility on the southeastern slope of the Acropolis.

Having spent over three hours on the hill we decided it was time to return to the Attalos and check on the health of Leo. Jenny determined that she was fit enough to make the descent on foot, so we made our way slowly back down the hill. She was able to cover the ground without much difficulty and we returned to the hotel to find Leo feeling much better.

Well past noon by now, we decided to find a location for lunch. Since Jenny had not been into the Plaka, we decided it was time for her to explore the narrow, cobblestone streets of the old town. We made our way a couple of blocks and entered the ancient neighborhood. We worked through the streets window shopping until we came upon a small, tranquil square with a highly recommended restaurant. The Taverna Platanos is an old, family-run establishment right on this little plaza. With seating inside in a pleasant dining room, or outside under the trees, we chose the alfresco route on this warm, sunny day.

It was a glorious afternoon of around seventy degrees with no breeze as we sat down at the table for four under the trees. Promptly a waiter arrived bringing us English menus and taking drink orders. We had read in the guidebook that they made their own wine on the premises and we ordered a carafe and a large bottle of water. Our waiter returned with our drinks and we placed our orders. We sat under the trees in this peaceful setting and ate some pita bread, fresh olives and drank the homemade retsina.

I must confess to not being a huge fan of retsina, largely because I think it tastes like what I believe turpentine might taste like. But, I must say this wasn't too bad, and I think that I could grow to like it in the absence of other alternatives. Our orders arrived, and we all enjoyed plates of Greek salad with grilled lamb and French fries. We took our time enjoying the weather and the food, but finally decided it was time to move.

We took a quick tour through the rest of the Plaka, stopping at several of the little stores. Jenny and I came upon a very nice, little carpet shop, and spent some time looking for a new rug for the baby's room. We found a very nice rug that would do perfectly, but were unable to come to a deal so we decided to come back later.

Jenny was now understandably tired and wanted to return to the hotel for a rest. It was obvious to me that she was going to need to take a rest, or nap, each afternoon because of the rigors associated with traveling while with child. We returned to the room and both of us ended up taking a nap for a couple of hours.

When we awoke we met our fellow travelers at the rooftop bar for a drink. Leo was feeling better, but had decided not to venture too far that evening for dinner. Keith suggested that he was going to hang with Leo and we should feel free to make our own plans. I turned to Jenny and asked her if she had any interest in fried fish, if so I knew the perfect place in the Plaka. I had been there before on my last time in Athens and I thought she would like the joint.

Before I knew it, we were finishing our drinks and leaving the gents behind. We walked back toward the Plaka and followed our map to Bakaliarakia o Damigos. The basement taverna has been in business since the American Civil War, and specializes in deep-fried cod with French fries. We walked down the half flight of stairs and found an empty table. The place has old firearms on the wall and large wine casks lining the back wall. I find it loaded with charm and devoid of any pretense. This is truly my kind of place.

A middle-aged waiter with a broad mustache came over to the table and brought us menus. He took our drink orders, Jenny had a bottle of water and I had a small carafe of their house wine. He returned promptly with the water and a small copper pitcher filled with their homemade retsina. I sat and drank the tasty wine from a small juice glass while we made our dinner decisions. We both decided to eat the house specialty, the cod and fries.

We watched the cooks prepare our dinner in the small, open kitchen which is visible from the dining room. It didn't take them long to batter the fish and deep fry it, while also preparing the French fries. It was served to us still so hot that we had to wait a couple of minutes to start eating. I drank my wine and waited for it to cool.

The waiter had also left us a bowl of a creamy, garlic sauce that he recommended we try on the fish and the fries. When they cooled, I tried the concoction and it was a perfect complement to both the fish and fries. We absolutely loved the food and the taverna. We were having such a good time that I ordered some more wine and we just sat and talked about life and the coming change we were about to encounter, for quite a while.

I could see that Jenny was beginning to tire, so I paid the bill, and we set out for the hotel. It was a very pleasant night for a walk and the Plaka is a wonderful location for a stroll. As we came to the street which dead ends into Monistiraki Square, we looked to our left and saw the Acropolis all illuminated in yellow cast flood lights. It is a beautiful sight to behold and you can just sense the centuries of history that lies before you.

We returned to our room and Jenny called Leo to see how he was doing. He was much better and he and Keith had gone out for something light for dinner. We were to meet in the morning for breakfast. We prepared for bed and shut the light out, hoping for the same kind of sleep we had gotten the night before.

We awoke the next morning to another sunny and pleasant day. We cleaned up and went downstairs to meet Leo and Keith for breakfast. Leo seemed to be back on top of his game and we had a nice meal. After we finished our hot beverages we decided to go up the street to the Athens' Central Market. We gathered our things and headed up the street a couple of blocks to see what was selling that day.

We always enjoy going to the markets in cities to see what food stuffs and other products are for sell. I believe that this tells you a lot about the culture you are visiting. You learn about what they eat and drink, as well as, what resources are readily available by what is on display.

That morning, and I suspect as every morning, the Central Market was a beehive of activity. The first area we entered was the meat market, and one of the first things we saw was a whole lamb hanging before us. The butchers were hard at work cleaving beef, lamb, and pork to the perfect cuts for their awaiting customers. The next place we visited was the fish area, where every manner of seafood that plies the nearby waters were on display. The aroma was a little strong and Jenny needed to move through pretty quickly for fear that it might upset a delicate stomach.

We moved through the fish market to the area selling fruits and vegetables. This colorful area had some of the best looking and largest fruit I had seen in my life. We also checked out the huge section selling olives and cheeses. You are free to sample some of the finest olives you will find anywhere on earth, and the feta cheese looked divine. We spotted a couple of interesting looking, working-class restaurants in the market that we decided we would come back and pick one for lunch.

After our tour of the market we decided to take a walking tour of the city. We continued up Athinas Street, the home of the Attalos and the Central Market, toward Omonia Square. The first public square in modern Athens, it is often considered one of the most dangerous areas of the city. Apparently, at night the area becomes a denizen for prostitutes and junkies, but we saw none of that on this day. The area looked more modern than where we had been with department stores, shops and restaurants. We were told that large public celebrations are often held in this area such as for sporting victories and political campaigns.

From Omonia Square we walked several blocks down Panepistimiou Street past the University of Athens and its impressive buildings until we reached Syntagma Square. Probably the most important and famous plaza in Greece, also known as Constitution Square, it is home to the Greek Parliament among other imposing structures.

Here you will also find the Tomb of the Unknown Soldier which is guarded around the clock by the Presidential Guards. We happened to be there in a timely manner and witnessed the changing of the guard which occurs every hour on the hour. If you happen to be in the neighborhood, and in all likelihood you will be sometime during a visit to Athens, it is worth a few minutes of your time to observe this ceremony.

The area around Syntagma is the commercial and political hub of the country. Not only does the Parliament meet here, but the large banking institutions can be found here along with posh hotels, boutiques, shops and restaurants. Do keep an eye out if you visit the area because the long-standing democratic traditions of Greece are often on display in the form of demonstrations taking place. On the day we visited one such activity was transpiring and it became somewhat violent when the demonstrators clashed with police over some topic unknown to us.

Observing this clash prompted us to move along quickly and we headed back into the Plaka which borders the square. We cruised through the area and did some shopping until we got hungry and decided to return to the Central Market for lunch. We had spotted a couple of restaurants when we had visited earlier and decided to give one of them a try.

We ended up deciding to try a restaurant that was in the basement of a dilapidated building next to the market. Diporto Agoras is a true throwback place, which you enter by descending a set of well-worn, narrow steps. Once inside there are several, long wooden tables crowded onto the concrete floor. We joined a few elderly Greek men who we guessed, based on their blood-spattered aprons, worked next door as butchers at the meat market.

The simple place had no menu, just a friendly waitress, and the proprietor who spoke no English. We ended up communicating with them by pointing and gesturing, but we eventually were successful. One wall was lined with wine casks, our waitress moved to one of the casks and drew up an aluminum vessel full of a tasty, white wine along with three glasses. Seeing Jenny was pregnant, she returned with a cold bottle of mineral water for her. Next the food began to arrive, beginning with a loaf of bread, which was placed directly on the paper tablecloth in front of us, to be torn by hand.

Soon the waitress returned with bowls of garbanzo bean soup and Greek salads. They were so delicious and so fresh, undoubtedly the ingredients had come from the market that morning. This was followed by more wine and plates of fried fish with Greek potatoes. They were at least as good as the previous course. We sat there and enjoyed the feast, the amazing atmosphere, and watched the locals interact. There were lively discussions occurring all around us, and we understood none of it, but it was all good.

Clearly, this type of experience is why I love to travel. This was a peek behind the cultural curtain that one does not get to see every day. I could have stayed there for hours, but the place was very busy and others were waiting for a place to sit. I began to feel like an interloper when our waitress returned and informed us what we owed by scratching some numbers on the paper tablecloth. I don't remember what we owed, but I do remember it was cheap, and I gladly paid the bill for the four of us. We thanked our gracious hosts and departed as others scrambled to take our now vacated seats.

We headed back out into the bright sunlight and Jenny informed me that she probably needed to take a rest. We walked back down the street a couple of blocks to the Attalos and went inside. It was now after two o'clock and I went to the room with Jenny and got her down for a nap. I met back up with Leo and Keith and we roamed the streets in the neighborhood.

Ultimately, we ended up at a little taverna where I had lunch on my earlier visit to the city. There we sat at an outside table under a shade tree overlooking the ancient Agora and drank a cold beer. We sat and looked at the ancient marketplace below us and the Acropolis above it and mused about how we never dreamed as kids growing up that one day we would trod the same ground as Aristotle and Socrates. Athens can be a truly heady experience.

It had been a couple of hours since I had left Jenny and I decided it was time to check in on the expectant mother. The others decided to join me as I walked back to the hotel. We piled onto the elevator and decided to meet upstairs for a drink, and another view of the Parthenon at six. I slipped quietly into the room where Jenny was still sleeping. I decided to sit on the balcony until she awoke, took my book, and sat down outside.

A few minutes later she awoke and came out to join me on the porch. We sat and chatted for a while, and then moved into the room and caught up on the world news with CNN. After a time we decided to freshen up and move upstairs to meet the guys for a beverage before dinner. It was a clear evening and the rooftop view of the Acropolis was absolutely stunning. We drank a quick beer and decided it was time to move out for dinner.

We descended the grade down toward Monistiraki without a firm plan as to where to go to eat. We reached the square and I think unanimity quickly was reached, we were standing in front of the Taverna Sigalas-Bairaktaris and there seemed to be no better option. We had such a good meal there on our first night, we were bound to repeat.

We took a table outside again, this time under a white, canvas tent as it had just started raining. Our waiter from the night before last was back again to serve us. We started with a carafe of house white wine and a large bottle of water. Not as hungry as our previous trip, we kept the food order to a minimum. We all selected an entrée which came with a salad and a side. This time I chose a full plate of the fried calamari with French fries.

Our salads were served promptly along with some warm pita bread. The entrees soon followed, and my calamari did not disappoint. I squeezed the juice of a lemon all over my order and dove in. It was perfectly prepared and delicious. About the time we were finishing our meals a wind blew up and nearly knocked over our tent. We decided that this must be an omen, and we needed to move on. We paid our bill and thanked our waiter for his fine service.

The rain had let up as we went up the street for one last time. We were all headed to Chania on the island of Crete in the morning, and needed a good night's sleep before we traveled. When we arrived back at the hotel we parted company with the guys and headed to our room. We did a little packing and decided to call it a night. Since our flight was not until noon the next day, we didn't have to set an alarm. We drifted off to sleep with thoughts of Crete on our minds.

We awoke the next morning and, after showering, headed downstairs for breakfast. We got a table and started on a beverage when the guys joined us. We had plenty of time so we enjoyed a leisurely meal. After several cups of coffee, we returned to our room and finished packing. We went downstairs, checked out, and then headed down the street for the subway.

We caught the subway for the airport and about forty minutes later we arrived. We grabbed a free trolley and piled our luggage on the cart and headed for check-in. We were flying on an Aegean Airline flight that day, which I had arranged through Europebyair, and were quickly able to locate their counter. The kind airline clerk noticed Jenny's status and immediately offered us seats on the bulkhead which I quickly accepted. These seats came with extra legroom, something that is in short supply in most airplane seats.

We soon were boarding the small jet and were winging our way across the Aegean Sea toward the island of Crete. About fifty minutes later we arrived in Chania after a smooth flight. We gathered our bags at baggage claim and went outside to find a taxi for our hotel. Since the taxis were small, we grabbed two, and headed toward the city about ten miles down the road. In about fifteen minutes we were pulling up in front of our hotel.

The Amphitri Hotel is a small hotel with about twenty rooms on a narrow street overlooking the Old Harbor in Chania. The street was so narrow that we parked at the bottom of the hill and walked up past a few buildings to the hotel. We lugged our bags from the taxi and entered the dimly-lit lobby of the hotel. It was much like entering someone's living room with couches and easy chairs and knick knacks all round. But, beyond through the large picture windows, there was a terrific view of the Old Harbor. We waited a minute until an aging woman came to greet us. She spoke no English, but was pleasant and we were able to get checked-in.

The old lady showed us up the stairs to the second floor where we had reserved two adjoining rooms which shared a huge balcony overlooking the town and harbor below. Our room was small with one queen-sized bed, an armoire, a small desk and chair, and a small, full bathroom. Leo and Keith had the room next door which was much larger and brighter, but the balcony was clearly the selling point of these rooms, and the view was unrivaled.

We did some minor unpacking and joined the fellows on the rooftop outside. We looked over the Old Town and harbor of Chania which was a very impressive sight. Chania was a very old city which had been under the control of the Venetians and Turks for much of its history. The architecture of the buildings below us clearly reflected the dominance of these rulers. The Old Town was built around a natural harbor which is a large, elliptical shape. At some point in time the Venetians erected a wall around the Old Town which included a bulwark that protected the harbor and decreased the size of its opening. On the tip of the bulwark there is a small lighthouse marking the way for sailors.

The harbor is lined with decaying multi-story buildings on all sides. Some are painted in pastels, and most are products of the Venetian occupation era, which started in the thirteenth century and lasted until 1645 when the Ottomans overran the city. One distinct mark of the Turkish period is a lovely, little mosque that sits below our rooftop. During World War II, the city took a pounding from Nazi bombers and some of the buildings remain in disrepair from these attacks to this day.

It was now nearing two o'clock and hunger was starting to become our foremost concern. We could see from our rooftop balcony that the harbor was lined with cafes that looked very inviting. We decided to find one of these that met our needs. We exited the hotel and walked down the street until it dead ended, turned right a few paces and were on the square which is at the center of the Venetian harbor. Immediately to our right was a largely, open-air café which was within spitting distance of the water and looked perfect for our needs.

The Remezzo Café had ample, comfortable seating some inside, some outside under cover, and other tables completely alfresco. Given it was an absolutely gorgeous, sunny day with blue skies with only a few white, puffy clouds, we opted for the latter. The young women who greeted us and showed us to our table ended up being our server. She brought us extensive menus, and took our drink orders.

The fellows ordered a cold, local beer and Jenny stuck with a bottle of still water. We examined the menus and all decided on different items. Overdue for some pasta, Jenny and I went that direction, she had a fettuccini carbonara, and I, penne Bolognese. We sat and sucked on our drinks enjoying the beautiful sunshine and the magnificent vista. Our meals came and were met with much approval. Our pastas were perfect for the occasion and Leo and Keith enjoyed the large salads they had ordered.

It was so pleasant that another round of drinks were in order. We sat and finished our large bottles of beer, and watched the gentle waves lap against the seawall directly in front of us. I could tell that Jenny was beginning to fade, so we paid our bill, and took a short stroll part way around the harbor. We then returned to the hotel for her to get a nap before we ventured out for the evening. While Jenny slept, I went in search of a laundry to drop off our dirty clothes the next day. I was successful in this mission and found a nice little place near the large Catholic Church in the newer part of the city.

After she awoke from her sleep, we all congregated at the table on the rooftop. The fellows had picked up a bottle of a local wine while they were out, along with some orange juice for Jenny. We sat on the rooftop and enjoyed the flavorful beverages and watched the sun fade away. After we finished our wine we decided it was time to strike out for our evening meal. Leo had spotted a restaurant which specialized in seafood in the Old Harbor area and we decided to give it a try.

Just as we were departing some threatening clouds opened up and it began to rain. We hastily retraced our steps from earlier that day and passed the Remezzo Café as we moved along the east side of the Old Harbor. Near the end of the walkway along the harbor, just before reaching the protective seawall, the Apostolis Restaurant sits. The attractive little taverna had tables lining the harbor, but not tonight as we scurried inside to get out of what was now a driving rain.

The proprietor met us at the door and ushered us to a table with a great view of the stormy harbor. This was one of those nights when Leo just sort of took over the meal. He order for everyone and we shared our plates. He started us out with an appetizer plate that included shrimp, sardines and mussels. He then order the main course which included stuffed calamari with me in mind, and a couple of whole fish, a sea bass and a sea bream. These came with assorted sides.

Rainbow over the Chania Harbor.

Then Keith and the owner picked a dry, white wine to compliment the meal and it was poured before we began this bacchanalian endeavor. The appetizers were served and all passed the approval of the restaurateurs, I particularly enjoyed the large shrimp. This was followed by a large Caesar salad which was shared by all. It was simply perfect in my book. The main courses were served and we watched as the server deboned the two large fish. We shared the fish and calamari, which I particularly enjoyed.

As we finished our plates the owner came to our table and sat down beside us. He tempted us with deserts, but we all passed having already eaten too much. He hailed one of his waiters and he returned with a large bottle of homemade ouzo, some coffee beans and a hot tea with lemon for Jenny. He prepared small snifters of ouzo for all by pouring the beverage into the glasses and then adding a few coffee beans for flavor. He then insisted we all toast the pending birth of our child, which we all did joyfully.

After repeating this procedure a few times, we had more fun than we should have. The owner was a hoot and just wanted to make sure his new friends were having a good time. Thankfully, Jenny wisely paid the bill for us and we thanked our Greek friends as we departed. Jenny led us back to the hotel that dark night and we went directly to bed, agreeing to meet for breakfast the next morning.

We awoke the next morning and the first thing I did was to swear off after-dinner drinks. It seems that the ouzo had left me with a bit of a headache, which was an unwanted side effect of the previous evening. I walked out on the rooftop patio as a rain shower had just ended and some rays of sunshine were breaking through the clouds. A beautiful, full rainbow was forming to our south and I ran inside to get Jenny to see this natural wonder.

By the time we returned, the fellows were out of there room and there was now, not one, but two complete rainbows. One rainbow ran just to the south of the harbor and the other was just beyond the breakwater to the north. We scurried inside to grab our cameras to save this moment for prosperity and were able to do so. Amazingly, the day turned out to be one of those that sudden showers would appear, and then the sun would come out. On several occasions we saw rainbows, including another occurrence of a double. What a lucky day.

We finished cleaning up and went downstairs for breakfast. The meal was served in a room off the lobby and had large windows with a great view of the harbor. Breakfast at the Amphitri Hotel was a pretty simple event, some yogurt with honey, cereal, bread and jam, juice and hot beverages. I really enjoyed the yogurt and honey, and the rest did me good on overcoming my headache, that and a couple of Advil. We all drank several cups of coffee, or tea, and plotted our day.

After breakfast the fellows were headed out to explore the island. Their main destination was Samaria Gorge several miles south of Chania. Keith had learned of this place and had made arrangements for them to travel to the sight and hike the trail through the gorge. This was far too rigorous for us given that Jenny was seven months along, we wished them well, and told them we would see them for dinner.

After they departed, we gathered up our dirty clothes, and headed to the drop-off laundry I had located the day before. We left our things with the kind woman that was in charge and told her we would collect them before they closed that afternoon. We thanked her and set out to see the sights of Chania.

We decided to first visit the City Market to do some souvenir shopping. Located in the center of the city, several blocks south of the Old Harbor, the market is a bustling place. The covered building is an attractive structure built in the early twentieth century. The structure contains over seventy-five shops ranging from butchers to souvenirs.

There are a number of specialty shops selling locally-produced goods including food stuffs, wines and spirits, carpets, clothing and assorted other items. We spent the next couple of hours nosing around these shops. We stopped at a coffee shop for a hot beverage and a local pastry which was filled with honey, and was delicious. We spent some time trying to figure out if we could possibly get some olive oil and honey home with us, but decided that wasn't a good idea.

We checked out some shops near the market and moved on to visit the Chania Archeological Museum. We walked back to the Old Town and located the museum which is housed in an old Catholic Church. The museum traces the history of the area from the Minoan era, through Roman and Venetian times. The museum contains an impressive collection of Minoan and Roman artifacts. It doesn't take an hour to view the entire offerings, but it is certainly worth the time, and low cost to stop by for a visit.

When we were leaving the museum Jenny spotted a carpet shop where they were hand weaving rugs and carpets on traditional looms. We ducked into Roka Carpets and watch the artisans ply their trade, but eventually decided that their products did not match up with our décor. We thanked the workers and moved back out into the now sunny day.

Well past noon we decided to begin to look around for a spot for lunch. We had meandered past an interesting looking taverna the night before on the way to dinner which we decided to check out. O Mathios Taverna is located at the Venetian harbor near the very end. To get there we walked around the mosque and continued along the water until we came to the restaurant on the right near the seawall.

The nautically-themed restaurant looked inviting to us the night before, and equally so in the daylight. We took a table on the inside because a cool breeze had kicked up and we were afraid that a shaded seat on the exterior might be chilly. Our waiter came and brought us some bread and olives. We ordered a large bottle of water and looked at the menu. The special of the day was a fish and chips, and we both decided to give it a try. After all, we knew it would be fresh.

Our table was on the front window so we had a good view of the harbor, watching the small boats bob up and down on the windswept water. We munched on the bread and fabulous olives until our orders came. Our waiter returned with two plates covered with freshly fried fish and chips. He also brought along some garlic sauce similar to what we had in Athens a few nights before. It was all quite good and we enjoyed our lunch and the wonderful view.

We finished our meal and it was now approaching three o'clock. We decided to head back to the hotel for Jenny to get some rest. We returned just in the nick of time as another cloud burst hit. By the time we got Jenny down in the bed and resting the sun was peeking through and another colorful rainbow appeared.

Since the rain had stopped, I decided to run out and pick up our clothes at the laundry. I entered the cleaners to a warm welcome from the lady who ran the place. She scurried around and found our big bag of clothes and I paid her the modest sum we owed her. On the way back to the hotel I decided to duck in a convenience store and buy a couple of beers.

I returned to the hotel and slipped into the room as quietly as possible. Jenny was still sound asleep, so I decided to take my book onto the rooftop patio and read while sipping on the cold Amstel's I had just purchased. This plan lasted about fifteen minutes until another pop up shower hit, forcing me back inside. Unfortunately, this time I made enough racket that I woke Jenny up from her nap. She was nice about it saying that it was time for her to get up, but I still felt badly about waking her.

We laid on the bed and talked a while until we heard the guys return from their big day of exploring the gorge. Once more the rain had stopped and we congregated on the balcony to have a drink and talk about our day. Leo and Keith had caught a bus and ridden to the Samaria Gorge about twenty-five miles south of Chania. There they hiked through the apparently spectacular ravine. Samaria is a National Park and the gorge is the longest in Europe running about thirteen kilometers in length. The hike took them about five hours and they were met by a bus on the other end which brought them back to Chania.

They made the trek and the gorge sound incredible, I just wish we had been able to join them. However, they were clearly pooped and all they wanted to do was to have a drink, get something to eat, and call it a night. We decided to make the night's meal a rather simple one and determined that a return trip to the Remezzo Café was in order. The café was close by, had a great view and the seating was very comfortable, all things that were appealing to the guys after a long day hiking.

We left the hotel and walked down and around the corner to the Remezzo. It was a clear, cool evening so we took a table inside which was surrounded by thick cushioned chairs. The same waiter we had the day before at lunch appeared and we placed a drink order. I had a Stella Artois, Jenny some juice and the others ordered something stronger. We reexamined the menu and placed our orders when the drinks arrived. Jenny went for the chicken souvlaki with roasted potatoes and the other three of us had pizzas with various toppings.

Our meals arrived promptly and all semblance of a conversation pretty much ceased as we all were hungry and began to eat. My pizza was quite good, with ham, onion and mushrooms in a tangy tomato sauce and smothering in hot cheese. All the others liked their choices and we reordered drinks while we finished our meals. We finished our food and beverages and paid our bill. We took a little stroll around the Old Harbor checking out the other establishments that surrounded it, stopping along the way for a small scoop of ice cream.

We made our way back to the hotel and said goodnight to the guys. We slept as late as we could, but were still downstairs for breakfast by eight-thirty. We beat the guys and began to have some breakfast. They appeared shortly and joined us for a cup of coffee. They informed us that they had decided to go to the Remezzo for an omelet, passing on the blasé fare at the Amphitri. Having already eaten most of a meal, we told them we would finish here and join them for a beverage later at the café.

It was a bright, warm morning as we made our way back to our favorite café to join Leo and Keith. When we arrived, they were sitting in the sun eating their ham and cheese omelets. I ordered a coffee and Jenny a tea and we relaxed in the perfect weather. This was a transition day, so we were going to enjoy a little down time before we moved on.

Jenny and I were flying back to Athens early that afternoon. There, we were to be picked up by our friend, Louis Stergiopoulos, and driven down to the Peloponnese Peninsula where he was born. The guys were going to stay on in Crete for a couple more days and do more exploring of the island. They were then flying back to Athens where Leo was joining us for more travel, and Keith was headed back to Delaware to celebrate Thanksgiving with his family.

Our plane wasn't scheduled to depart Chania until about 1:30 that afternoon. This gave us a little time to do some more nosing around the area before we had to leave. After we finished our drinks at the Remezzo, we went back to the hotel and packed our bags. We checked out of our rooms and left our bags at the front desk while we wandered the streets.

Leo and Keith had picked up a rental car and were headed in the direction of Iraklion, the capital and largest city on the island. We helped them pack up their little car and said good-bye to them and watched them pull away. We decided to walk around to the far side of the Old Harbor and see more of that side of the town. The area was lined with interesting little shops, bars and restaurants. We bought a few small gifts at one boutique and decided to grab a quick gyro at a stand before we headed to the airport.

We made our way back to the hotel, picked up our bags and walked down to the bottom of the street to meet the taxi which we had arranged to pick us up. Our ride to the airport took around twenty minutes and was very uneventful. We arrived in plenty of time to check-in and claim good seats on the bulkhead again. Our plane arrived from Athens and unloaded its passengers and their bags, and we were called to get on.

The flight went perfectly and we had an on-time arrival into Athens. We deplaned and made our way to the exit. There was some sort of a commotion in front of us which blocked the exit and delayed our departure. When the doors cleared we could see a large crowd of people standing just outside the exit waiting to pick up departing passengers.

Right in the middle of this crowd stood our friend, Louis, neatly dressed in a business suit holding a large bouquet of roses waiting for our arrival. Jenny rushed to greet him nearly crushing the beautiful flowers in their embrace. I joined in the hugs and tears of joy to see our friend in his home country. We were all anxious for this part of the trip because we could spend time with Louis, and he could introduce us to his homeland.

We had become friends with Louis and his family after becoming patrons at their restaurant, the Greek Islands. This small, blue and white building sits just south of downtown Indianapolis and serves up some of the best Greek dishes this side of Athens. The family-run business is managed by Louis and his three children, George, Angela, and Penny.

It is one of the homiest places you could ever visit and, if you are ever in Indianapolis, I would strongly recommend you give it a try.

Louis helped us with our bags and we headed to the attached parking garage to locate his car. We arrived at his sparkling clean, hunter green Pontiac which he had shipped over to Greece sometime earlier. We put our luggage in the trunk and piled in for the hour-long trip to Corinth.

Louis turned the ignition key and nothing happened. He tried it repeatedly and could not get the car to crank. Agitated, Louis got out of the vehicle, opened the hood and tried to figure out what was wrong with the automobile. We both fiddled with the battery cables, removed them, did our best to clean them, and replaced the cables onto the battery. Louis got back in the car and tried the key again to no avail.

With frustration mounting and not knowing exactly what to do next, Louis remembered that he had a pair of jumper cables in the trunk. He opened the trunk and fished the cables out. Louis now began to search for someone to give us a jump. Just then a kind couple were getting into their car down the row of parked automobiles. Louis persuaded the gentleman to pull his car around and assist us in starting his vehicle. We hooked up the jumper cables and, sure enough, the car started right away.

We thanked the kind couple and were soon on our way down the multi-lane, superhighway headed west for Corinth. The trip would take a little over an hour from the airport, which gave us some time to catch up with our friend. Louis enjoys returning to the country of his birth on a regular basis, often times staying for several weeks visiting with family and friends that still live in the small village he was born in just outside of Corinth.

At that time, Louis was such a frequent traveler home, he maintained an apartment in his village. He offered for us to stay with him, but we didn't want to be an imposition, and were able to dissuade him before we arrived in Corinth. The sun was beginning to set when we crossed the Corinth Canal and we pulled off the highway. We pulled up to a modern-looking hotel perched nearly on the edge of the canal.

We entered the Isthmia Prime Hotel which is a gleaming white property with a large lobby area. We walked across the white marble floor to the front desk and Louis sprang into action. He talked to the initial clerk and then the manager, finally turning to us and telling us he had arranged a deal, and we should now check-in. I filled out the necessary forms, gave them my credit card information while a bellman was getting our bags from Louis' car.

The bellman showed the three of us to the room which was on the second floor in the rear. Louis came along to make sure the room was correct, and in good shape. It was. The bellman opened the door and we entered our two-room suite. The first room contained a king bed and a sitting area, the second room was a parlor room with sofa, easy chairs and a kitchenette. The rooms were both done in muted, earth tones and were very attractive. Both rooms had a balcony, each with a view of the canal and the mountains beyond. I don't remember what exactly we paid for the room, but I do know that Louis had worked a very fine deal for us.

Satisfied that he had done well by us, Louis departed to see if he could get someone to look at his car to figure out what was wrong. He promised to return in a couple of hours so we could all go to dinner. Jenny and I settled into our suite, flipped on the satellite television which featured several English-speaking channels and relaxed for a while.

Before we knew it Louis was calling us from the hotel lobby ready for us to venture out to dinner. He had been unable to roust anyone out to look at his car, so he left it running in the parking lot for fear it would not restart. It was now very dark and we climbed into his car for a little ride around the city of Corinth. We then crossed over the canal into the resort town of Loutraki where Louis had decided we should have dinner.

Loutraki is a modern, seaside resort located on the Gulf of Corinth. Noted for its fine beaches and it thermal springs, the area is awash with sun-worshipers during the high season. This was clearly the off-season, but there was still activity in the area as it is also home to one of the largest casinos in Europe. Although it was dark you could see that the city had natural beauty with a mountain in the background and the city spilled down its side to the sea.

We pulled into the center of town where Louis parked the car on the side of the street. He excused himself for a moment while he left us for a conversation with some taxi driver waiting at a nearby cab stand. He returned, armed with the necessary information, and we headed out up the side of the mountain behind us. It seems that Louis had gotten the name and address of a taverna that served some excellent food, but was a typical restaurant for the area.

Louis knew us well enough that he understood we would appreciate a local place that served good food. We certainly did not require anything fancy. Shortly we were pulling up in front of the restaurant, which appeared to be formerly a house, and was up on the hill a short walk above the street. We climbed the walk to the entrance and pushed the door open. It was like stepping into someone's home. The small, warm place had one dining room with several tables, but was mostly empty that evening.

The multi-generational family that owned and operated the taverna were crowded around a table in the back of the room watching a basketball game on the nearby television. A very pretty, long-haired blond got up from the table and greeted us. She and Louis began to converse in Greek and shortly she seated us and spoke to us in English. We sat at a large table at the front of the dining room near a large picture window which had a great view of the city lights below and the sea beyond.

Louis told us he would do the ordering, and returned to his conversation with the woman in Greek. There seemed to be some sort of disagreement between the two, but it was quickly resolved and the woman left for a minute returning with a couple of large bottles of beer and a large bottle of still water. We asked Louis what was up and he told us that they were discussing the type of lamb chops they had that evening. Louis preferred to order the old lamb, and she was attempting to persuade him that the young lamb chops were better that evening, or vice versa, I don't recall the specifics.

The upshot of the conversation was that a compromise had been struck. We were going to have both kinds of the lamb chops, so we could compare, and decide for ourselves. We sat and enjoyed our beers, the conversation and the view. Soon, plates of food began to arrive.

First the attractive woman brought us a classic Greek salad of cucumber, tomatoes, olives and onion in an oil-based dressing. It was terrific. This was followed by two huge platters of lamb chops, one young and one old lamb. There were way too many chops for three normal people to eat. Each platter had to contain at least a dozen, large, meaty chops. Next she produced plates of fried mushrooms and some sort of cooked greens. Louis informed us that these vegetables were freshly harvested and had come from the mountainside that was behind us.

Louis insisted that the only way to eat the chops was by hand and we didn't argue. We dove into this incredible meal like there was no tomorrow. We ate and ate, and then ate some more. I could not come to a conclusion which type of lamb chop was superior, but could distinguish the difference under Louis' tutelage. Ultimately, I agreed with my host, but I can tell you they were all good.

In the final analysis, we amazingly ate nearly everything that was placed in front of us, washing it all down with several of the large beers. I swear we each ate at least six lamb chops. This is one of the most memorable meals of my life. Today we seem to be preoccupied with the farm to table movement, but in Greece it has been a way of life forever. Jenny and I were so lucky to have experienced that evening and the wonderful meal. I could never thank Louis enough for this opportunity. This was my favorite meal in Greece, but I have no idea what the name of the taverna was, or even if it had one. I just have the indelible memory of that fantastic meal.

As we thought we were preparing to leave the server returned with baklava and a carafe of ouzo. I had the good sense to only take a small bite of the baklava, which was wonderful but I was too full to consume anymore. But, Louis and I did have a couple of glasses of the ouzo to settle our stomachs. Louis insisted on paying for the dinner, which I am still upset about, but there was little I could do to change his mind.

Jenny standing in the orange grove with our dear friend,
Louis Stergiopoulos. Notice the size of those oranges.

It was now growing late and time for us to leave. We climbed back down the hill to the car and, luckily, it fired right up. It was a pleasant ride back to the hotel. We were all incredibly full. Louis dropped us off at the front door and we thanked him profusely. He would call us in the morning and come get us for a day of sightseeing. Hank, I know you love lamb chops and your mom and I now trace it back to that unbelievable meal when you were in utero.

We awoke the next morning to a sunny, clear day which promised to exceed seventy degrees. We cleaned up and went downstairs for breakfast. The hotel offered a sumptuous buffet with a wide variety of choices from scrambled eggs and sausage to yogurt and muesli, and everything in-between. Louis arrived during our meal and joined us for a little food and some coffee.

After we finished eating we decided to go check out the Corinth Canal while it was daylight and such a pleasant day. The canal was constructed near the end of the nineteenth century and is an engineering wonder. The four-mile long trench was built to allow ship traffic to cross the narrow isthmus which connects the Peloponnese Peninsula to the Greek mainland. The canal enabled ships to traverse the route from the west to Athens and beyond without having to circumnavigate the entire peninsula, thus saving over two hundred miles of the journey. The waterway was built by dynamite blasts through sheer rock about three hundred feet deep. We approached the edge and peered down into the chasm while a ship was passing through. We could easily see from end to end of the canal and were amazed by the short length, and the depth of the rock which they were forced to remove.

We walked back to the hotel and got in Louis' car to go see the sights. Louis was still experiencing difficulty with his car starting and he was continuing to seek resolution to this issue. Thankfully, the car started and we headed toward his village. Pergiali is a small settlement just to the west of Corinth and was the birthplace of Louis. Louis took us through modern Corinth on the way to his hometown, and I must confess that this gateway to the Peloponnese was not too much to see.

We arrived in Pergiali and Louis parked his car in front of the building that housed his apartment. We went upstairs to look around his modern, two-bedroom place. It was very functional, but not fancy. We left the apartment and walked across the road to Louis' hangout, a coffee shop/ bar, where Louis wanted us to meet his friends. The place was perfect for Louis, filled with locals drinking strong Greek coffee.

We went inside and all ordered a drink, coffees for Louis and me and a hot, dark tea for Jenny. We went back outside into the sun and sat at a table and consumed our beverages. My coffee was so strong that the spoon would literally stand up in the cup for all the sediment in the bottom.

We sat long enough for Louis to drink a couple of coffees and for us to meet his cronies. They were an interesting lot, and I could see why Louis enjoyed coming home and hanging out with his friends. I believe that many of his days consisted of drinking coffee with the guys through the first half of the day, and turning to beer sometime after noon. He could get something light to eat at the bar and spend the day just relaxing with friends he had known all his life.

Our next stop on the tour was to visit the Stergiopoulos family orange grove. Just outside of the village the orchard had been in Louis' family for several years. When we got there workers were in the process of picking the biggest oranges I had seen in my life. About the size of a grapefruit, Louis picked and pealed a couple of the sweet fruits for us to sample. They were quite delicious and refreshing on that sunny day. We walked through the rows while Louis checked things out and we enjoyed the sights and smells.

We next went to visit Louis' brother and sister-in-law who lived in the Stergiopoulos family home in Pergiali. Louis' younger brother, Kostas, and his wife, Kiki, did not speak much English, but were very pleasant and gracious hosts. We had no more than arrived when Kiki prepared us nice snack of tea, coffee, light sandwiches and a tasty pastry. We sat in the living room of the lovely home and enjoyed the refreshments while looking at photo albums and learning the Stergiopuolos family history. It was an interesting way to spend some time.

Louis next drove us to Ancient Corinth, the ruins of what was once one of the most important cities in the world. We pulled up to the site of the ancient ruins at the same time three tour buses were unloading. The fact that the ruins were already crowded, coupled with the fact that new busses were unloading, discouraged us from staying. We looked over the fence and Louis pointed out the highlights of the ancient city including the Temple of Apollo which was visible from our vantage point.

It was now well past noon and hunger had set in. We returned to Louis' car and pointed it back in the direction of Loutraki. Louis had another restaurant in mind for lunch and, after the great meal we had the night before, we were not about to argue with him. We crossed the bridge into the city and followed the street that ran parallel with the sea until we reached the destination. We parked the car on the street and walked down to the beach where Louis had selected another small taverna for our midday meal.

We entered the eatery which was really more of an open pavilion on three sides fronting on the beach. The place was under roof, but the front was all open to the beach. The small kitchen in the back was producing some great smells. We found an open table on the concrete floor near the beach. Our waiter appeared and, much like the previous evening, Louis conversed with him in Greek and arranged the whole meal.

First, large bottles of beer for Louis and me arrived with a cold carafe of still water for Jenny. Next a Greek salad appeared along with a fresh loaf of bread. We had just begun our salads when the mains arrived consisting of two preparations of calamari; one fried, one cheese stuffed and covered in a rich, tomato sauce, and an order of fileted, fried grouper. The fish dishes were accompanied by a massive plate of home-cut French fries and a couple of more beers.

Again, we had enough food for twice as many people than were seated at the table. But, once again we did our best. Louis squeezed a couple of full lemons on the fried calamari and the fish, and we started to eat. The fried calamari was incomparable, the grouper was perfectly prepared and the stuffed calamari was delicious, but terribly rich. I focused my attention on the fried calamari and the marvelous French fries. The three of us ate and drank to our heart's content enjoying not only the food, but the wonderful daytime view of the sea and mountains.

It was truly a beautiful setting and the food was very tasty. However, Jenny was now beginning to tire out from the long couple of days of travel. We asked Louis to take us back to the hotel for a rest. We paid the bill and headed back to the car. This time we weren't quite so lucky because the car wouldn't start again. We were very near the taxi stand where we had stopped for directions the night before and Louis quickly arranged for a jump from one of the cabbies.

Soon we were on our way back to the Isthmia Prime. By the time we got back to our room, Jenny was not only tired, but she was not feeling well. Something she had eaten was not setting well and before I knew it she was in the bathroom driving the porcelain bus. It was not a pleasant time and I worried that something could be wrong with the pregnancy. Finally able to get her up off the floor, we put her to bed and she got a good nap, sleeping until after the sun set.

When she awoke, she still did not feel well. About that time Louis called and we discussed the situation, deciding that we would pass on dinner that night and regroup in the morning. He was still trying to get his car fixed properly and was still full from lunch. Louis agreed to meet us at our hotel at seven-thirty the next morning, have breakfast with us, and drive us back to the Athens Airport.

I tried to stay out of Jenny's way so she could rest. I took a walk down the highway toward the canal where there were a few shops and restaurants to see what they had to offer. They offered the usual assortment of souvenirs and some light fare like gyros and fries. I ended up buying a couple of bottles of beer for myself and a lemon-lime soda for Jenny hoping it might help settle her stomach.

I returned to the room and poured Jenny some of the soft drink which she took down readily. I decided to order a little dinner from room service and settled on some spaghetti with meat sauce. They also brought us up some soda crackers for Jenny with the order. We sat in the parlor room and ate our dinner, such as it was. The spaghetti was actually better than average and the crackers seemed to help perk Jenny back up. By now, although it was only a little after eight o'clock, I was tired too. So we just went into the other room and crawled into the king bed, shut off the light and fell asleep.

I awoke the next morning at by around six. I got up and showered, dressed and started packing for our trip that day. Jenny awoke and was now feeling just fine, but hungry which I took as a good sign. We were both ready and packed up by seven-thirty. We went downstairs to meet Louis for breakfast. Sure enough, he was waiting for us in the lobby when we got there. We went into the restaurant and enjoyed another fine meal.

After breakfast we grabbed the bags out of our room, checked out, got in Louis' car, and headed east toward Athens. It was another nice day which helped make for a pleasant drive to the airport. Jenny and I had a plane to catch for Malta which departed a little before noon. When we arrived at the airport and were saying our goodbyes to Louis, Leo appeared seemingly out of nowhere. Louis and Leo met and we finished thanking Louis for all his kindness and departed into the terminal in search of the Air Malta ticket counter.

We found the Air Malta counter and joined a short queue for check-in. We soon were standing in front of a polite, uniformed desk attendant. She took our ticket information, checked our bags for departure, and assigned us seats. She took one look at me, sized up my height, observed Jenny's condition and gave us three seats in the first row of the economy class. We thanked her and moved on to clear security and customs for departure.

We moved toward our gate and had a few extra minutes so we stopped for Leo to have one last Greek coffee which he had come to enjoy. Jenny got a tea and I an American coffee, and we waited for the plane to begin to load for our departure. We were soon called to our gate and the plane loaded for an on-time takeoff.

MALTA

Malta is a small, independent island country in the middle of the Mediterranean Sea south of Italy. The flight time from Athens was about an hour and a half and we fortunately had smooth skies for our flight. We were just above ten thousand feet when our flight crew sprang into action. First, we were served drinks. This was followed by a meal of pasta with a red sauce, accompanied by a green salad, and a piece of white cake for desert. I am always amazed that foreign carriers are able to serve you a meal in the same amount of time our domestic airlines are unable to serve you with a drink.

We finished our lunch and soon were landing in the country of Malta. The former British colony has a reputation as an efficiently run place, and their arrivals procedure was no outlier to this theory. We breezed through customs, gathered our bags, cleared immigration and were on our way to Valetta, the capital. But first, we made a quick stop at the Malta Tourism Office in the arrivals area to pick up a map and some guides to enhance our visit. This is a procedure we try to follow when arriving in any new location, check to see if a tourist office exists at your point of entry and stop for information. I think this can save you time and money in the long run.

We stepped outside the modern terminal, looking for a taxi to our hotel. In no time we found the cab stand and were being whisked to our hotel in the Maltese capital. The airport is only a few miles from Valetta and even with traffic the ride only took about ten minutes. We arrived in front of our hotel which sits on a hill overlooking the Grand Harbor in Malta. Thanks goodness we took a cab from the airport because the climb up and down the hills to reach the hotel would have been difficult.

The British Hotel, our home for the next three nights, is an old stone structure and is a pretty basic place. We entered the lobby with its vaulted ceilings and made our way across the room to the front desk. There an overweight, middle-aged man with a decidedly English accent checked us into our rooms. We climbed on a rickety, old elevator which took us up a few floors to our rooms.

Jenny and I had a small room with a king-sized bed, but a huge rooftop balcony. Our only drawback was a very small bathroom. However, the real kicker was that I practically had to fold myself in half to get in to the toilet. We began to unpack when Leo knocked on the door and came in to check out our room. He looked around and offered to change rooms with us. He claimed his room was twice the size of ours with a big, nice bathroom with a human-sized entry.

He insisted we come down a flight of stairs to check it out ourselves. We all three scurried down to Leo's room and, clearly, he had a superior room to ours. I felt somewhat guilty, but we ultimately decided that we should accept his offer and exchange rooms with him. We made the room switch and returned to the rooftop balcony to reconnoiter and enjoy the view. The British Hotel enjoys a commanding view of the picturesque harbor below and the cityscape on the other side of the water. Included in this vista is an interesting old fort that juts out into the water directly across from the hotel.

We finally got the itch to move on, so we decided to begin exploring the city of Valetta. Armed with our maps from the tourist office, we exited the hotel to the left and turned left at the next street for the climb back up the hill to the center of the town. It was quite a hike up the narrow, pedestrian passageway to the reach the flat part of the city. It seemed that all the buildings we passed were made of stone and were centuries old. You quickly got a real sense that you were surrounded by history.

We reached Republic Street which is the main street of Valetta and started checking out the activity. The streets were now bedecked for the holidays with decorations strewn from side-to- side overhead as we walked down the streets. The narrow little roadways were nearly pedestrian-only because they were not wide enough to support much vehicular traffic. This made walking a pleasure and we took advantage of it on this sunny afternoon.

We traversed Republic Street from one end to the other checking out the shops and businesses until Jenny decided it was time for her to take a rest. Leo and I escorted her back to the hotel, and made sure she was asleep, and then decided we should explore further. We climbed back up the hill and darted down a side street. Not too far down the street we came across an inviting little pub which was playing some good music.

The Pub is as English a pub as you will find this side of London. They poured us a good pint of a local beer and we settled in for a little people watching. The crowd in this small bar seemed to be increasingly populated by Maltese who were finishing work for the week. They all appeared to be ready to unwind from their workweek and were ready for a good time.

Leo and I sat there listening to the classic rock music and observing the happenings for a couple of beers. We finally decided it was time to head back down the hill to check on Jenny. We stopped on the way down the hill at a little store and bought a Diet Coke for Jenny and a bottle of a local red wine for us to drink later.

We arrived at the room and Jenny was awake painting her nails. She lamented that she had not gotten much sleep because of the loud church bells, that when they would ring they would resonate throughout the room. Our room had a large, glass enclosed porch, but some of the windows were open to let in the fresh air. I started to go over and close them when the five o'clock hour passed. Soon Leo and I learned firsthand how loud those bells were, as their sound reverberated off the plaster walls. It was nearly deafening.

Night was now closing in and the three of us repositioned ourselves to the enclosed porch in the room. There were comfortable chairs and a lovely view of the activity on the harbor below. Leo and I cracked into the bottle of wine and Jenny drank her soda. We watched nightfall and the city light up across the water. Finally, completely dark we noticed a celebration at a church across the water. Soon there was a delightful fireworks display shooting into the night sky. It was a beautiful sight which was doubled by the reflection in the water below.

We finished our drinks and decided it was time to venture back up the hill to find some dinner. Leo and I had spotted a nice-looking little restaurant when we were wandering around earlier and decided to check it out. After about a five minute hike up the hill we arrived at our destination. The Café Jubilee sits on a quiet street not far from the center of Valetta. The place is very warm and cozy, kind of a cross between an Irish pub and a French bistro.

We were greeted warmly by a smiling waitress who found us a table in the back corner. We all ordered beverages while she returned with menus for us. We looked around the dining room enjoying the many quirky things attached to the walls and ceiling. There were several old-looking movie posters from classic pictures which also adorned the walls.

We looked over the menu which was a fusion of pub food and Italian. Jenny went for the homemade, meat-filled tortellini, Leo the house ravioli, and I tried the penne Bolognese. We noshed on fresh bread until our orders arrived in about ten minutes. We were all pleased with our wonderfully fresh entrees.

We finished off our mains and Jenny decided it was time to try one of their homemade dessert offerings. She ordered a warm apple pie with cinnamon ice cream. Leo and I ordered another glass of wine and hoped we would get the opportunity to sample Jenny's dessert. Sure enough when her pie arrived piping hot she offered to share a bite with each of us. It was simply amazing. The pie baked to perfection and the ice cream tasted like the finest Italian gelato, an excellent combination. **(See Appendix 26 for the recipe)**

We finished our drinks and decided it was time to go down the hill to the British. It had been a long day of travel and we were tired. We made our way back to our rooms and arranged to phone each other the next morning before we went downstairs for breakfast. I made sure the windows on the porch were shut in an effort to block the sound from the church bells, and shut off the light for the night.

We awoke the next morning to bright sunlight streaming in through the windows on the porch. It was another pleasant day and we showered and prepared for the day. Jenny called Leo and he was ready to meet us for breakfast, so we descended the stair at the end of the hall to the restaurant.

The meals were served in a very pleasant dining room with the same view we had from our balcony. We scored a real nice table on the window so we could look out on the harbor. Unfortunately, the food did not match the view. Their breakfast offering was pretty much a standard continental one, a couple of cereal choices, yogurt, bread and jam, coffee, tea and powdered juices. But, the view was great.

We finished breakfast and decided it was time to see the sights that Valetta had to offer. We ascended the hill and to the main part of town. Sightseeing is not difficult in the city, as the entire place has been declared a UNESCO World Heritage Site. Our first stop would be St. John's Co-Cathedral, an incredible Catholic Church in the center of this old city.

No strangers to Christianity, the Maltese were first converted to the Christian faith by St. Paul who was shipwrecked on the island in 60 A.D. The St. John's Co-Cathedral is probably the finest example of their devotion to their faith. The church was built by the Knights of St. John, a Western Christian military order famous during the Crusades. The Order, after moving from place to place during the crusades, was given Malta and neighboring Gozo by Charles I of Spain in 1530. After settling in Malta, the order commissioned the construction of the cathedral as a tribute to their fallen members.

We entered the large church which is a rather plain-looking stone structure from the outside. We purchased our tickets and proceeded into the nave. We were nearly shocked to see inside. The church is considered to be the finest example of high Baroque architecture in the world. Designed by the Maltese architect, Girolamo Cassar, the interior is as ornate as the exterior is simple.

We spent well over an hour wandering through the nooks and crannies of the structure. The walls are intricately carved stone and the vaulted ceilings are painted in great detail. Much of the artwork is a tribute to life of St. John and features the masterpiece, Caravaggio's Beheading of John the Baptist. The cathedral is the final resting place for many of the Knights of St. John's, as many of the sons of Europe's noble family are buried here. Their graves are marked by intricate, marble inlaid headstones.

After Jenny lit her candle in memory of her family members, we decided it was time to move on. In keeping with our medieval theme we walked down the street to the Palace Armoury and the Palace State Rooms. We first visited the Palace Armoury which is an incredible collection of amour and armaments used by the Order of St. John's and it is still housed in its original location. We browsed through the impressive displays of the weapons of destruction of the era and their protective suits. If you are ever curious about the devices that were used to kill the Muslims during the Crusades, this is the place to come.

We then moved next door to the Palace State Rooms. Originally it was built as the home and seat of government of the Grandmaster of the Knights of St. John's. Subsequently, it also served as the official residence of the British Governor of Malta. Today it fulfills the role as the site of the Office of the President of the Republic of Malta, and home of the Maltese Parliament.

We were able to visit many of the state rooms in the palace. Not only are there impressive chambers to visit, but the palace is filled with art that has been collected by its various occupants over the past 400 years. There are some lovely 18th century French tapestries, beautifully painted ceilings, paintings from the eras of its existence, and a collection of portraits of the rulers of the Maltese Islands from the Knights of St. John's until today.

We enjoyed our visit to these two museums, but it was now past one o'clock and our stomachs were telling us it was time to find something for lunch. We exited the Palace and headed down the street for a trattoria Leo had read about which was highly reviewed. As we strolled down the street we passed the ubiquitous McDonald's restaurant. The only thing that made this significant was the fact that a children's choir had assembled in front of the establishment and were singing Christmas carols.

They were a true delight and we lingered in the street to hear them sing several songs until we could not withstand our hunger anymore. We left and walked the few blocks to the Da Pippo Trattoria. The cozy, little restaurant was doing a thriving business and we were lucky to squeeze into a small green and white checked table with matching green slat-backed chairs. The ochre colored walls were filled with works of art, and the patrons were all happily eating.

The person who directed us to our table returned shortly and told us what was available that day to eat. The restaurant is only open for lunch and the menu varies by the day, depending on what is available at the local markets. Leo and I ordered a bottle of the local red wine, Jenny still water, and we asked the waiter to return while we decided on our luncheon choices.

The waiter promptly returned with our drinks and plates containing cheeses, olives, hard meat and some bread. This was apparently a complimentary appetizer served to all patrons. We placed our orders, Leo and I went for a pasta dish with seafood, and Jenny asked for the salad of the day. We sat and sipped our drinks and enjoyed the nice vibe that was in the trattoria. The waiters were cheerfully moving around at a brisk pace, and the patrons all were in engaged in lively conversations while merrily munching on their lunches.

Our orders arrived in no time and we could see why everyone was so pleased. Our dishes were out of this world. Leo and I received a hot pan of seafood marinara which was served over a linguine. Jenny had a fresh salad of assorted greens, cheeses, ham and olives served with a vinaigrette dressing. We drank our wine and ate our wonderful meal until we could eat no more. Jenny and Leo split a home baked pastry of some sort and I had a lemoncello to finish off a fabulous meal. This was a very close call for my favorite meal in Malta.

After this fabulous lunch we decided it was time to return Jenny to the British Hotel for her afternoon rest. Now past three in the afternoon, we got her back and in the bed for a rest. She was complaining of a sore back, and I could see why lugging the future little Hank around in her tummy up and down this hills. I closed the porch windows and slipped out with Leo to do some more exploring of the city.

We spent the rest of the afternoon walking several of the parallel streets which run the length of the old part of the town. We did a little shopping and scouted out some stores that we wanted to bring Jenny back to before we moved on to Rome in a couple of days. Again, we stopped to buy a bottle of wine and a diet soda to take back to the room for a pre-dinner drink on the porch while enjoying the Grand Harbor below.

We worked our way back down the hill to the hotel and I went to the room to check on Jenny. She was awake and reading in bed, something to get her prepared for pending motherhood. We sat and talked for a while and Leo came and joined us. We poured a glass of wine, Jenny a diet cola, and headed to the porch to watch the Saturday evening traffic on the harbor.

The last bit of sunlight was fading as we sat down for our drinks. A large commercial, container ship was plying the waters below and the parish party was still on, as it was the night before. We sat hoping that there would be another fireworks display like the previous night, and sure enough there was. In fact, if anything it was grander and a few small pleasure crafts were idling in the harbor below us also enjoying the sights.

We decided it was time to head out to dinner. We finished our bottle of wine and all prepared to depart for an unknown destination up the hill. We had little doubt that our cuisine would be Italian, or a reasonable facsimile thereof, because it had become obvious to us by now that Maltese cooking was very much like Italian. This only stands to reason given the proximity of the two countries. It also was not a problem for us because we are big aficionados of Italian cuisine.

We were all in the mood for some beef, specifically a nice steak might be in order. In our house, Jenny and I make it a practice that Saturday night is steak night, and so the urge was upon us. We ended up at a nice bistro called the Malata Bar and Restaurant. Located right off the Palace Square, we had seen the establishment while we had been touring earlier that day.

We decided to give it a try and pushed open the front door only to be greeted by a host who quickly found us a table. The warm, well-appointed restaurant had vaulted ceilings with candlelit, white linen covered tables. It looked quite nice, I just hoped the prices didn't match. Our waiter soon arrived and brought us menus. Leo and I decided to stay with the wine theme and ordered a carafe of the house red, Jenny a diet cola.

We all looked over the menu, but it didn't take long to decide. We all decided to go for the rib-eye steaks with confit potatoes. Our waiter returned with our drinks and some bread and olive oil. We snacked on the bread and mused at the caricatures of what must be famous local people that adorned the walls. The red wine was quite tasty and the bread dipped in the olive oil tided us over until our meals arrived.

In due time, our waiter returned with large plates containing big slabs of steak and a generous helping of the potatoes which had been baked in olive oil. The rib-eyes were all grilled to perfection, medium-rare, and the potatoes were soft and delicious. This was a perfect Saturday night meal for us. It did not take us long to eat everything that was served to us. We passed on a tempting array of dessert offerings and headed back to the hotel for the night.

We awoke the next morning to the sound of the seemingly incessant, church bells ringing the parishioners to mass. We cleaned up and met Leo at the same table in the restaurant for breakfast. We ate a little yogurt and bread with jam and drank hot beverages. It was another sunny day and we intended to get out and enjoy the environs.

We decided that the first thing we would do was to visit the Sunday morning market that is a Valetta tradition. The Monti market is located near the city gates and Triton Fountain on every Sunday. We wandered down the street through the city gate, outside the fortress, past the landmark fountain to where the market takes place.

We walked each row of the market looking for a deal we could not pass up, and pretty much came up empty. The market consisted largely of clothes, some linens, CDs, and small electronics, items we were not particularly interested in obtaining. We were hoping to find locally produced handicrafts. We struck up a conversation with one of the vendors and he pointed us in the direction of the Artisan's Centre back through the City Gate in Valetta. He felt confident that if we wanted local products, we could find them there.

We made our way back down the street and located the shop. We walked inside and soon realized we had hit the mother lode of Maltese handicraft shopping. The store contained all sorts of interesting items from objects made from hand-blown glass, ceramics, jewelry, lace, and brass works, to name a few.

We found the prices good and decided to do some Christmas shopping. I ended up buying two hand-blown vases for Jenny, who is a vase collector. The uniquely designed pieces are quite colorful and are displayed prominently in our home. I also found small gifts for my assistants at work and my mother. I know that Jenny and Leo both made purchases, so it was a genuine find for us. These types of shops that deal in truly local wares are our favorite places to shop. You have the opportunity to support local artists and can acquire unique gifts at the same time.

Having had a light breakfast and now well past noon, we decided to begin looking for somewhere to have lunch. We stumbled along one of the streets in downtown Valetta when we spotted a pizzeria which had a couple of vacant tables in front along the street. We sat down in the warm sunshine at an open table and a young waitress appeared bringing a menu to us. Unlike most pizza places you encounter abroad, this joint made large pies big enough to serve the three of us. We agreed on a ham and mushroom and placed our order.

We sat in the warmth and drank our soft drinks waiting for them to finish making our pizza. Our waitress finally appeared with a very large, hot, cheesy, thin-crust pie. We all dove in, it was very good with a very tangy tomato sauce. We acted like we had not eaten in days as we mowed through the offering. The sun felt particularly good on our faces while we ate and we enjoyed the meal.

We paid our waitress and set out to see more of the city. We decided to examine some of the city's fortifications which had been built in large measure by the Knights of St. John's in the sixteenth century. These high stone walls and ramparts encircle Valetta, and in some areas give way to nice green spaces and parks.

We ended up in a nice, little park just down the way from our hotel. We all sat on a stone bench with a good view of the Grand Harbor and watched the pleasure craft ply the waters. We enjoyed the time together until Jenny finally decided it was time for her afternoon nap. We all strolled along the city wall back to the British Hotel where Jenny laid down and Leo and I headed out in search of a happy hour drink.

After a couple of beers in a nameless little pub just up the hill, Leo and I bought a couple for the road, and headed back to the hotel. It was nearly dark when we returned. Jenny appeared particularly refreshed when we arrived and started our evening ritual of sitting on the enclosed balcony for a pre-dinner drink. We were in luck, because the festival across the way had not ended and the best fireworks show of the trip took place that evening. When it was over we headed out for our final dinner in Valetta.

We decided to return to the Jubilee for our last evening in town. We had enjoyed the coziness of the place, the servers were very friendly and the food was good. I really think we liked the quirkiness of the place best of all. It was another busy night, but we were fortunate to be given another nice table. We all ordered our drinks and looked at the menu.

Our waiter returned with the beers and water and we decided to place our orders. Having eaten very well the entire trip we decided that a sandwich was in order that evening. Leo and Jenny went for the club and I had an Italian sausage sandwich on a French baguette with caramelized onions and Dijon mustard. When the server brought them out, they looked and tasted delicious. They were all served with medium cut, golden brown fries. Once again, we enjoyed the food and the experience. If I am ever in Valetta, I will definitely return to the Jubilee.

We slowly walked back to the hotel. The streets seemed quite deserted and nearly black that night. In fact, if it weren't for the lovely, illuminated Christmas decorations it would have been very dark indeed. We knew as we made our way that we had to catch another Air Malta flight in the morning, departing around nine-thirty. So, we called it another early night as we figured we would need to depart the hotel a couple of hours before our flight. We said goodnight to Leo and headed to bed.

ITALY

The next morning we awoke to the ringing of the phone in our room, the front desk giving us a wakeup call. We hastily cleaned up, packed our bags and went downstairs to meet Leo for a quick breakfast. We sat by the window and drank in one last, long look at the beautiful view of the Grand Harbor below our hotel. We ate our breakfast and hoped that our next hotel would have a better selection of food for the morning meal, and better coffee and tea.

We went to the front desk and settled our bill and asked them to call us a cab while we grabbed our bags from our rooms. By the time we got back downstairs with our things, the cab was just pulling up and we piled in for our ride to the airport. It was another clear day and looked like a great day for flying. We arrived at the Malta airport and checked in with Air Malta for our flight to Rome. We cleared customs and had a little time so we all grabbed a hot beverage, the best we had since landing on the island nearly four days before.

Our flight was on time and we departed a little before ten that morning. We were once again seated on the bulkhead and once aloft we were served beverages and a light meal. We arrived in Rome at the main international airport, Leonardo de Vinci, where we once again were forced to clear customs and immigration. We collected our bags and caught the train for downtown Rome.

Once we arrived at the Roma Termini, Rome's main train station, we grabbed a cab for our hotel. Our driver pointed his shiny Mercedes in the direction of our hotel and took off. However, it turns out that our cabbie didn't know exactly where the hotel was located, and finally just let us out in the neighborhood to figure it out for ourselves. It was a little tricky to locate because the entrance was through a large gate and back in a courtyard, but we found it without much difficulty.

This was my first time to stay at the Hotel Parlamento, although I had been to Rome a couple of times before. The one thing I did know about the hotel was that it was well situated, in my opinion. Located between two famous landmarks, the Spanish Steps and the Trevi Fountain, and nearly across the street from the Italian Parliament building, the hotel was in the hub of activity for Rome.

We pushed our way through the big gate and found the elevator up to the fourth floor reception and check-in. We exited into the small lobby which is filled with antiques covering a white marble floor. There we were greeted by a middle-aged man, George, who was extremely helpful. He checked us in and showed us to our room, a very well-appointed one right off the breakfast room near the front desk. The room contains a king-sized bed, a love seat, desk with a television hooked up to a satellite feed, and a largely marble bathroom.

We were well pleased and did a little settling in before we walked Leo down the street to his hotel. Leo had decided to join us after we had made our hotel reservations and, unfortunately, there was no room at the inn for him. We had hoped that something might open up, but when we arrived George informed us that no such luck had occurred, all twenty-three rooms in our small hotel were taken.

Before we could leave the hotel to walk Leo down the street for his check-in, George stopped us and provided us with maps of the city and detailed directions to Leo's hotel. This was most helpful and we thanked him and headed out the door. Once back outside, we took the short three block walk to Leo's hotel. We got him all checked-in and went to his room with him. The room turned out to be a bit of a disappointment to him and, later that afternoon while Jenny was resting, he changed to a nicer hotel even closer to ours.

After Leo checked into his original hotel we decided it was high time to find some lunch. Since we were starving we decided to just stay in our neighborhood to find something to eat. It was now well past two o'clock and a sense of urgency descended upon us. We stopped at one of the first places we came across, a little pizzeria on the street between our hotels.

The warm, little restaurant was a typical hole-in-the-wall with red and white checkered table cloths with Chianti bottles on the table. We all surveyed the menus and each of us chose an individual pizza. I order a sausage, ham and onion, and Leo and I decided to split a bottle of house red wine. Our orders came quickly which probably saved us from gnawing off our arms. The pizza was good, a thin-crust pie with lots of sauce and cheese. Leo and I both enjoyed the wine which was very dry and bold.

We all finished our plates of food and decided it was time to begin to look around the area. Being nearly four o'clock, we decided to confine our sightseeing to the immediate neighborhood. Leo had been to Rome before also, and we thought the best place to start was the Spanish Steps.

We walked the few blocks to the famous staircase which takes its name from the Spanish Embassy which used to be located nearby. Given it was a sunny day, the steps were filled with young people enjoying what could be one of the last seventy degree days of the year. A carnival-like atmosphere existed with street performers and vendors filling the plaza at the base of the steps.

We checked out some of the wares which were for sale, and did a little people watching before deciding to move on to our next stop. We made our way through the winding, narrow streets to the Trevi Fountain. The over three hundred year old Baroque fountain is an interesting piece of artwork and a favorite spot for tourists. The fountain is fed by an ancient

Roman aqueduct. Tradition holds that one should throw a coin in the fountain for good luck.

We all decided to keep with tradition and throw a coin in the fountain using the proscribed technique; chucking the currency with the right hand over the left shoulder with our backs to the water. We had a long day by now and Jenny was observing her feet were beginning to swell up. We decided that we should return to our room so she could at least get her feet up for a few minutes. Leo decided to return to his hotel, this is actually when he changed accommodations, and he agreed to come to our room before we went to dinner.

When we got back to the room we both laid down on the bed and Jenny dozed while I watched CNN. Around six o'clock we had a knock on the door, it was Leo bearing gifts. Somewhere along the way he found a liquor store and bought a bottle of vodka for me and a gin for himself. He also had a Diet Coke for his sister. I went to the front desk and procured a bucket of ice and we proceeded to continue the tradition of having a party in our room prior to dinner.

After a couple of drinks we decided it was time to go to dinner. We checked our guidebook and decided the nearby Otella alla Concordia sounded good to us. We left the hotel and headed in the direction of the Spanish Steps. The restaurant sits on a side street close to the landmark, amid the toney shops of the neighborhood.

We arrived at the address and walked back into a courtyard to the main dining room. The large room with vaulted ceilings was beginning to fill up with dinners. We were seated at a table in the back of the room and immediately were brought fresh, warm bread with the menus. There was a menu of the day and an extensive, reasonably-priced wine list. Our waiter returned and we ordered a bottle of Italian red, Barolo I believe, and some tap water for the table.

When the wine was served we placed our order. We all chose from the menu of the day and started with prosciutto with melon, a favorite of mine. We all ended up having the pasta of the day which was a homemade fettuccini with a Bolognese sauce. The server promptly returned with our appetizer. The waiter had recommended that one was large enough for the three of us to split, and he was right. The cantaloupe was perfectly ripe and flavorful, and the ham was delicious, which made for a perfect combination. I had eaten this dish before several times, I enjoy it greatly, but it had never tasted so good to me.

We all enjoyed several pieces of the delicacy and were just finishing when our entrees arrived. The plates were teeming with pasta which was generously covered in a rich-looking sauce. It was quite possibly the best fettuccini alla Bolognese I had ever eaten. Jenny and Leo, who was a top notch chef, both concurred with my assessment. We really enjoyed that meal. We had fine service, great food, and the atmosphere was at a high standard. I have had the good fortune of making several trips to Italy and eating many terrific meals there, but none surpassed that night.

(See Appendix 27 for the recipe)

We polished off our bottle of wine and resisted the temptation to order dessert. The check came and I gladly paid for the modestly-priced meal. As we headed out into the cool night air, we all were in a great mood because of the meal, and the convivial nature of the dining experience. We had to resist the temptation to eat all our meals here the rest of the trip.

We walked along and shortly came to Leo's new hotel. He invited us in to see his room which we did. We could understand why he liked it better than the previous hotel. The real kicker was his old hotel let him leave at no charge and the two rooms were priced the same. So, he made out well in the trade. As we were preparing to leave, Leo insisted that we have a quick drink in the small bar in his new hotel. We obliged him, and I drank a nice glass of grappa, an Italian after dinner drink.

Jenny was tiring out and we said goodnight to Leo and headed for the door. We agreed to meet at our hotel in the morning after nine o'clock to set out for our day of sightseeing. Jenny and I walked arm-in-arm back to the hotel. Even though she was now less than two months from delivering our child, she looked and felt great. We got back to our room, disrobed and went to bed.

The Colosseum in Rome. Amazing!

The next morning we awoke to the sounds of people eating breakfast directly outside of our room. It was not a big problem, but we had not noticed how close the entrance to our room was to the actual breakfast area. It was just right there. We cleaned up and joined the other patrons for breakfast in the fashionable, but cramped dining area. The Parlamento served a nice breakfast with a fine array of cereals, fresh fruit, yogurt, cold meats and cheeses, breads and jams and hot drinks. They would gladly fix you an espresso or latte, and Jenny raved about their selection of hot teas.

We squeezed into a small table directly outside our door and a server brought us a basket of bread with jellies and took our drink orders. We then helped ourselves to the breakfast buffet while they made our hot drinks. We were enjoying a nice meal, and I was finishing my second flavorful latte when Leo arrived. He had already eaten, but the server quickly brought him a latte also.

As we finished our beverages, we plotted out tour strategy for the day. We decided that we would focus on ancient Rome, beginning with the Colosseum and the adjacent Forum. We noticed that our friend, George, was working so we went to see him for advice. Jenny and I were also running out of clean clothes, so we began by asking him if there was a nearby laundry we could drop off our clothes to be washed and dried.

George pointed us in the direction of a very nice little laundromat only a few blocks away very near the Parliament building. He then called them for us to see if we could bring them our clothes that morning, and have them finished by the end of the day. He reported to us that they could if we got there within the hour.

He also directed us to the nearby bus lot across the street and told us which bus to catch that went directly to the Colosseum. Not only did he give us directions on which bus to take, he reached into his wallet and fished out three bus tickets that he gave us to get us going. I tried to refuse his act of kindness, but he would hear none of it. He finally agreed that I could replace them later when I had an opportunity to get to a kiosk and buy tickets. We were absolutely blown away by such great customer service, and the kindness of this fine man.

We went to our room and gathered our dirty clothes and headed directly for the laundry. We arrived a couple of minutes later to a warm greeting, they had been expecting us because George had called them as we left the hotel. They seemed quite nice and competent, and assured us that our clothes would be ready any time after three, but we should collect them before they closed at seven o'clock. We told them that would be no problem, thanked them, and headed out to catch our bus.

Almost directly across the street from the building that housed our hotel, there is a large piazza which also serves as a big, open-air bus station. Here there are numerous stations where buses congregate to pick-up and drop-off passengers for destinations all over Rome. We found the proper bus that George had told us to catch and hopped aboard for the Colosseum.

We found seats in the front of the bus and enjoyed the views out of the front window as we made our way. Leo and I had both been to Rome before, but this was Jenny's first trip. I still remember the moment when the bus turned the corner and the Colosseum came into full view. It is a majestic sight and Jenny was amazed, as was I when I had been there previously, at seeing the former home of the gladiators.

The edifice is so large and imposing, and it sits in the middle of downtown Rome. The Colosseum, not unlike the Acropolis from earlier in the trip, is one of these historic sites that when you see it, you are absolutely wowed. It is like I said before, seeing these types of significant pieces of history are something I could only dream about doing one day when I was growing up. I kept feeling all the while it was somehow probably not attainable.

The bus stopped about a block short of the Colosseum and we jumped off into the warm sunshine of the day. We walked the couple of minutes to the ticket office and were quite lucky that there was almost no one in line that day. We purchased our ducats and walked in. We spent the next hour exploring this incredible structure. We climbed to the highest reaches of the arena we were allowed to, and snapped pictures from every conceivable angle. It was a wonderful experience.

We had finally exhausted the experience and decided it was time to depart for the Roman Forum, which is practically next door. We wandered around looking for the entrance for a time, passed the Arch of Constantine, and finally relied on the kindness of strangers to point us in the right directions. We arrived at the entrance and purchased our tickets. We entered unescorted with some literature which provided us some guidance as to what we were about to see.

The former hub of ancient Roman government, society and life, is now clearly a ruin. You need a bit of imagination to figure out what it must have been like a couple of centuries before, but it is nonetheless a worthwhile experience. We spent over an hour climbing around on the remnants of ancient temples, libraries and marketplaces. We trod the same streets that the most famous Romans walked in the Golden Era.

We decided it was time to move on and thought that we would visit the site of the Circus Maximus before departing the area. Located behind the Colosseum, just short of Palatine Hill, the area is the former site of an arena that could seat around a quarter of a million Romans for various games. Often home to chariot races, the Circus Maximus today is a large open space with tiers of benches laying in ruins. Tired from our walk, we sat on the ruins and imagined what it must have been like to sit there and watch the races with 250,000 other people. On a nice day like this one, it is a pleasant heaven in the midst of the bustling city.

We were now hungry and decided to strike out for the other side of the Colosseum where civilization today rests. After about a pleasant ten minute walk, we came upon Restaurante la Cicala e la Formica. We followed our noses, not a guidebook to this quaint little trattoria tucked down a side street off the busy Via Cavour. There were a few tables out front in a little courtyard that were shaded from the sun by umbrellas, so we took a seat at one.

A server soon arrived with the menu of the day and did a rough translation in somewhat broken English. Leo and I decided to try a carafe of the house red which turned out to be a very good decision. When the waiter returned we all had decided, so we placed our orders. Leo started by selecting a rabbit dish, one of his favorites. Jenny went for a tubular pasta filled with porcini mushrooms and a smoked cheese and I selected the cheese-filled ravioli covered in a meat sauce.

The waiter returned with salads for all. A mixed greens dish with tomatoes and some cheese sprinkled on it, the dressing was a tasty vinaigrette. We were all quite hungry by now so we wasted no time in diving into the salads and the hot bread he had brought. We had finished with our salads for a while when our entrees arrived, but they were worth the wait. We all found our selections truly delicious and really enjoyed our little find.

We decided it was time to move and requested the bill from our waiter. We paid our bill and decided to make one more stop before heading out for our neighborhood for some rest. I had visited a nearby church on my first visit to Rome several years before which contained a Michelangelo sculpture. I thought with the help of a map I could find it again, so we headed out in search of the church.

As it turns out the church, St. Peter in Chains, was only a couple of blocks from the restaurant. Back down a little side street on the other side of Via Cavour, the church is rather unassuming from the outside. We climbed the steps to the entrance and swung open the door to find a lovely, somewhat ornate nave. Inside the church the chains that bound St. Peter before he was executed are on display.

However, for me the real prize of the church lies in an alcove, Michelangelo's sculpture of Moses. In the marble statue, Moses is depicted with horns that symbolize the light, or radiance, of the Lord. This large sculpture is often compared favorably to the David which I had seen on an earlier trip to Florence. I am not sure I would go that far, but it is an amazing piece and well worth the effort to see if you are in the neighborhood of the Colosseum. Clearly, it is a masterpiece.

We had walked a great deal by now and my pregnant wife was beginning to feel the effects of being on her feet all day. We determined that we should head back to the hotel for Jenny to take a rest. We walked back down to the Colosseum and caught our bus for the quick ride back to our neighborhood.

We all three parted company, Jenny headed to the room, Leo to his hotel, and I to pick up the laundry. We agreed to rendezvous with Leo back at our room in a couple of hours at six for another happy hour. I headed back down the street to the laundry doing some window-shopping for potential Christmas gifts for Jenny. The laundry had all our clothes finished and neatly folded up and bagged for my arrival. I paid the kind folks and headed back to the hotel to get a little rest as well before Leo came over.

I entered the room as quietly as possible and Jenny was out like a light. I pulled off my shoes and took out the guidebook to begin looking for the right place for dinner. I figured with all the distance we had covered on foot that day, we would be best served staying in the general area of our hotel. Thankfully, there were a lot of good restaurant choices in the area which made this task quite easy. I picked out a couple of potentials to show Leo when he arrived, so we could make a decision.

Promptly at six Leo arrived and I got some ice from the person at the front desk of the hotel. We settled in for a drink and a discussion about where to eat that night. Over a second glass of our favorite clear liquids, we decided to try Da Mario near Leo's hotel. One of the guidebooks rated it highly, and it sounded like it had a good menu.

We finished our drinks and headed out to see if we could get into Da Mario's for dinner. The short walk of a few blocks toward the Spanish Steps was not a difficult one, but we did notice that the fall chill was beginning to fill the air. We arrived at Da Mario's, a pleasant and cozy place which was about half-filled. The host showed us to a table in the corner of the main dining room, a warm room with dark paneling half way up the walls.

Our waiter came by, a pleasant chap who spoke passable English. He informed us that they had a special, boar stew, which Leo immediately announced he would be having. We had read that the place specialized in game dishes and Leo hoped the review was correct. The waiter convinced us that we should try the fried vegetable appetizer, which turned out to be quite delicious. Jenny had an order of spaghetti carbonara and I had the parpardelle with a rabbit Bolognese.

We all enjoyed our meals with Leo especially blown away by the stew. Jenny is a fan of carbonara sauces and felt this was the best she had on the trip. Leo and I drank an inexpensive Chianti which the waiter recommended, and it was spot on, also. We finished our meals and refused the appetizing looking desserts, deciding instead to go in search of some Italian gelato.

We had seen a gelato shop near the Trevi Fountain the day before which had a huge line in front. We reckoned that meant the place was good, so we decided to give it a try. We walked the few blocks to the fountain and located the shop which was still open, and busy. We joined the queue and peered through the case trying to decide which flavor to get. When my turn arrived I chose the hazelnut which was out of this world.

We retreated to a good place to view the Trevi which is very attractive when fully illuminated. We all greatly enjoyed the gelatos, the Italian version of ice cream. Or should I say, the superior Italian ice creams. Clearly, the milk fat content of these marvelous concoctions are a great deal elevated over their American counterparts, but it is worth it. We liked it so much, we made a pact that we would return each night the rest of the trip.

We walked Leo back to his hotel and wished him a good night. We decided to meet up an hour earlier the next morning so we could head to the Vatican Museums by no later than nine o'clock, in hopes of getting ahead of the rush. Jenny and I headed back to the Parlamento and fell into our bed. The day had taken its toll and we were asleep in a matter of minutes.

We awoke again the next morning to the sounds of our fellow travelers taking their breakfast just outside our door. We cleaned up and joined them for another nice breakfast. I remember that morning we were served, in addition to our regular fare, a basket of breads that included a chocolate filled croissant that was just delicious. As we were finishing up Leo appeared and joined us for a latte before we headed out to sightsee.

We finished our beverages and departed to visit Vatican City that morning. We headed out walking toward the Spanish Steps where there is a subway stop on the line that runs directly to the Vatican. We found the entrance, purchased tickets, and went to the platform to catch the train. Shortly after we arrived at the platform our train pulled up and we were whisked away westward toward the Holy See.

This is the most efficient and cost effective route from this area to visit all the Vatican sites. However, I caution you to be very aware of the activities around you if you ride the subway in Rome. I have taken the train to St. Peter's on four occasions now, and each time there was a pickpocketing event that occurred directly in my vicinity.

The thieves work in teams and are very quick, so be alert. They tend to use the "bump and run" technique where one member of the team jostles you, distracting you, while an accomplice lifts your wallet. Before you know it they have jumped off the train as the doors are closing, and you are down the tracks to the next station before you can get off. By then the thieves are on another train and probably picking someone else's pocket. The safest way to protect yourself is to carry all valuables in your front pockets and pay very close attention to all around you.

We arrived at the nearest subway stop and disembarked. We exited the subway station into a sunny day and made our way down a broad boulevard toward the Vatican. Shortly before entering the gate which leads to St. Peter's Square, we made a right turn and followed the Vatican wall westward to the Vatican Museum ticket office and entrance. We joined the queue to purchase tickets for the museum and were fortunate that the line was not too long that day.

Today, you are able to purchase advance tickets online for admittance to the Vatican Museum and the Sistine Chapel. In my opinion, this makes all the sense in the world to take advantage of this opportunity. First, you are assured entrance on the day you desire to go. Secondly, you get to skip the line and enter the museum directly. This can save you a great deal of time on most days.

This type of service is now available at a number of major museums around the world, and can represent a considerable time savings for you. However, many times there are additional fees associated with the online reservation process, so you have to weigh the costs and benefits which come with the added charges. Also, sometimes these services are provided by a third party, so you need to identify exactly who is offering these early reservations to be sure they are authorized to provide the service.

At the time of this trip no such service was offered by the Vatican Museum folks, so we waited our turn in line and bought our tickets. We caught a good day and were through the process, and inside the museum within fifteen minutes. We felt like we had been lucky, and were not standing in line for over an hour as I had on my first visit.

The Vatican Museum can be an overwhelming experience. The Catholic Church has acquired an amazing collection of various forms of art over the centuries, and it is ostentatiously displayed in the various rooms. You are led through various salons and down numerous hallways which contains works of art from before the birth of Christ through the Renaissance, and beyond. It is truly a wondrous museum. One is reminded that the Catholic Church had, and has, immense wealth and power.

Your tour of the museum culminates in the visit to the Sistine Chapel. We wound our way to the chapel's entrance and were surprised that the usual throng was absent. Luckily, we found seats on the wooden benches that line the sides of the chapel. We sat on these hard seats for over half an hour marveling at the incredible sights that lie above our heads. Our stay was much longer than most because of the absence of the omnipresent crowd.

Michelangelo was commissioned by Pope Julius II to paint the ceiling of the Sistine Chapel. Michelangelo considered himself a sculptor, not a painter, and was contemptuous of the assignment. He spent the next four years, from 1508-1512, working on the arduous project. The task was so difficult that he suffered permanent damage to his eyesight. Throughout the task he had to contend with the pope's insistence that he speed the project to completion.

Michelangelo focused the painting on the Book of Genesis, painting nine panels depicting various stories from this scripture. The human form is glorified in his works. The most famous of the panels is one which depicts the expulsion of Adam and Eve from the Garden of Eden. Given that the artist undertook the project against his wishes, there is certain irony in the fact that the paintings are heralded as his most famous works.

Numerous other famous Renaissance artists including Botticelli, Roselli, and Signorelli, painted works on the side walls. These frescos can easily be overlooked by visitors when they are compared to the masterpieces created by Michelangelo on the ceiling.

When Michelangelo was in his sixties, he returned to the chapel to paint the fresco on it's alter. His depiction of the **Last Judgment** presents a view of God sitting in judgment as sinners are plunged into hell. Seeing these works by Michelangelo are well worth the trip to Rome and the Vatican, and should be on your list of things to see in this life.

We began to feel that it was time to move on to allow new visitors to take our spots in the chapel. We exited the room and began to proceed toward the exit. However, we did make a stop at one of the several gift shops inside the museum to make some purchases for our good Catholic family members and friends back home. Jenny stocked up on rosaries and prayer cards for those on her list, and we made our way outside into the sunshine.

Our next stop was St. Peter's Basilica, the huge Renaissance structure that dominates Vatican City. We exited the museum and made our way to the large cobblestoned, St. Peter's Square. We crossed the square which is the site of weekly services. These are often presided over by the pope when he is in residence. The shear sight of the cathedral was awe inspiring to Jenny, as it was her first time to see this pilgrimage site in person.

We mounted the stairs to enter the church. I recalled for Jenny and Leo the story of my first visit to St. Peter's over a decade earlier. My friend, Bill Schreiber, and I were visiting Europe in November of 1989, which happened to coincide with the fall of the Berlin Wall. As we entered the basilica on a Sunday morning, mass was in session. We had barely entered the building when a round of thunderous applause erupted. Bill turned to me and speculated that the clapping was not for our arrival.

He was correct, the adulation was not for us at all. We looked up and saw what had precipitated the commotion. At that moment Pope John Paul II was making a seemingly unexpected appearance at the service. Bill and I stood in the back of the church and listened to the pope's remarks and believed that they pertained to the events that were transpiring in Eastern Europe. We think that with his Polish background he was relaying to the audience the importance of the break-up of the Soviet Union, and its potential impact on the Catholic Church.

Whatever the reason for the appearance and the message he imparted, this visit to St. Peter's would be much less dramatic. There were no formal ceremonies transpiring, merely a large number of pilgrims milling about the beautiful structure. The basilica is one of the largest churches in the world and certainly one of the most dramatic.

We walked into the nave on its marble floors taking in the giant marble columns that support its ponderous roof. As we entered further the huge dome of the church came into view. Rays of light were floating through the window in the ornate dome making for a very holy atmosphere. We wondered around the church viewing its numerous chapels and burial places for a number of Roman Catholic leaders, not the least of which was the tomb of St. Peter.

As we were making our way back to the entrance we stopped to observe another of Michelangelo masterpieces, the *Pieta*. The large marble sculpture depicts the body of Christ, after the crucifixion, draped across the lap of his mother, Mary. The stirring piece is truly something to behold. The sculpture was attacked in the 1970s by a deranged geologist named Lazlo Toth. Using a hammer Toth broke several pieces of marble from the statue before he was suppressed. Some of the broken marble was taken by onlookers and never returned. Artists have long since repaired the damage taking marble from Mary's back to replace that which was marred.

After having spent over an hour taking in what the basilica has to offer, we decided to attend to a basic need, hunger. We exited the church and walked across the sundrenched square stopping to snap several pictures in a favorable light. We left the square through the same gate we had entered and headed up the street in search of a place for lunch.

We exited the Vatican City walls and ducked down a side street that runs parallel to the walls. These streets are lined with shops and small eateries. We were in search of Restaurante IL Matriciano which had come recommended in our guidebook. Within a few blocks walking we came upon this quaint establishment. We were warmly greeted by a mustachioed host who seated us at a table in the first dining room.

It felt good to sit down at the white linen draped table. The padded, slat back chairs were comfortable and provided relief to our weary bodies.

The smells emanating from the kitchen only heightened our appetites. Our waiter appeared with a basket of hot bread and English menus. He told us about the specials and we ordered drinks while thumbing through the menu.

Leo and I decided to split a carafe of house red wine (something unusual for us on this trip) and Jenny got some cold water. The waiter brought our drinks and we ordered. As we sipped on our drinks we tore into the bread basket and slathered the hot pieces with fresh butter. The red wine was a very pleasant full-bodied offering with long legs. Soon our waiter reappeared with our lunches, Jenny and Leo had a risotto special and I went for the penne arribiatta.

Our dishes were delicious and quickly devoured. My penne was nice and spicy and had a good garlic kick. We sat a while after finishing our pastas, as we finished the wine and Leo drank a cappuccino. Jenny was spent, so we paid our bill and headed up the block for the subway station. Our arrival at the station coincided with an eastbound train, so we made a mad dash and were able to just catch it before it departed.

We returned to the station at the Spanish Steps and walked the couple of blocks back to the Hotel Parlamento. When we arrived in the lobby our friend, George, was working and handed us our room key. We stopped to chat for a while and he recommended a nearby restaurant to us for dinner. He was glowing with his praise for the place, so we asked him to make us a reservation for that evening. He called them immediately and we were set for eight o'clock for a party of three.

Leo and I got Jenny ensconced in the bed for a nap and headed back out to do some shopping. I enjoy buying jewelry for Jenny when we travel, and I had noticed that several small shops around our hotel specialized in Cameos. I decided to try and find Jenny a Cameo necklace for Christmas, and Leo agreed to help me pick one out. We told Jenny we would be back in a couple of hours and hoped she would get some rest.

Leo and I decided to head away from the Spanish Steps and toward the Pantheon in our search, thinking that we might find a better value in this seemingly lower-priced neighborhood. We spent the next couple of hours plying the streets that are in the area of the Pantheon and the Piazza Navona looking at Cameos in small jewelry shops. We successfully eliminated several places and decided on the size and style we liked, but arrived at no final decision. I had two more days to make up my mind, and decided to use it all.

Leo and I headed back to the hotel and stopped at the front desk upon our arrival to ask George for a bucket of ice. George obliged us and we went to the room where Jenny was awake watching the television. We made drinks and relaxed for a time before we had to leave for our dinner reservation. Leo and I polished off a couple of cocktails and we spruced up before departing for the restaurant.

The place that George had recommended to us was across Via Del Corso, the main north-south street near our hotel. We walked past the back side of the Italian Parliament building and reached the small, neighborhood eatery. Trattoria Da Gino's is far from fancy, but is a very comfortable place that features homemade cooking. We were seated in a small dining room that has frescoed walls depicting scenes of the Italian countryside.

George had told us that the house red wine was delicious, so we order a liter along with a large bottle of water. He had also recommended that we try whatever the pasta special was, we could not go wrong. It turned out that the homemade pasta of the evening was a linguine with ham and peas in an olive oil sauce, and we all went for it. Everything turned out to be just great. The house wine was bold and flavorful, the bread was delicious, salad very fresh and crisp, and the pasta was remarkable. George had not steered us wrong in the least. We absolutely loved it.

We finished our pastas and drank the remnants of the red wine and asked for the check. We paid the very reasonable bill and headed out into the cool, clear night in search of our nightly fix of gelato. We returned to our favorite little ice cream shop near the Trevi Fountain and ordered our sweet treats. We sat on a bench facing the fountain and enjoyed the gelato and the moon-lit evening.

We finished our desserts and headed back toward our hotel. We walked Leo back to his place and agreed to meet at nine the next morning in our breakfast room. Jenny and I strolled hand-in-hand back to our hotel. We reached the lobby where George was still on the job. We thanked him profusely for his restaurant recommendation and filled him in on our evening. He gave us our key and we turned in for the night.

We awoke the next morning at nearly eight o'clock, a very good night's sleep for us. We could hear the breakfast being served out our door, so we cleaned up, and secured what by now had become our favorite table right just outside our room. We were eating another fresh, hearty breakfast when Leo arrived and got a cappuccino. We finished our breakfast and discussed our agenda for that day.

We decided to explore the area around the Pantheon and the Piazza Navona that day. We realized it was Thanksgiving Day back home, so we were going to try to make it a special day in Rome. It was Leo's last day and Jenny and I would be following him on Saturday. We headed out into the morning. The weather had changed growing much cooler and it was foggy, almost like a heavy mist was clinging to the air.

Our first stop of the morning was only a few blocks from our hotel. The Pantheon, which is a building dedicated to all gods, is one of the oldest remaining structures from ancient Rome. Built in 27 B.C., the building is an architectural marvel. The Pantheon is 142 feet tall and 142 feet wide and is a perfect sphere sitting on a cylinder. A large hole in the center of the roof allows light to emit throughout the interior of the space. The concrete structure is the final resting place to some luminaries including the Italian master, Raphael. It is a truly impressive structure and should not be missed if visiting Rome.

After finishing our tour of the Pantheon we stood outside and tried to take some pictures of the building, but the weather would not cooperate and supply us with ample light. We next headed to a nearby church which contains a sculpture made by Michelangelo. Only a block south of the Pantheon, St. Maria Sopra Minerva Basilica is one of the only Gothic churches in Rome. The basilica sits at the back of a square which is dominated by a statue of an elephant supporting an Egyptian obelisk.

The church itself is a rather plain-looking building. However, inside the cathedral is quite ornate and well worth a visit. We entered the structure and browsed around looking at the crypts of the various religious leaders that are buried inside. We soon located our reason for visiting the basilica, the statue carved by Michelangelo.

The marble sculpture of the muscular Christ carrying a cross was finished in 1521 for the church. The artwork sits to the left of the apse and was at the time a very approachable item. In fact, we all three reached out and touched the incredible work, which left us each feeling a little guilty. But hey, when do you get an opportunity to actually touch a Michelangelo?

We decided to move on to the area around the Piazza Navona which is a few blocks to the west of the Pantheon. We wound our way through the narrow, crooked streets which separate the two landmarks and soon arrived at the large opening which is the Piazza Navona. The piazza is an oval shaped public space that was once a Roman arena, or place which hosted games and chariot races.

Today the huge square is home to some lovely fountains, a market, and numerous vendors. The sides of the piazza are lined with shops, bars and restaurants. At Christmastime the square is transformed into a large Christmas market. We browsed the area and found a great Christmas shop which sits on a street on the east side of the square. Here Jenny and I bought several ornaments that still don our tree at the holidays.

We were now thinking about lunch and decided to walk back toward the Trevi Fountain to try a little restaurant we had seen when we were walking about earlier on the trip. We window shopped, I was keeping my eye out for a Cameo, and made our way back to the Il Miraggio. The restaurant is located on a very small street that runs parallel to the Via Del Corso near the Trevi.

We arrived at the well-appointed, little trattoria and were seated immediately at a table next to a large window. We watched the pedestrian traffic flow down the busy shopping street. Our waiter arrived with a basket of hot bread and English menus. I ordered a beer and the others a large bottle of cold water, no gas. Jenny and Leo decided to try some homemade pasta and I went for a pizza.

We enjoyed our beverages and ate the delicious bread which was still hot enough to melt butter. Soon our orders arrived, Jenny had a tagliatelle with a mushroom sauce, Leo got a penne with salmon and I got a ham and mushroom pizza. Everyone liked what they got. My pizza had abundant toppings, the tomato sauce was tangy, and the whole pie was covered in thick, gooey cheese. I ordered another beer as we finished our lunches.

Full, we decided to head out and do some more shopping at a nearby market which runs along a street between the Via Del Corso and the Trevi Fountain. Along this street you could buy anything from fresh fruits and vegetables, meat and fish, and local handicrafts. We browsed the kiosks and Jenny picked up a few small items to give as gifts for Christmas which was now only a few weeks away.

Jenny decided that she needed to nourish her unborn child by stopping at a gelato shop for a cup of rocky road ice cream. Leo also caved in and got a mango cone and I abstained, for once. We sat down on a bench outside the shop and discussed what to do with the rest of our day. We all decided that we would return to the Otella alla Concordia, the restaurant where we had eaten the first night, for our Thanksgiving dinner that night.

Leo volunteered to drop by the Concordia and make a reservation for that evening as he went back to his hotel to begin packing to leave the next morning. Jenny was tiring and wanted to go back to the room and rest. When they finished their desserts we all headed toward our respective hotels. I dropped Jenny back at the room and headed out to visit a couple more jewelry stores that I had seen during our travels earlier that day.

After another day of indecision on a Cameo, I headed back to the hotel to see if Jenny was up from her nap. Sure enough, she was awake watching television when I arrived. I had no more than laid down on the bed when Leo knocked at our door. I opened the door to find him with a bucket of ice declaring that it was cocktail time at the Parlamento. We fixed a couple of drinks and prepared to go out to dinner, as he had been successful in acquiring a dinner reservation for us.

We toasted to Thanksgiving, finished our drinks and headed out into the cool, night air. We arrived at the Otella alla Concordia just in time for our eight o'clock dinner reservation. We were seated in the same dining room as the previous evening at a table in the back corner with a commanding view of the room. We ordered a bottle of a Tuscan red and Jenny splurged with a Diet Coke.

We examined the English menu and found no turkey available, so we all settled on steaks. We started out with a fried calamari appetizer which was served with a red sauce for dipping. It was a wonderful start to a terrific Thanksgiving dinner. Next we were served fresh, green salads with an oil and vinegar dressing. We had no more than finished the salads when our large, rib-eye steaks arrived. Lapping over the sides of the large plates, they looked incredible, and were.

The steaks were prepared to perfection and were accompanied by roasted potatoes which were equally good. We sat and enjoyed one of my favorite Thanksgiving dinners I have had away from home. Barely able to finish the tasty steak, we passed on dessert, but kept the option open for another trip to the gelatoria after dinner.

As Leo and I were finishing the bottle of wine, our waiter brought us each a complimentary glass of limoncello. Nearly frozen in the glass, the lemon liquor was quite refreshing, and since Jenny was not drinking due to her condition, I was forced to drink hers. It was quite the sacrifice, but as an expectant father it was one that I was willing to make.

Goofing on a couple of young Asian women with
my hand in the Mouth of Truth.

We finished our drinks and paid our bill. We headed back out into the cool, dark night. Leo had to catch an early flight back to the States in the morning and decided he was spent. He talked us out of seeing him off in the morning because of his early departure. So, we dropped him at his hotel and said goodbye to our travel companion. We had enjoyed his company greatly and hated to see the trip come to an end. But, we had one more day and decided to head back to our hotel to get some rest.

We wanted to sleep as late as possible the next morning and awoke quite refreshed at nearly nine o'clock. We showered and dressed quickly so we could grab some breakfast before they closed it down. We were able to take our favorite little, corner table and had another great, healthy breakfast. We lingered over several hot beverages, as they fixed me several lattes and Jenny enjoyed a strong black tea.

We decided over breakfast that we would stay in the neighborhood and explore the area to our north that we had not been to yet. We finished our meal, grabbed our jackets, and headed out for our last day in Rome. We stepped outside just when the skies opened up with a steady rain. Fully equipped with rain jackets with hoods, we were undeterred by the weather. We walked to the Via Del Corso and turned right headed to the Piazza del Popolo.

We started out with a good pace stopping occasionally to peer into the windows of an interesting shop. Clearly, Jenny had a real pep in her step and was enjoying the walk immensely. We covered the ground to the piazza in really good time and arrived at the beautiful square in the middle of the street just as the clouds really let loose with a downpour. We found a little café on the south side of the plaza and grabbed a tea and a coffee.

We sat by the window and enjoyed our drinks and the view. The Piazza del Popolo is a large public square that is dominated by an ancient Egyptian obelisk which is positioned in the center of the piazza. Legend has it that Nero's remains were originally buried here and that he has haunted the area since. The open space is really quite attractive with nearby fountains and churches.

We finished our drinks and made our way across the street and roamed around the area. Satisfied that we had seen enough, we headed back down the Del Corso toward the ancient city. Jenny was feeling great and was quite eager to walk. In fact, we walked from the Piazza del Popolo to the Piazza Venezia, a distance in excess of two miles, without breaking stride.

We wandered around the vicinity of the Piazza Venezia and ended up walking further to the Bocca della Verita at the church of Santa Maria in Cosmedin. Jenny had seen the "Mouth of Truth" in the old movie, *Roman Holiday,* which starred Gregory Peck and Audrey Hepburn. She wanted to see the marble image, so we walked to the church. Under a portico we found the man-like face with its open mouth.

Legend has it that if you tell a lie while you hand is in the Mouth of Truth, your hand will be bitten off. When we arrived under the portico two young Asian women were standing around the face acting a little tentative. So, I seized the moment and thrust my hand into the mouth and said something to Jenny. Soon I let out a yell and removed my hand, sliding it up my sleeve so it would appear to be missing. Goofy as it may seem, the two Asian women thought I had lost my hand. Finally, we all laughed and the other three took their turn placing their hands in the mouth.

Tiring by now, we caught a bus back to the Piazza Venezia and went in search of a place for lunch. Consulting our guidebook once again, we decided to try Enoteca Corsi for our midday meal. A couple of blocks north of the Piazza Venezia sits this unpretentious wine bar which only serves lunch. We were fortunate that the host found us a place to sit at a table in the back where we joined two elderly Italian gentlemen.

I, of course, could not pass up the opportunity to sample a glass of the house red wine which came as a generous pour. We were informed of the specials of the day and we both started with a fabulous bowl of Tuscan bean soup. The piping hot dish was quite delicious and apt for this wet, chilly day. Jenny chose the spaghetti carbonara and I went with a three cheese and mushroom pasta.

We absolutely loved our dishes. We sat and ate and tried to converse with the two kind gentlemen with whom we shared our table. They were eating some good-looking fried cod with French fries and a garlic sauce which reminded me of our earlier days on the trip in Greece. We finished our meals and paid our bill, bidding the two Italians chow.

By now, Jenny was beginning to feel the effects of all the walking, but she insisted on walking back to the hotel for her rest. Instead of walking directly back along the Via Del Corso, we took side streets which wound near the Pantheon. We eventually made it back to the hotel, where Jenny collapsed on the bed. She barely got her shoes off before she was asleep.

I decided that I had to go out one last time in search of the perfect Cameo for her Christmas gift. I had pretty well narrowed it down by now, so I went to the little jewelry store between our hotel and the Pantheon. The pleasant, sixty-something lady who had shown me the collection earlier, was there to meet me when I entered the door. She pulled out my two favorites and informed me that they were prepared to reduce the price on the larger pendant. That was all it took for me to decide, as I am a true sucker for a sale.

The kind lady took my credit card and we finished the transaction. She then offered to gift wrap the present and I took her up on her offer. I watched as she meticulously folded and taped the gold paper to the small box and finished it off with a small, red bow. I thanked her and headed out the door for the Parlamento. When I returned Jenny was still a sleep, so I quietly read a book and waited for her to awaken.

When Jenny woke up, we had our evening cocktail party, and pulled out the guidebook for one last time to choose a restaurant for dinner. Our criteria that evening was that the eatery be close to the hotel, and must serve a mean plate of pasta. We both love Italian cooking and really can't get enough of their terrific pasta while we are there, so we weren't going to miss this final opportunity for a plate of these fabulous noodles.

We chose a restaurant we had walked by earlier on the trip. The Maccheroni Ristorante is a small rustic place that is about a five minute walk from the Parlamento Hotel. In search of a good plate of pasta for our last night, how could we go wrong at a place named for a popular noodle? We walked through the crisp evening air toward the Pantheon in search of the trattoria.

We arrived at the Maccheroni at seven-thirty as they were just opening up for dinner. They graciously seated us at a window table in the front dining room. The white linen covered tables were of heavy wood with heavy wooden arm chairs surrounding them. The dining room was dimly lit that evening with candles on the tables augmenting the low lights.

It was a very romantic setting for our last meal of the trip. We ordered a bottle of still water and perused the options available on that evening's menu. We both decided to start out with a Caesar salad. Jenny opted for a fettuccini carbonara with meatballs and I decide to try the penne arrabiata.

Our efficient waiter brought us a basket of bread and our water soon after we placed our orders. Quickly he returned with our fresh Caesar salads and a wedge of parmesan cheese to add to our salads and pastas. The salads were crisp and refreshing and really hit the spot with us. We made quick work of them and when our waiter returned to clear our plates I ordered a glass of Chianti to go with my penne.

The server arrived with our main courses which were so piping hot that you could see the steam rising from them as he placed them on the table. I sampled my glass of wine while the dish cooled, it was very tasty and full-bodied. Finally at a sufficient temperature for eating, we dove into our choices.

Jenny really liked her carbonara and was particularly intrigued with the meatball pairing, instead of the customary diced ham she usually received. My penne arrabiata was very spicy, which I prefer, and I added copious amounts of the fresh parmesan cheese for a complimentary flavor. We drank in the atmosphere and ate our generous portions of pasta.

Finishing our meal, we decided to pass on dessert in favor of a final walk to our favorite gelatoria. We paid our check and headed back in the direction of the Trevi. As usual the ice cream shop was busy, so we fell into the line. We soon received our two scoops of the rich, creamy offering, and stood gazing at the fountain for one last on this trip.

We finished our gelato and headed back to the Parlamento to pack our things for our departure the next morning. When we arrived our friend, George, was there to greet us. He informed us that he had arranged for the car service to pick us up at seven-thirty in the morning. Trying to come up with a small thank you for all he had done, we offered him the left over gin and vodka we had in our room. He graciously accepted and assured us that he would put it to good use.

We thanked him for all his kindness and bade him a good night. We hurriedly packed our bags and hit the hay, we had an early start to a long day ahead of us. We both actually got a pretty good night's sleep, a bit of a rarity on the last night of a long trip. We awoke, cleaned up, finished our little packing, and grabbed a little breakfast before our ride for the airport arrived.

I slipped away from the table to settle our bill while Jenny took a few last swallows of her tea. I had no more than finished paying than the driver called the front desk to let us know he had arrived. We loaded up our bags and headed downstairs to meet the car. Waiting in the courtyard of the building was our driver who helped us with our bags.

We crawled into his big shiny, black Mercedes and he chauffeured us smoothly to the airport. He dropped us off very near to our check-in position and we pulled our bags inside heading directly for the priority lane. A raven-haired desk clerk assisted us with checking our luggage and supplied us with boarding documents. We breezed through security and spent our remaining time before boarding in an airline lounge.

Our plane was finally called and we headed to the gate. We were seated in the front row on all our flights on the return. We headed to Amsterdam, then to Boston, on to Detroit, finally arriving home in Indianapolis late that night. All our flights went smoothly and we had ample time to discuss the life changing experience which was about to occur for us.

In January, Jenny was to give birth to you, Hank. Obviously, your birth would change our lives forever and we had done our best to plan for it before we left on vacation. Jenny would tell you that the vacation also went a long way in helping her to prepare for childbirth. She strongly contends that all the walking we did on the trip helped her to get in shape for the delivery.

In fact, she and I did a great deal of walking after we returned so she would not lose her edge. On January 20, Inauguration Day, George Henry "Hank" Fleetwood, II, was born at St. Vincent's Women's Hospital in Indianapolis, Indiana. Checking in at 7 pounds, 10 ounces, and 19 and a half inches long, he arrived over a week early. It was a relatively easy delivery, aided by the walking of travel. Little did this baby boy know, but he would be destined to a life of travel.

Hank, you would be going with us on our next international trip. At the ripe age of three months you would be traveling to Ireland and Northern Ireland. And, you would handle it like a pro.

APPENDIX 1

Luxembourg

Café Francais – Mussels in White Wine Sauce (Given directly to us by the
Manager of the restaurant)

Ingredients

New Zealand mussels (chef's recommendation)
Elbing wine – a Luxembourg dry white wine (chef's choice)
Carrots
Celery
Onion
Salt
Pepper

Directions

Empty bottle of wine into cooking vessel. Julienne vegetables and add
to pot. Salt and pepper to taste. Bring pot to boil and add mussels. Boil
mussels for 8 minutes (for 600-700 grams).

Place contents in large bowl. Serve.

APPENDIX 2

Belgium

<u>Chez Leon – Brussels (Provided from their website)</u>

Special mussels

Easy, economical, tasty, this is a recipe that has to be followed to the letter with first-class ingredients, no cream or wine and a very exact cooking time. The flesh should be cooked exactly right to retain its flavour.

For 4 people

Ingredients :

2 kilos of Zealand mussels
2 onions
2 branches of celery
butter, water, salt and pepper

Instructions : Thoroughly wash and brush the mussels. Chop onions and celery into small cubes. Take a high-sided and deep receptacle such as a casserole dish or stewing pot. Put butter and vegetables in the pot and cook for 3 minutes. Add water. Bring to the boil and keep boiling on a high flame. Throw in the mussels. Allow to cook for 7 minutes exactly. Season to taste. Serve scalding hot from the casserole dish accompanied by thickly-sliced French fried potatoes or a salad.

APPENDIX 3

Netherlands

Cafe De Prins – Amsterdam – Pea Soup (Provided from their website)

Ingredients (for 14 liters of soup)

2 Kg pork shoulder on the bone
1 kg leeks in rings
1 kg onion rings and 1whole onion
1 kg celeriac cubed
1 kg potatoes cubed
2 bunches of celery
1 bunch of fat leafy parsley
3 kg split peas rinsed
5 bay leaves
10 cloves
2 tbsp nutmeg
2 tbsp ground black pepper
20 cl beef stock
6 Dutch smoked sausages (or frankfurters might do)
Marmite

Preparation

Bring peas to a boil in 8 liters of water and cook until tender. Cook the meat in 1.5 liters of water with the bay leaves, cloves, nutmeg, pepper, stock, and unpealed whole onion in a pressure cooker. Puree the peas. Add leeks, onion rings, potatoes and simmer. Stir occasionally. When the meat is done, debone, cut in small pieces and add to peas. Strain the meat juices and add as well. Simmer until the vegetables are cooked. Slice the sausage and add to the soup. Warm thoroughly, remove from the fire and add the chopped parsley and celery.

Season with Marmite. Serve with rye bread and bacon.

England

Taormina Restaurant – London - Seafood Marinara

Hi George
I'm sorry for being so slow getting back.

We've never written weights down for our recipes, just ingredients and by sight! So please, experiment yourself as everyone has a different taste, but here are the basics.

Might get a long winded, so apologies again.

We use fresh mussels, squid, shell on prawns, sometimes king prawns and baby clams (no shells as unless they are in season, can be very gritty and sand has been known to chip teeth, so that why we use no shells).

I always add shell fish to oil infused with garlic and white wine. Heat them until the clams start to burst/pop. Medium to high heat. Salt?

Not too much oil at this stage, but enough wine to cook shell fish without burning them. Maybe add drop of fish stock to help here.

Once they are popping like crazy, add some tomato sauce.

This can be fresh tomatoes, passata or even tinned chopped tomato. I prefer passata with a few cherry tomatoes cut in half, as get better colour.

Remember, you are not making a soup, so not too much, just enough after reducing to cover the pasta in a layer of red!

Add a couple of basil leaves ripped up.

After a couple of minutes, add the pasta (spaghetti is best I think for marinara or linguine).

At this point, just before serving, I add olive oil. Depending on taste, more garlic and touch of chilli oil. Maybe pinch of salt? I also add chopped parsley here. Not essential, and normally I don't like parsley, but somehow I find it works! Stir/flip a minute.

Place in a round past bowl, add another basil leaf or two, e via!

Note on the fish.

Squid can be tough, so we pre boil it. Longer you boil, softer it becomes.

King prawns taste nicer if grilled first!

To avoid problem with "bad" mussels (there are always a couple), we also pre cook them and get rid of the ones that don't open.

Of course, at home, better to cook all at once and keep your eyes open!

Hope that helps and all the best!

Giancarlo

APPENDIX 5

Scotland

After repeated attempts to contact the restaurant and receiving no response. Since I have received no response, I have decided to turn to a superior source for this recipe, my mother, Nancy Fleetwood. It is as follows:

INGREDIENTS

Servings 4

- 4 potatoes
- Cooking oil
- 1 lb halibut, cod or other lean fish fillet
- 1 cup of flour
- $\frac{1}{2}$ teaspoon salt
- ½ teaspoon of ground pepper
- $\frac{1}{2}$ teaspoon baking soda
- 1 tablespoon vinegar
- $\frac{2}{3}$ cup water

DIRECTIONS

1. Cut potatoes lengthwise into strips.
2. Heat oil (enough to cover) in deep fryer or skillet to 375 degrees.
3. Fry potatoes 5 to 7 minutes or until golden brown; drain on paper towels.

4. Cut fish filets into 2 x 1/-1/2-inch pieces. Pat dry with paper towels.
5. Mix flour, salt and pepper.
6. Mix baking soda and vinegar.
7. Stir vinegar mixture and water into flour mixture; beat until smooth.
8. Dip fish into batter, allowing excess batter to drip into bowl.
9. Fry 4 or 5 fish pieces at a time for about 3 minutes, turning fish once, until brown. Drain on paper towels.

Wales

After repeated attempts to reach the good folks at Austin's Guesthouse for their recipes for their English breakfast, I have given up on my efforts. I will assume that you, the reader, will be able to grill up bacon and sausage, and have experience at frying an egg. To me, the most outstanding feature of the meal was their baked beans. Quite honestly, having baked beans with breakfast was a new concept to me and one that I really enjoy. Since I have received no response, I have once again turned to my mother.

Please find below Nancy Fleetwood's baked bean recipe:

<u>Ingredients</u>

2 large cans of pork and beans (approximately 30 ounces each)
¾ of a cup of brown sugar
1 large onion – diced
1 cup of tomato catsup
1 Tbsp of yellow mustard
3 strips bacon

<u>Directions</u>

Place beans, brown sugar, onion, catsup and mustard in shallow baking vessel. Stir ingredients together. Place bacon strips on top of the beans. Bake in oven at 350 degrees for one hour. Remove and serve.

Andorra

La Borda de Can Travi – White Beans and Sausage

Dear Mr. Fleetwood,

Thank you so much for your comments; we are glad you had a great meal at La Borda de Can Travi.

At the moment the restaurant is not open any more but our group of restaurants has the same kind of cooking so we also offer the White Beans and Sausage in other restaurants: Can Cortada, Can Travi Nou and El Pintor (all of them in Barcelona city).

You can check the restaurants at our website: www.gruptravi.com

I give you our recipe: "Botifarra amb seques" Typical Catalan dish

Ingredients

"Botifarra" Big pork sausage 1 per person
200gr. White beans (dry)

Garlic and parsley
paprika
olive oil
garlic
salt

Preparation

1) Make the sausage grilled on wood until they are tender inside and outside toasts.
   If you don't have the barbecue on the grill, try a little prick them and making them virtually without oil. Sausages cooked with its own fat.
2) In the same pan you can skip the beans. If they are dry you can hydrate and boil previously. In Catalonia we can buy good quality beans cooked.
3) In a mortar, chop garlic and parsley and then add a little red pepper. Add the mixture to the beans and add Virgin olive oil and salt.
4) Finally serve the sausage with beans.
   Sometimes we add to this recipe our famous allioli sauce.

Allioli

Servings: Makes About 1 Cup

10 garlic cloves, peeled

Pinch of salt

Spanish extra-virgin olive oil

Place the garlic in a mortar along with the salt. Using a pestle, smash the garlic cloves to a smooth paste. (The salt stops the garlic from slipping at the bottom of the mortar as you pound it down.) Drop by drop, pour the olive oil into the mortar slowly as you continue to crush the paste with your pestle. Keep turning your pestle in a slow, continuous circular motion in the mortar. The drip needs to be slow and steady. Make sure the paste soaks up the live oil as you go. Keep adding the oil, drop by drop, until you have the consistency of a very thick mayonnaise. If your aioli gets too dense, add water to thin it out. This takes time – around 20 minute of slow motion around the mortar to create a fence, rich sauce.

Bon Appetite!!
Sílvia Badal
Sales and Marketing Manager
Telf. +34 **934 280 452**
www.gruptravi.com

APPENDIX 8

Spain

Dear George,

I am so sorry but the "Cheff" is no longer working with us. However I can send you the ingredients and quantities of the Lamb Shank. Hope this could be useful.

Best regards

Lamb shoulder

	0.18
sage	0.04
garlic	0.08
mild olive oil	0.10
salt	0.10
pepper	0.10
sour potato	0.00
vanilla pod	0.10
pack choy	0.10
vegetable broth	0.10
sake	0.05
sakura	
Maldon	

APPENDIX 9

Portugal

Sol Dourado – Lisbon - Carne de porco a Alentejana (pork stew with clams)

Hello, George, how are you?

Here is the recipe for our Carne de porco à Alentejana (Alentejana Pork):

- Marinate pork meat with garlic, bay leaves, ground pepper spread, white wine and coriander for at least 12 hours
- Fry (with swine grease), adding a bit more of white wine for refreshing.
- Halfway through the frying, add the clams. Don't add clams too soon or they will taste dry.

We hope you enjoy our recipe and thank you again for your contact.

Best regards,

Russia

<u>1913 Restaurant – St. Petersburg – Hunter's Steak</u>

Dear Mr. Fleetwood!

Sorry for late answer. We waited for our chef from vacation, he alone knows this recipe. He came up with it 20 years ago. And in our menu, this dish has been missing for 8 years. Now there is a reason to bring him back to our offers!

Meat pork carbonate or neck.

Cut a piece of 2 cm thick. Lightly beat off, salt and fry on both sides with vegetable oil and cook until ready in the oven for 15 minutes at 180 degrees Celsius.

Sauce. Fry in vegetable oil chopped onions and bell peppers, than add fresh mushrooms add a little tomato sauce and cream, salt and evaporated for 5 minutes on low heat.

When serving pour the steak sauce and garnish with parsley summarized.

Bon appetite!!!

Andrey Aboimov (G.M.) 8-812-911-257-02-87 <u>1913@sp.ru</u>
p.s. the name of chef- Sergey Semenov!

APPENDIX 11

Poland

After repeated attempts to contact the restaurant, Gospoda C. K. Dezerterzy, I was unsuccessful. However, in its stead I am including a fabulous recipe for ribs from one of my favorite restaurants, **Sawasdee Thai Restaurant** in my hometown of Indianapolis, one of the most outstanding eateries I have eaten in anywhere. The proprietor, **Mr. Ty**, supplied us with the following:

<u>Ingredients</u>

3 slabs baby back ribs
Water
1 Tsp sugar
¾ Tsp salt
1 Tsp fresh, chopped garlic
Barbeque sauce (your favorite)

<u>Preparation</u>

Arrange three slabs of baby back ribs tightly in double-layer, oven-safe cooking vessel.
Combine sugar, salt and garlic.
Rub mixture thoroughly on the ribs.
Cover ribs completely in water.

Cover vessel with aluminum foil.
Bake at 250 degrees for 2 and a half hours.
Shut off oven, but leave ribs in oven for another half hour.

Remove from oven and allow to cool for one hour.
Separate pans.
Coat bottom of underneath pan in barbeque sauce.
Add rib pan with ribs back into bottom pan.
Cover ribs with sauce.

Cover with aluminum foil.
Place in freezer overnight.

Thaw ribs.
Place on grill to heat through.
Serve and enjoy very tender ribs.

Austria

Unfortunately, this is the reply I received from the good folks at the Augustinerkeller. It is too bad, because their golash is really terrific.

Dear Mr. Fleetwood,

thank you very much for your e-mail.
We are honored to hear you liked our beef goulash so much and also write about it in your book J

After consulting with our management, I'm unfortunatley not allowed to give you the recipe of our goulash, because it's an old secret family recipe.

I hope you'll come back again and enjoy a goulash at our restaurant.

Have a nice weekend!

Best regards,

Nora Prochaska	Augustinerkeller | Vinothek
Reservierung und Verkauf	| Bundesbad Alte Donau
	Augustinerstraße 1, A-1010 Wien
	| +43/1/533 10 26 30 info@
	bitzinger.at | www.bitzinger.at

Josef Bitzinger, Gastronomiebetriebe e.U. |
Ing. Josef Bitzinger | Firmensitz: Reitschulgasse
2/2/3, A-1010 Wien | FN: 5914y | UID: ATU
49008103 Handelsgericht Wien

However, you might like the enclosed recipe, again from my mother.

INGREDIENTS

Servings 8-10

- 4 lbs stew cut meat, cut into bite-sized chunks
- flour seasoned with salt and ground pepper (about 1 cup flour, 1 Tbsp salt & pepper)
- 2 large, sliced onions
- Olive or vegetable oil, for searing
- 1 tablespoon hot paprika
- 1 -2 teaspoon mild paprika
- 2 garlic cloves, sliced thin
- 1 small lemon, zested
- 1 tablespoon caraway seed
- 2 tablespoons tomato paste
- 4 cups tomato sauce
- ½ cup beef or ½ cup chicken stock
- salt & pepper
- flour(for searing meat)

DIRECTIONS

1. Use a large Dutch oven with a lid for best results. Add just enough olive oil to coat the pan and turn the heat high enough to make the oil shimmer, but not smoke.
2. Pat the meat dry and dredge in flour, seasoned with kosher salt & cracked pepper.
3. Add one piece of meat to the hot oil to make sure that it sizzles. Add the remaining meat, and sear for about 3-4 minutes per side. You want a golden crust that will give the gravy good flavor.

4. Cook the meat in batches, if necessary and set aside in a bowl-- to collect the juice.

5. When all the meat is seared, turn the heat to medium and add a little more olive oil to the pan and cook the onion until tender-- 3-4 minutes. Add the sliced garlic and cook until fragrant-- 30 seconds or so.

6. Add the tomato paste and paprika, and cook for 1-2 minutes.

7. Add the tomato sauce, caraway seeds, lemon zest and chicken stock and stir well.

8. Bring to a simmer for about 15 minutes and taste for seasoning. Adjust as necessary. If the sauce is too thick, thin with a little more chicken stock or water until it is the consistency of a gravy.

9. Simmer for 2 hours, or you can use a slow cooker for 4-6 hours.

10. This stew tastes even better if made one day in advance. Serve on buttered egg noodles.

APPENDIX 13

Slovakia

I made several attempts to reach the folks at the Hotel Dukla, now the Apollo Hotel. Since I received no response, I would recommend you try the recipe provided by the good folks at 1913 Restaurant in St. Petersburg. It can be found above in Appendix 10. For a different taste you might substitute round steak as your meat.

Sweden

Regretably, the Hot Wok Café has closed for business. This seems to be an all too often occurrence in the restaurant business. Again, in its stead I am including a fabulous recipe for a hot wok chicken dish from one of my favorite restaurants. **Sawasdee Thai Restaurant** in my hometown of Indianapolis. The proprietor, **Mr. Ty**, kindly supplied us with the following:

Thai Basil Chicken

Ingredients - per serving
One thinly-sliced, boneless chicken breast
One small loose handful of fresh basil leaves
One half, thinly sliced bell pepper
One half, thinly sliced banana pepper
One small, chopped yellow onion
Fish sauce, to taste (1 to 1½ tsp.)
Garlic cloves, chopped (1/2 tsp.)
2 dashes of white wine vinegar
Ground chilis, to taste
½ tsp. sugar
2 Tsp. chicken broth for desired consistency

<u>Preparation</u>

In very hot wok coat bottom with vegetable oil

Add and stir in approximately half the chopped garlic

Stir until soft

Add chicken and stir fry until soft and cooked through

Add remaining chopped garlic

Add sliced peppers and stir fry until soft

Add basil/chicken broth/fish sauce

Add chilis, to taste

Add black pepper, to taste

Remove from heat. Plate along with steamed white rice.

Lithuania

Lokys Restaurant– Vilnius – Cepelinai (As provided by restaurant)

- Dumpling Mixture:
- 8 large potatoes, peeled and finely grated
- 2 large potatoes, peeled, boiled and riced
- 1 medium onion, peeled and finely grated
- 1 teaspoon salt
- 1 teaspoon black pepper
- .

- Meat Mixture:
- 1 pound ground pork or 1/3 pound pork, 1/3 pound beef, 1/3 pound veal
- 1 medium onion, peeled and finely chopped
- 1 teaspoon salt
- 1/4 teaspoon pepper
- 1 large beaten egg
- .

- Gravy:
- 1/2 pound bacon, diced
- 1 large chopped onion
- 1 cup of sour cream
- Black pepper to taste
- **Prep Time**: 45 minutes

- **Cook Time:** 25 minutes
- **Total Time:** 70 minutes

Preparation

1. In a large bowl, mix all the meat ingredients thoroughly. Refrigerate until ready to use.
2. Add a drop or two of lemon juice to the grated potatoes so they don't turn brown. Place them in a fine-mesh cheesecloth or cotton dish towel and twist over a large bowl to get rid of the excess water. Pour off the water, reserving the potato starch at the bottom of the bowl.
3. Unwrap the cheesecloth and place potatoes in bowl with the potato starch you reserved from the bottom of the bowl. Add the riced boiled potatoes, grated onion and salt. Mix well.
4. Put a large stockpot of water on to boil. To form the zeppelins, take about 1 cup of dumpling mixture and pat it flat in the palm of the hand. Place 1/4 cup or more of meat mixture in the center and, using slightly dampened hands, fold the potato mixture around the meat into a football shape, sealing well. Continue until both mixtures are gone.
5. Carefully lower dumplings into salted, boiling water to which 1 tablespoon of cornstarch has been added (to prevent dumplings from falling apart). Make sure water returns to the boil and continue boiling for 25 minutes. Remove dumplings, drain briefly on a clean dish towel and place on a heated platter.
6. While dumplings are boiling, make the gravy. Fry the bacon and onion until tender. Drain and combine with sour cream and black pepper. Thin with 1-2 tablespoons milk if necessary. Drench dumplings with gravy or pass it in a gravy boat at the table.

APPENDIX 16

Latvia

Unfortunately, I discovered during my writings that the Arba has ceased to operate. Thus, I have turned to my good friends at the Greek Islands Restaurant in my hometown of Indianapolis for a similar recipe. We are fortunate to have such good friends who run such an appetizing establishment and are willing to share their recipe with us.

Chicken Souvlaki

Ingredients

2 pounds Chicken Breast (boneless and skinless)
2 tomatoes (medium)
2 onions (medium)
1 large green pepper
4 12 inch wooden skewers (soak in water for ten minutes)
1 lemon cut in 4 wedges

Marinade

½ cup of Extra Virgin Greek Olive Oil
1/3 cup of Lemon juice
½ tsp salt
1 tbsl garlic
1 tsp black pepper
2 tbsp Greek Oregano

Directions

Cube chicken about two inches all around.

Place chicken in container, pour marinade and mix.

Cover and let stand in refrigerator for up to two hours.

Cut tomatoes, onions and green peppers, then build skewers with marinated chicken.

Pre-heat skillet with Extra Virgin Olive Oil on stove top and brown for about 3 minutes of each side.

Then place in oven at 425 degrees for ten minutes, then turn for five minutes or until thoroughly done.

Place on plate with Greek Salad and lemon wedge.

Greek Salad

Ingredients

2 Tomatoes

1 Cucumber

Parsley

Onions

Feta Cheese (cubed 6 to 8 pieces)

Kalamata Olives

3 tbsp Extra Virgin Olive Oil

1 tbsp vinegar

1 tbsp Greek oregano

Directions

Cut tomatoes in wedges, slice cucumbers, julienne onions, and chop parsley. Cube Feta and Kalamata olives and add olive oil and vinegar and Greek oregano and toss. Serve with crusty bread.

Appendix 17

Estonia

I discovered that the Donkey's Stable is no longer in business. But, please see Appendix 10 for a recipe for Hunter's Steak which you might enjoy.

APPENDIX 18

Finland

Although the Café Engel continues to exist in Helsinki, I was unable to find an email address for the restaurant so I could communicate with them. The breakfast they serve is truly outstanding, but for me the highlight was the baked goods they served us. The eggs and breakfast meat were delicious, but the pastries were the coup de grace.

However, since I was unable to obtain the recipes from the Café Engel, I have decided to share with you another of my mother's recipes, this time for cinnamon rolls. These delectable treats were a family favorite of ours for all major holidays while I was growing up. If my mom chose to make another occasion special, she would fix these special morsels. I guarantee you these are at least the equal to anything served at the Café Engle.

Nancy Fleetwood's Cinnamon Rolls

Ingredients (24 rolls)

1 package of yeast
1 tsp sugar
½ cup of lukewarm water (110-115 degrees)
1 cup milk – scalded
1/3 cup butter, melted
1/3 cup sugar
2 tsp salt

1 egg beaten

5 cups flour (approximately)

Preparation

Dissolve yeast and tsp sugar in water. Melt butter, add milk, sugar and salt. Add to dissolved yeast. Add eggs. Add half the flour, beat well. Add remaining flour. Knead. Grease top of dough with melted butter. Refrigerate for at least 24 hours (will keep for a week).

After time in refrigerator, remove.

Take ½ of dough – roll out to ¼" thickness – do not use too much flour in this process. Make dough into a long narrow shape. Pour on 1/3 cup of melted butter and cover with sugar and cinnamon. Roll, pinch together, and slice in approximately 12 equal parts. Place in pan which has a light coating of melted butter and brown sugar. Repeat process until you have prepared all the dough into approximately 24 rolls. Put all into pan and let sit for 2 hours.

Bake at 375 degrees for 15-20 minutes until golden brown. Serve.

APPENDIX 19

Norway

I made several efforts to contact at Brasserie 45. They were apparently unwilling, or unable, to assist. So, I have improvised with the following recipe I acquired for Pepper Steak, again from my mother's recipes.

INGREDIENTS

Servings 4

- 2 tablespoons black pepper
- $\frac{1}{2}$ teaspoon hot pepper flakes (optional)
- 4 (6 -8 ounce) boneless sirloin or 4 (6 -8 ounce) filet mignon steaks, well trimmed
- 3 tablespoons vegetable oil
- 1 tablespoon butter
- 2 cups sliced mushrooms
- 2 tablespoons cognac, brandy, bourbon or scotch or 2 tablespoons beef stock
- $\frac{1}{2}$ cup whipping cream
- salt, to taste

DIRECTIONS

Combine peppercorns & hot pepper flakes and rub on sides of steaks.

Heat 1 tablespoon vegetable oil with butter in a heavy frying pan.

Add mushrooms to frying pan and cook over medium heat, stirring and turning them occasionally until they are wilted (approx 5 minutes).

Increase the heat to med-high and continue cooking until the liquid from mushrooms have evaporated and they are lightly browned. With slotted spoon, remove them from the pan and set aside.

Add remaining oil to frying pan. When hot, add the steaks.

Fry until brown, about 2 min on each side. Continue cooking until desired temperature is reached.

Remove steaks from pan and allow to rest.

Pour off all fat from pan. Add alcohol or stock and bring to boil, stirring and scraping browned bits from bottom of pan.

Add cream and return to a boil. Boil 1 minute.

Stir in mushrooms & reheat them. Check seasoning & then pour sauce over steaks.

Serve.

APPENDIX 20

Denmark

I found out during my research that the Faergekroen Restaurant at Tivoli has been reborn as a brewpub. Unfortunately, they no longer feature labskovs on their menu. I tried repeatedly to contact another restaurant at Tivoli which has the dish on their menu. I received no reply.

My wife, Jenny, and I developed the following recipe based on notes we took from our waiter at the Faergekroen, and trial and error.

INGREDIENTS

Servings 6

- 4 tablespoons butter or substitute
- 1 $\frac{1}{2}$ lbs stew beef, cut into 1 inch cubes
- 3 medium chopped onions
- 3 cups beer, preferably a blond
- 3 cups beef stock
- 1 teaspoon salt
- 12 ground pepper
- 2 bay leaves
- 6 medium potatoes, peeled and cut into cubes
- ¼ cup of chopped green onion tops (optional)
- One bottle or Worchester sauce (optional)

DIRECTIONS

1. Brown meat and cook onions in the butter, stirring occasionally.
2. Add stock, beer, bay leaves, salt and pepper.
3. Cover and simmer for 20 minutes.
4. Add potatoes and continue to simmer for 2 hours.
5. Mash any remaining pieces of potato, so that you have a thick, smooth consistency.
6. Serve.
7. Sprinkle with onion tops
8. Douse with Worchester sauce to taste

APPENDIX 21

Monaco

Here is the reply I received from the management at Café de Paris. If you
refer to Appendix 25 there is a very nice Bolognese recipe from Malta. In
fact, it could be superior to the one I ate in Monaco.

Dear Sir

I am sorry to hear that the Chef did not answer you. I guess he wants to
keep the recipe secret.

Best regards

Christelle Calippe
Coordinatrice Banquets
Brasserie Café de Paris
Monte-Carlo SBM - Hotels & Casinos
T. +377 98067607

Appendix 22

San Marino

I received no reply from Ristorante Pizzeria del Ghetto, despite repeated attempts. I believe the real key to the success of their pizzas was their wood-burning oven. Unfortunately, I do not believe many of us possess ovens, so it would be very difficult to replicate.

Liechtenstein

My efforts to contact the New Castle Inn bore no fruit. Thus, I have resorted to including the following substitute recipe which I acquired from my mother.

<u>INGREDIENTS</u>

Servings 4-6 Yield 8 wiener scnitzels

- 1 lb boneless veal or pork cutlet, pounded thin
- $\frac{1}{2}$ cup flour
- 2 large eggs
- 1 tablespoon milk
- 2 cups fresh breadcrumbs
- 3 tablespoons vegetable oil
- Lemon wedge

<u>DIRECTIONS</u>

Dredge cutlets in flour.

Place the eggs, milk, and tablespoon of vegetable oil together in bowl and beat together.

Dredge each of the cutlets first in flour, then egg wash and then the bread crumbs.

Set aside the coated cutlets on a platter.

Heat a large, heavy skillet, with remaining vegetable oil to medium heat.

Place the coated cutlets into the hot oil to fry.

Cook about 2 minutes per side.

Drain the cutlets on a paper towel.

Serve with lemon wedges.

Switzerland

Restaurant Zeughauskeller – Zurich – Pork Knuckle and Rosti

Dear Mr. Fleetwood

We thank you for the compliment about our "outstanding" food and I apologies for delay in response due to the fact that I was on holiday.

One can cook pork knuckle very easily.

- Season the meat well
- Then place in the hot oven – simmer until the knuckles are tender

For "Rösti" one need:

- semi-hard-boiled potatoes – peel and grate them
- in the frying pan with butter until it gets golden-brown – lightly season with salt

That is it, enjoys the meal.

We wish you further success.

Freundliche Grüsse

Gabriela A. Hammer
Mitglied der Geschäftsleitung

Restaurant Zeughauskeller SA
Bahnhofstrasse 28a
8022 Zürich

Greece

In my research I discovered that the wonderful Taverna Sigalas-Bairaktaris has not emerged into the electronic age and has no website, nor email. Thus, I turned to my dear friends at the fabulous, cozy Greek Islands restaurant in my hometown of Indianapolis. The Stergiopoulos family and I have been friends for decades. They turn out some of the best food in the city. George, their son and one of the current operators of my son's favorite restaurant in the world, provided me with this family recipe.

Stifado

Ingredients

1.5 kg stewing beef, such as chuck or top rump, trimmed and cut into 7cm pieces
24 baby onions
4 ripe tomatoes, or 1 x 400g tin of chopped tomatoes
4 tablespoons extra virgin olive oil
1 tablespoon tomato purée

MARINADE

3 cloves of garlic
2-3 fresh bay leaves
1½ teaspoons allspice berries

6 whole cloves
1-2 sticks of cinnamon
1 teaspoon dried oregano
125 ml dry red wine
4 tablespoons red wine vinegar

Place the beef in a large non-reactive bowl. Add the marinade ingredients, peeling and finely slicing the garlic first, then cover and refrigerate for at least 6 hours, or preferably overnight.

Peel the baby onions. If using fresh, peel and roughly chop the tomatoes.

Heat the oil over medium heat in a large saucepan and sauté the onions for 5 minutes or until softened. Remove with a slotted spoon and set aside.

Sauté the beef, reserving the marinade, for about 8 to 10 minutes, or until browned on all sides.

Return the onions to the saucepan, add the marinade, tomatoes and tomato purée and enough water to just cover the stew.

Season generously with sea salt and freshly ground black pepper. Bring to the boil then simmer for 1½ to 2 hours, or until the beef is tender and the sauce has thickened.

Serve with pasta and grated hard cheese, such as kefalotiri, pecorino or Parmesan.

Malta

Café Jubilee – Valetta – Pasta Sauce (as provide by the restaurant)

Ragu Recipe

Ingredients:
1 kg minced beef
Olive oil, salt, pepper
1 onion, finely chopped
2 garlic cloves, finely chopped
2 glasses red wine
2 table spoons tomato paste
2 tea spoons sugar
1 tea spoon mixed spice
1 tea spoon mild curry powder
1 table spoon Worchester sauce
3 litre tomato puree
4 Bay leaves
2 glasses water

Method:

Heat some olive oil in a deep pot and put in the garlic and onions. Fry on medium heat for few minutes until they start to brown. Add, the tomato paste, sugar and mix well.

Add the minced beef to the pot and turn flame on high heat. Add the mixed spice, curry powder and Worchester sauce. Stir the mix continuously until the meat browns. Then, add the wine and tomato puree and season with salt, pepper and bay leaves. Leave to simmer for 40/50 min while stirring occasionally. (You can add water accordingly while the sauce is simmering).

Italy

Below is the reply I received from Otella alla Concordia. I thought Julia was going to share their recipe with me, but it appears that sarcasim does not translate well. If you would like a good Bolognese recipe, see the previous appendix.

Gentile Signor George,
sono Giulia, una delle nipoti di Otello e una dei proprietari del ristorante, Saremo felici di inviarLe la ricetta delle nostre fettuccine al ragu' (bolognese). Provero' oggi a farmi raccontare tutti i segreti dal nostro chef e a inviarle il tutto domani.
Grazie di averci scelto!
a presto
Giulia

Dear George, I'm Giulia, one of the grandchildren of Othello and one of the owners of the restaurant, we will be happy to send you the recipe of our fettuccine al ragu (bolognese).

I'm going to try today to make me tell all the secrets of our chef and send them all tomorrow.
Thank you for choosing us!
soon Julia

Printed in the United States
By Bookmasters